CW01671565

PHOTO ACTIVE

PHOTOGRAPHING LANDSCAPE WHATEVER THE WEATHER

By

TONY WOROBIEC

RHE MEDIA LTD

www.RHEMediaPhotography.co.uk

This book was first published in 2016 by:
RHE Media Ltd
5 Pennsylvania Crescent
Exeter
EX4 4SF

ISBN 978 1 910226 42 1 (Paperback)

British Library Cataloguing in Publication Data
A catalogue record for this book is available from the British Library.

Print, bind and distribution by **Printondemand-worldwide.com**
9 Culley Court, Orton Southgate, Peterborough, PE2 6XD.

RHE
MEDIA LTD

www.RHEMediaPhotography.co.uk

CONTENTS

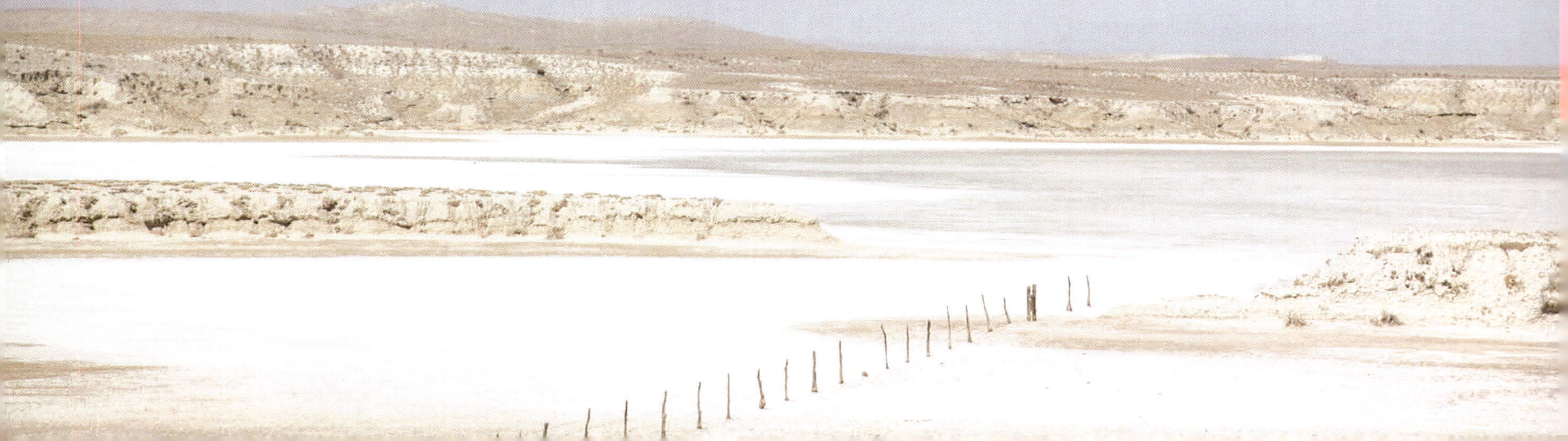

Introduction

In the mind of some, a great 'landscape' needs to conform to some ideal paradigm – a sun-kissed Caribbean beach bathed in rich sunlight, or a snow-capped Alpine shot with a cluster of conifers in the foreground – and they are seemingly unaware that the moment we step outside we are entering 'landscape'.

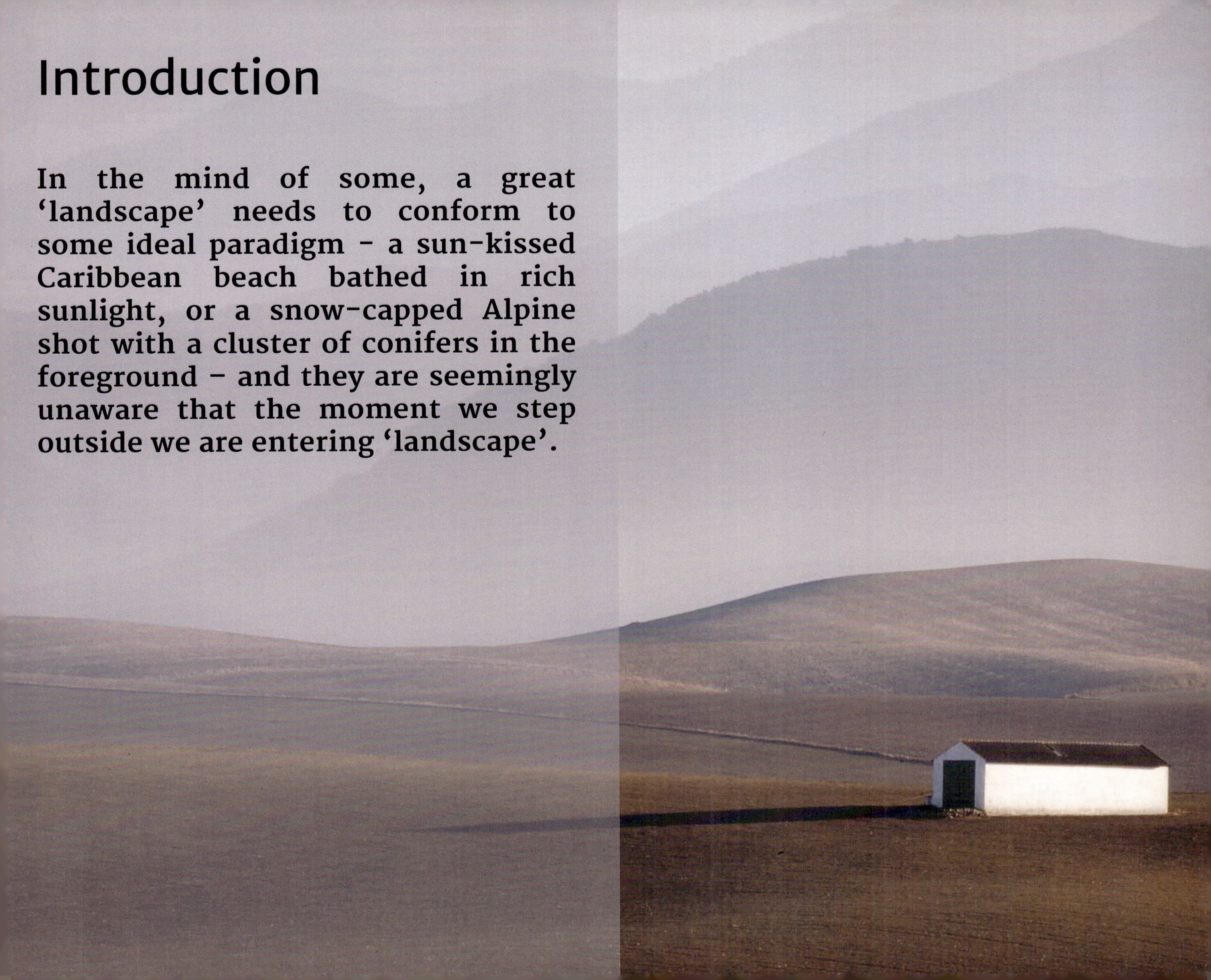

The first thing we need to appreciate is that landscape photography is an extremely wide-ranging genre. While of course there will always be a place for the bucolic scene, we need to appreciate that 'industrial landscape', 'coastal landscape' and of course 'urban landscape' are also worthy subjects. It helps to understand that every location will have its golden moment and it is simply a matter of being in the right place at the right time. Moreover, photographers can often be quite disappointed when visiting a photographic 'honey pot' because it does not appear quite as they had expected. It is only when we understand that the defining quality of any landscape is the weather, as it governs the two most important features notably lighting and mood, that we are truly able to master landscape photography.

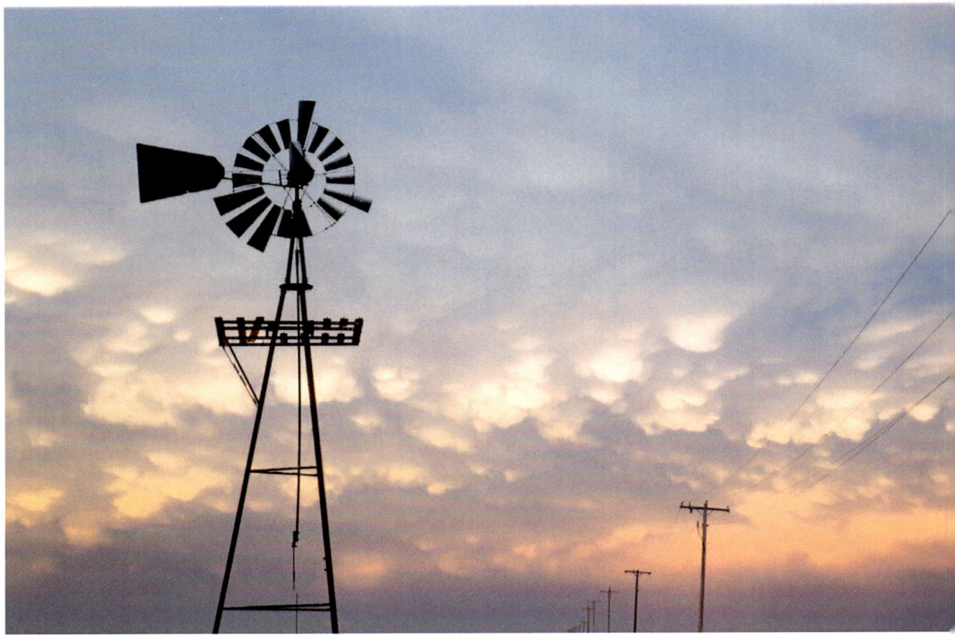

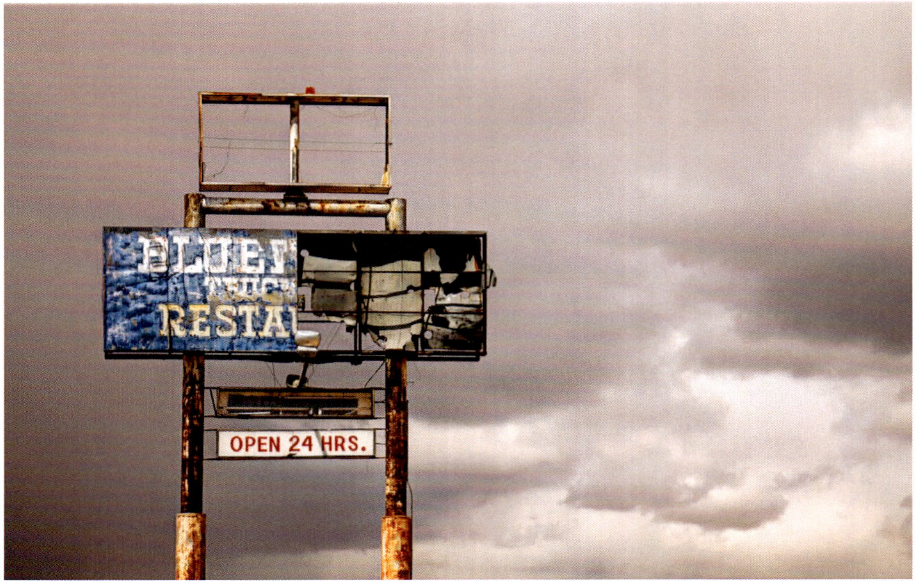

Figure 1 (Left) Bluewater Restaurant. This wrecked and abandoned sign, photographed on old Route 66, conveys a sense of pathos and sadness consistent with the dark and threatening sky. While this is a subject that would have been just as easily photographed under sunny skies, that all important sense of mood would have been lost.

Figure 2 (Above) After the storm, near Havre, Montana. Many photographers are discouraged by rain, but the lighting we see, often after a heavy storm, can be spectacularly beautiful. When this shot was taken the area had been afflicted by passing tornadoes, although shortly afterwards the sky was filled with a magnificent display of mammatus clouds. The old adage that 'there is a silver lining under every dark cloud' certainly applied.

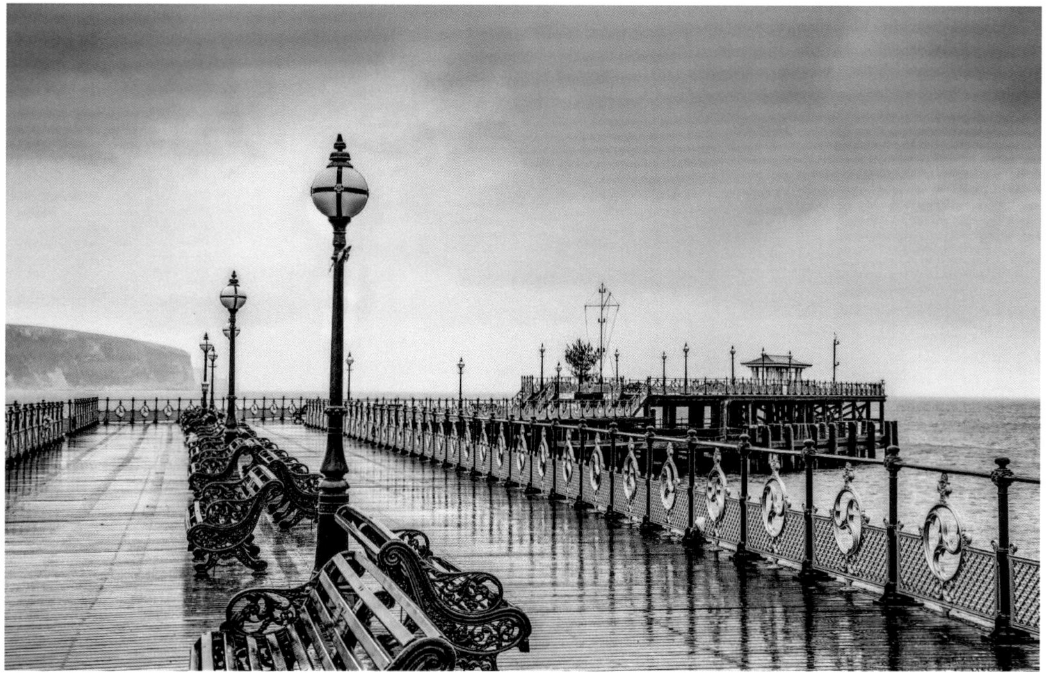

Figure 3 **Swanage Pier in heavy rain**. It is all too easy to convince yourself that there is no point in venturing out when it raining, but to do so is to miss a wonderful opportunity. The mood you are able capture in these conditions just about surpasses all others. Obviously you do need to take certain precautions to ensure that water doesn't get into your camera, but these can be very easily overcome. In this example, I had already anticipated the aperture and ISO rating required prior to walking out onto the pier and only took my camera out of my bag at the last moment.

While we have some control over where we visit, we have no control over the weather. I am often saddened when I listen to some photographers complain that the weather was not kind to them. Rather than determine where you wish to photograph on any specific day, it is often far better to assess the weather, then choose a location that best suits. For example, while strong sunshine might benefit a field of sunflowers, it will prove less advantageous when trying to capture that lovely silky effect one can achieve when photographing waterfalls using a slow exposure. Some urban or industrial landscapes convey a sense of pathos that is more suitably photographed under dark or thunderous skies.

Some of the most interesting examples of photography feature the same landscape taken on different days, with each shot revealing the unique climatic characteristics of that day. The great American photographer Joel Meyerowitz is a personal hero. In one of his publications, *Bay/Sky*, he focused on a single stretch of shore and photographed it repeatedly, capturing the subtle nuances of the changing weather day by day. What Meyerowitz understood with this remarkable project was that it is not just the location but the weather that truly defines the landscape.

While I have made every attempt to keep all the illustrations free of manipulation, there are occasions when a little help from editing software can help.

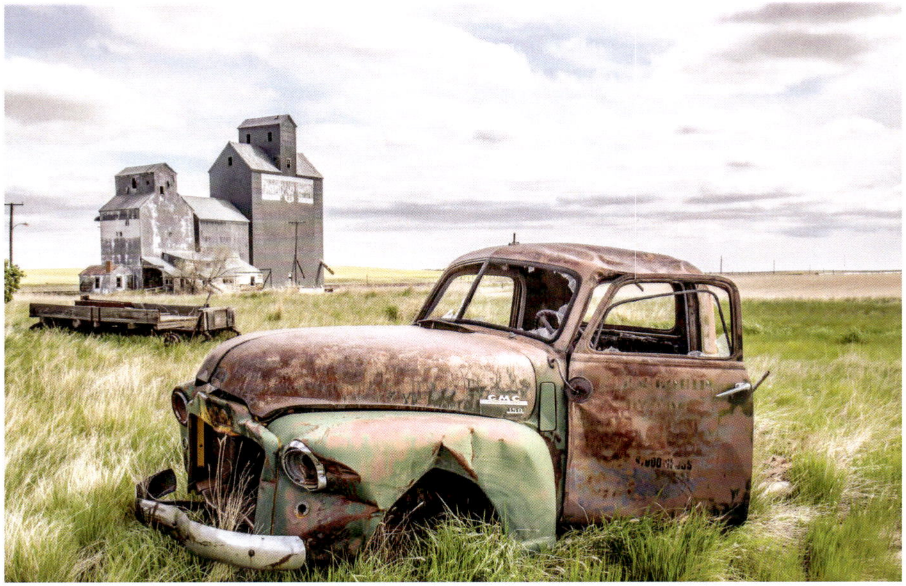

Figure 4 **Abandoned pickup**. There are, of course, numerous occasions when the weather conditions are 'ideal'. Here, for example, there was little wind, there was no threat of rain and it proved moderately warm. Never one to stare a gift-horse in the mouth, I made best use of the benign weather, but we would be cheating ourselves if these were the only conditions we were prepared to work under.

Although DSLR cameras have greatly improved in recent years, knowing how to retrieve 'lost' shadow and highlight detail is invaluable. From a technical standpoint, the essence of good landscape photography is balancing out the light and dark areas, and a knowledge of how certain filters work also helps. But the single most important skill is to develop a sensitivity to how the prevailing weather affects the mood of the landscape and then how best to capture it.

This is a particularly accessible genre of photography. By recognising that landscape can be photographed irrespective of the weather, and that landscape exists outside your back door, it becomes available to everyone. There is no need to buy the most expensive camera; in fact, very impressive landscape photographs can be taken with quite modest equipment. What is more important is to develop an open-minded approach to the potential that exists on a daily basis.

The purpose of this publication is to encourage you to photograph landscape, irrespective of the prevailing weather. While we are all quite comfortable shooting landscape when the weather conditions are benign, we should also be aware of the excellent opportunities that exist when the weather proves challenging. Whether it is sunny or raining, calm or blowing a gale, freezing cold or baking hot, each of these weather conditions will help to define the landscape; it's a matter of learning how to respond. So, when you wake up in the morning and assess the weather for the day, view it as an opportunity to take meaningful and original landscapes.

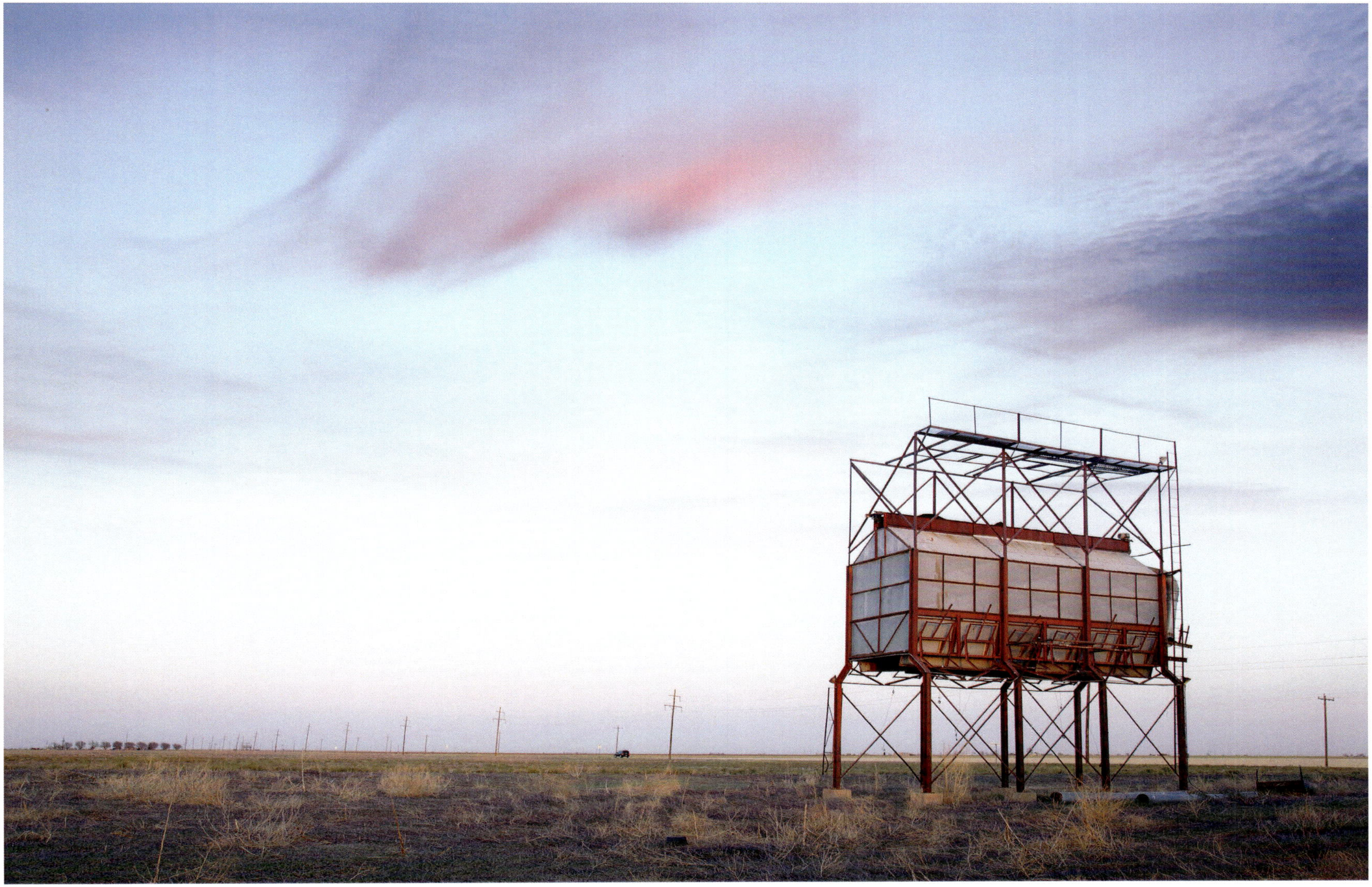

Figure 5 **Silo**. It had been overcast for much of the day and seeing a photograph in this location certainly was a challenge. But, as the cloud started to break, I became aware of how the small cluster of pink clouds in the sky served as a counter-balance to the silo in the bottom right of the composition.

1 Understanding the Weather: Getting Started

It is windy, you have a crucial meeting, you are trying to collect important papers together and, as you step out of your car, a sudden gust dishevels your hair and generally roughs you up, so it is hardly surprising that you have a negative view of wind. On a similar tack, you think you are adequately dressed for the conditions but, while the forecast suggests the temperatures will remain well above freezing, you had not taken the wind-chill into account.

On the other hand, there is of course a positive way of looking at weather. If we have the time it can be fun leaning into a howling wind on the side of an exposed hill, or to visit the coast when it is blowing a gale and marvel at the gigantic waves crashing on to the shore. I'm sure you will all have noticed that children just love dodging the spray as the tide smashes into the promenade.

ADOPTING THE RIGHT MENTAL ATTITUDE

How often have you set off on a walk unaware that you are likely to encounter rain and, when you arrive at that point where there is no opportunity for shelter, the heavens open? Unprepared you hurry back but, with the rain in your face, it is hard to imagine moments less pleasant. If, however, you have anticipated it and are suitably dressed, then the experience is completely different. Because you remain dry, you are comfortable with the conditions; playing in the rain becomes fun as we indulge in simple pleasures such as splashing in puddles.

While we may dream of a 'White Christmas', when it does snow it can prove an enormous hindrance. Before we set off to work, the car needs to be cleared and the ice scrapped off the windscreen. If that is not bad enough, when you do finally hit the highway everybody in front of you is travelling at a greatly reduced speed, guaranteeing that you will be late for work. When you find a parking place and step out of your car, you have to contend with wet sludge. The plus side, of course, is that if you are able to escape into the countryside and see how wonderfully it has been transformed by the snow, it will be prove to be an experience you will want to record and share with friends. Even a simple walk in the park becomes a joyous pursuit.

I hope I have made my point? As a photographer you can view the weather conditions either as a negative or as a positive. If you are put off by the cold, the rain or the wind, then you will find that your opportunities for taking photographs are severely reduced. Alternatively, you can embrace weather as an exciting challenge and, providing that you are suitably prepared, it should always be a pleasure. If that was not enough, taking photographs in adverse weather conditions usually results in particularly interesting and unique images.

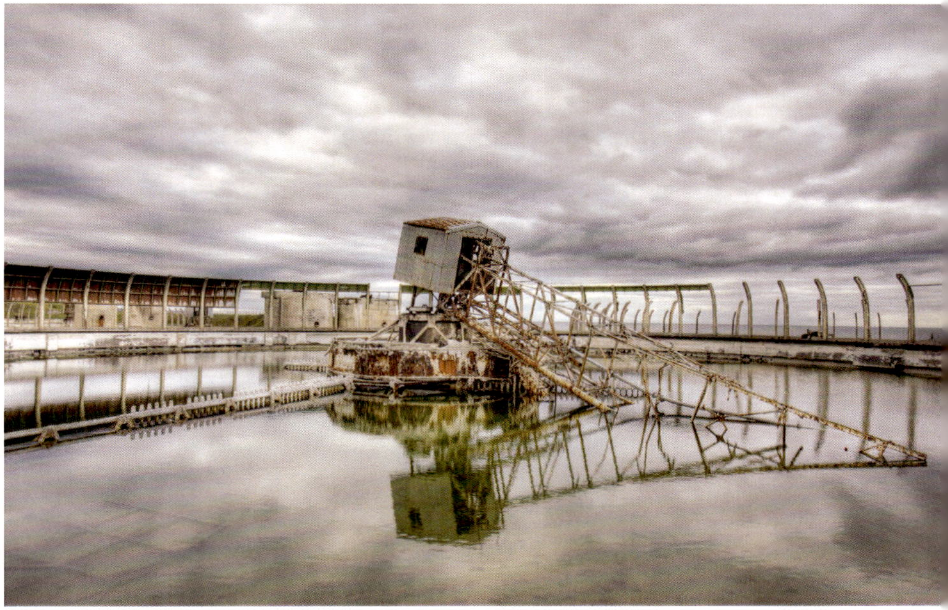

Figure 1 **Industrial wreck**. Once you convince yourself that you are able to take interesting photographs irrespective of the weather conditions, your definition of 'landscape' quickly expands. I would not have considered taking this photograph in more benign weather conditions, but the grey and threatening sky seems to chime well with this particular scenario.

Figure 2 **Trees in mist**. Prior to taking this shot, the weather outside looked grey and unpromising and I certainly questioned whether it was really worth venturing out. As ever, it is when you can be bothered to give it a go that really interesting pictures materialise. Weather conditions what we see and, while this cluster of trees might easily have gone unnoticed under more normal lighting conditions, it is a scene that appears completely transformed when photographed in a heavy winter mist.

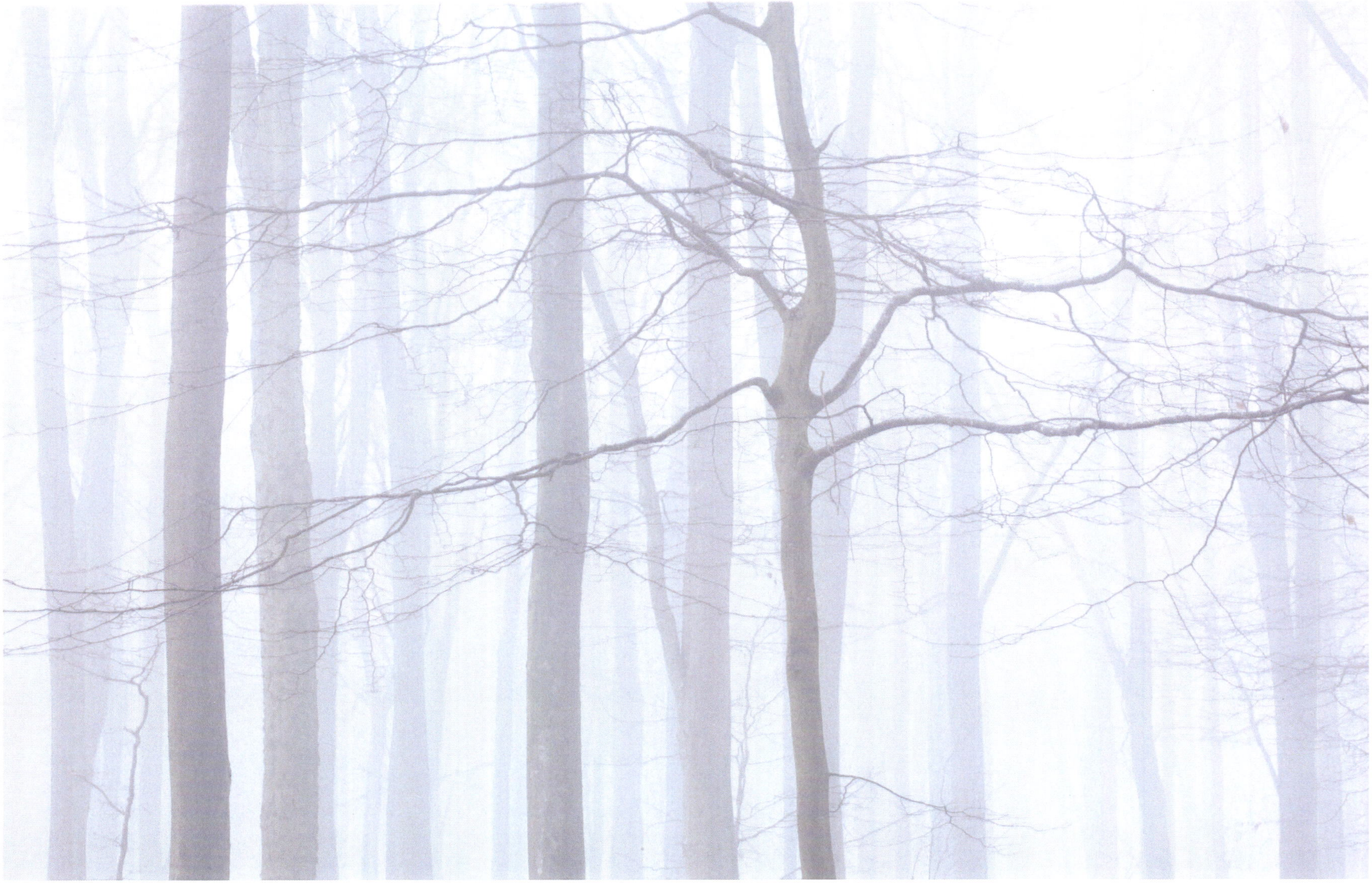

Figure 3 **Irrigated fields**. When photographing landscape you should not always feel compelled to include the sky. If it is not particularly interesting, don't include it. Using a telephoto lens certainly helps in this respect.

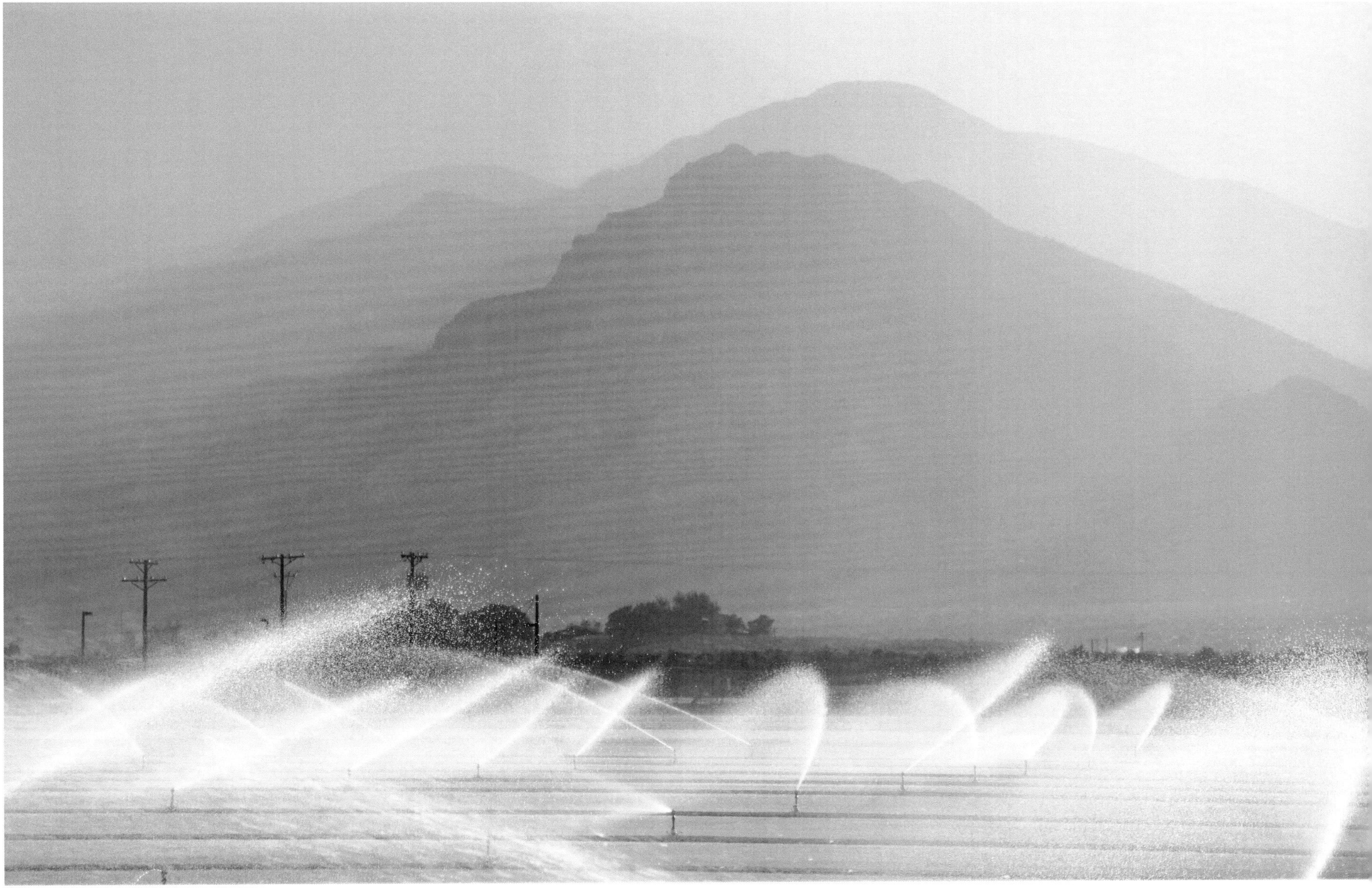

As I explained in the previous two pages, most people enjoy being out in even the most adverse weather conditions, providing they are well prepared for it. This means being suitably dressed for the weather. Whether it is blowing a gale, pouring with rain or freezing cold, being out in the elements can be spiritually uplifting but, more importantly, it offers some of the best conditions for taking great landscape photographs.

Protection against rain

Without stating the obvious, you clearly need to wear garments that are waterproofed in some way and there are a variety of materials currently available. The ambient temperature is also a factor as you can experience rain both in warm and cold temperatures. Either way, it is far more comfortable when wearing a garment that can breathe. Most photographers opt for a cagoule with an attached hood that offers excellent protection for the upper part of the body. A good cagoule can be surprisingly expensive but, when you factor in the attention to detail regarding its manufacture, particularly regarding the seams and zips, they are generally worth every penny you pay. The best cagoules are made from materials that are laminates and the best known of these is Gore Tex. This is a membrane bonded to other protective fabrics. The membrane is constructed of tiny pores that prevent water passing through yet allow water vapour (i.e. sweat) to evaporate from the inside, hence its 'breathable' qualities.

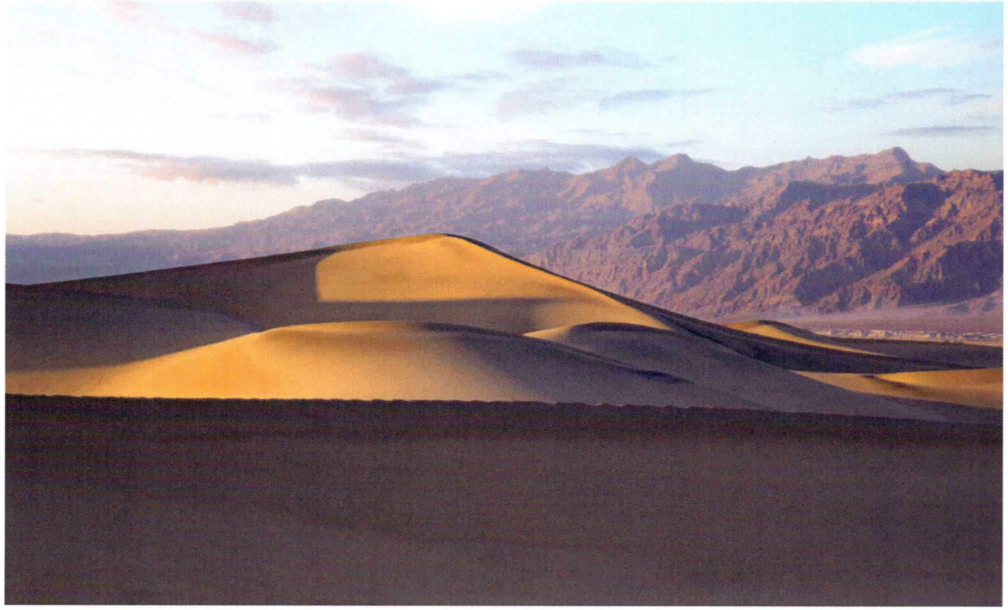

Figure 4 **Death Valley**. On the day I took this shot, the midday temperature rose to 47 degrees Centigrade, which was not just uncomfortable but potentially dangerous. In order to escape the excessive heat, I took this shot just as dawn was breaking.

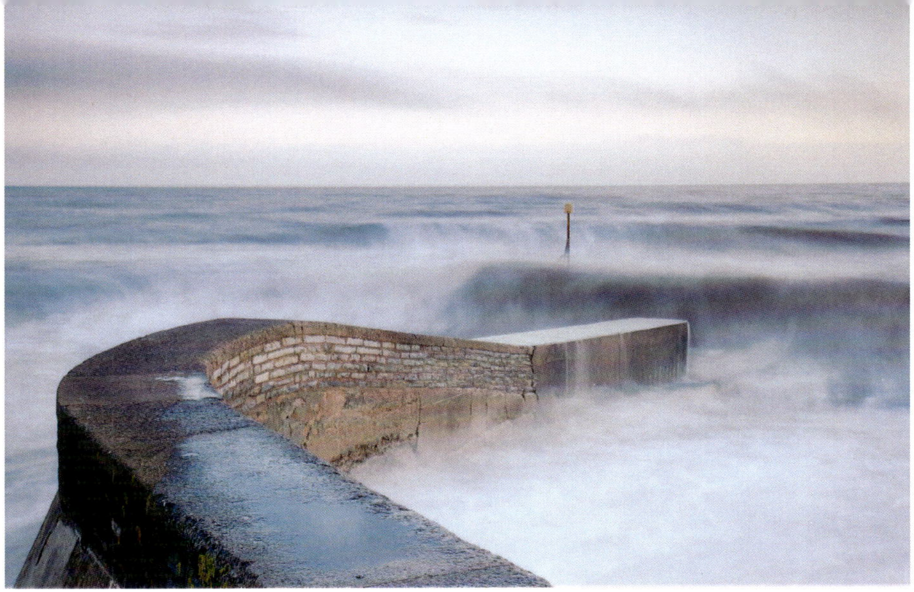

Figure 5 **Sidmouth**. A raw and windy day in January, it was not the perfect evening to be standing outside. Making sure that I was warmly clothed, with a wind-cheating cagoule, made the experience far more tolerable.

Something that is often overlooked is what trousers to wear. Denim jeans are popular and are ideal for walking when the weather is fair, but offer very poor protection when it is raining as they just soak it up. Once your legs get wet, particularly if it is windy, walking becomes uncomfortable. If you are anticipating being out in the rain you should consider wearing rain trousers. These are considerably cheaper than cagoules and are designed to be worn over your regular trousers. They are light and compact, and can easily be packed into your camera bag in case you should need them. When buying a pair, make sure they have wide legs or at least a zip part way up the leg so that they can be easily put on or removed even when you are wearing shoes. You should also think about pockets. Many of these rain trousers will have gaps that allow you get to the pockets of your regular trousers.

It is not just walks in the rain that you should protect yourself from. If you are photographing the coast, particularly in windy conditions, you need to be aware of sea-spray. On a similar note, when photographing waterfalls one often experiences swirling mists that can soak you in minutes so good waterproof clothing certainly is essential. Finally, while an umbrella might be useful protection against the rain when out for a casual walk, if you are on your own it is a positive hindrance when you want to take photographs. You need both hands when handling a camera, which makes an umbrella next to useless (however, see Chapter 3 for ideas for using an umbrella with a tripod).

Protection from the cold

Equally important as staying dry is to keep warm. Feeling cold can very quickly dampen your enthusiasm for photography, particularly if you are waiting for the light to change. Evidence shows that you lose most of your body heat from your extremities, so it is so important to keep your head, hands and feet warm. You don't need to be a rocket scientist to appreciate that a warm pair of socks, a thick woolly hat and a pair of gloves are a useful start.

The key to staying warm is to wear plenty of layers. This not only traps the warm air in but, of course, it allows you to remove layers. Garments made of wool are particularly suited to cold weather, although you may wish to wear something made of cotton directly on the skin, as wool can be quite scratchy. Wool is an excellent natural insulator. It is also important that the clothing you wear is the right size. If it is too tight, then it can constrict the blood flow, which will make it more difficult to stay warm. One of the best innovations for staying warm are thermals; these are inner garments usually made of a synthetic material that are designed to remove moisture from the surface of the skin so that you continue to feel comfortable.

What is often underestimated is how debilitating wind chill can be. You may have planned an expedition on the understanding that the temperatures would remain above freezing, but failed to account for the predicted winds. If you are not suitably dressed these can prove devastatingly unpleasant, making photography absolutely impossible. The discomfort is directly related to the strength of the wind. To give you an example, if the measured temperature is 1 degree Centigrade, with a wind of 25 mph it can feel like -9.

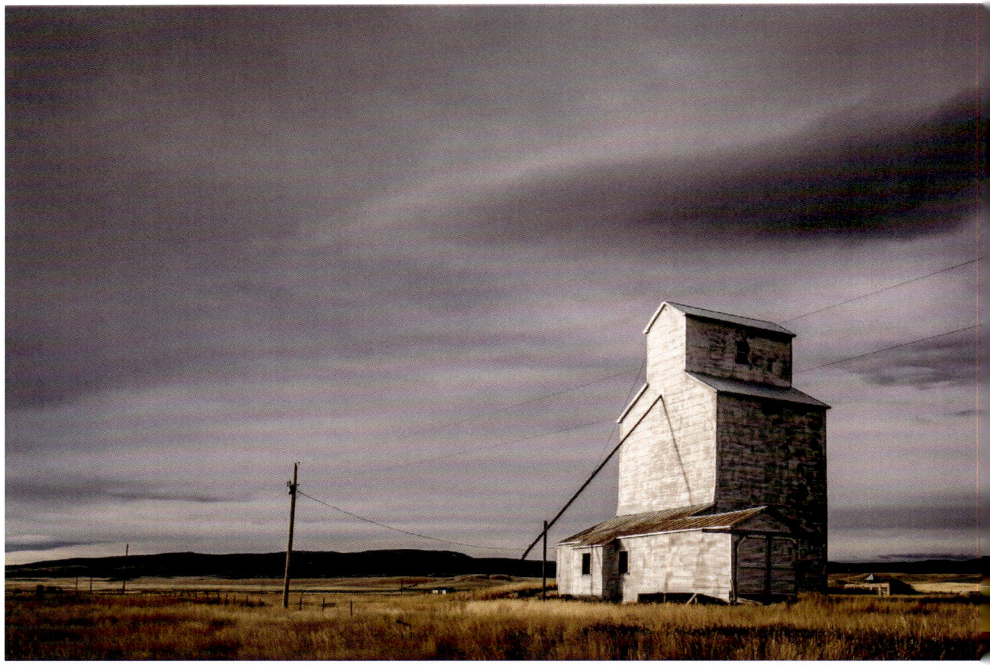

Figure 6 **Elevator under grey sky**. Cold and grey coupled with a howling wind, it took a certain level of commitment just to stop the car, never mind get out. But if you are suitably dressed you are able to take advantage of any situation, irrespective of the weather.

Protection from excessive heat

It had never occurred to me that this could be a problem until a recent trip to Death Valley, California, which is one of the hottest places on Earth. It was mid-September, so I assumed that the worst of the high temperatures had passed, but I was wrong. For the three days I was there, the maximum daily temperature averaged at 47 degrees Centigrade, which made photographing through the day impossible.

Unlike extreme cold, there is not a great deal you can do to counter heat. One thing you should not do is to remove clothing as the sun's rays can burn you very quickly. In fact Middle Eastern tribes used to these sort of temperatures ensure that most of their bodies remain covered. Wearing a large-brimmed hat helps to keep the worst of the sun off your face, but all areas of skin that might be exposed should be covered with sun-block. However, the best solution is to take your photographs early in the morning, when the sun is still low in the sky, or in the evening.

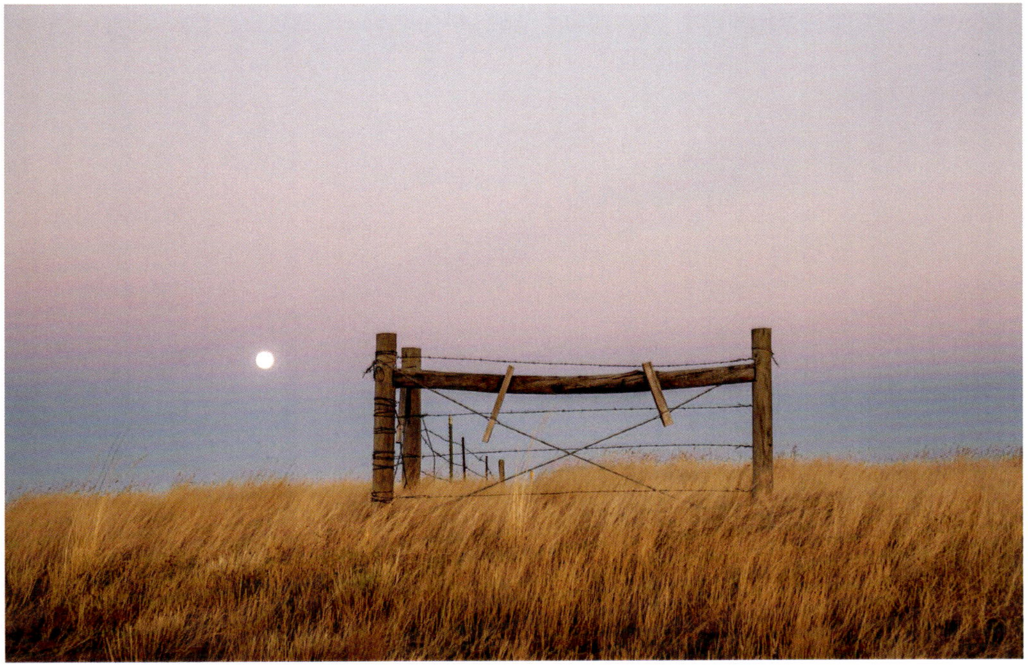

Figure 7 **Fence and moon**. While you can tolerate a certain level of cold when you are walking, it can become considerably more uncomfortable if you are standing around for any length of time. In this example I needed to wait for 40 minutes before I got the lighting conditions I was after but, as I had come prepared with plenty of layers, the waiting was not so bad.

Suitable footwear

Footwear is another issue that should not be overlooked. Obviously you need to ensure that what you wear is comfortable, but also that it is well suited to the weather conditions you are working in. For example, if you are photographing in rain or in generally wet conditions, then a pair of Wellington boots will prove invaluable. Even if it has stopped, you may want to work from a particular vantage point that requires walking through deep puddles. Fields and pastures get muddy when it is raining and walking through them when wearing shoes is a distinct disincentive. Similarly, if you ever engage in coastal photography, you will constantly encounter streams or rock pools so being able to walk through them rather than round them will be more convenient. However, wellies are not the most comfortable footwear, so wear a pair slightly larger than your normal shoe size and wear an extra pair of thick socks. Admittedly, driving with Wellingtons is not ideal, but changing back into your normal shoes should not pose a problem.

On a similar tack, light shoes are comfortable, but they are not suited to cold weather. The ideal footwear is hiking boots, which will not only protect you from the elements but also offer sufficient grip to allow you to walk over ice and snow. As with cagoules, hiking boots are wonderfully engineered, so do expect to pay a fair price. The best (and usually the most expensive) are those with full-grain leather uppers. As they are durable and water resistant, they tend to be the natural choice for serious hikers, although many are now opting for synthetically constructed boots with a Gore-Tex lining. These are excellent for keeping your feet dry and are relatively inexpensive.

Other sundries

If you are anticipating hiking, there are several things you should consider taking along and the most obvious of these is a mobile phone. Thankfully we rarely experience a true emergency, although it is quite easy to slip and fall or sprain an ankle, so being able to contact a friend or relative is certainly reassuring. Moreover, most smart phones now have a GPS facility that allows you to find your way home should you get lost. Also, carry a small torch in your camera bag; these can prove particularly useful if you need to get back home in the dark.

Finally, while this section considers how to protect you from the elements, it should be noted that your camera needs protecting as well. This will be dealt with as we consider each of the varying weather conditions.

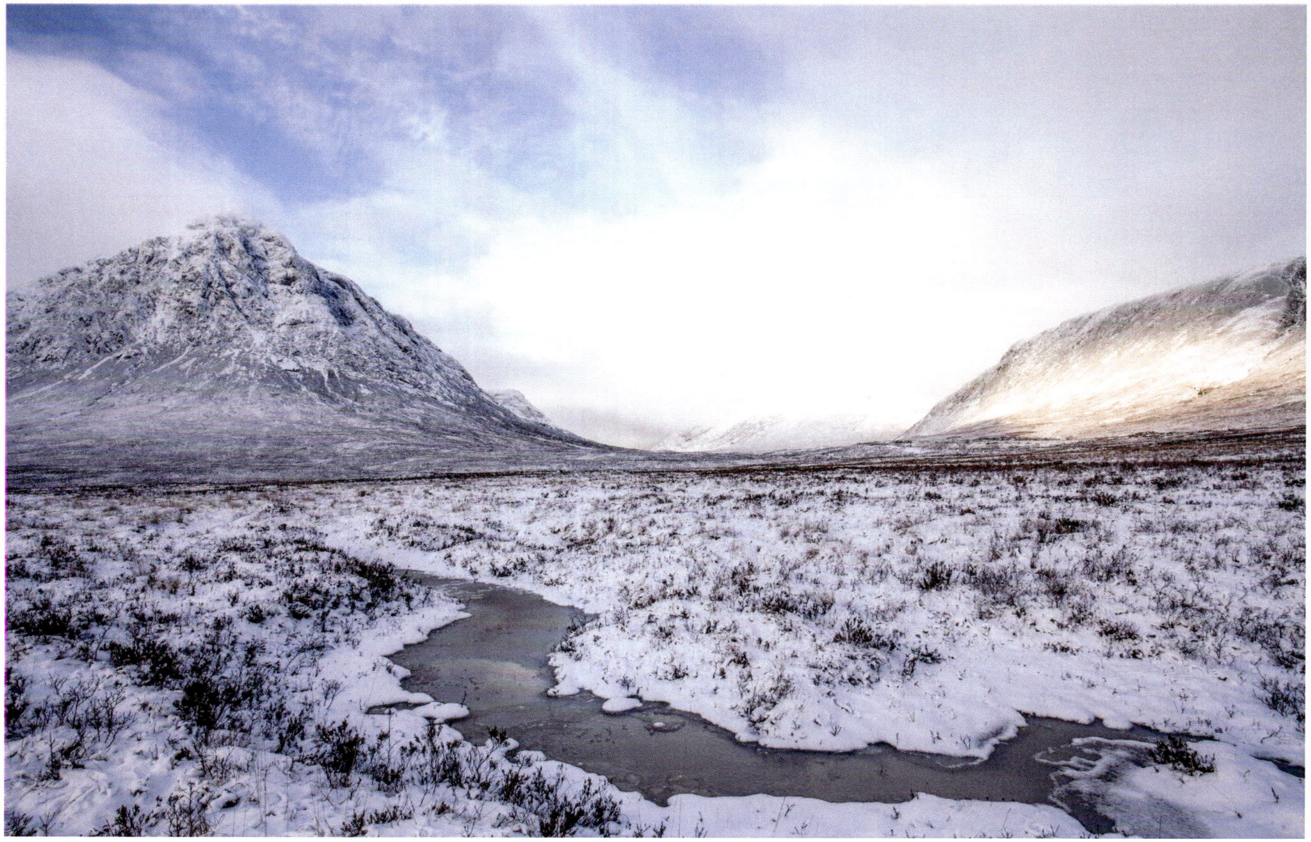

Figure 8 Rannoch Moor. Wearing suitable footwear in snow and ice is an absolute must. Not only does it need to be waterproof, but warm also. If your feet are cold, so is your entire body.

USEFUL FILTERS

While you may be dazzled by the variety of filters available to the photographer, some are especially useful when photographing landscape in adverse weather. Not only do you need to protect the lens, but you will often encounter difficult lighting conditions. There are various types of filters that help to resolve this problem.

What is a filter?

A filter is simply a glass or plastic screen that you put in front of your lens in order to reduce or control the light reaching the sensor. They come in many shapes and sizes, but there are two generic designs:

1. there are the screw-on types typically manufactured by Hoya and B&W;
2. there are the modular types that require placing a rectangular filter in an adapter and holder, made by Lee Filters and Cokin.

Useful lenses to use

UV filter

The general advice with filters is to only buy on a needs-must basis; some are particularly expensive and should only be considered if they positively help your style of photography. However, there is one filter I would strongly recommend you buy with each new lens you get, and that is the simple UV filter. The UV filter is designed to remove the bluish haze caused by particles in the atmosphere; by introducing a very gentle pinkish tint, the sky will appear cleaner so, in terms of improving clarity, it does serve a useful purpose. But the main reason I would recommend using this filter is because it serves as a guard for your lens. If you are shooting in rain or snow, then you certainly do not want water appearing on the front element of your lens. On a similar tack, if you are shooting in windy conditions, you are exposing the lens to dust and possible scratch damage. Relatively speaking these filters are cheap and, while they have only a minimal effect on the image, they can serve to protect your very much more expensive lens. Sometimes it is important to remove it, particularly when you want to add another filter such as a polariser as leaving the UV filter on can result in vignetting but, otherwise, always keep this filter firmly secured to your lens.

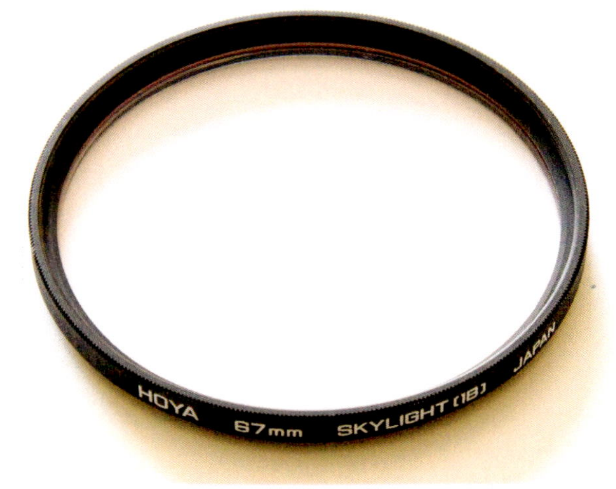

Figure 9 **UV filter**. While the UV filters remove the bluish haze in the atmosphere, they also serve as protection for the lens.

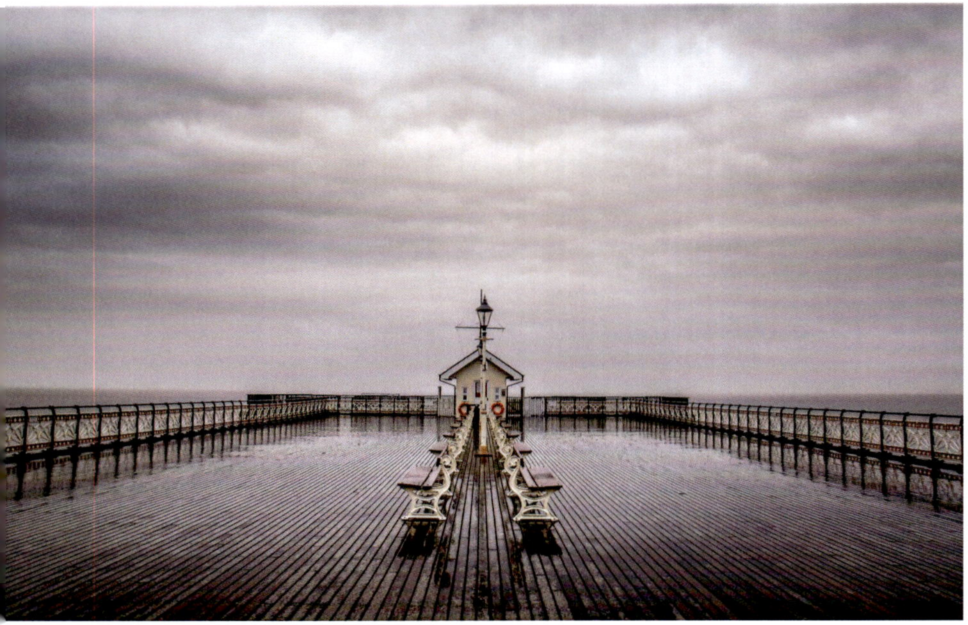

Figure 10 **Penarth Pier in rain**. It was pouring with rain as I took this photograph but, as I had a UV filter attached to the lens, I was able to regularly wipe it with a microfibre cloth without worrying about possibly damaging the lens.

Graduated Neutral Density Filter (ND Grad)

One of the major problems when photographing landscape in adverse weather is excessive contrast, which is why a graduated neutral density filter can prove so useful as it helps to balance out the disparities of exposure. When making a light reading there might often be a three or four stop difference between the foreground and the sky. If you expose for the sky, the foreground will appear too dark, but if you meter for the foreground, the sky will appear burnt out. All the graduated filter does is to correct this disparity without changing the colour balance. While it is possible to buy a screw-on graduated filter, they are more commonly part of a modular system such as Lee or Cokin. In essence it is a half grey and half clear sheet of acetate that is positioned in front of the lens. By ensuring that the darker part filters out the lighter part of the scene, an exposure balance is restored.

Graduated filters come in different strengths. For example, you can have a '0.3' (which equates to a one-stop reduction of light), a '0.6' (which equates to 2 stops) and a '0.9', which reduces the light by three stops. These filters also come as hard or soft. This describes the transition between the grey and the clear areas, which can be gentle or harsh. It is also possible to use two filters in combination so that the overall exposure is reduced, which is useful when you wish to achieve a low light effect in normal light. Used in this way they become, in effect, a neutral density filter. They may also be 'stacked' in order to increase the strength of the filtration, but don't overdo this as the sky should normally appear marginally lighter than the foreground.

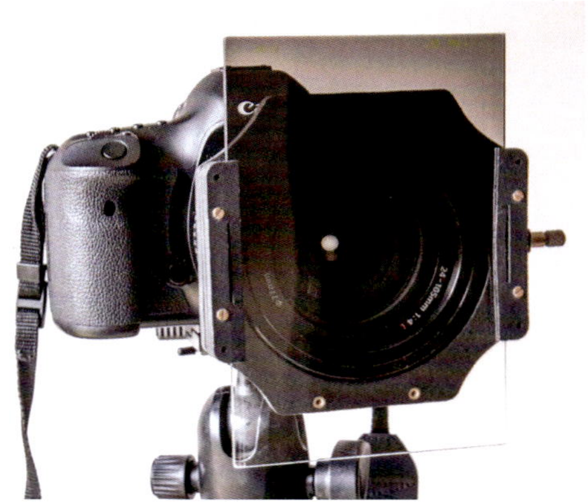

Figure 11 **Neutral Density Grad**. One of the most useful filters for landscape work as they help to balance out the sky and foreground. They come as 'hard' or 'soft'.

Metering with a graduated filter

This can prove problematic, as the metering system on the standard DSLR can easily be fooled, resulting in the foreground appearing too light. There are ways to overcome this.

- Take two independent light readings, one of the sky and one of the foreground, set the camera to expose for the foreground, then select the appropriate ND graduated filter in order to achieve an overall balanced exposure. It should also be noted that, while the effect of the filter can be seen through the viewfinder, it is being viewed with its maximum aperture. By using the depth of field preview facility you can see the effect the filter is having with the aperture you have selected, particularly when using a hard grad filter. If the effect is too harsh, then you may wish to use a larger aperture. Alternatively, you can use live view.
- Meter the subject first without the filter, use the camera's auto-exposure facility to memorise the reading, then add the filter and expose.
- Meter manually without the filter, make the necessary camera adjustments, and then put the filter over the lens.
- Bracket; working digitally, this is easy to do. Find 'Exposure Compensation' in the camera's menu and set it to expose one stop higher and one stop lower. This will give you three exposures including a standard exposure.

Examples of images taken with graduated filters

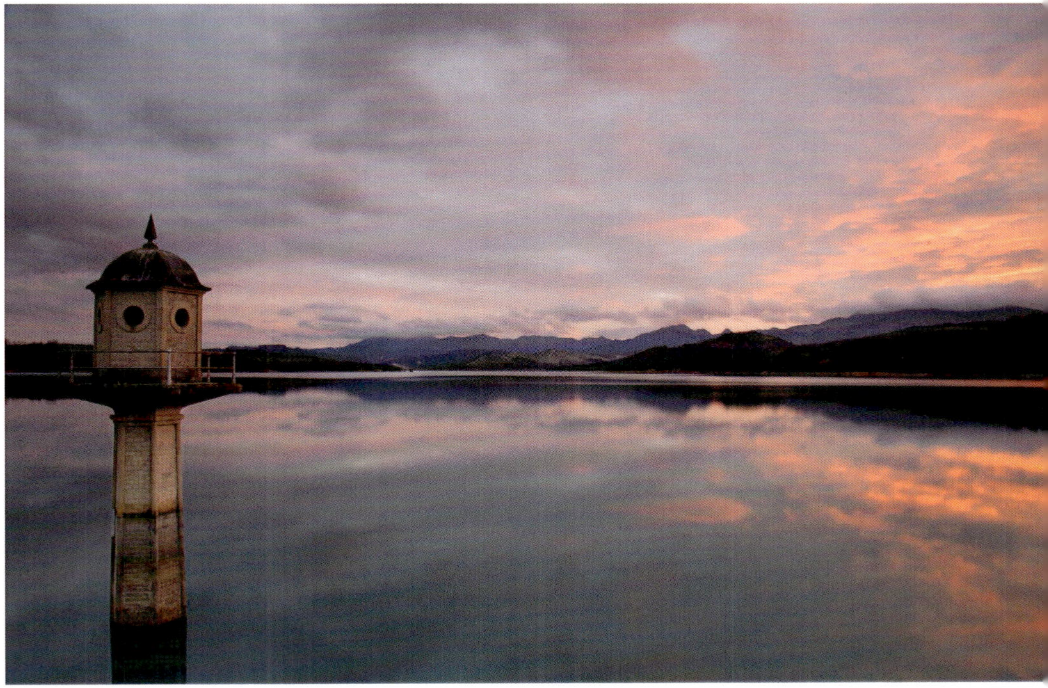

Figure 12 **Reservoir, Andalusia**. When taking this photograph I was particularly keen to retain detail both in the sky and in the reflections in the water. In order to balance out the exposure I used a graduated neutral density filter.

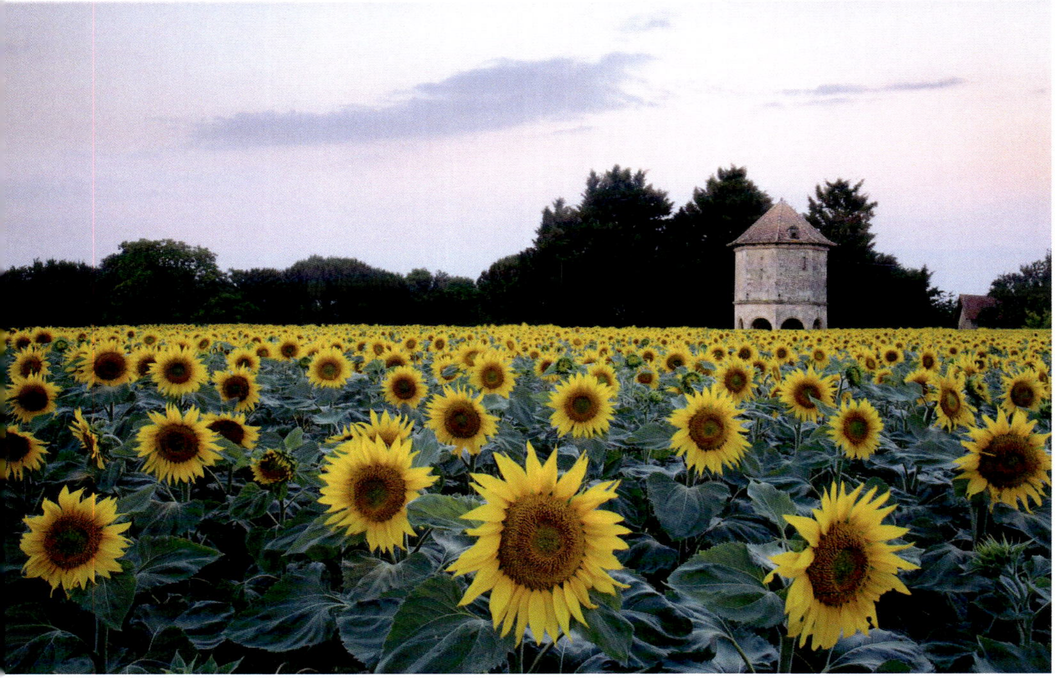

Figure 13 Sunflower field and pigeoniere. Photographed just after sunset, I was particularly keen to capture this single altostratus cloud drifting over a field of sunflowers. As the exposure difference between the sky and the foreground was over three stops, I decided to use a soft graduated filter.

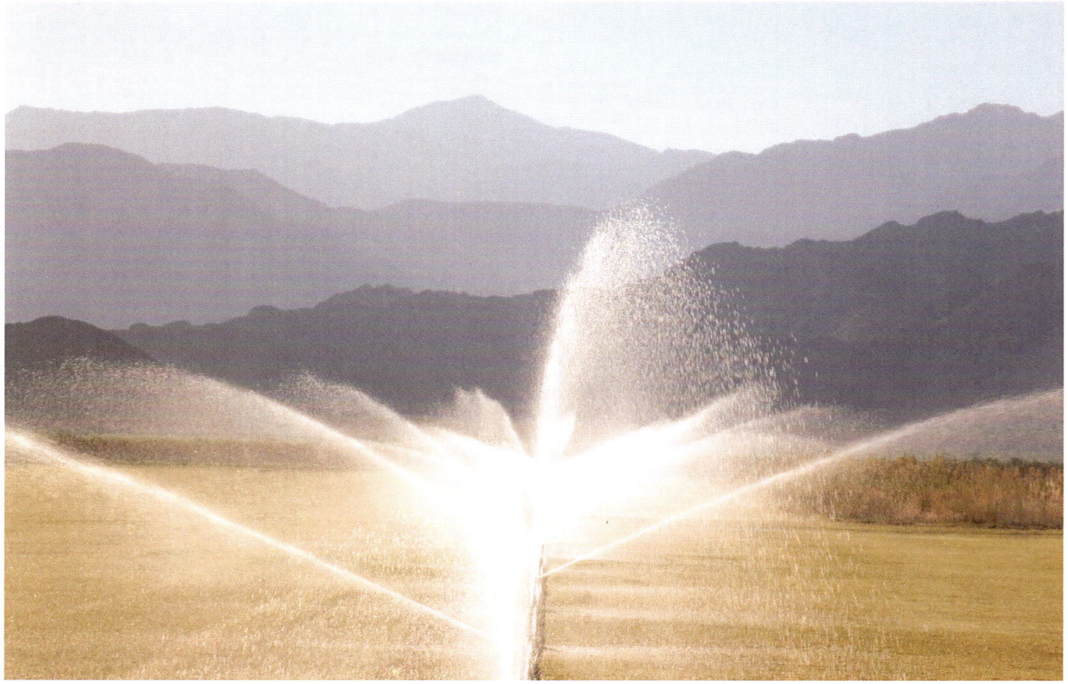

Figure 14 Irrigated fields, California. In order to lend emphasis to the spraying water at the bottom of this composition, it was important to darken the sky. This was effectively done by using a soft grad filter.

A Neutral Density filter (ND filter)

A Neutral Density filter is like a graduated filter except that it reduces the light evenly across the entire frame. They are most commonly manufactured as screw-on filters and act rather like a pair of sunglasses. A neutral density filter is used to reduce the amount of light reaching the sensor by absorbing the same amount of all the wave lengths, therefore it does not alter the colour in any way. As it effectively reduces the ISO rating it is often used to simulate the effects of low light photography when there still is plenty of available light.

Why would you wish to use a ND filter?

- You may decide that you want to use a very wide aperture, but you are unable to do this because the available light is too bright.
- You are photographing a location and people keep getting in the way. By considerably reducing the shutter speed, they will appear as a blur or disappear entirely.
- When photographing waterfalls, many photographers wish to capture the silky gossamer effect that one achieves when using a slow shutter speed. If the lighting is too bright, using this filter will counter it.
- You wish to capture the movement of the wind but there is too much light, which prevents you using a very slow shutter speed. By using a ND filter you are limiting the amount of light reaching the sensor, therefore you are able to greatly increase the exposure time. So, if your camera's metering system tells you that for a given aperture a shutter speed of 1/60 second is required, by applying a neutral density filter this could change to seconds or even minutes, depending on the strength of the filter. Obviously you will then need to re-set your camera accordingly, using it either in Manual or Bulb mode.

ND filters have an overall grey appearance and on first inspection can be confused with a polarising filter. They come in different densities:

- an ND 2 filter, which allows 50 per cent of the light to reach the sensor, reducing your speed by one stop;
- an ND 4 filter, which allows 25 per cent of the light to reach the sensor, reducing your speed by two stops;
- an ND 8 filter, which allows 12.5 per cent of the light to reach the sensor, reducing your speed by four stops.
- One slight problem you will encounter when using some of the stronger ND filters is that, because of the almost opaque nature of the glass, it is impossible to see through them. The only way round this is to compose and then focus with the filter off, and then carefully place it on the lens once you are ready to take your shot.

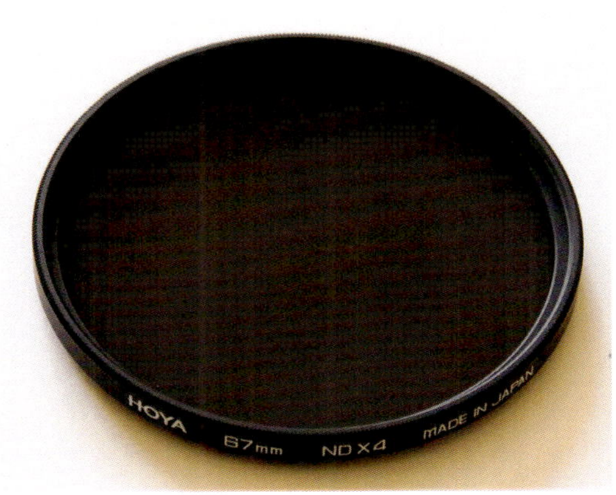

Figure 15 Neutral Density Filter. Plain, dull and grey, neutral density filters don't look very exciting but they truly are one of the most creative options in your toolbox.

Examples of images taken with a ND filter

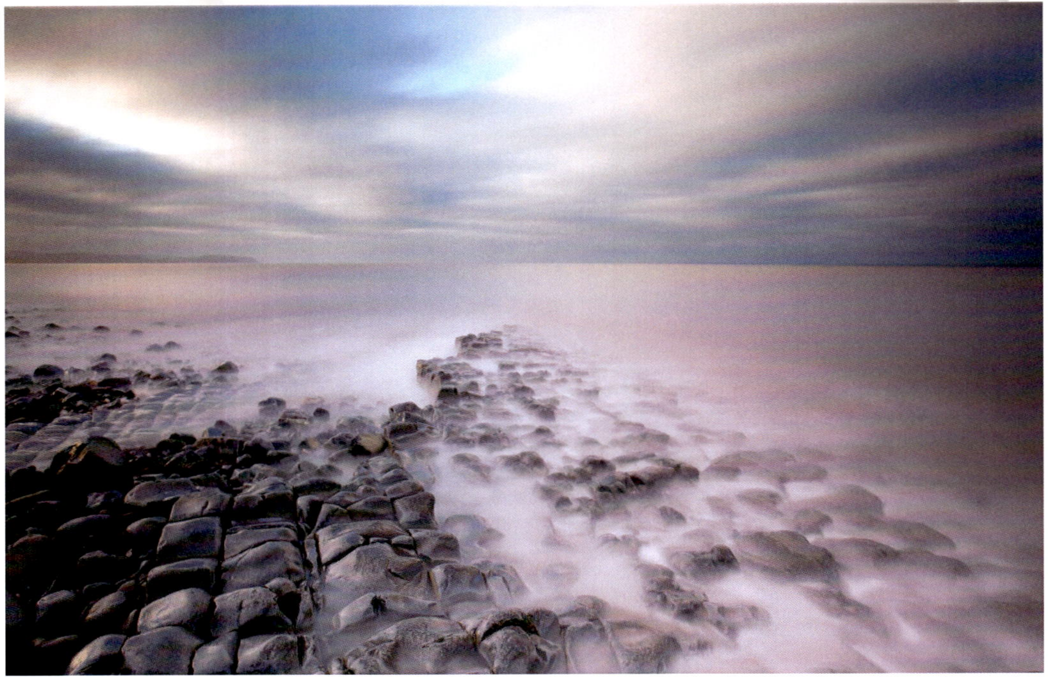

Figure 16 Rocks at Kilve. When I took this shot it was a cold and windy day. I was particularly impressed with the scuttling clouds driven by the wind. In order to make a feature of this I decided to use a neutral density filter, which greatly extended the exposure time.

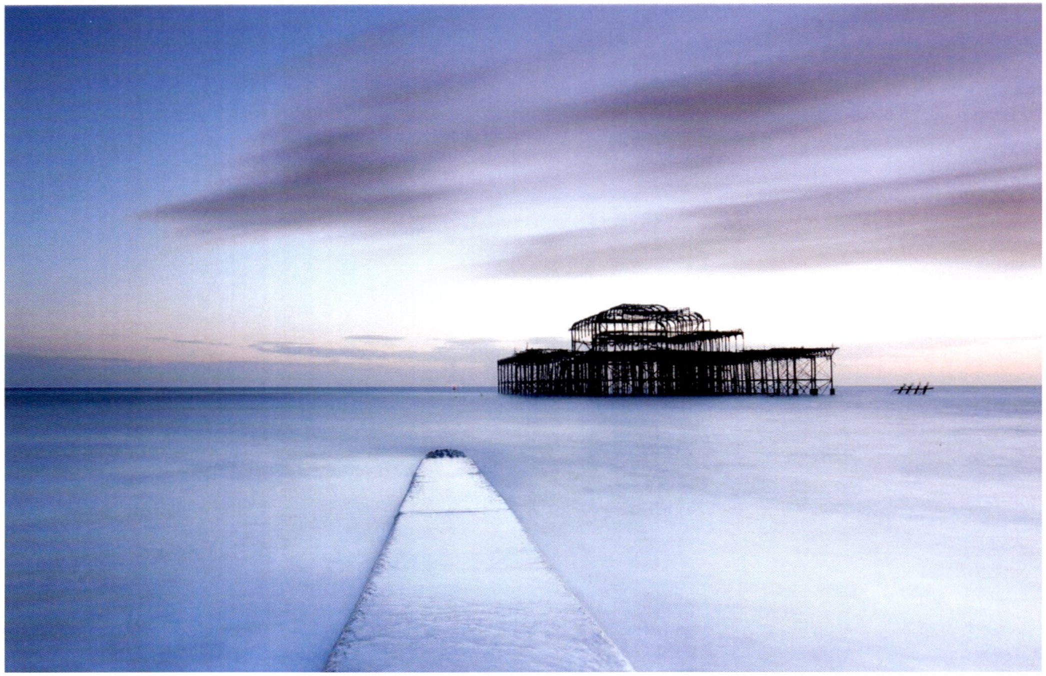

Figure 17 Derelict pier. In common with the previous image, it was the formation of clouds that I found particularly interesting. Even though the sun had set, there was still too much light. By attaching a ND filter the wonderful drama of the moving clouds has been successfully captured.

A polarising filter

This is possibly one of the most useful filters a landscape photographer can use as they help in three ways. First, they eliminate unwanted reflections making water and other reflective surfaces appear more transparent. The effect varies considerably depending on the angle to the water so, for example, if you take your shot at an oblique angle the results will be minimal but, if you are able to take your photograph directly over water, the results can be dramatic. Second, they reduce the reflection from plants and leaves, increasing saturation and, as a consequence, making colours look more intense. Third, a polarising filter can be used to improve saturation or just to increase contrast, particularly if a sky is included in the shot. This filter is most widely used by landscape photographers to intensify a blue sky, but you need to appreciate that it only works to its full potential when the lens is pointing 90 degrees to the sun. The effects can be dramatic, particularly if there are some white clouds present. By removing the reflection of light from the minute water droplets present in the atmosphere, the polarising filter produces more saturated and slightly darker skies.

There are two types of polarising filters, the linear and the circular. The linear versions were cheaper to manufacture and worked well on older SLR cameras. However, they can create problems with the metering and focusing of modern DSLRs. For these you need a circular polariser that is designed to work with the camera's exposure and auto focus systems.

While a polarising filter has benefits, there are also some drawbacks. The purpose of this filter is to reduce the amount of light reaching the sensor, therefore expect to lose between two and three stops when using one. This could mean the difference between hand-holding your camera and putting it onto a tripod. They can be over-used resulting in an unnaturally dark blue within the sky. Polarising filters are notoriously tricky to use with wide-angle lenses, sometimes resulting in an uneven effect across the frame. They are helpful filters but they should be used with care.

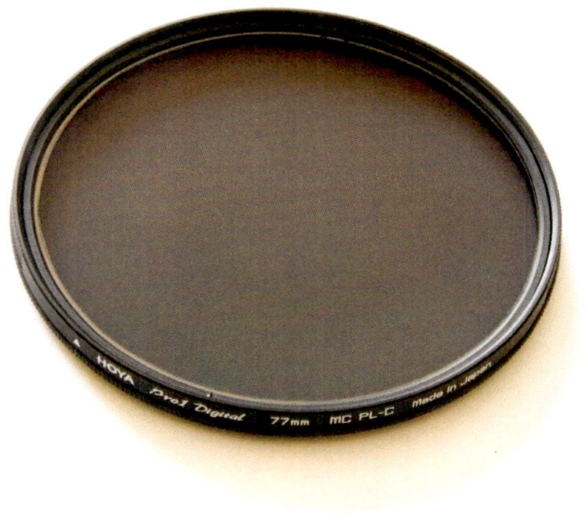

Figure 18 **Polarising filter**. A polarising filter can be used to improve saturation or just to increase contrast, particularly if a sky is included in the shot.

Examples of images taken with a polarising filter

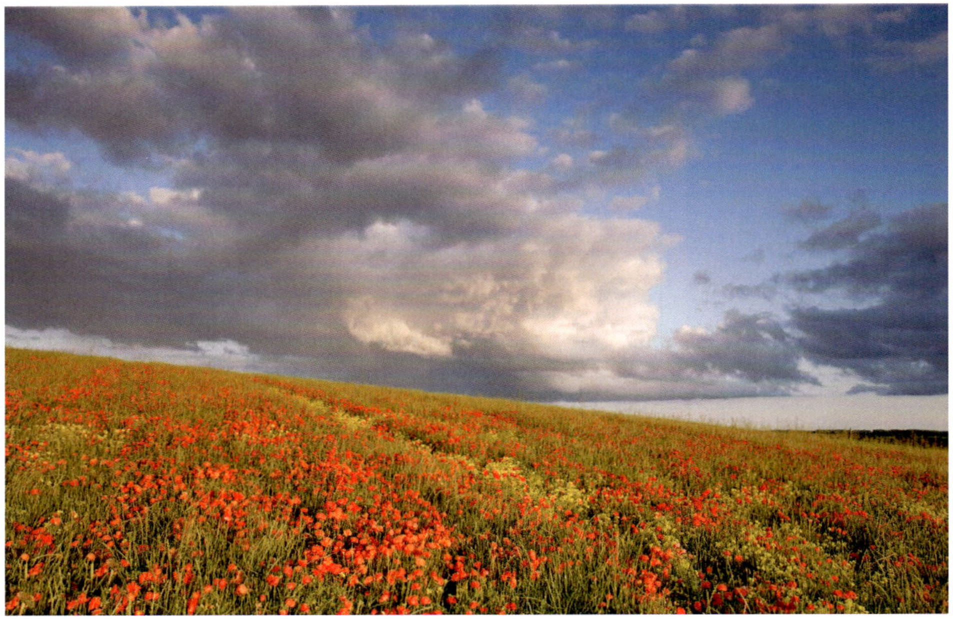

Figure 19 **Poppy field and evening sky**. Irrespective of what appears in the foreground, it is often the sky that sets the mood in the landscape. By using a polarising filter not only does the sky appear more dramatic but also any possible unwanted reflections from the poppies have been subdued.

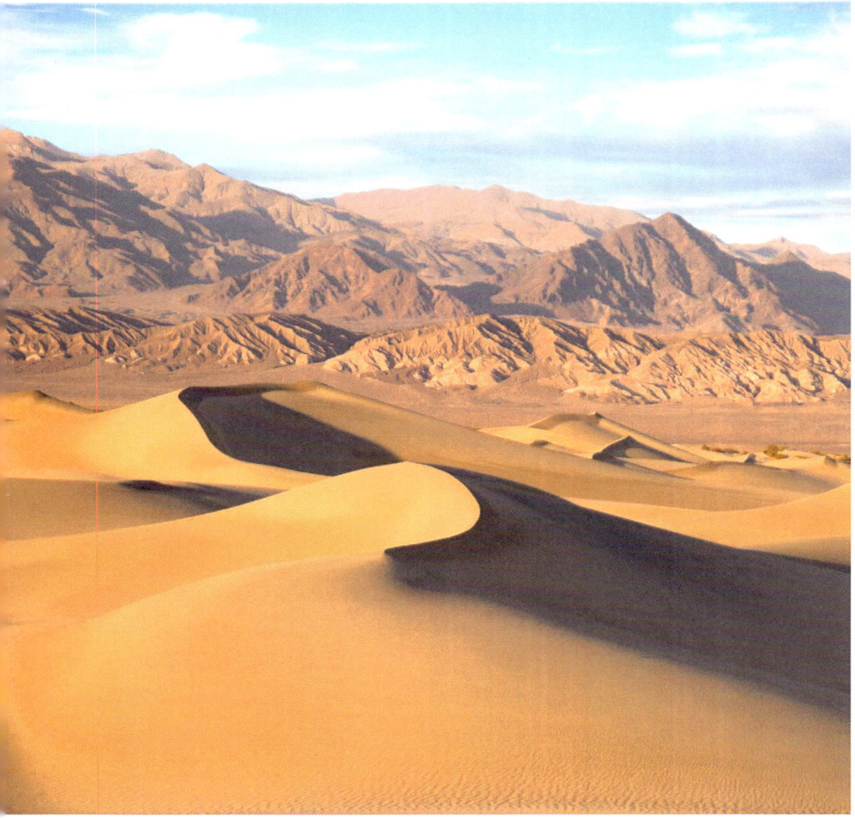

Figure 20 **Cirrus clouds and sand dunes**. In order to heighten the contrast between the dunes in the foreground and the distant blue sky, I have used a polarising filter. Not only has this acted to darken the sky, but it has also emphasised the delicate cirrus clouds. Great care needs to be taken when using a polarising filter so that the sky does not appear unevenly polarised. This can be particularly evident when using a wide-angle lens.

GETTING A RELIABLE WEATHER FORECAST

When considering the vexed issue of forecasting weather, the first thing you need to do is to distinguish between 'climate' and 'weather'. Climate takes a long-term view of the weather, describing the average conditions for a given region. For example, you may discover that an area to which you wish to travel averages 10 hours of sunshine daily within the month of June. That, of course, doesn't mean that you will get 10 hours of sunshine; you could be unlucky and see none.

As a photographer what you actually need is a detailed forecast of the weather you are likely encounter on days you intend to take photographs. The information you need will vary – sometimes all you need to know is the medium-term forecast for the coming week. Alternatively, you may need a forecast for the day, giving you a breakdown hour by hour. Finally, if you intend to work on the coast, having some awareness of the tides is invaluable because the opportunities for photography vary enormously depending on whether the tide is in or out.

The media: television, radio, newspapers

As a first call many of us use the media, namely newspapers, radio and television, to supply us with weather information but, sometimes, it is not sufficiently up-to-date. Newspapers in particular are not able to give information much more than 24 hours in advance. As radio and television operate for nearly 24 hours, they are more accurate as they are capable of regularly updating their information. The problem with all established media outlets is that they cannot afford to be specific. A radio or television forecaster will have just five minutes to describe the weather, which at best will be generalised. As we all know, it is possible for a town just 20 miles away to be enjoying sunshine while you are experiencing dull overcast weather. What you need is a forecasting service that gives you an hour-by-hour forecast in precisely the area you intend to work. This is where the internet comes in.

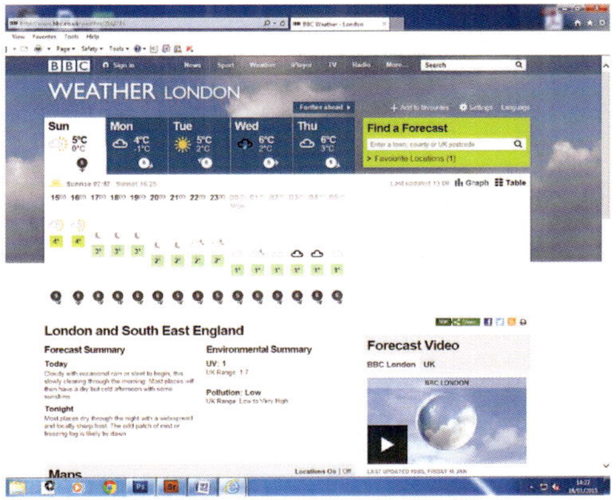

Figure 21. Websites such as The BBC are an excellent facility for finding out what the weather is likely to be at any given location on an hour-by-hour basis.

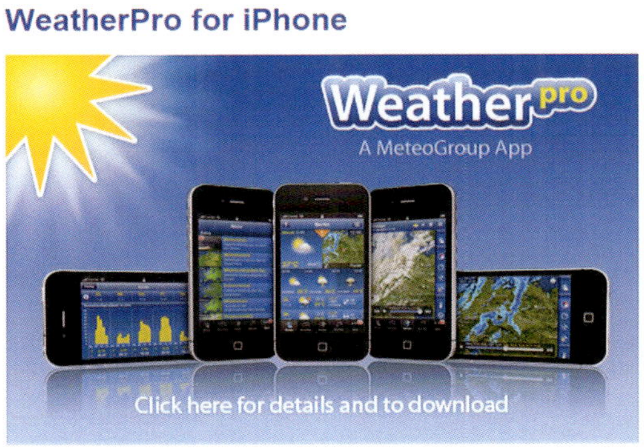

Figure 22. With the increasing popularity of smart phones, there is a host of excellent apps that you can download to allow you to keep tabs on the weather, even as you travel.

There are numerous excellent weather websites that allow you to pinpoint a specific area, giving you reliable hour-by-hour predictions. The information will have been gathered from sophisticated computers that are capable of making trillions of calculations per second. On a similar tack, we are all now able to download smart phone apps that provide an identical service. WeatherPro HD, for example, is capable of accurate seven-day forecasts or hourly reports depending on your requirements. Gleaning its information from global satellites, you are instantly able to assess the weather for your selected location. Other Apps you may wish to consider include Accuweather Platinum, which is highly regarded but it doesn't come free. If you are looking for a free option then try Yahoo Weather.

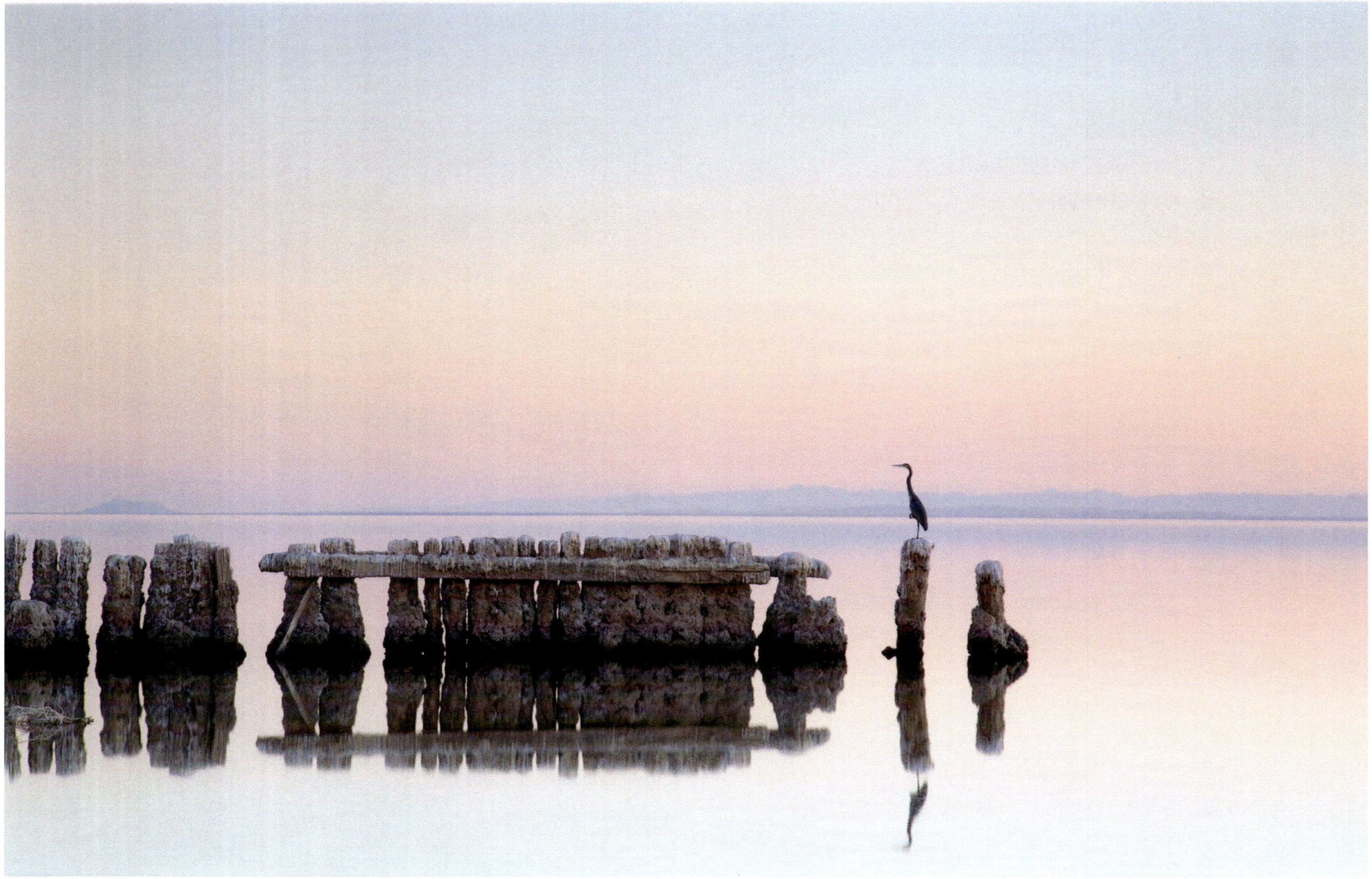

Figure 23 Becalmed. In order to get this photograph, I needed to make a round trip of 80 miles, so I wanted to be assured that the journey was worth my while. Being able to access an up-to-date weather forecast using my smart phone proved particularly helpful.

When looking at a forecast, you are able to plan both for the immediate and the longer term, ensuring that you can make best use of the weather.

Planning for the immediate term

1. Wind

If the forecast predicts winds, establish whether this means gusts or just a steady breeze. If you are likely to encounter severe gusts and plan on working with a tripod, you will need to find a location that offers some shelter. Alternatively, if you have no option but to work in the open, consider using your camera bag to 'anchor' your tripod. Moreover, if you are likely to encounter strong winds, take note of the ambient temperature as well. If they are predicting low temperatures and winds, you need to anticipate the 'wind-chill' and dress accordingly.

2. Rain

As discussed in Chapter 3, rain should be viewed as a positive element that can greatly enhance an image, but it does help if you can plan for it. It is easy to work in drizzle or light rain but, if you are likely to experience both heavy rain and strong winds, then once again aim to work from a sheltered location. Don't be deterred, it is just that you may need to consider your vantage point more carefully. It also helps to think about the direction of the rain. If it is predicted to come directly into the camera, then you might need to assess your options. Finally, establish if the rain is likely to be torrential. Working in these conditions does pose problems (although they are not insurmountable) and torrential downpours often pass quickly leaving the landscape wonderfully transformed.

3. Find out what conditions you can expect at dawn and dusk

Dawn and dusk are often the times of day most landscape photographers want to work in, not least because of the dramatic colours you see in the sky. It undoubtedly helps if you are able to determine whether there will be any cloud cover at these important times of the day. You are also able to establish the sunrise and sunset times by consulting a weather forecast and websites on the internet are particularly accurate in this respect. It should also be noted that they can vary quite surprisingly, even within a small country.

4. Check the tides

If you are planning a photographic shoot by the coast, checking the tides is essential. There are locations where you will get better shots when the tide is in while, on other occasions, you will be better served when it is out. You also need to know if a 'spring-tide' is anticipated, as the extent of the tidal changes will be greater. All this information can be obtained from the Met Office.

Planning for the longer term

Why not try anticipating the weather yourself? By studying the developing air masses you should be able to do that with reasonable confidence. An air mass, whether warm or cold, usually remains fairly uniform, although things can get quite interesting when it is likely to collide with another air mass at what are known as frontal boundaries, which can create 'lively' and potentially exciting photographic conditions.

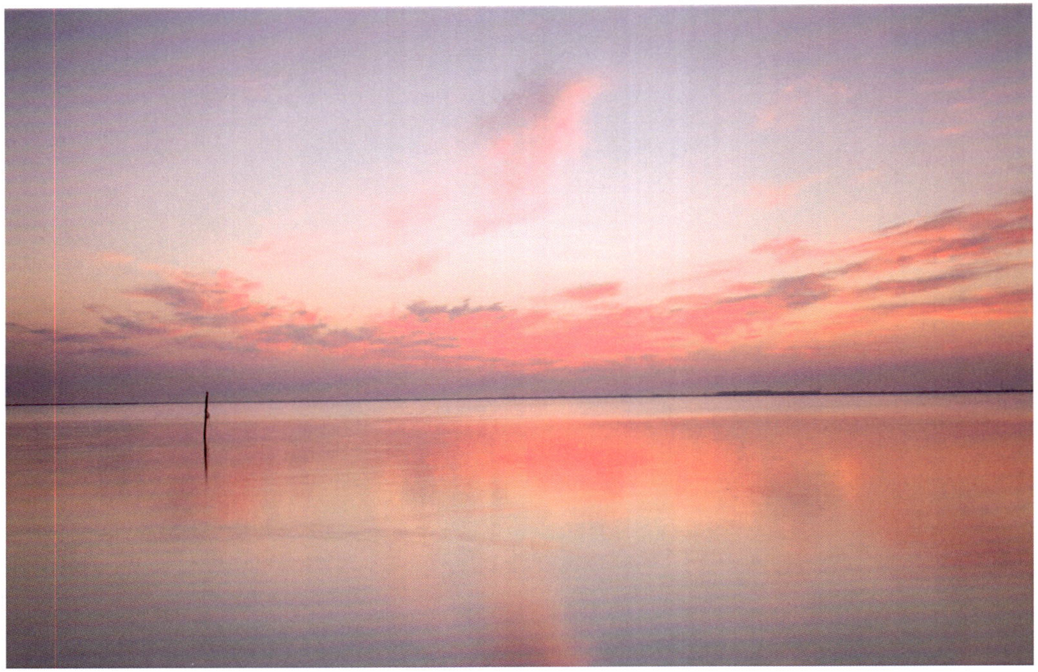

Figure 24 **Dawn light**. By getting an accurate weather forecast for a specific location, you are more likely to travel in order to make best use of the pre-dawn light. I certainly would not have taken the chance just on a whim.

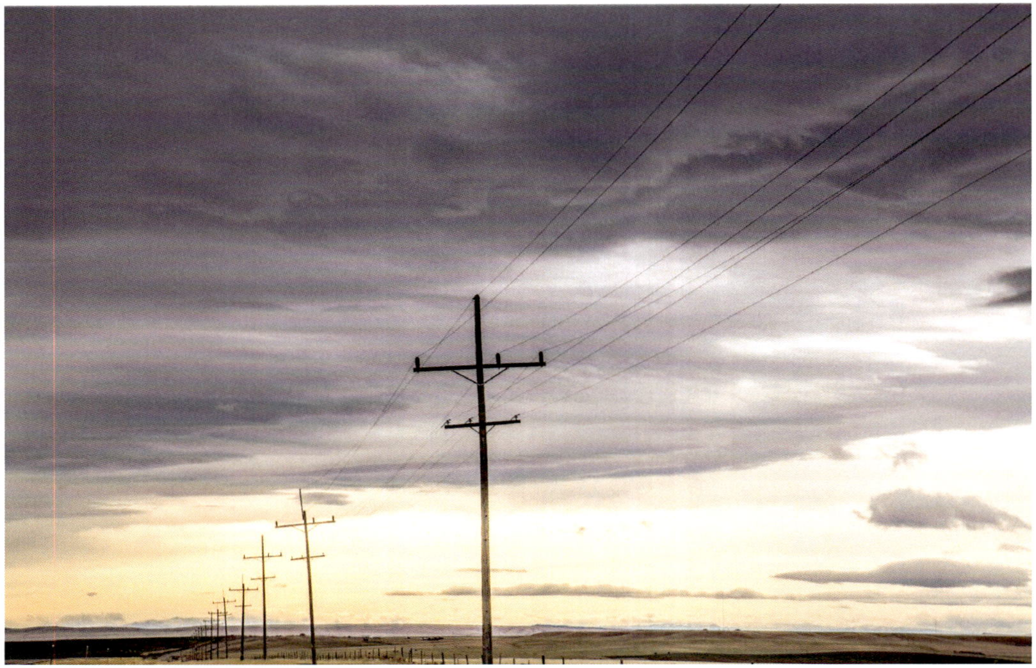

Figure 25 **Receding telegraph poles**. This was taken while travelling through America. Having carefully studied the weather forecast I specifically chose to head in this direction as I wanted to capture a landscape under a sombre and threatening sky. I was well rewarded.

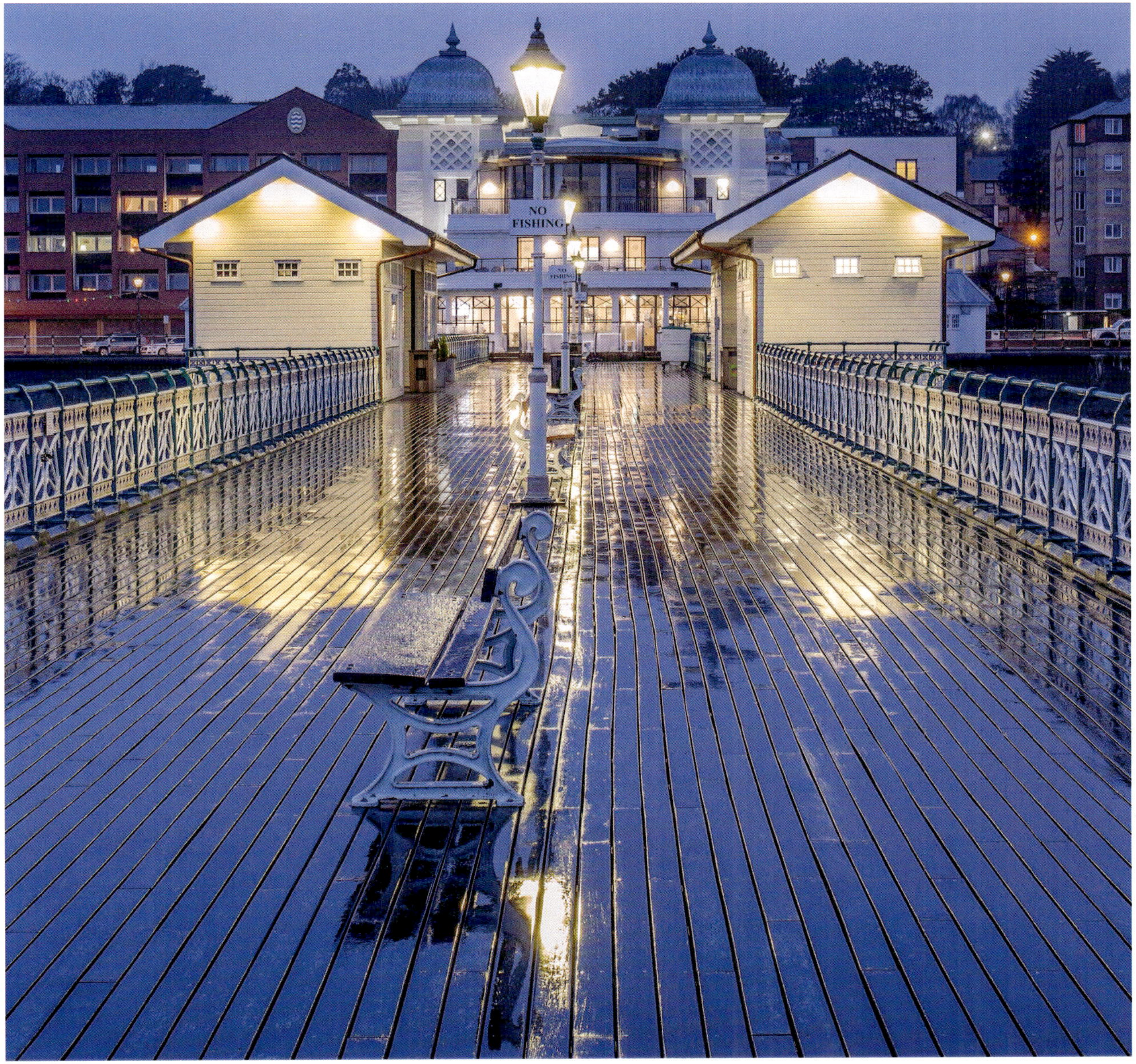

Figure 26 **Pier in heavy rain**. This is a classic example of where it helps to consult an up-to-date weather forecast. Mindful of the orientation of the pier, I was able to establish that the wind and rain would be blowing into my back (rather than into the camera), therefore making my journey worthwhile.

Viewed from space, it is quite illuminating to see how much of the Earth's surface is covered in cloud at any one time. Obviously some areas are more prone to cloud cover than others but, rather than view this as a problem, it should be seen as presenting you with fresh opportunities. In the eyes of many professional landscape workers, there is no other visual element that conveys mood more effectively than cloud. Somehow it conveys a unique character that is special to that moment. Even if a particular location has been well photographed in the past, the uniqueness of the clouds will make it special to you.

It is not just the variety of clouds that make them so interesting but when within the day they are photographed. A cumulus cloud, for example, can appear fluffy and white in the middle of the day but, if it is photographed early in the morning or late in the afternoon, it can appear pink, yellow, golden or peach depending on the strength and direction of the sun. In order to be able to make best use of clouds, it helps to know their various classifications and to understand how they are formed.

Common cloud types

1. Stratus

Stratus are low-lying clouds; they are typical on those days when you look out and the sky appears grey and featureless. Moreover, because of the low nature of this cloud, if you climb to a higher elevation you are quite likely to enter the cloud and experience a mist or drizzle. In fact, some meteorologists view a stratus cloud cover as 'high fog'. The parallels are clear. Stratus forms when a body of relatively warm moist air rises and then depressurises. This can often result in light rain, sometimes lasting for days, which is why it is not everybody's favourite cloud formation. From a photographic standpoint it is grey and featureless, and many view this as difficult conditions to work in but, in common with all weather conditions, stratus does suggest a distinct mood.

Figure 27 Stratus. Low lying and featureless, from a photographic standpoint it is easy to dismiss stratus clouds, but they are capable of injecting mood into landscape, particularly if you are working in monochrome.

2. Cumulus

The best way to describe cumulus clouds is as those that are often used 'decoratively'. White and fluffy set against a blue sky, cumulus clouds often feature in illustrations featuring idyllic landscapes; highly idiosyncratic, children love to include cumulus clouds in their landscape drawings. 'Puffy' and 'cotton-like', they certainly are both common and distinctive. Cumulus are low-stage clouds rarely forming above 3,000 feet. They can appear individually, in lines or in clusters, which adds to their visual appeal. One rarely experiences precipitation as a result of cumulus, just the occasional and sometimes welcome shadow although, under certain circumstances, they can group and then grow into more threatening cumulonimbus clouds. Photographers are keen to use a scattering of cumulus clouds as a way of breaking up an otherwise featureless blue sky.

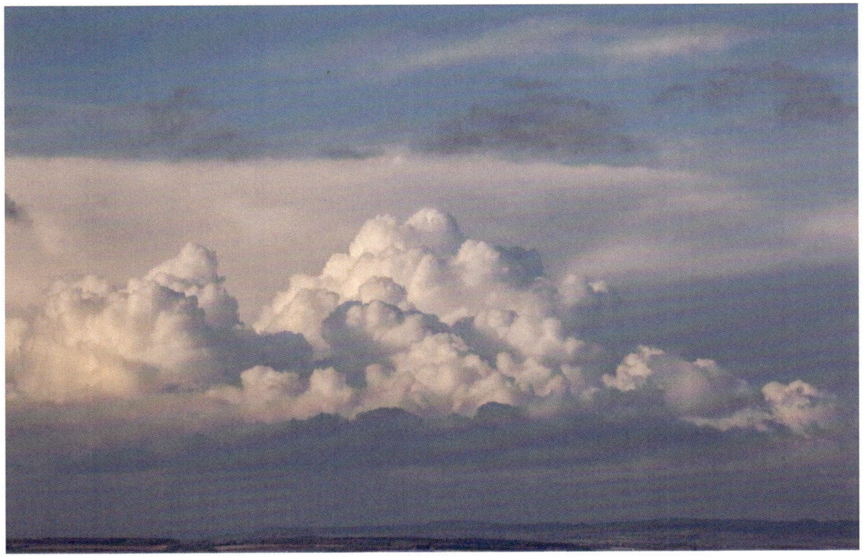

Figure 28 Cumulus. The best way to describe cumulus clouds is as those that appear in idyllic landscapes. It is surprising how frequently cumulus clouds feature in postcards as a way of breaking up a blue sky.

3. Stratocumulus

Once again this is a common type of cloud that forms below 6,000 feet. It tends to be thicker than cumulus, often appearing as a sheet of grey or white cloud formed into regular bands or rolls. The cloud cover can often appear patterned and regular across the entire sky, with just small patches of blue peeking through. It is a cloud form that is more likely to occur during the winter months, usually when there is a period of high pressure, producing little if any rain, although they can also be a sign of worse weather to come. With little direct sunshine and free of harsh contrasts, stratocumulus offers relatively easy lighting conditions for landscape photography. Moreover, the rather beautiful mosaic effect this cloud cover offers is often used as a feature, particularly with monochrome enthusiasts.

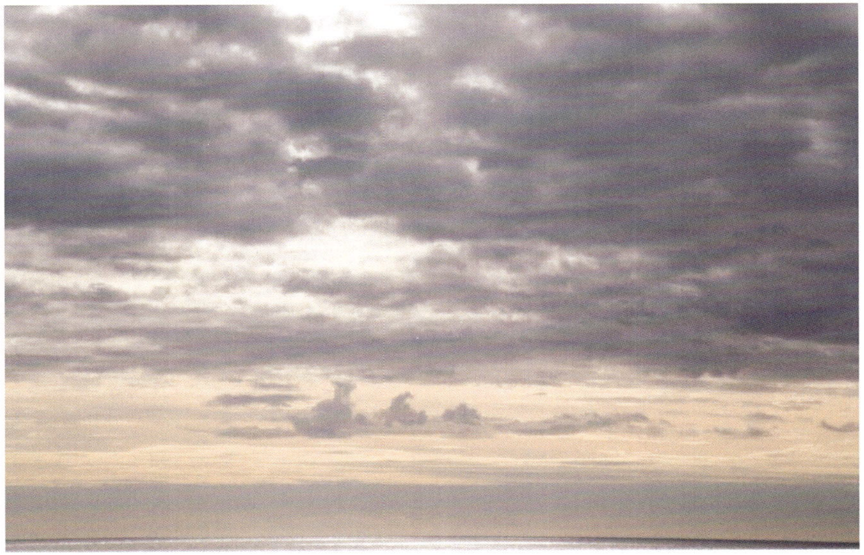

Figure 29 Stratocumulus. From a photographic standpoint, this is a type of cloud that has distinct 'character', creating an interesting pattern across the entire sky.

4. Altocumulus

From a visual standpoint altocumulus clouds are visually similar to stratocumulus clouds, except that they form higher in the atmosphere. Typically, they form between 6,000 and 20,000 feet. The patterns created can be stunning and are capable of sustaining sufficient visual interest in their own right, particularly if photographed at dawn or dusk. Altocumulus are most commonly found between the warm and cold fronts of a depression, although they are often hidden by lower cloud. However, once this clears (surprisingly often in the evening) you will be rewarded with one of nature's truly spectacular shows. This is a cloud formation that can cover quite a large area and is often referred to as a 'mackerel sky'. This notion of course is very much part of our folklore, stimulating phrases such as 'with a mackerel in the sky, three days dry'. Clearly it is a metrological feature that has long caught our imaginations.

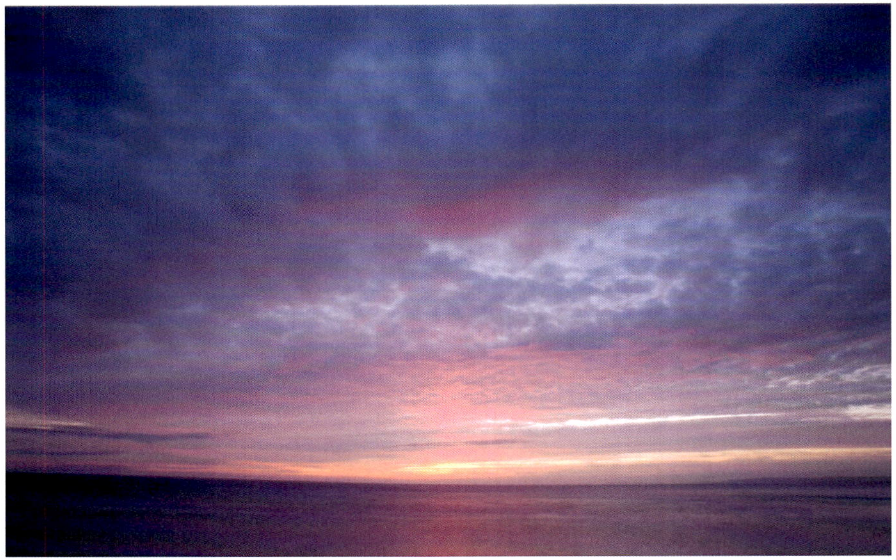

Figure 30 **Altocumulus**. Often referred to as a 'mackerel sky', they can appear spectacularly beautiful when photographed at dawn or dusk.

5. Altostratus

As you might guess, altostratus clouds are simply stratus clouds that exist much higher in the atmosphere, usually between 6,000 and 22,000 feet. They are similar to stratus clouds insofar as they blanket the sky and are relatively featureless, although you can sometimes see rather interesting yet subtle wavy patterns that are caused by wind shear. They tend to be a light grey to bluish-grey colour and, while the sun or moon can be seen through them, particularly in the thinner parts of the cloud, the effect is pale and watery. We tend to see altostratus cloud prior to a period of continuous rain or snow so it does have negative connotations although, of course, it does bring with it its own unique beauty. I do find this cloud formation photographs particularly well at night.

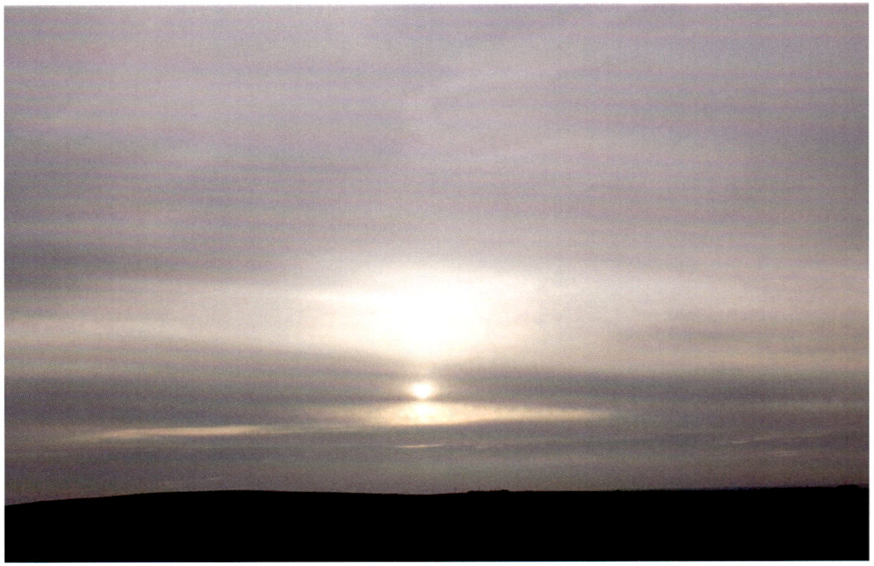

Figure 31 **Altostratus**. Featureless and flat, altostratus are easily confused with stratus clouds, except that they form at higher altitudes. Where they thin, it is possible to see a watery sun or moon shining through.

6. Cumulonimbus

By way of contrast to the altostratus, the cumulonimbus is a dramatic cloud formation that reaches high into the sky and is usually associated with stormy weather. They normally start as cumulus clouds at lower elevations but then grow vertically, often quite spectacularly into its tell-tale 'mushroom' shape. The base of a cumulonimbus cloud can be several miles across so it certainly is a dominating feature on the skyline. While it starts at altitudes of as low as 500 feet, in extreme cases it can reach up to 20,000 feet. What makes this cloud formation so distinctive is its flat, anvil-like top, which is caused by the winds at the highest altitudes that shear off the top of the cloud. These dramatic clouds can form what are known as 'super-cells', which are a prelude to severe thunderstorms. The photographic appeal of these metrological giants is obvious as they can add drama to just about any landscape.

7. Cirrus

One of the most charming of cloud formations is cirrus, which tends to form between 18,000 and 40,000 feet, so it certainly is a high altitude cloud. They are characterised by their wispy strands that resembles a horse's tail, which is why they are often referred to as 'mares' tails'. Much of the delicacy of these wonderful formations is created by powerful high altitude jet-streams that appear to elongate and stretch the cloud. Because of their height, cirrus clouds are composed almost entirely of ice crystals. They tend to be semi-transparent and appear particularly white when set against the deep blue of the upper atmosphere. They are, however, a sign of wet and stormy weather to come. While similar to cirrostratus, what marks out cirrus clouds is that they appear as relatively small scattered clouds. They really are worth photographing as they can add character to the most uninspiring landscape. Shot either in daytime or night, they always appear spectacularly beautiful.

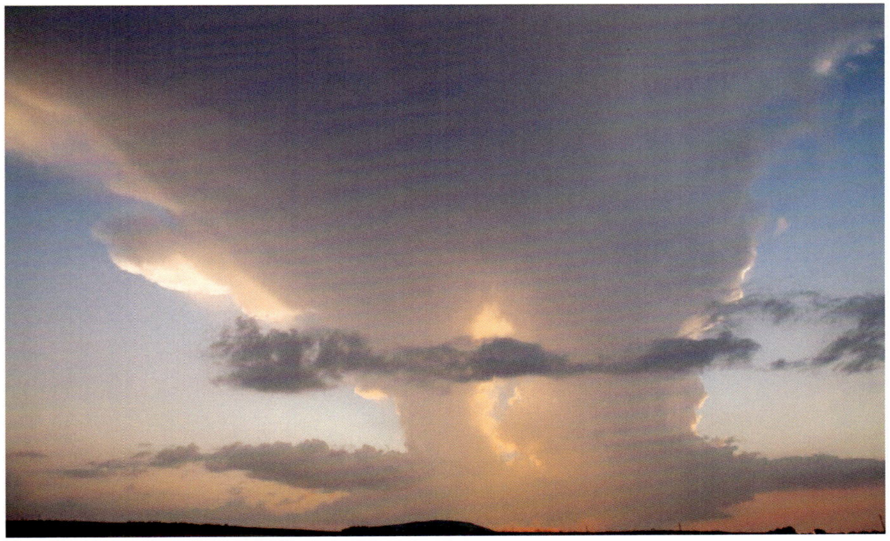

Figure 32 **Cumulonimbus**. Cumulonimbus can prove spectacularly beautiful whether photographed in the middle of the day or in evening light. What makes them so distinctive is their height and their distinctive anvil-like top.

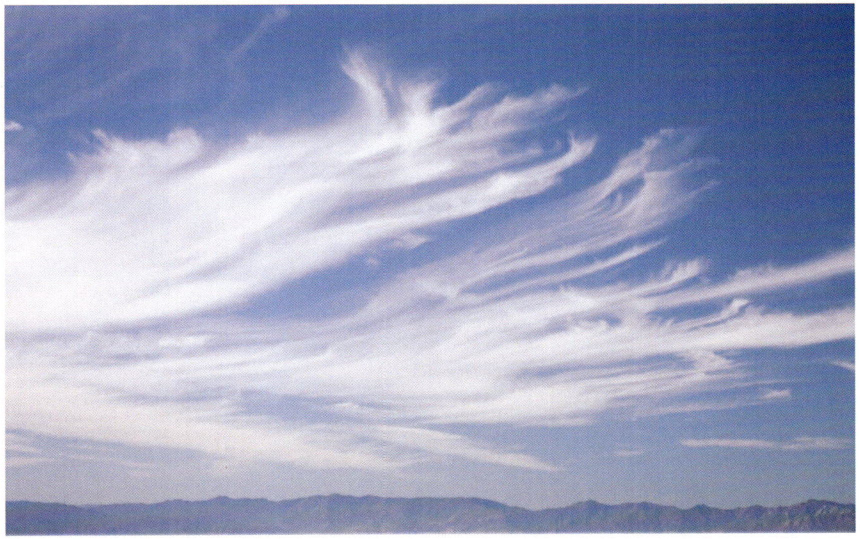

Figure 33 **Cirrus**. This is one of the most delicate of cloud formations. Whether you are working colour or in monochrome, the inclusion of cirrus will immediately add character to your landscape.

8. Cirrocumulus

Together with cirrus and cirrostratus, cirrocumulus is the last of the three 'high altitude' cloud formations. It seems amazing, but they appear between 3 and 7 miles above the earth's surface. Due to their altitude, the majority of the cloud comprises ice crystals, although they may also include some liquid water droplets as well. Due to their relative distance from the earth's surface, each individual cloud appears small. The sky appears noticeably patterned, in a way not dissimilar to a typical 'mackerel sky' one associates with an altocumulus cloud formation, except the cirrocumulus pattern is considerably finer. Moreover, cirrocumulus clouds appear marginally more translucent and are often seen together with cirrus clouds. Often when looking at these wonders of nature, it strikes me how much they look like a human fingerprint. From a visual standpoint, cirrocumulus always look attractive, but can look especially striking when seen at sunset, or just before sunrise as the tiny clouds reflect the orange, red and yellow rays of the rising or disappearing sun.

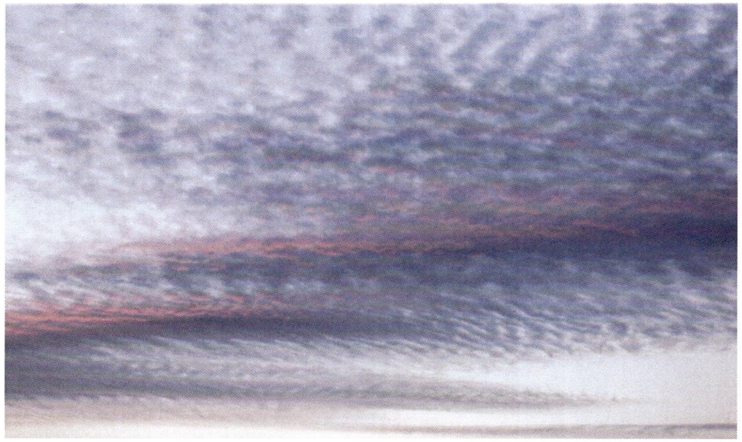

Figure 34 **Cirrocumulus**. An example of a high altitude cloud formation; in appearance cirrocumulus can often be confused with altocumulus.

Photograph clouds for their own sake

Some photographers, when viewing an awe-inspiring unfolding cloud formation, become concerned that they cannot find a suitable foreground, unaware that it is not always necessary to include one. It is a simple principle, but the more dramatic the sky, the less important the foreground becomes. I greatly enjoy photographing skies and I have established various local viewing points I can use when the sky gets interesting. The horizon needs to be simple and uncluttered. It is not necessary to know the various cloud types; just appreciate that they are beautiful in their own right and can offer fabulous opportunities for photography.

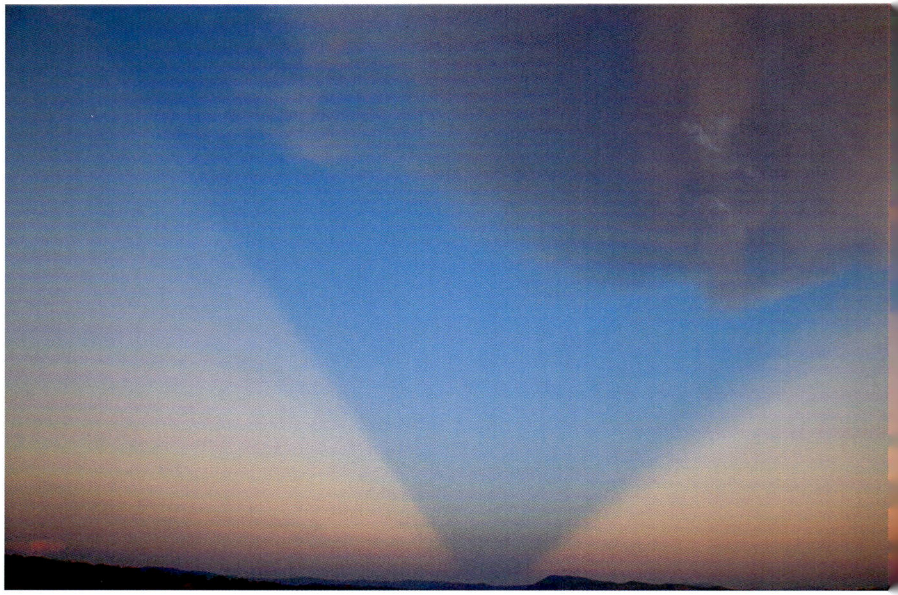

Figure 35 **The blue triangle**. Not all cloud formations conform to a specific type as there might be a varying weather system at play, which results in some unusual, yet extremely dramatic skies. I was travelling along a motorway when I first spotted this, so I pulled off at the first convenient intersection and quickly found a suitable vantage point.

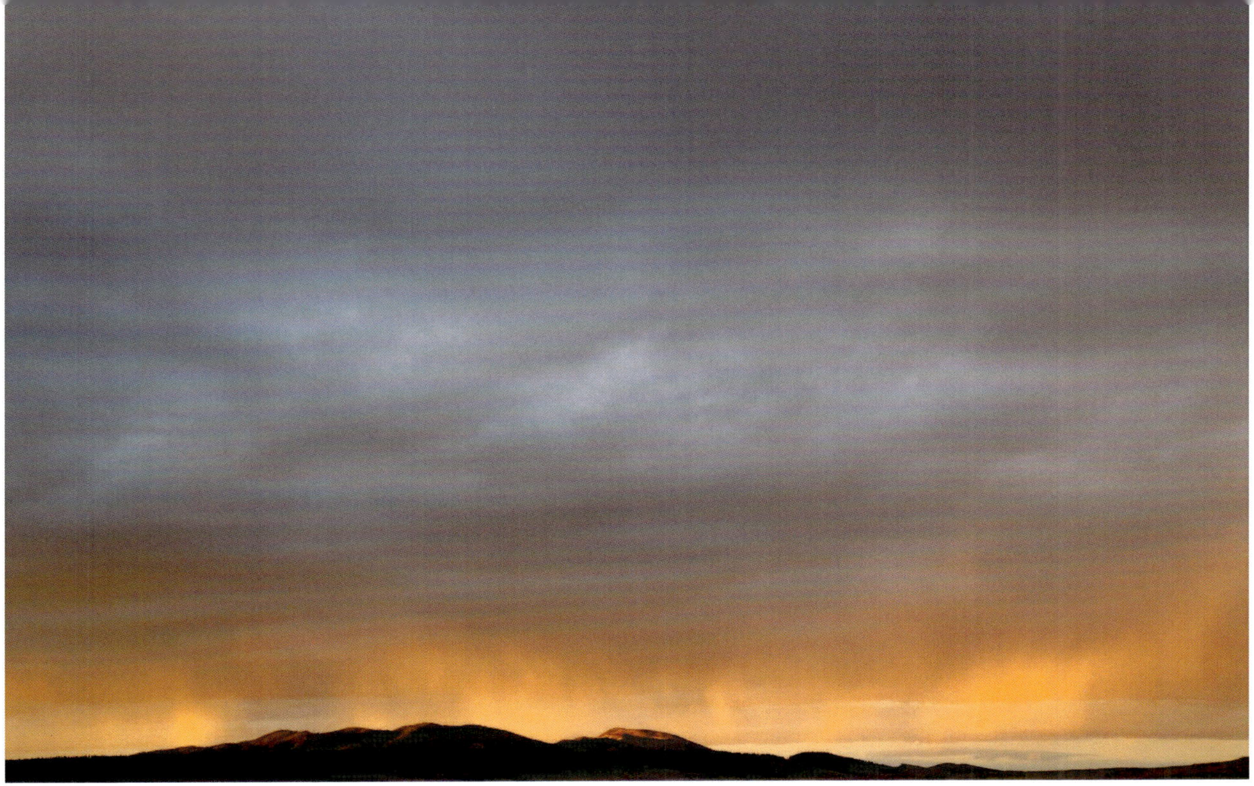

Figure 36 Simmering orange. Photographed at dusk, we had experienced a prolonged period of rain. The stratus clouds were just beginning to break which allowed the low rays from the rapidly disappearing sun to penetrate beneath them, producing this fabulous and dramatic combination of colours.

The best locations for photographing skies

- While I do understand that this might be inaccessible for many, the coast offers the ideal location for photographing skies. With a perfectly uninterrupted skyline, it should be possible to capture the entire panorama without compromise.
- A lake or a large stretch of inland water will offer the same advantages as the coast. There will be the odd possibility of an unwanted structure such as a pylon on the skyline, but that can be easily removed post-camera using your preferred editing software.
- Any stretch of reasonably flat landscape will do, although if you can find a high vantage point you should be able to secure an uninterrupted vista. Once again, check the skyline to ensure that there are no unwanted elements.
- If you find yourself witnessing a spectacular sky and cannot find a suitable location, just point your camera upwards. It is not always necessary to include the horizon.
- Sometimes including the odd unintended element to a sky picture can add interest. A silhouetted tree in the corner, or the gable-end of a building adds scale to the picture.

It helps to understand that a cloud formation is a constantly changing element, so do not always assume that the shot you have just taken is necessarily the best. Allow yourself time to watch and record this fascinating metamorphosis, as the cloud changes volume, shape and form. The colour changes, particularly when viewed at sunset or sunrise, can prove particularly alluring. Once you have taken your shots, why not group several of the images together, showing what is, in effect, a time lapse? The results can prove surprisingly illuminating.

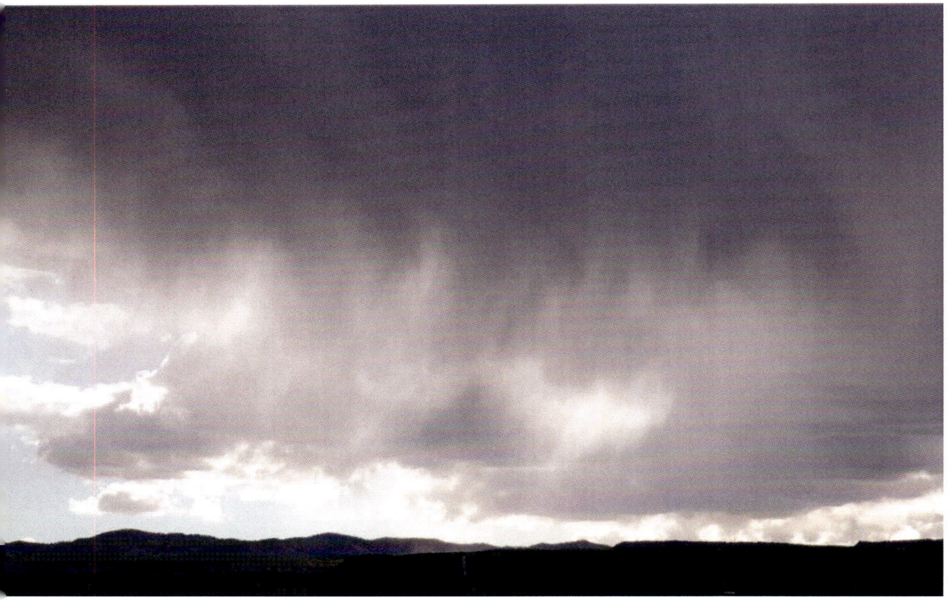

Figure 37 Distant rain. Caught on the edge of a large cumulonimbus cloud formation, rain was inevitable and clearly visible in the distance. The contrast between the overhead clouds and the distant horizon introduces a distinct sense of drama into the landscape.

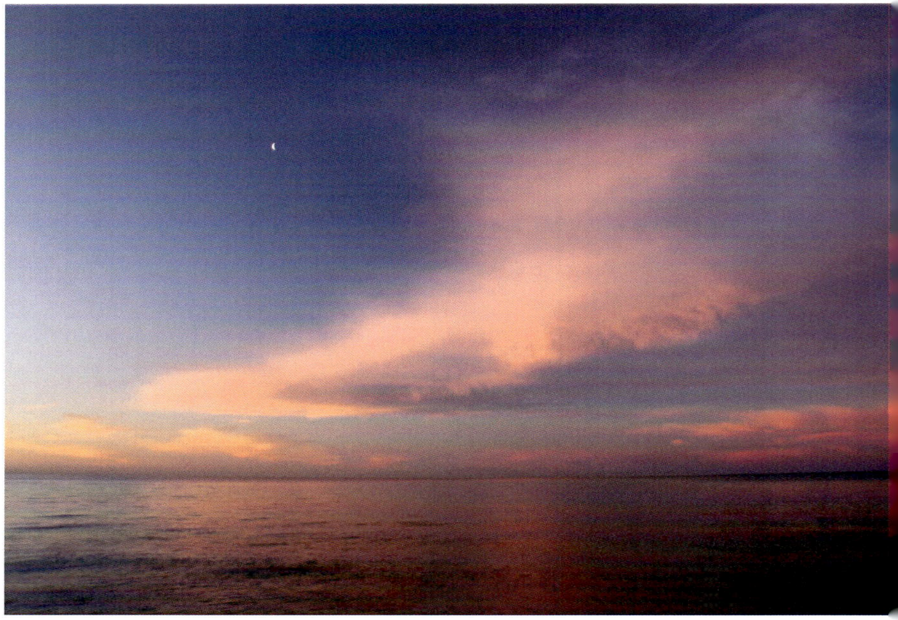

Figure 38 Cloud formation photographed pre-dawn. Unquestionably, one of the best times to photograph the sky is pre-dawn, just before the sun emerges.The intensity of the colours can be particularly spectacular at this time of day.

The technical issues relating to photographing clouds

The most obvious consideration is which lens to use. The sky is a large expanse, therefore there is an inclination to use a wide-angle lens and often it proves to be the most suitable. Occasionally the real drama is restricted to just a limited part of the sky, which is when a telephoto lens will prove useful. Gauging the correct exposure is also important. The sky is usually much brighter than the foreground, so point your camera towards the sky in order to get the best exposure setting. This often means the foreground appears silhouetted, but that can be a good thing. Depending on the position of the sun, you might experience an unevenness when photographing the sky, particularly when using a wide-angle lens. There are two ways of remedying this. First, use a soft-graduated filter but position it horizontally (rather than the conventional vertical orientation) in order to balance out the exposure. Second, deal with the problem post-camera. Whether you are using Photoshop or Lightroom, by making a graduated selection this problem is easily corrected.

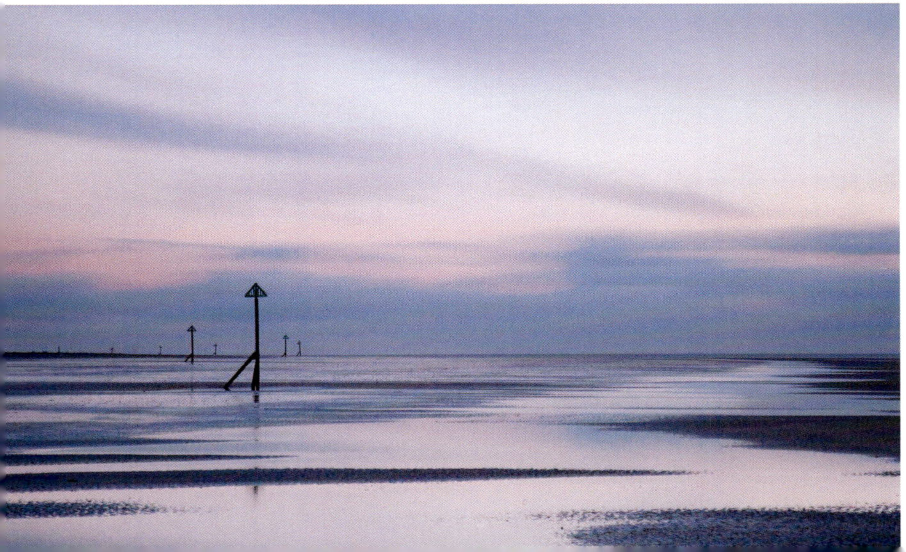

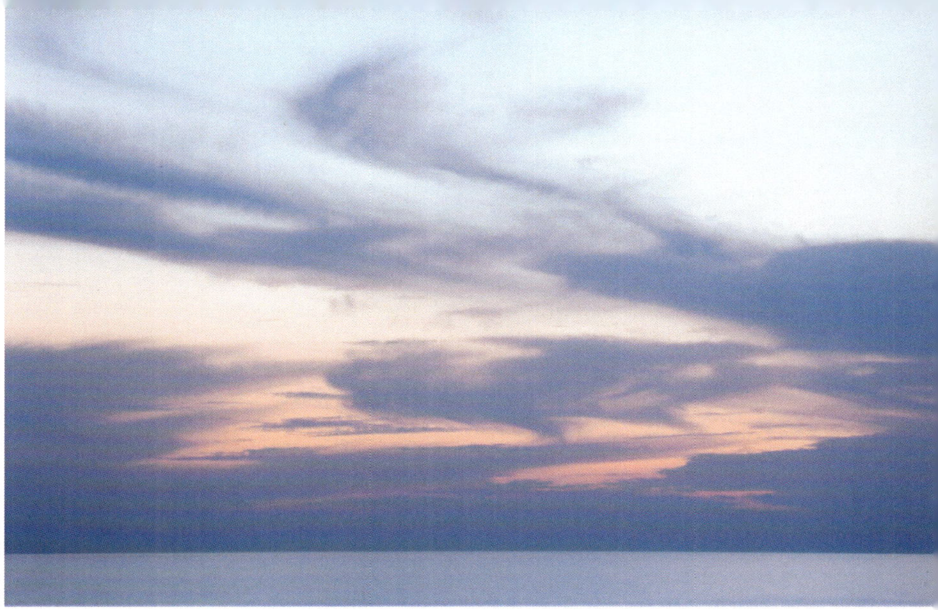

Figure 39 (Above) **Peach and blue**. Some skies are just so beautiful that there is no need for a foreground. Photographed over the coast in pre-dawn light, the subtle interplay between the pale blue and peach evokes a very gentle mood.

Figure 40 (Below left) **Beach with groynes**. What makes this image interesting is that the interplay between the jagged light and dark shapes on the beach are echoed in the sky, which introduces a strong sense of cohesion.

Exploring the 'character' of the cloud

While I have largely concentrated on the cloud formation and disregarded the foreground, it is worth noting that each cloud formation will have its own unique character that could visually chime with certain landscapes. To dismiss that would be to ignore a fabulous photographic opportunity. For example:

- You might encounter a rocky landscape revealing a regular pattern, with the rocks

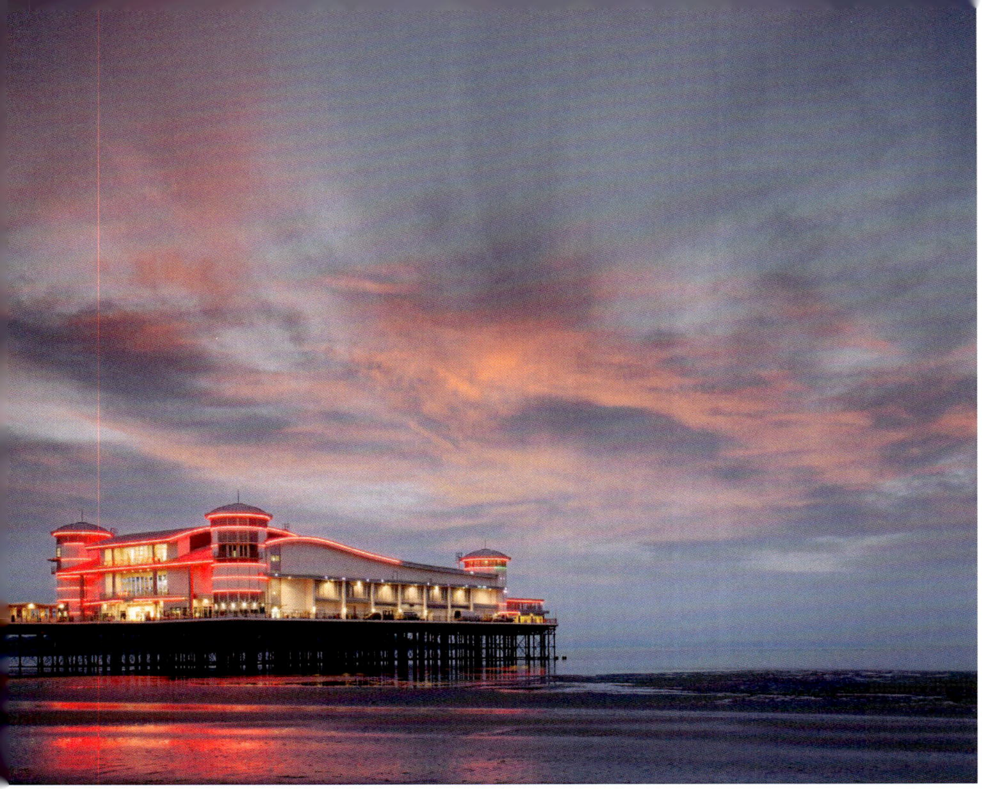

appearing quite large in the foreground and with those in the distance appearing to attenuate. Groups of clouds, particularly cumulus, seem to do the same, as if the sky is mimicking the foreground. Both the rocks and the clouds diminish on the horizon.

- The gentle rhythm of wind passing through a field of cereal crops can create a similar effect, except that it might work far better if there is a simple display of cirrus clouds in the sky that echoes the foreground.
- It might just be the colours that chime. For example, when photographing a building or structure illuminated by red neon in the evening, you may also notice a dramatic blush of red in the sky. This coincidence is far more common than you might think.

Figure 41 **Pier and red sky**. The vibrant colour in the night sky echoes the red neon on the pier and its reflection in the wet mud. The echoing colours introduce a sense of cohesion throughout the image.

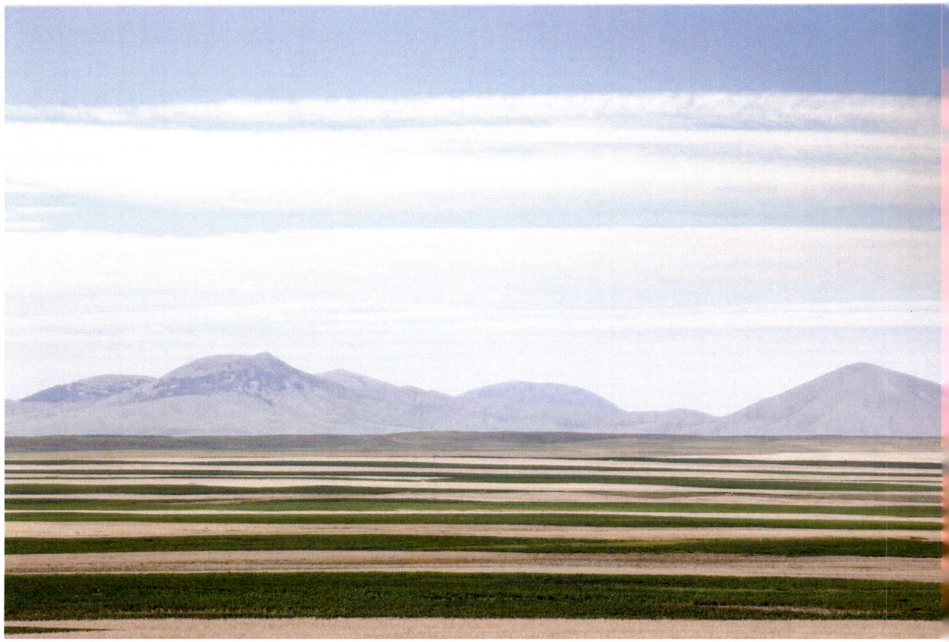

Figure 42 **Strip-farming**. We occasionally encounter a situation where the pattern in the sky parallels that in the landscape. In this example the scene is dominated by a sequence of horizontal light and dark strips, a theme that is subtly mirrored by the horizontal bands of cloud in the sky. I have used a telephoto lens to compress the design and thus emphasise the patterns.

- The patterns in sand, whether in a desert or on a beach, will have been created by wind, which creates a highly idiosyncratic rill. If you look to the sky you will sometimes see similar patterns, which are of course also created by the wind.
- It is not uncommon to see agricultural land that has been strip-farmed (see Figure 42), which creates a distinctive banding pattern. On a similar tack, stratus cloud can appear very similar, particularly as they are being burnt away by the sun.
- The most obvious example where the land appears to mirror the sky is when you find an area of still water that mirrors its every detail. Lakes and reservoirs are the most obvious locations to explore, but even a simple puddle after a period of rain can offer worthwhile opportunities.

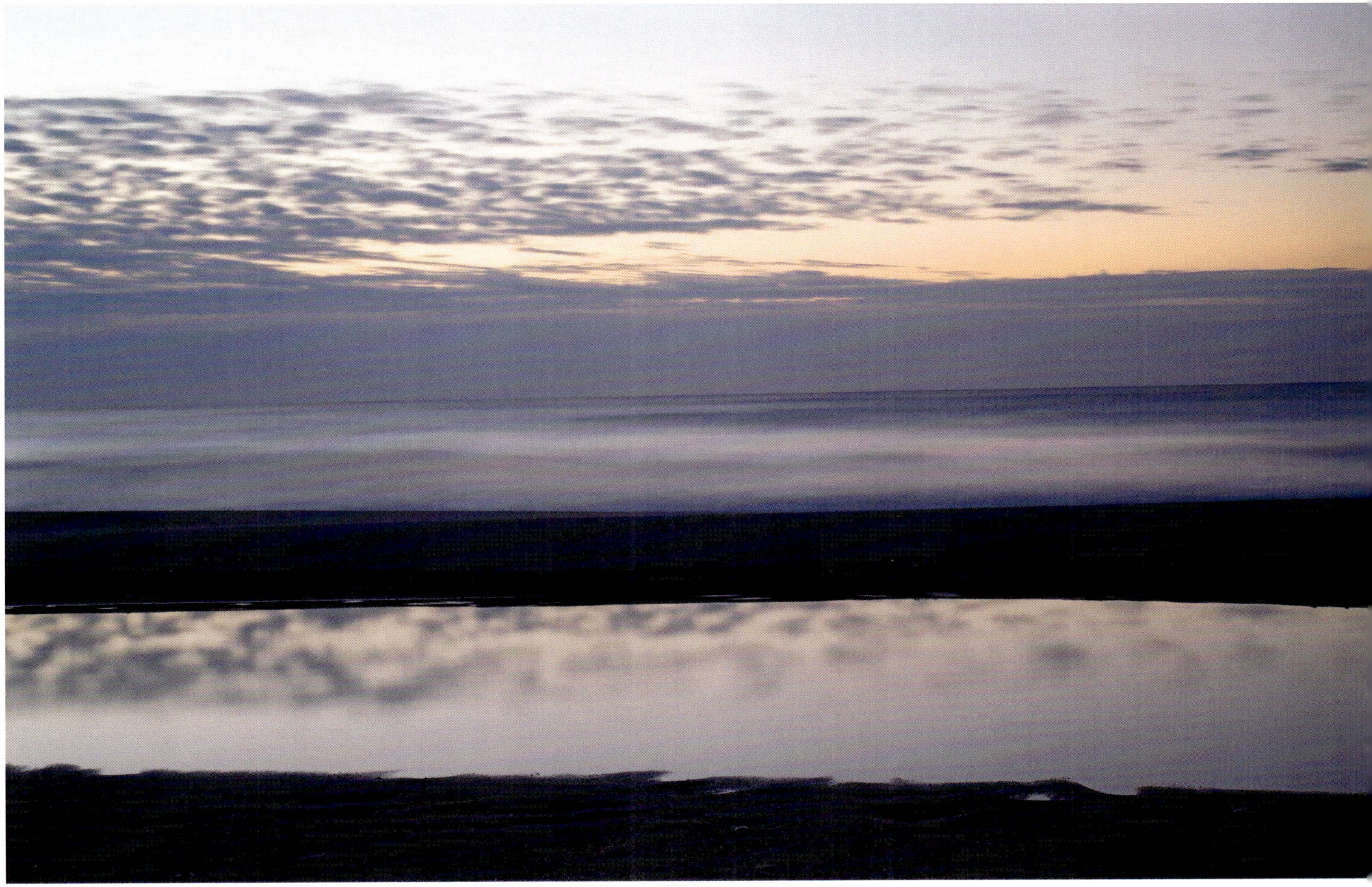

Figure 43 Sky reflected in a beach puddle. Puddles are to be found everywhere, whether on a beach or within an urban environment immediately after rain. If you get down low you can often see the sky beautifully mirrored within them.

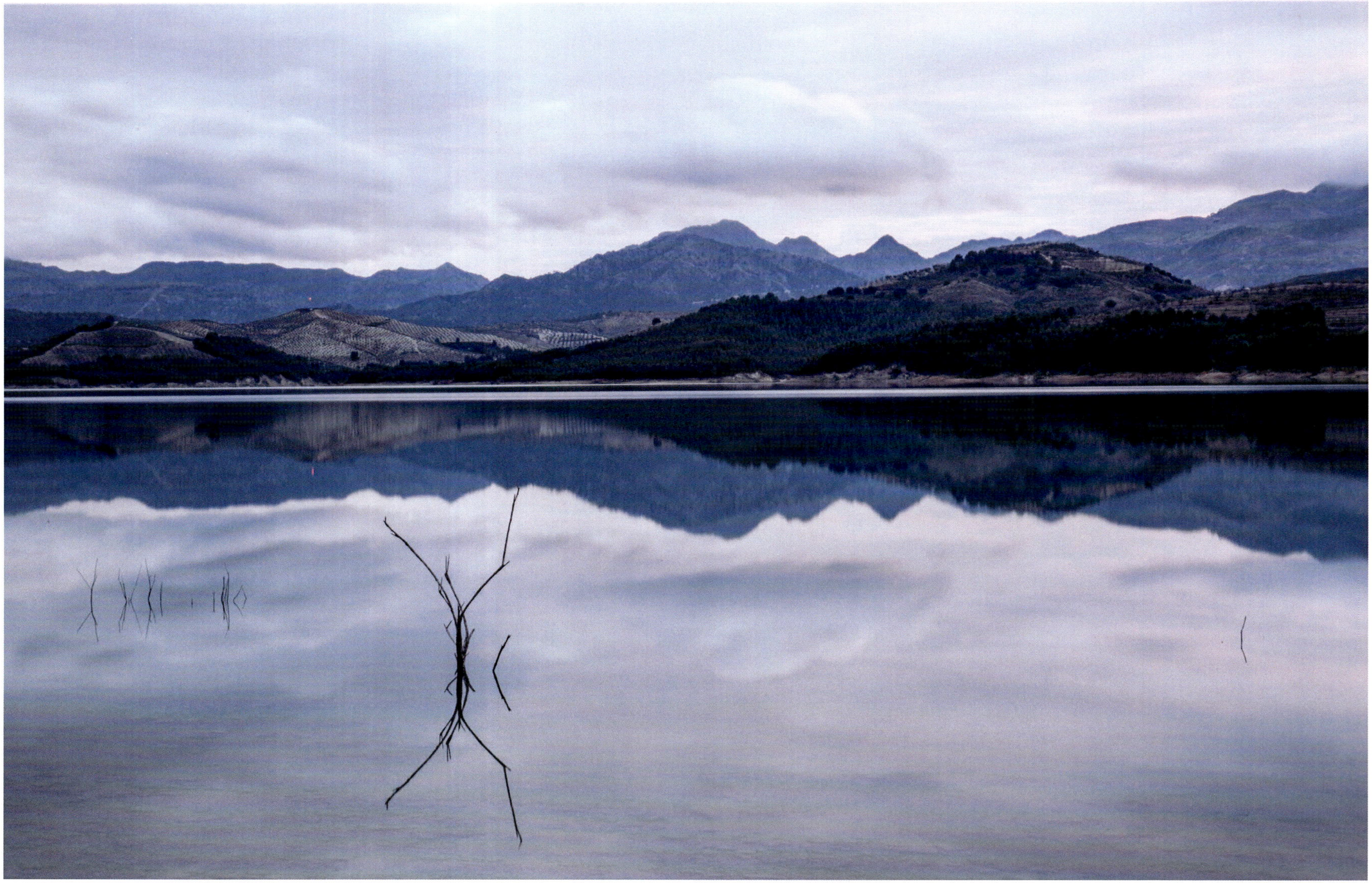

Figure 44 **Reflections in water**. If you find a suitably reflective surface, the sky need not appear particular dramatic in order to secure an interesting picture. The low-lying stratus cloud was offering very little detail although it is its very simplicity that appears to enhance the mountains in the distance. The bluish cast is as a result of photographing the landscape after sunset.

2 Every Cloud has a Silver Lining

Most of us will experience some measure of cloud cover just about every day of our lives, which, for photographers, is something of a blessing. While an uninterrupted blue sky is viewed by the advertising industry as the nearest thing to Nirvana, even when on holiday we generally appreciate the odd cloud floating across the sky. What makes cloud so interesting is that it is so varied, which offers photographers a multitude of opportunities. For those of us who indulge in 'landscape' photography, the presence of cloud sets the tone for the final image.

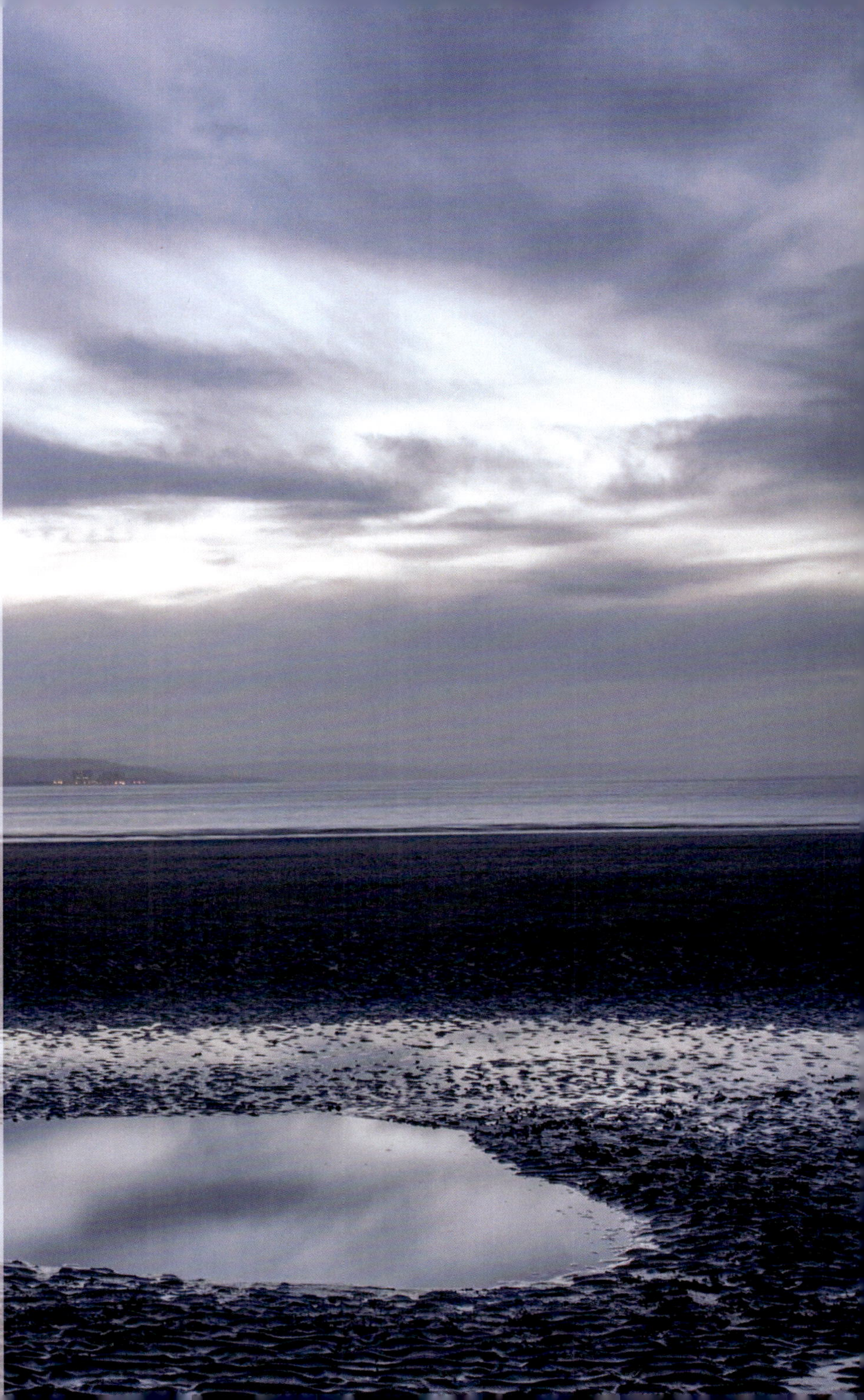

CELEBRATE THE DRAMA OF A STORMY SKY

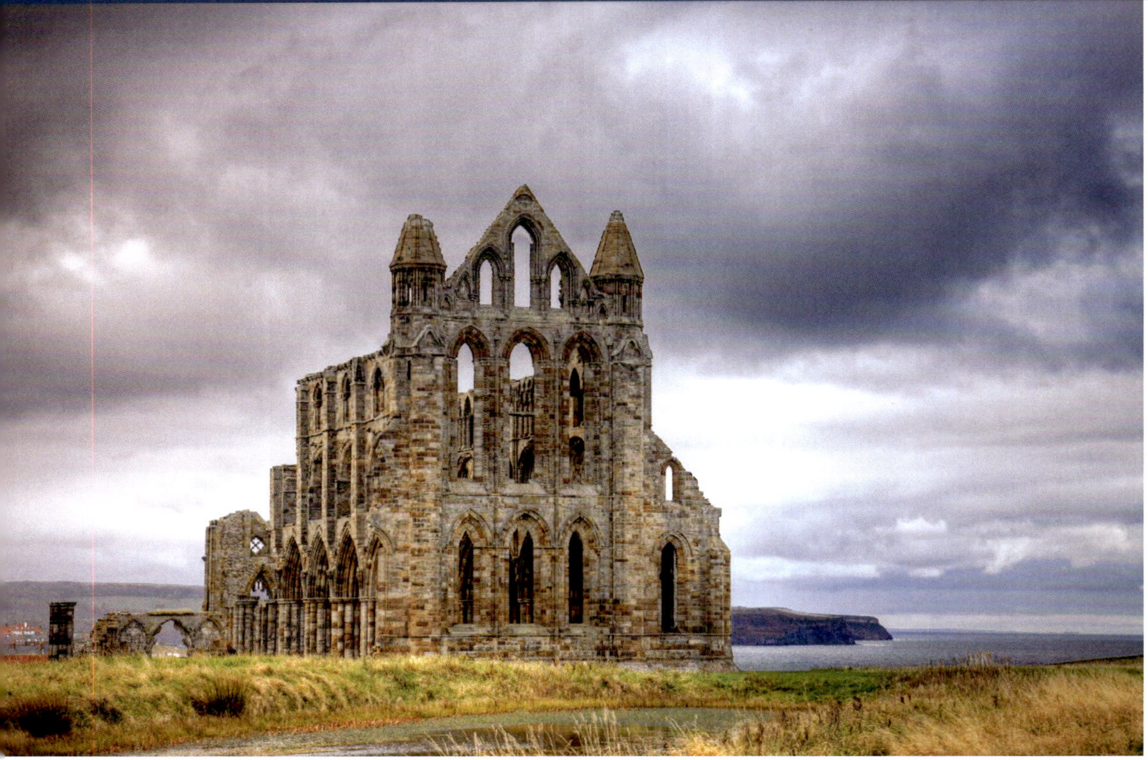

Figure 1 **Whitby Abbey**. The alleged inspiration for Bram Stoker's *Dracula* so it is only fitting that it should be photographed under a 'threatening' sky. One of the most important considerations when photographing the weather in landscape is to match the sky with a suitable foreground.

First, let's consider the most dramatic of cloud, namely the thunderous sky. I have suggested that by introducing weather into our landscape work we are able to promote a heightened sense of mood, and this is particularly evident when photographing stormy skies. The best photographs evoke an emotional response, something a threatening sky is capable of suggesting. The word 'storm' covers many conditions, ranging from something as insignificant as approaching rain to a full-blown hurricane or tornado. I have no desire to witness weather quite as severe as the latter, but it is still possible to witness quite extreme thunderstorms without standing in harm's way.

It occasionally helps to step outside photography and consider how other visual artists have chosen to interpret weather. One of the most successful to have studied this theme is the great English Romanticist painter, J. M. W. Turner. Renowned for his seascapes, Turner believed that in order to understand a storm one needs to fully immerse oneself in the elements. It is alleged that, prior to painting his much celebrated *The Fighting Temeraire*, he had himself strapped to the mast of a ship during a particularly fierce storm. While I am not proposing that we photographers go to quite such lengths, being prepared to experience the power of a storm gives us a better understanding of the subject we are aiming to photograph.

How do thunderstorms form?

All storms are created when an area of low pressure develops within a surrounding area of high pressure, resulting in rapidly rising clouds. The results can be spectacular depending on how high the clouds rise. Often they are at their most impressive during the summer months. On a hot day the surface of the Earth warms up which, in turn, warms up the air directly above the surface. This causes the air to rise and the colder air above to sink, stimulating a process known as convection. The warmer the air, the more rapidly and the higher it will rise, creating amazing cumulonimbus clouds. Two of the most important ingredients required to produce a thunderstorm are moisture and unstable air.

What makes a suitable subject for a stormy sky?

Clearly any landscape will work, although some work better than others. If the cloud formation in the sky is especially dramatic, it becomes the main subject while the land plays a secondary role. In these circumstances lower the horizon within the frame when shooting. A landscape with a relatively uninterrupted horizon often works well. If you decide to include a figure within the composition, ensure it looks small relative to the sky. If there is a strong wind use it to enhance the scene. Photographing a woman with long hair or a person wearing loose clothing billowing in the wind all help to heighten the sense of drama. Think carefully about the position of the sun. Often with stormy skies, you will experience tiny breaks in the cloud resulting in spectacular illumination.

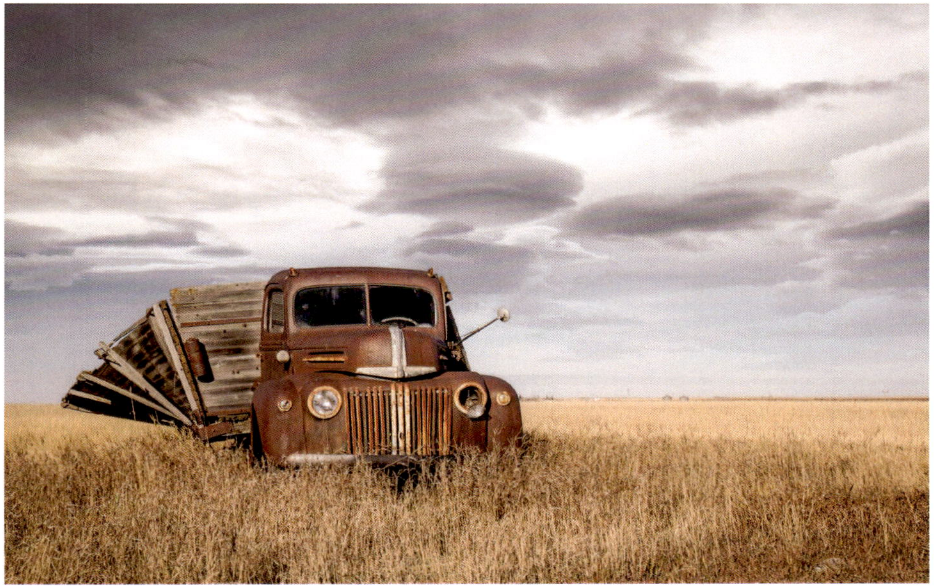

Figure 2 **Abandoned pick-up**. The colour palette is quite restricted which makes this a suitable subject for photographing under a stormy sky. The mood of the picture conveys a sense of pathos and sadness.

There are several technical issues you may wish to consider

1. When photographing stormy weather, you have various options. If you shoot in the middle of the day, the clouds will appear grey so, in order to introduce cohesion, make sure the foreground has a similarly restricted colour palette. Many photographers opt to work in monochrome in these situations, although some very subtle colour images can also be photographed under dramatically leaden skies. Another alternative is to take your photographs at dawn or dusk when the sky appears extraordinary and colourful. It is one of those occasions on which to pull out your wide-angle lens.

2. In order to enhance the drama, look in the direction of the sun; occasionally it will peep through producing a wonderful effect called 'back-lighting'. If you are fortunate enough to be near water, use it to mirror the sky. Obviously you have no control over whether the sun will appear or not, but be patient. If you are using a tripod make sure it is sturdy as you will invariably experience some buffeting.

3. Photographing skyscapes can almost become a daily routine, but never more so than when you have thunderous skies. Be prepared to use a variety of shutter speeds. While it is normal practice to use a shutter speed of 1/60th second or faster, fabulous images can be captured by setting your camera on a tripod, attaching a heavy neutral density filter, then using an exposure of 1 minute or more to capture the evolving formation of the cloud. The results can be spectacular!
4. Why not consider producing a panoramic shot of the sky when it is stormy? This can be done by stitching together various shots in Photoshop or some other editing software. Some cameras have a panoramic stitching facility that allows you to make several exposures while hand-holding the camera, although many do not. If your camera does not, set your camera on a tripod, then take several shots while methodically panning the horizon. The results can be both incredible and revealing.
5. Use a graduated filter. These allow you to balance the exposure of the foreground with a potentially much lighter sky. The main manufacturers of these filters are Cokin or Lee. If the sun is at 90 degrees you might experience an unevenness of exposure across the sky, so angle the graduated filter horizontally.
6. If you are shooting Raw (and most photographers these days do), enhance the Clarity Slider in the ACR in order to exaggerate the contrast in the mid-tones. (Both Photoshop and Lightroom have this facility.)

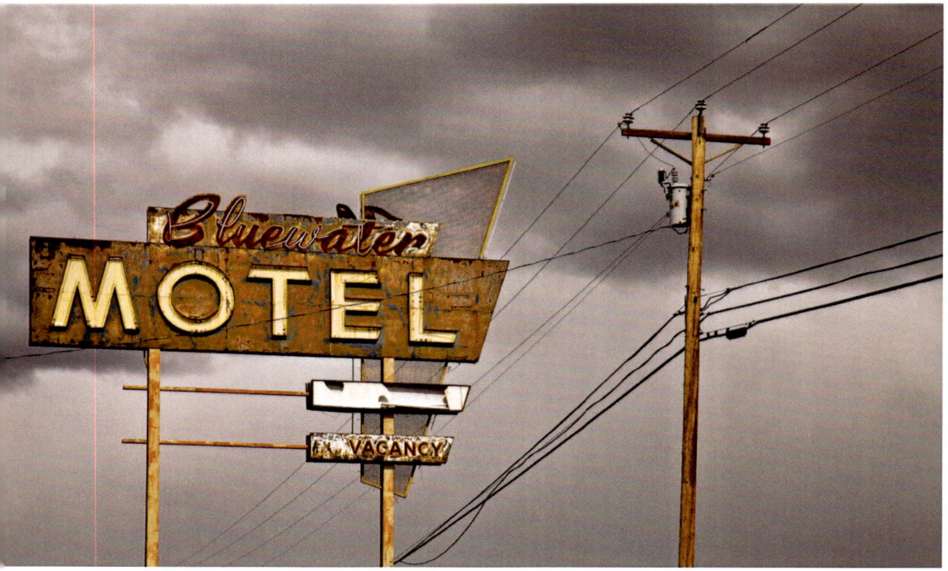

Figure 3 **Bluewater Motel**. This is an image that would certainly convert well to monochrome, and yet the subtle hues convey a very distinct mood.

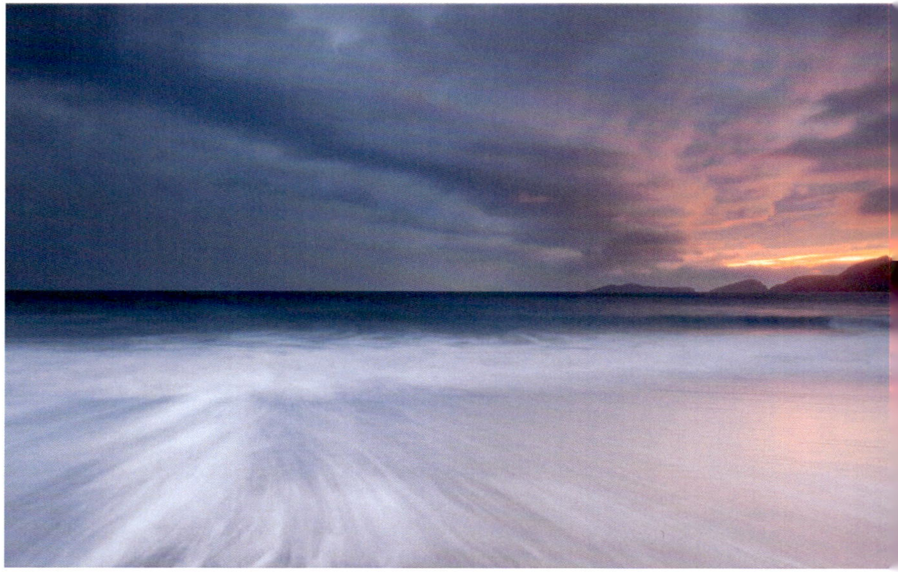

Figure 4 **Angry sky and receding tide**. When you are experiencing stormy clouds, consider taking your photographs at dawn or at dusk when the sky is likely to appear dramatic and colourful. It is also one of those occasions when using a wide-angle lens can prove advantageous.

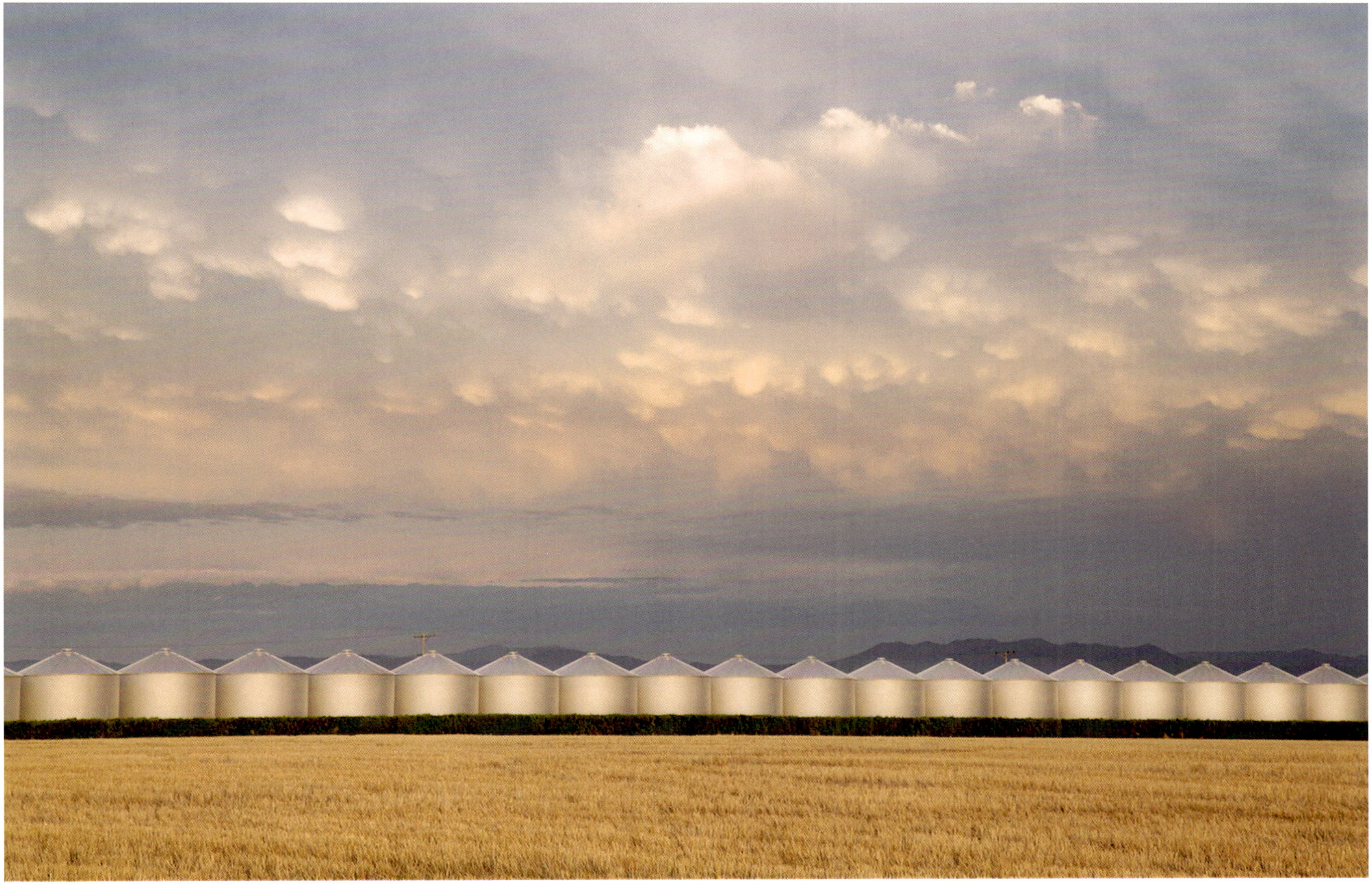

Figure 5 **Line of silos**. If you are fortunate enough to see a wonderful sky, make the best use of it by placing the horizon low down in the frame. This is certainly an example where 'the rule of thirds' should not apply.

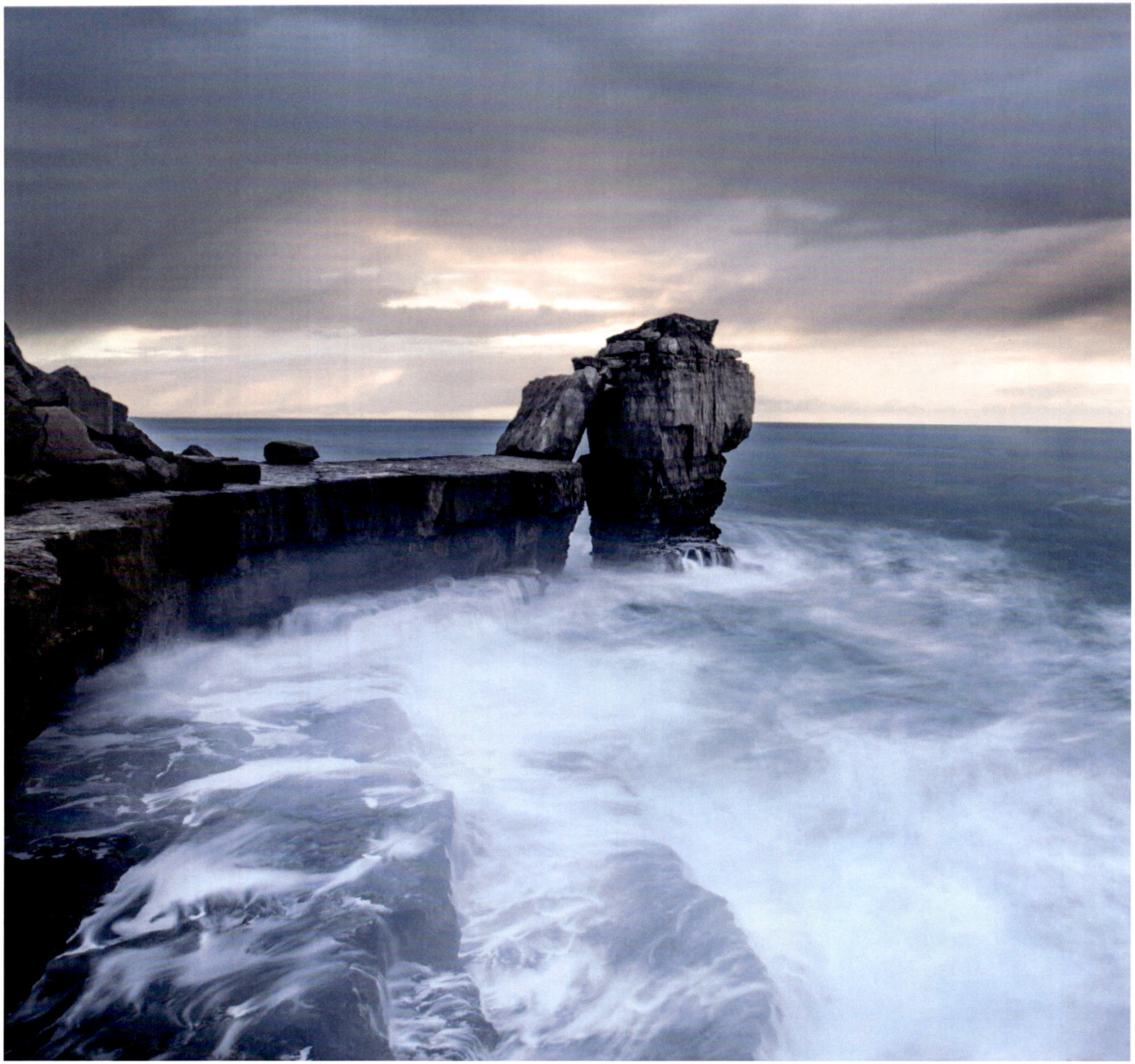

Figure 6 **Pulpit Rock, Dorset**. With the waves crashing into the rocks, this is a classic situation where the character of the stormy sky is mirrored by the foreground.

CAPTURE THE UNIQUE BEAUTY OF MAMMATUS CLOUDS

While all storm clouds have unique photogenic qualities, none can quite match the extravagant beauty of mammatus clouds. Also known as mammatocumulus, they are distinctive as a result of a cellular pattern of ‘pouches’ or bulges often attached underneath the base of a much larger cloud. The word ‘mammutus’ derives from the Latin *mamma* that translates as udder or breast, which gives a somewhat graphic description of these unusual cloud formations.

They are formed often in association with cumulonimbus or ‘anvil’ clouds, and are usually seen just before or after a fierce thunderstorm. While they normally appear at the base of a cumulonimbus, they can also form under altocumulus, altostratus and even stratocumulus clouds. Indeed, there are some photographs that also show them forming under volcanic ash clouds, so they do convey a sense of disaster. In fact, in some parts of

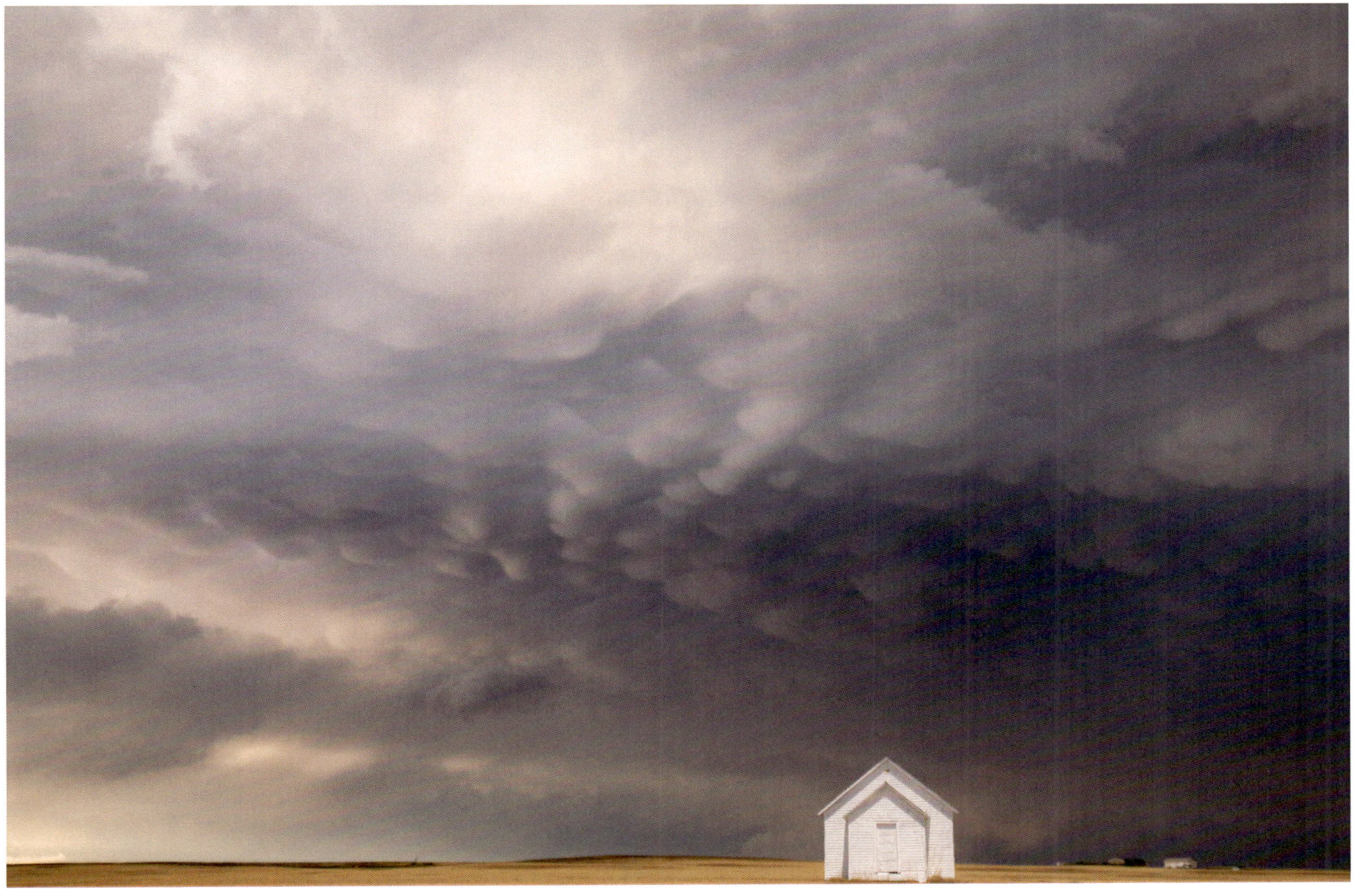

Figure 7 Small white school under stormy sky. These unusual mammatus clouds are often formed when there are tornadoes present. By making the school building appear very small within the frame, the suggestion of threat from the oncoming storm is greatly increased. Mammatus clouds are usually created in association with large cumulonimbus clouds.

the world, they are a prelude to particularly severe winds or tornadoes. Therefore, it is not surprising that in some cultures they are viewed as the harbingers of doom. Artists and graphic designers often use the sculptural qualities of this fascinating meteorological phenomenon as a source of inspiration.

These beautiful cloud formations can vary in appearance. The distinctive lobes sometimes appear ragged or lumpy, and they may look opaque or translucent. The way they clump together varies from quite small isolated clusters to a spread that extends for hundreds of miles. Each 'lobe' will average 1/4 mile across, which gives you a measure of the altitude at which this distinctive cloud formation develops. It is hardly surprising then that most of this cloud is composed of ice.

Mammatus clouds at sunset

Viewing mammatus clouds at any time of the day offers unique photographic opportunities, but never more so than in evening light. The rays from the setting sun are able to illuminate upwards, serving not only to dramatically emphasise the textural qualities, but also to introduce a truly magnificent spectrum of colours, typically yellow, orange, red and blue.

How to photograph mammatus clouds

This is a classic situation where you are advised to keep it simple. Spectacularly beautiful, but also complex, look for a simple foreground. In order to heighten the drama of the swirling cloud formations, keep the horizon low. Exploit the sense of threat this cloud formation is capable of suggesting so, if you do include any buildings, keep them small and isolated within the frame. These are clouds that possess almost allegorical qualities, so you may want to include elements that increase this sense of mystery.

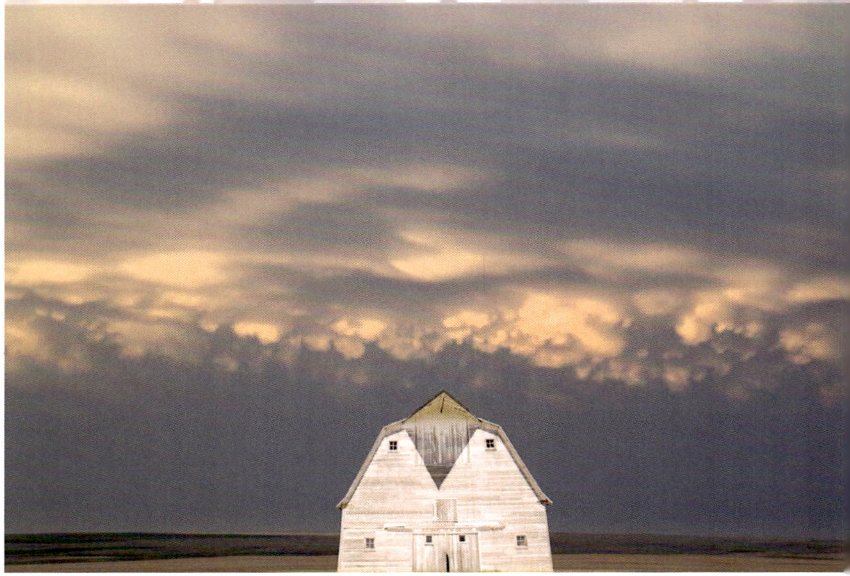

Figure 8 (Above) **Lone barn on prairie**. When photographing a cloud formation as spectacular as this, make sure that the elements in the foreground appear simple and relatively small in scale. Prominence should be reserved for the sky.

Figure 9 (Below) **Detail of mammatus cloud formation**. These clouds possess an almost mystical quality, so it is not surprising that they are the inspiration for examples of fine art and graphic design.

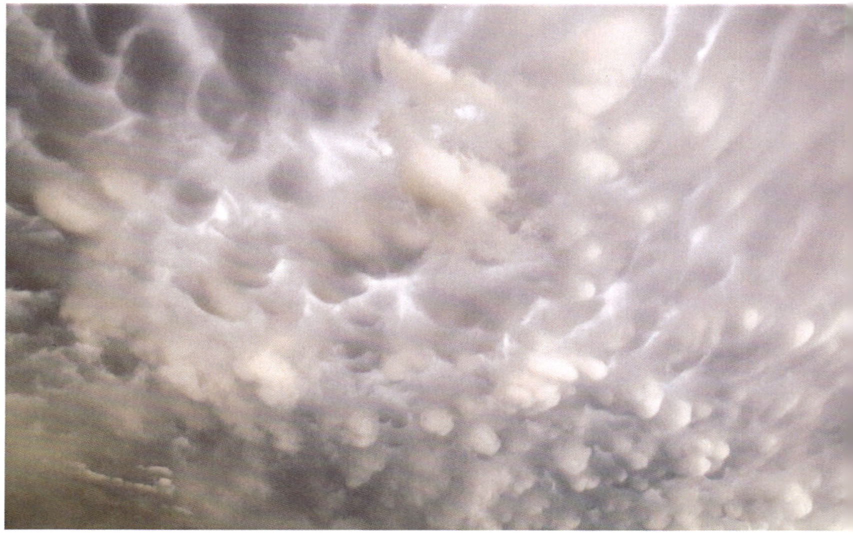

Another less common meteorological phenomenon is the dust storm. We tend to associate them with semi-arid regions although, of course, they can occur in any location where you have dry loose sand or dirt and wind. Dust storms have a history and were a major factor in creating agricultural poverty and the subsequent migration of thousands of families from the Oklahoma 'Dust Bowl' in the 1930s. One has only to see Walker Evans' deeply moving photographs to get an appreciation of the suffering these storms can cause. Of course this is still a common occurrence in parts of America today, and similar storms can also occur here in the UK, particularly in areas where you have large, flat and uninterrupted tilled tracts of land, although the severity and disruption caused cannot be compared with that in America.

So what causes a dust storm?

Dust storms can only occur when the soil is dry due to drought or arid conditions. They are more likely to occur in the summer months than in winter. As the wind passes over the loose particles on the surface of the ground, they start to vibrate, then 'saltate'. What this means is that these particles repeatedly hit the ground, thereby loosening further particles of dust, which increases the dust storm's severity. As the wind get stronger, it causes the particles of dust and sand to suspend, which produces a dust storm.

If you are visiting a desert region dust storms are a much more common occurrence. They are caused by strong pressure gradients, which greatly add to the ferocity of the wind within the area. The vertical extent of the dust storm is governed by the stability of the atmosphere directly above the ground and, of course, the relative weight of the dust particles. In some cases, the dust can be lifted to heights of over 20,000 feet and will therefore travel great distances so, occasionally, we in Northern Europe can see our cars covered in dust from a storm that started in the Sahara desert in Africa.

While few of us regularly visit desert regions, we can have our own 'dust storms' much closer to home. Where you have a large flat area of sandy beach, those parts that are not affected by the tide and thus remain permanently dry are subject to precisely the same forces. Anyone who is caught in a sand storm on an open beach will find it a distinctly unpleasant experience. We can even experience something similar when walking past a large building site; with a strong wind, clouds of light dust will billow in the wind.

So can you photograph a dust storm?

Yes, but with some difficulty. Something most of us see are those mini dust storms created by swirling gusts of wind passing over a dry and dusty stretch of tilled agricultural land. By using a telephoto lens you are able to capture it, but at a safe distance. One thing you might notice is that while the air may be relatively still from where you are photographing, it can change almost in an instant.

It is of course possible to photograph a full-blown dust storm, but it does pose certain hazards. The wind can prove particularly strong, so you will be severely buffeted. The dust is fine and can irritate your eyes and blur your vision. However, the biggest danger is to your camera. No matter how well sealed, it will be no match for a powerful dust storm unless you have it protected within a camera rain cover.

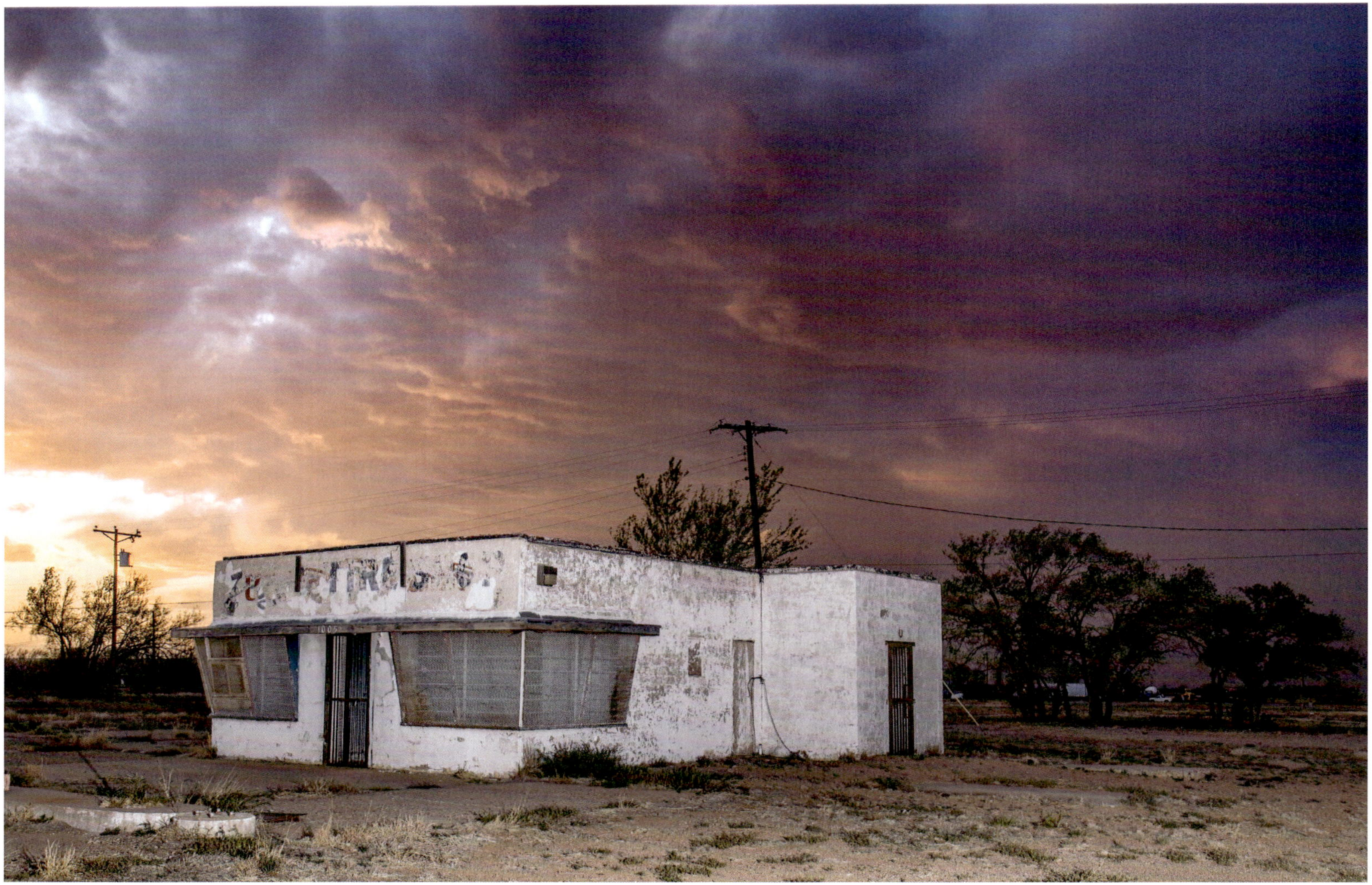

Figure 10 **Dust storm over Tucumcari, New Mexico**. Photographing this dust storm was quite an experience because, at the time, I had no idea what I was witnessing. Fascinated by the quickly evolving changing colours in the sky, I gave very little thought to what was causing this. It was windless so I had no reason to suspect that I was about to be enveloped in a dust storm. The clouds seemed to be getting closer and lower but, as I had never experienced anything like this before, I remained unconcerned. Then, almost without warning, I was hit by an incredible 'force of nature', so strong I almost could not make it back to my car. The wind was awesome and I had great difficulty seeing. The intensity of the storm lasted for just a short period, possibly just 20 minutes and then, almost without warning, it just disappeared.

The phase 'a grey sky' conjures a certain negativity; many non-photographers often complain of those days when they are deprived of sunshine, particularly during the winter months when the days are short. It is easy to get depressed under constant grey skies and yet there is a positive side to this type of weather. From a photographic standpoint, it can prove quite an asset.

The first thing to understand is that the term 'grey skies' covers a multitude of weather conditions ranging from a thick impenetrable cloud to a gentle scattering in an otherwise blue sky. Each carries its own unique opportunity. My own take on this is to recall that wonderful quote by the motivational speaker Paul F. Davis: 'the sun always shines above the clouds'. Cloudy skies bring their own special character to the day and, after all, when summer arrives you can indulge in a different style of landscape photography.

So what are the positives?

1. A layer of cloud helps to reduce contrast. When using a modern DSLR camera, while it

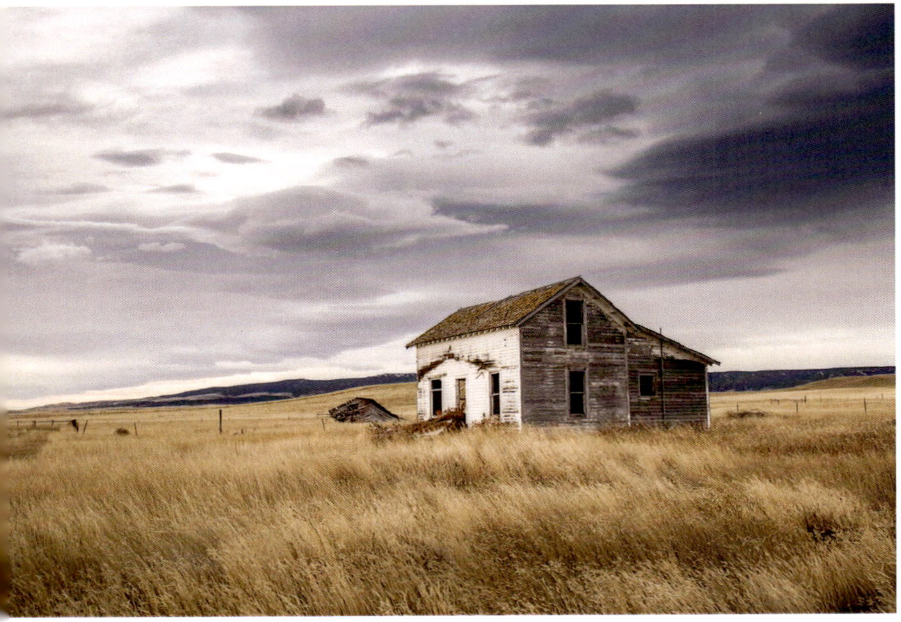

Figure 11 **Abandoned school on the prairie**. This image exudes a certain pathos which is heightened by the overcast sky. With a very restricted colour palette, the tonal values of the image become much more apparent.

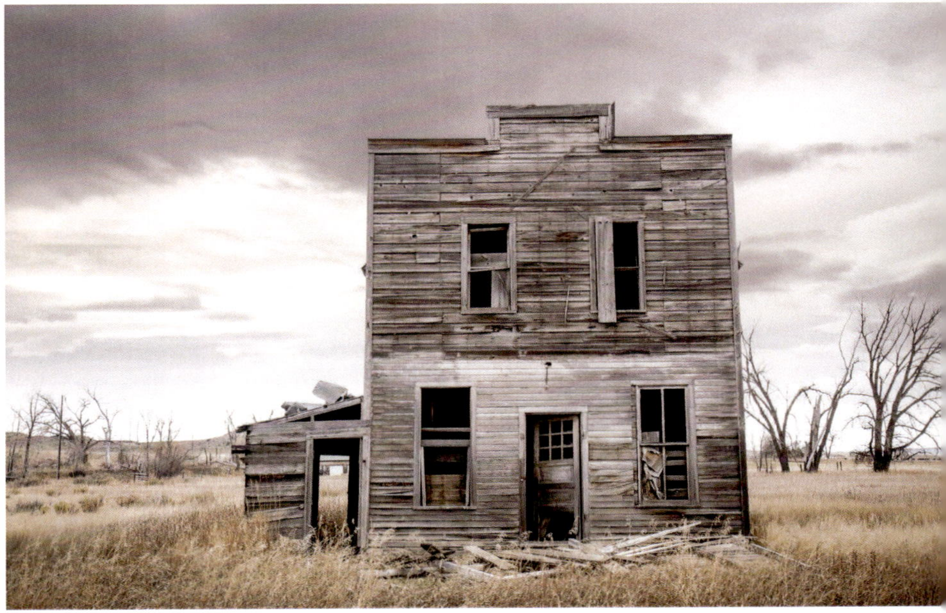

Figure 12 **Wrecked hotel, central Montana**. As in the previous example, the emphasis is on tone at the expense of colour. The tonal values in the sky have been expanded post-camera by using the Clarity slider in Lightroom.

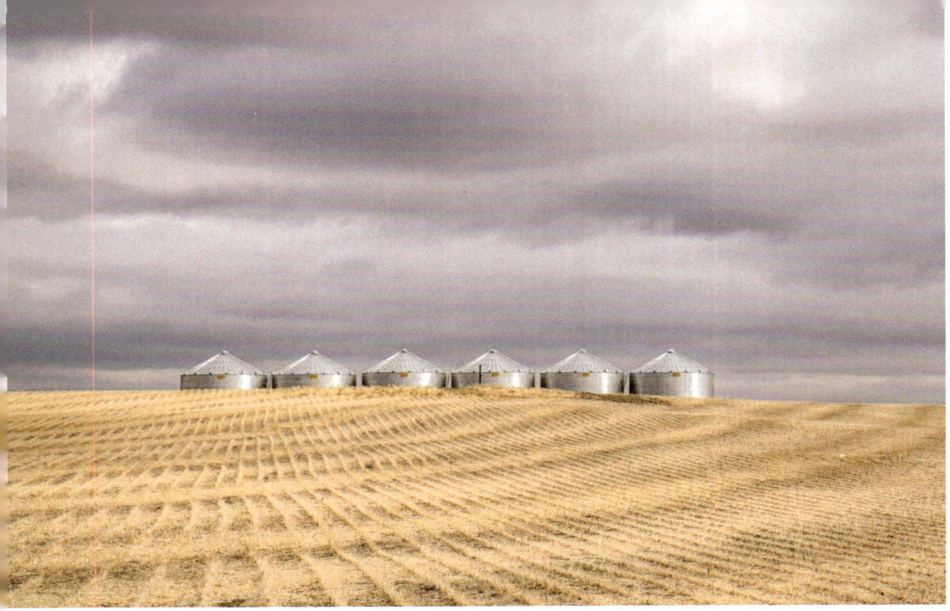

Figure 13 **A line of grain silos**. One of the best opportunities for shooting landscape under a grey sky is at that moment when the sun briefly appears directly behind you. While the foreground will look wonderfully illuminated the sky, by way of contrast, will seem even darker.

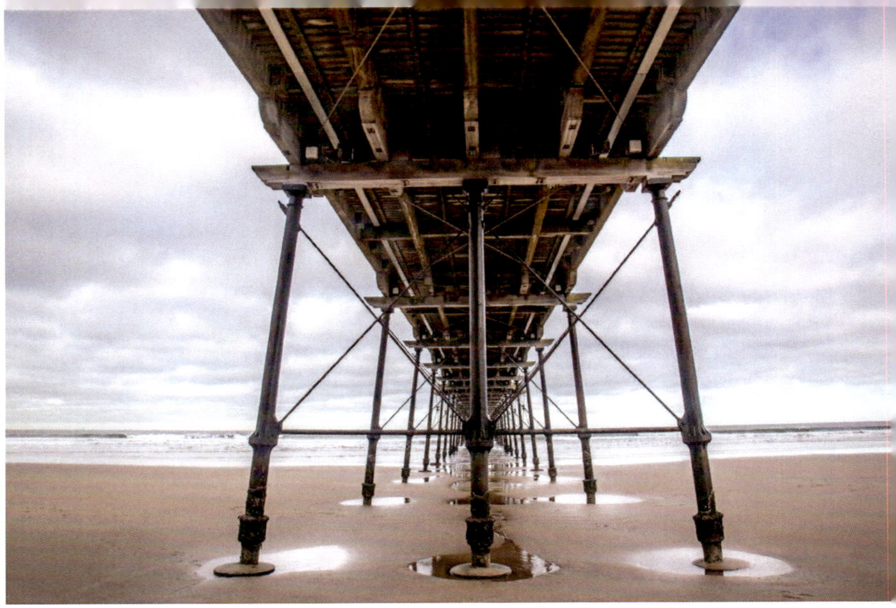

Figure 14 **Under the pier**. Had there been a blue sky, I would have experienced considerable problems taking this shot, as both the sky and the pier would have appeared unacceptably dark. When set against a lighter grey sky, I was able to introduce a reasonable element of contrast.

will have many assets, one of the main drawbacks is that the images are prone to appear too contrasty, especially in strong sunlight. This is rarely a problem when photographing in overcast light. Seasoned photographers will often refer to such weather as 'the soft box in the sky'. Should you wish to photograph a portrait or a figure out of doors, the result is far more flattering if it is taken under a grey sky.

2. A grey sky evokes a mood that works well in certain landscape situations. While we all respond to the picturesque landscape, the more experienced we become the more we want to explore fresh avenues, capturing landscapes that express pathos and sadness. Such scenes are complimented by a broody dark-grey sky. One of the key challenges when photographing any landscape is to ensure that the sky appears sympathetic to the mood of the picture.

3. Landscapes taken on a cloudy day often work well when presented as a monochrome. By eliminating colour, while emphasising the tonal values, the mood of the landscape becomes considerably more apparent. If you are using a DSLR and wish to follow this path, retain your image in full RGB and then convert

the image to black and white using your favoured post-processing software. This way you will retain the full image quality. A slight variation on this idea is to retain your image in colour but purposefully reduce the saturation; from an aesthetic standpoint such images can look stunning.

Technical considerations

1. Shooting without sun means that the strength of the light is reduced. This can be overcome by increasing the ISO rating, using a larger aperture, reducing the shutter speed or, if necessary, using a tripod. The quality of digital sensors has so greatly improved in recent years that none of these options should degrade your image in any way.

2. The emphasis of your images should be tonal; whether you decide to retain your images in colour, or decide to convert your images to black and white, the tonal values of the final image will be important and, specifically, emphasising the mid-tones is particularly useful when photographing under grey skies.

3. There is one very simple post-camera technique I would like to draw to your attention here – it is the 'Clarity' slider. You always have the option of shooting in either JPEG or Raw, although the reasons for using the latter are innumerable. The quality you can capture when shooting in Raw is impressive; when you are aiming to capture the subtle nuances of cloud cover you need every advantage available. In order to 'process' your Raw file, you need either to use ACR (which you are able to download free from Adobe) or, alternatively, to use Lightroom. Both offer a slider called 'Clarity'. If you isolate the grey sky in your photograph and then check the histogram, the tonal range will appear extremely restricted. You can expand the tonal range by increasing contrast, but that will affect the entire image. By using Clarity, contrast is increased, but only in the mid-tones, which can immediately add drama to an otherwise flat and uninteresting grey sky. You may feel this is cheating but, when looking at a grey sky, your eye is able to discern a considerable range of tones that do not appear in the final image. The Clarity slider is able to redress this.

4. While we are on the subject of post-camera technique, in order to heighten that sense of mood a grey sky can evoke, why not consider introducing added grain to your image? This can be achieved by either greatly increasing the ISO rating and thus possibly obviate the need to use a tripod or, alternatively, deliberately introduce grain by using one of the many post-production editing software programmes. By introducing an element of 'grittiness' you are able to explore the artistic feel of the image.

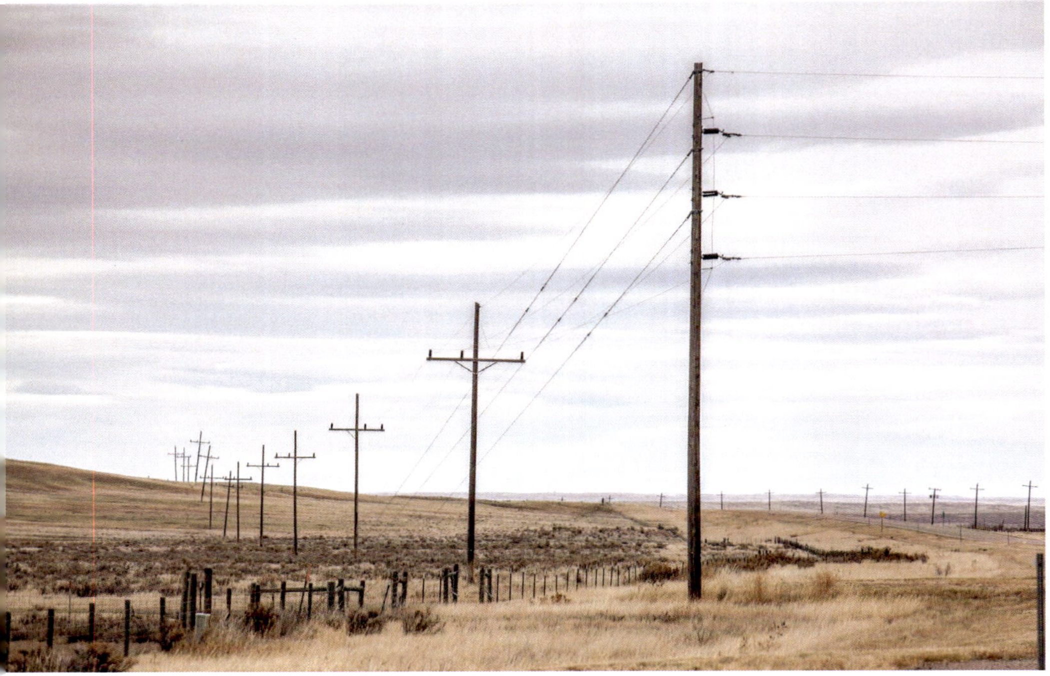

Figure 15 **Line of telegraph poles**. We are able to recognise different features depending on the prevailing weather. This rather delicate lines of telegraph poles could easily have been missed if it had been viewed against a more tempestuous sky.

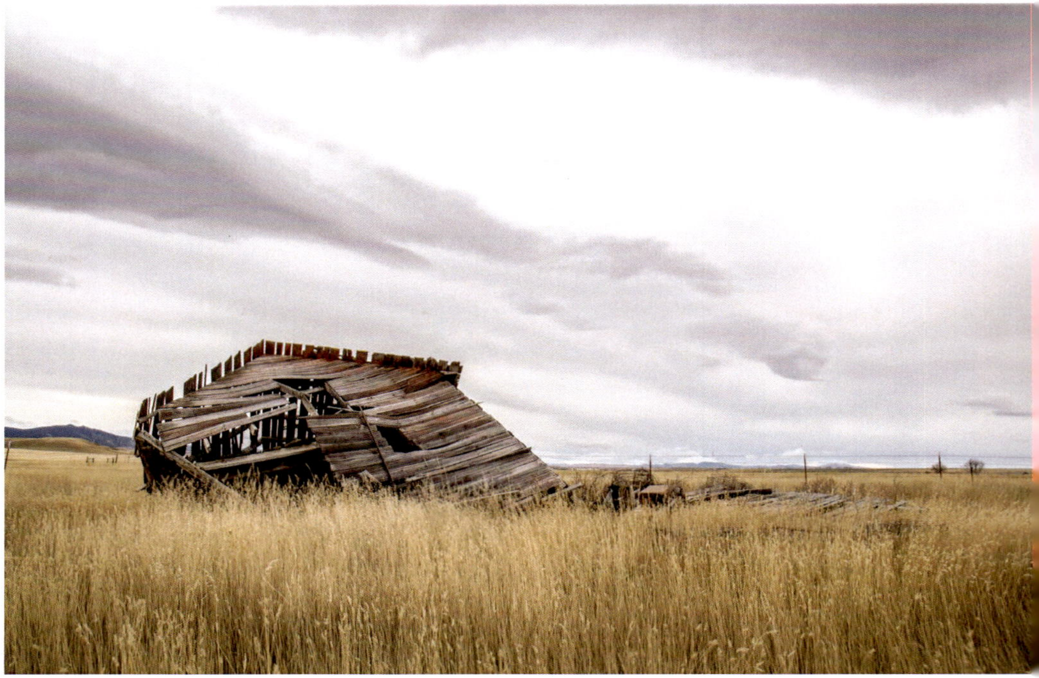

Figure 16 **Tumble-down homestead**. The character of the grey sky chimes perfectly with this tumbledown structure. Rather than view grey skies as a negative, understand that it opens up an entirely new genre when photographing landscapes.

EXPLOITING THE POTENTIAL OF BROKEN CLOUD

In the mind of many photographers, broken cloud offers some of the best conditions for 'pictorial' landscape photography. The great advantage of passing clouds in the sky is that you are offered two bites of the cherry. If you need the landscape to be brilliantly illuminated, wait for the sun to emerge from behind the cloud. Alternatively, there will be occasions when it helps having the foreground in shade, usually to ensure that there is not too much contrast, so just wait for the sun to disappear behind a cloud. The wonderful advantage of a broken sky is that you rarely need to wait for long.

The term 'a broken sky' does of course cover a variety of situations. It could, for example, describe a situation where the sky is predominately blue with just a gentle scattering of white clouds. Conversely it can also describe a sky that is largely covered in cloud, but showing small patches of blue. Either way, both are to be welcomed. If the sky is predominately blue it promotes a sense of optimism, which is why such skies are used so extensively in travel brochures. A sky that comprises largely of cloud introduces an entirely different feel, which can easily be interpreted as being sombre or dull. As each of these extremes promotes quite a different response, it does help to give the foreground serious consideration. For example, when photographing a joyous field of red poppies (a scene many of us would find positively uplifting), shooting them when the sky is largely covered in cloud might not make the best use of the situation.

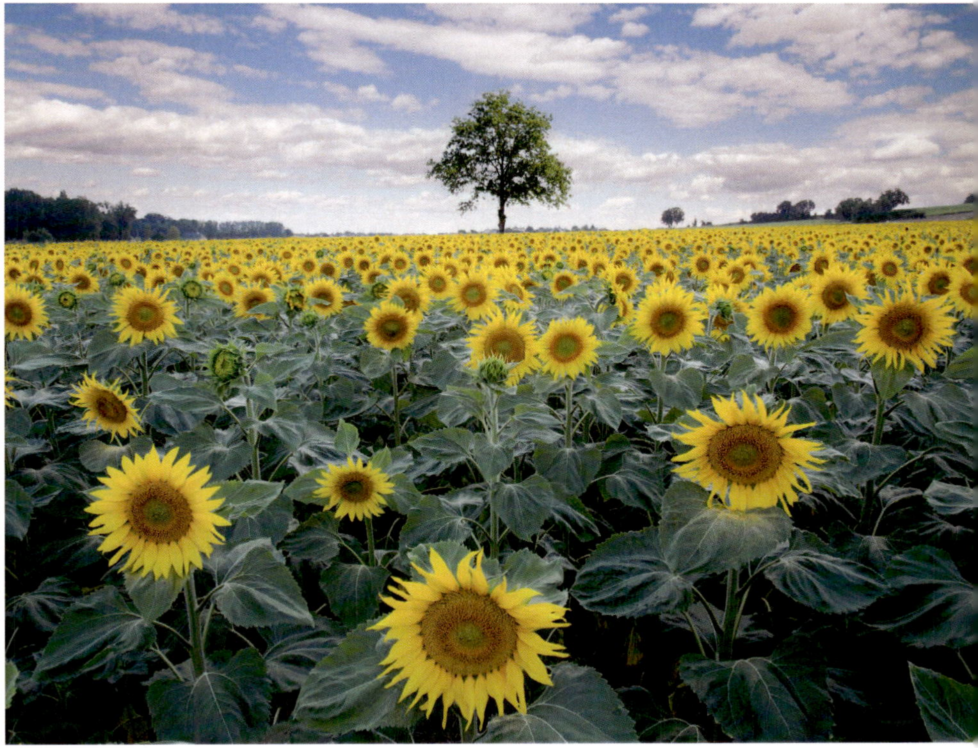

Figure 17 **Field of sunflowers**. A blue sky with a gentle smattering of white clouds induces a positive sense of optimism, so it does help to photograph a landscape that chimes with the mood. In this example, I waited for the sun to briefly disappear behind a cloud as I was concerned that the shadows cast by the sunflowers in full sunshine could appear distracting.

Technical considerations

Think about where to place the horizon

When you have an interesting sky, a balance has to be struck regarding the placement of the horizon. If the cloud formations are truly exciting, while the foreground is less so, then it clearly makes sense to place the horizon low within the picture frame. On a similar tack, if the landscape is clearly the main feature then it should dominate the composition. As a simple rule, placing the horizon on the thirds often works but, occasionally, the sky can appear so dramatic that you can get away with placing the horizon much further down.

Broken clouds and areas of still water

When you do witness a lovely broken sky, if you cannot find a suitably dramatic foreground then try and find a stretch of still water; often a large still puddle is all you need. By getting down low, you should be able to include both the sky and its reflection within a single shot, which immediately offers an impressive sense of cohesion. If you give this a go, you will find using a graduated filter particularly helpful as a way of balancing the sky with the foreground.

Use of a polarising filter

In order to add emphasis to the clouds, try using a polarising filter. By carefully rotating it you will see the areas of blue incrementally darken. If you are using a DSLR camera you will need to ensure that your polarising filter is a circular type.

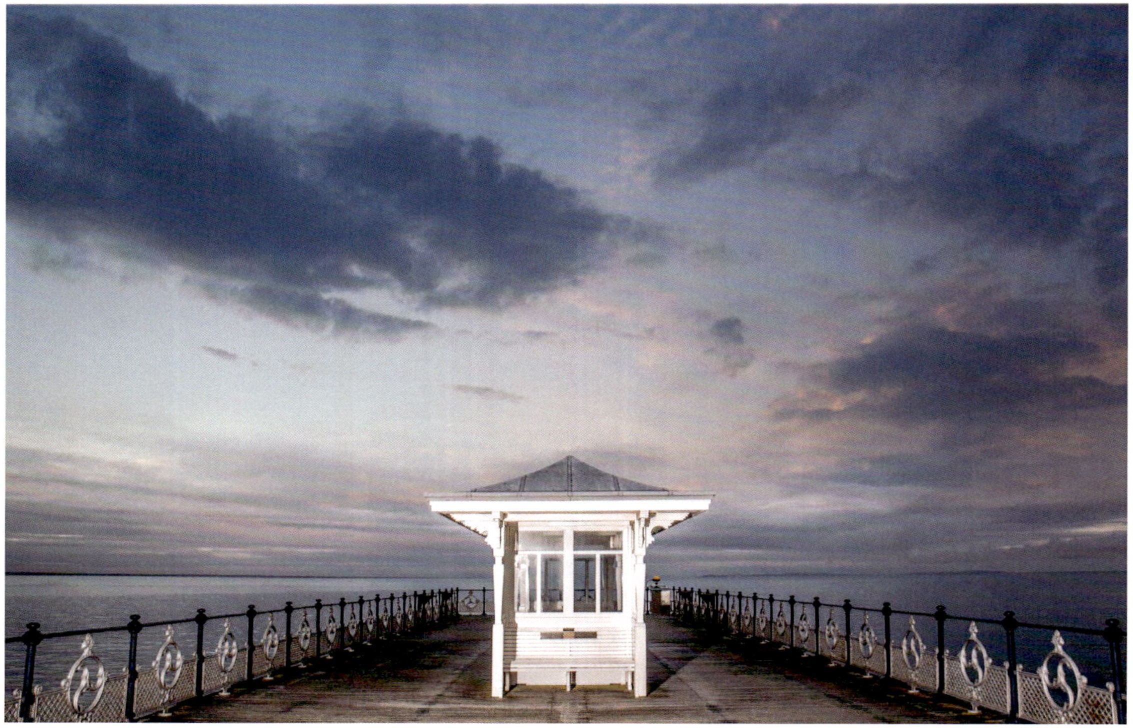

Figure 18 **Swanage Pier**. A great time to photograph broken cloud is in the evening or at dawn. With the sun so low it is capable of introducing a subtle range of colours.

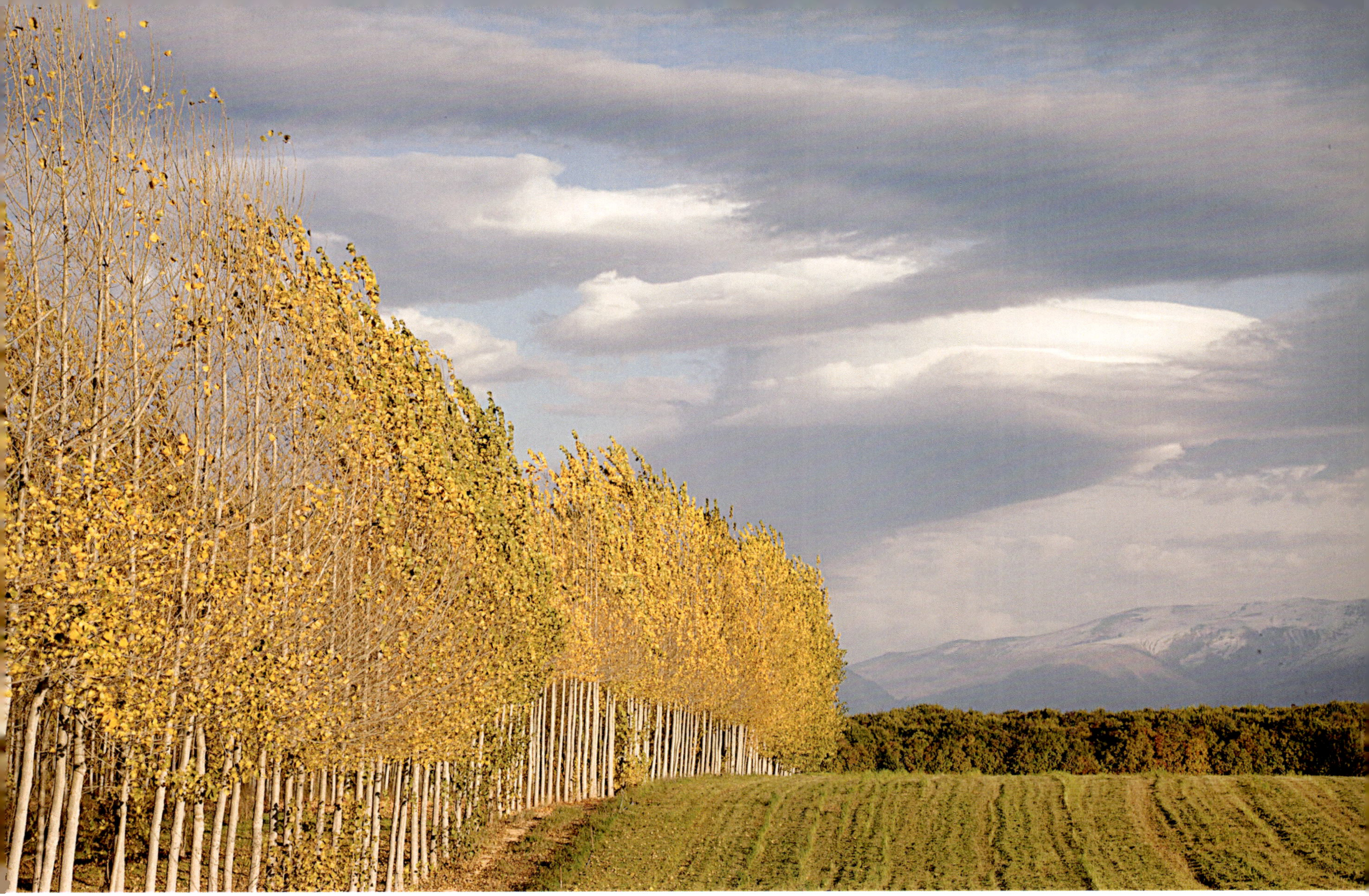

Figure 19 **A line of poplars**. What makes broken cloud so useful is that it not only offers detail in the sky, but you are also able to time your shot either when the sun is behind a cloud or, as in this example, when it is shining. This latitude is particularly useful for landscape photography.

PHOTOGRAPHING A LANDSCAPE WITH A SINGLE CLOUD

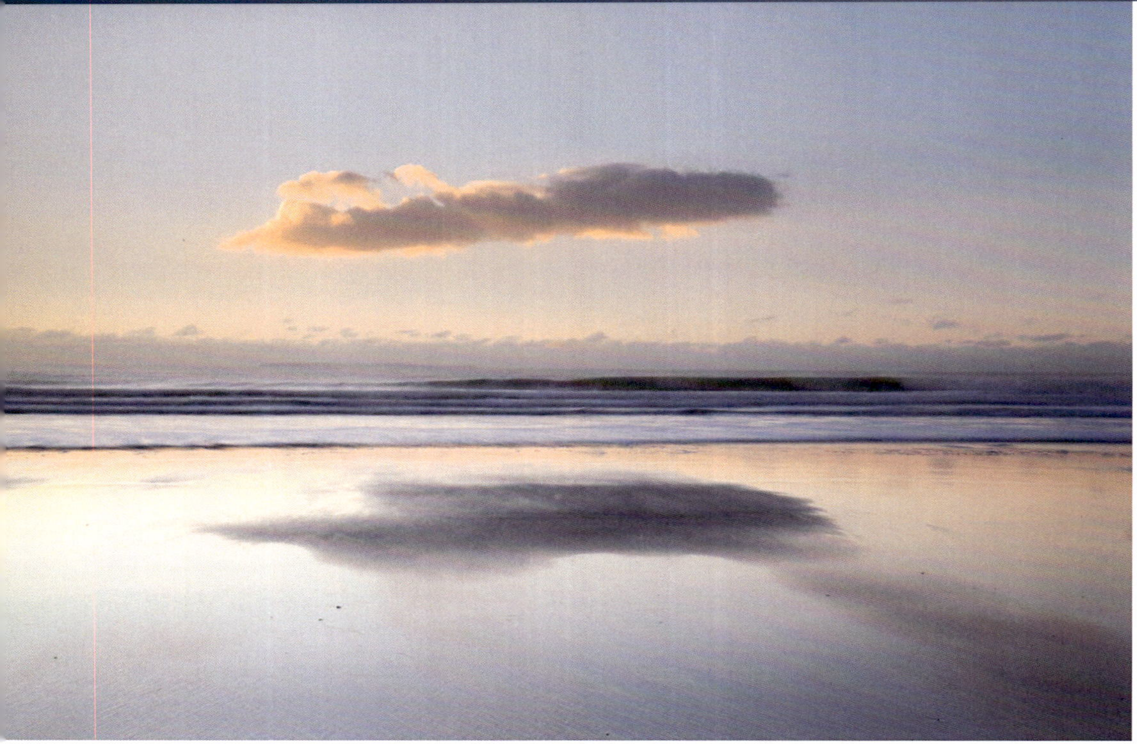

Figure 20 **Cloud over beach**. At first glance, it is easy to assume that the dark area in the foreground is the shadow created by this single passing cloud, but it has been created because it is a slightly raised part of the beach that has not been dampened by the incoming tide. It was coincidental that the shape of the cloud almost perfectly mirrors this dry patch of sand.

While an enhanced sense of character is introduced into a landscape when including a sky with broken cloud, a wonderful sense of cohesion is added if you can isolate just a single one. As the cloud cover starts to thin, you start to see individual clouds drifting across the sky that each offer unique opportunities. You certainly need to respond speedily if you are to make best use of these.

Each individual cloud has its own character. It is amazing how imaginatively children can identify anthropomorphic features when describing clouds they have spotted – it looks like a jumping dog or perhaps a speeding car. I'm sure you have done the same thing. The task as a photographer is to find a location that chimes with the character of the cloud. Sometimes it is an impossible task but, if you are aware of the concept, occasionally you will identify a cloud that appears to mimic the foreground. For example, it could appear elongated and cigar-shaped so, if in the foreground you found a puddle, a cluster of wild flowers or an isolated copse of trees revealing the same shape, then the image would have immediate cohesion.

Adopt a 'minimalist' approach

This is a genre that positively encourages a minimalist approach. Some landscapes can be described as 'busy', i.e. there are numerous interesting but conflicting elements within it. A 'minimalist' landscape is simple, revealing very few features of note, which is often why the inclusion of a single cloud can work so well. You will find that this style of photography is best done when using a medium telephoto lens. Not only will you be able to ensure that the cloud appears larger within the frame but also, as you are including less foreground, the landscape will appear much simpler.

Think carefully about the composition

The single cloud will be moving while the feature in the foreground is likely be static, so patience will be required to ensure that the cloud appears in the right place. The movement of clouds can prove frustratingly unreliable but that should not discourage you from giving it a go. A simple compositional strategy you may wish to try is to place the landscape feature fairly centrally, then wait for the cloud to drift directly over it. Some might be concerned that this does not conform to 'the rule of thirds', but that should be seen as just one of many design principles. The central meridian (where the image is composed relative to an imaginary central line) is another one that is used both by professional photographers and graphic designers.

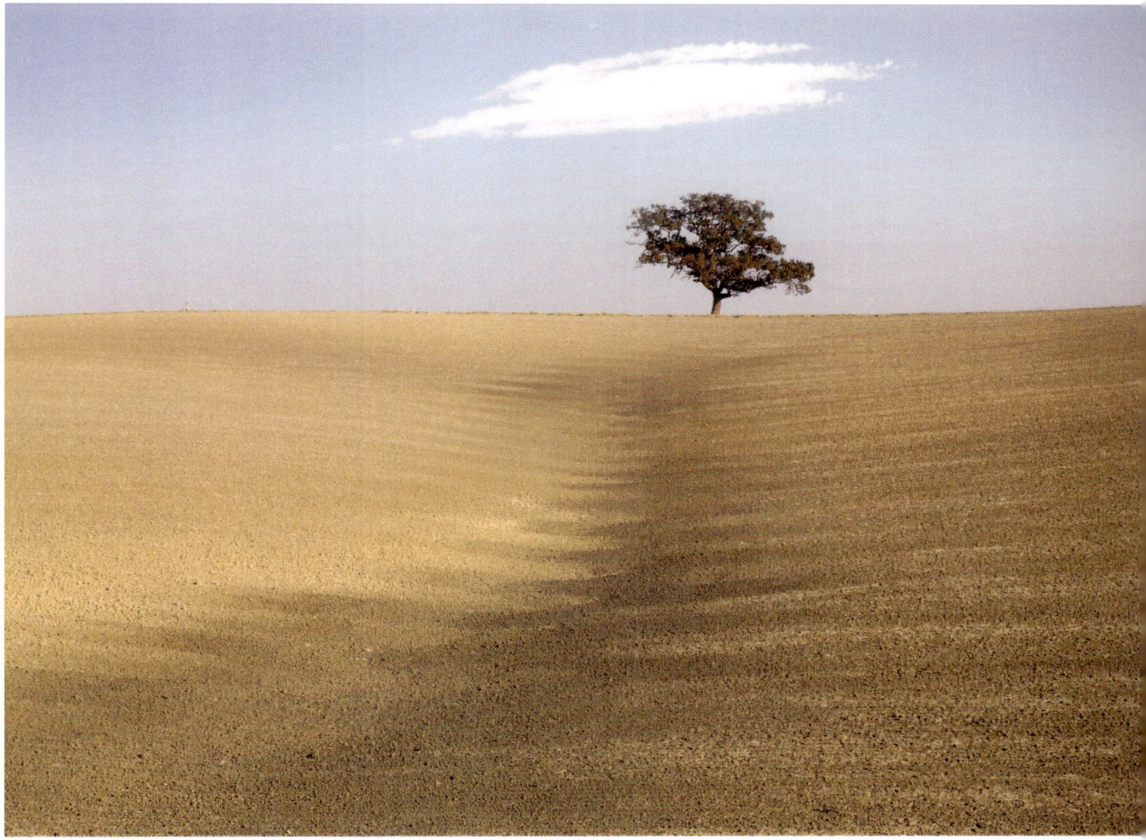

Figure 21 **Tree on horizon**. Having spotted this tree on the horizon, it was a matter of being patient and waiting for a single cloud to drift above it. When doing this kind of work, it certainly helps to use a telephoto lens.

Figure 22 **Wrecked pier**. Sometimes the visual relationship between the cloud and the foreground appears a little more tenuous. In this example, it would have been impossible to identify a cloud that mimics the shape of this wrecked pier. However, the width of the structure does appear to match that of the cloud, which offers an equally valid sense of cohesion.

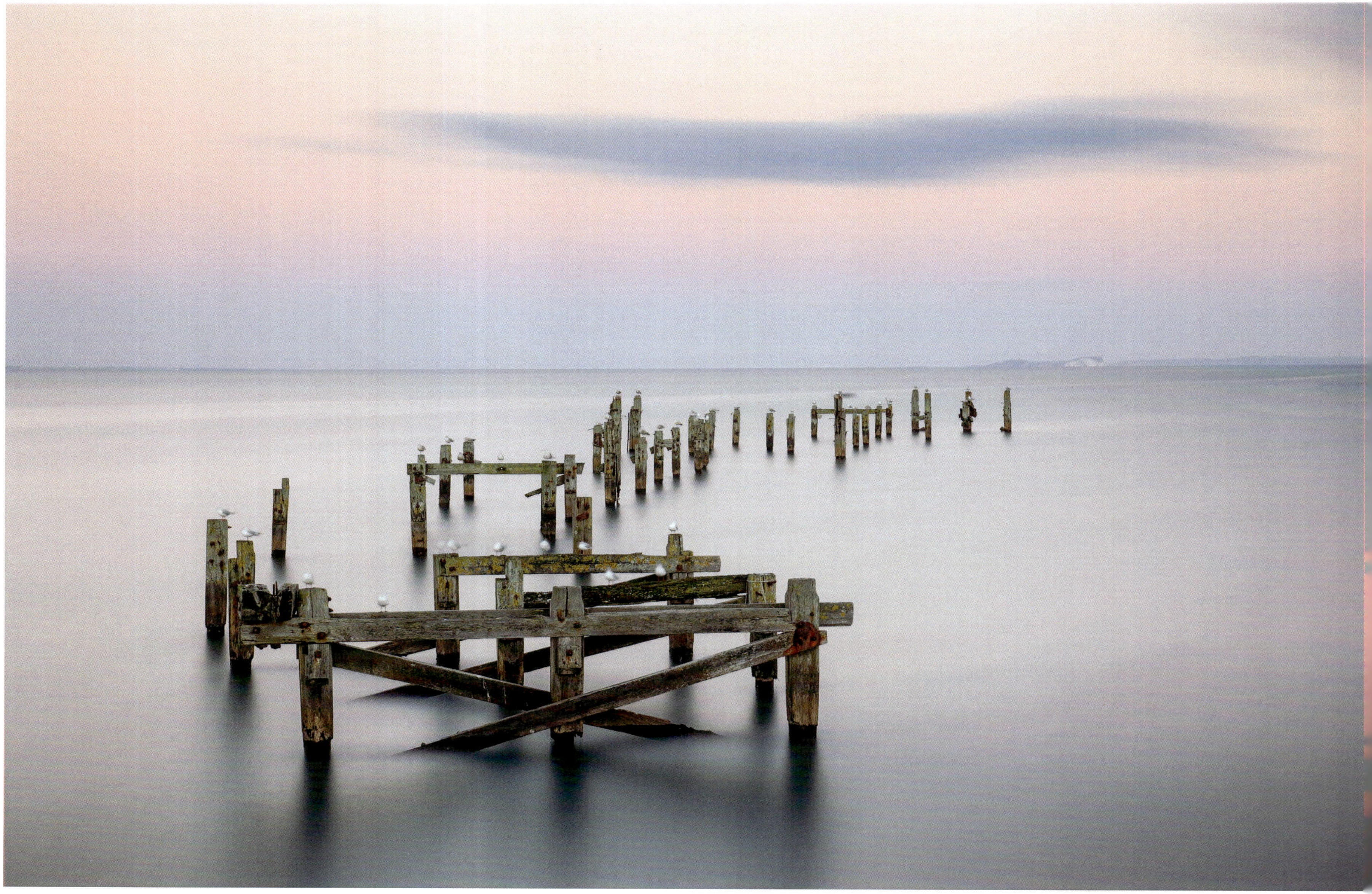

A CLOUDY SKY AT NIGHT

Some photographers might despair when they wake up in the morning only to face yet another 'grey day'. While much of this section is devoted to extolling the virtues of grey skies, it is of course not to everyone's taste. However, what some photographers do not appreciate is that what looks grey in daytime appears fabulously blue at night. When looking at the night sky with the naked eye, it appears black but, in reality, it is a dark blue. The human eye can only see an instant, while the sensor of the camera can absorb light over a longer period and thus reveal detail the human eye cannot possibly detect.

The sky appears blue even when it is cloudy

When we see a grey sky in daytime, it is because the light source is the sun, which comprises the seven colours of the spectrum. When all those colours are mixed, it comes out as grey. It is a strange irony but, once sunlight disappears and we enter night, our cameras record the sky as blue, even when there is an impenetrable cloud cover.

The beauty of broken cloud at night

A particularly interesting feature you may wish to photograph is broken cloud at night. The range of colours you should be able to capture can be awesome. How you choose to do this is a matter of personal taste.

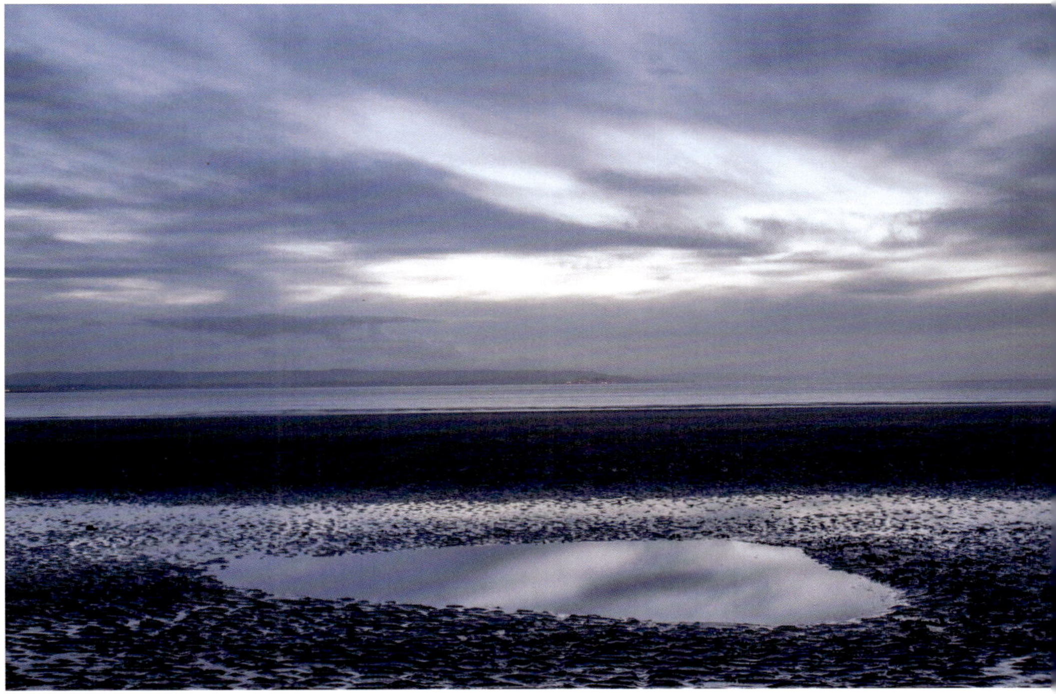

Figure 23 **Puddle on beach**. One of the interesting features of photographing a landscape at night is that it will appear bathed in a blue light, even under a cloudy sky. From a visual standpoint this offers a strong sense of cohesion.

1. You may decide to hand-hold the camera in order to capture the moving clouds. This will of course require greatly increasing your ISO rating; modern DSLR cameras have sensors that are capable of recording excellent detail even when using a very high ISO. Alternatively, if you are photographing only the sky and not including any foreground, then you can afford to open up your aperture and reduce the speed of your ISO a little.

2. Many landscape photographers opt to use a slow exposure instead. With the camera attached to a tripod, a low ISO rating is selected, which then requires an extended exposure. If more than 30 seconds is required, set the shutter speed to 'Bulb'. As the clouds are constantly moving, this motion is recorded as blurred streaks in the sky. If it is the streaking effect you most want to exploit, select the slowest ISO. When photographing at night, don't just trust your monitor. The image will appear brighter when seen at night, so check the histogram as well. Make sure that it is not 'bunching' too noticeably to the left.

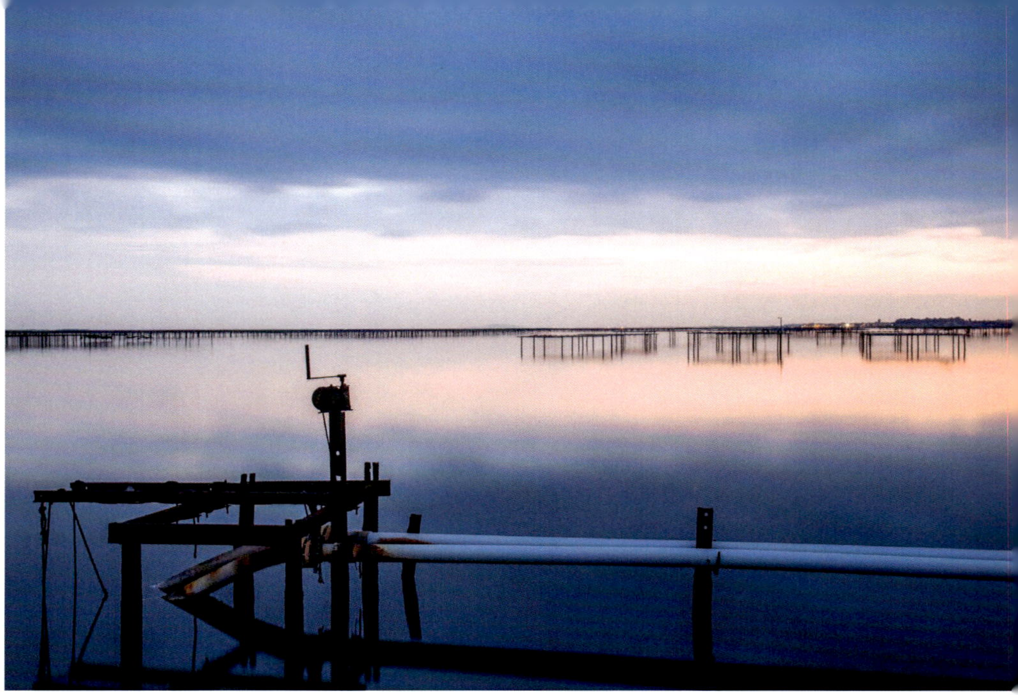

Some photographers are discouraged from doing extended exposures at night because they are concerned about 'noise' (the apparent graininess of the image). This should not pose a problem. First, it can be eradicated in-camera by selecting NR (Noise Reduction) in the camera's menu. Alternatively, you can address the issue post-camera using your preferred editing software.

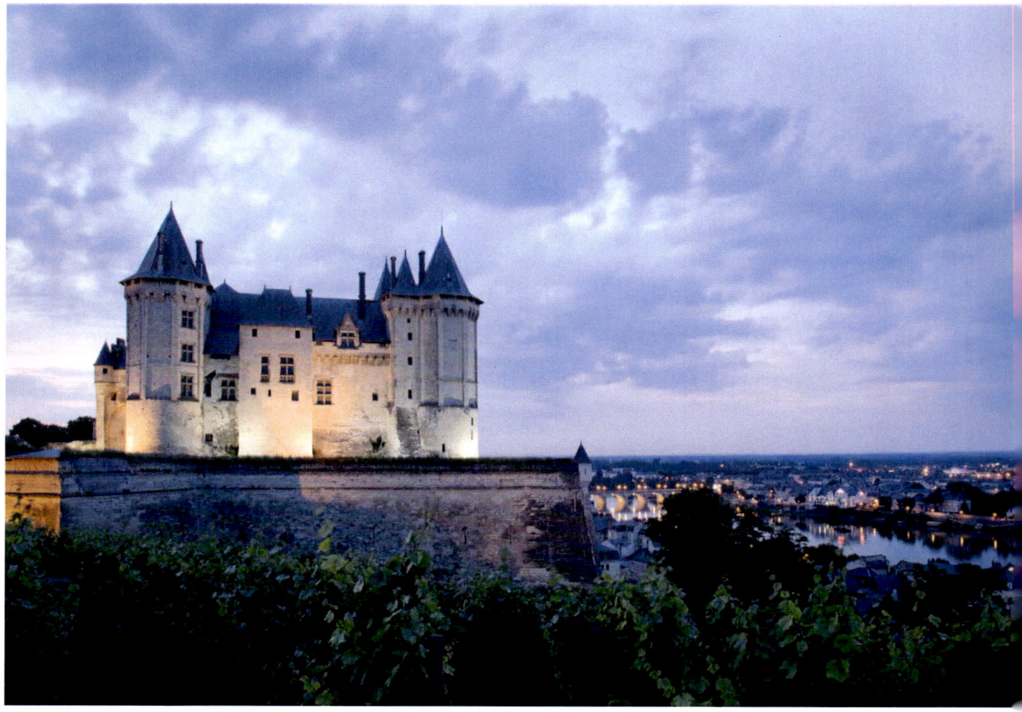

Figure 24 (Top) Oyster beds, France. With the cloud cover breaking on the distant horizon, the final embers of daylight are able to peep through, offering a wonderful colour combination of orange and blue.

Figure 25 (Bottom) French chateau. One of the interesting night-time situations is when you are able to photograph an illuminated building set against the night sky. The subtle orange of the tungsten lighting is complimented by the cerulean blue of the overhead clouds.

A FEATURELESS SKY

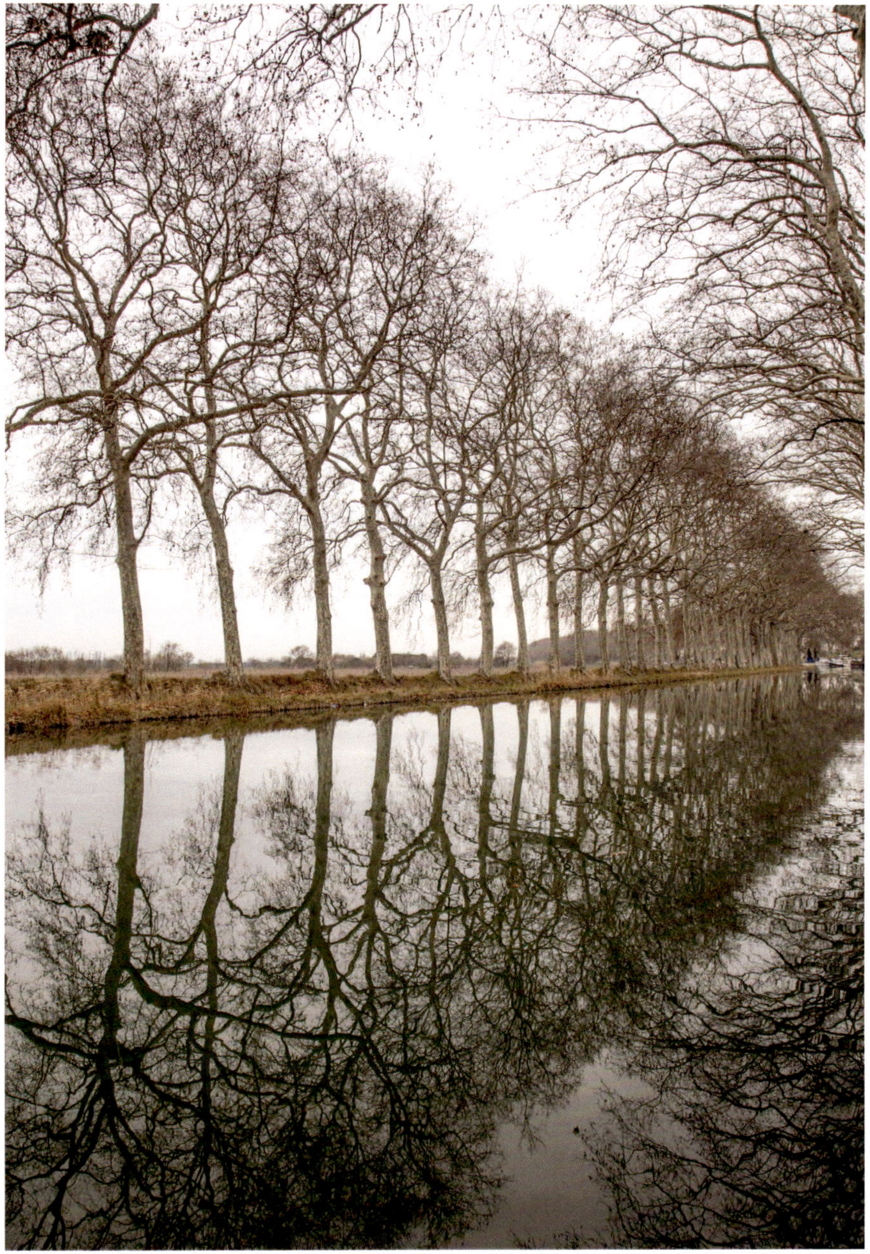

When I first started photography I can remember asking a landscape photographer I greatly admired 'what are the most difficult lighting conditions for shooting landscape?' After a bit of thought he replied, 'a white sky'. This is when there is a thin featureless blanket of light cloud that is just sufficient to block out the sun. Typically this is likely to be stratus cloud (which means 'flattened' or 'spread out') that forms no higher than 6,500 feet, although it can sometimes occur as low as ground level, forming a mist or fog. It offers none of the advantages of full sunshine and lacks the drama one can explore under a thunderous sky. A uniform pale grey or white, it is difficult to imbue any sense of drama in the landscape under such a sky but, as I have already suggested, there are no weather conditions that prevent us from taking interesting landscape photographs.

From a photographic standpoint, the height of the cloud determines how we respond. If it does drop to very low levels, then clearly it has the advantages of mist and fog (which is covered in Chapter 4), but what can be more challenging is when the cloud cover is much higher. Who wants a blank white sky you might ask. Well think of it in terms of a 'white canvas' - it can be filled with whatever you want.

Figure 26 **Line of trees and French canal**. While the sky was blank and featureless, it was not a disincentive to take landscape photographs; in fact, quite the reverse. When I first spotted this location the sky was darker and more dramatic, so that much of the delicate tracery of the branches was lost. By photographing this location when the sky was featureless, an interesting silhouette has been created.

How to fill a white sky

We often find in a landscape situation the delicate tracery of trees, the detail of which is completely lost when set against a darkened sky. If, however, they are viewed against a very pale sky, the simple beauty of these trees becomes immediately more apparent. Also, be prepared to expand your definition of 'landscape'. The countryside is awash with delicate manmade structures such as power lines, pylons and wind turbines that are similarly best photographed when set against a pale featureless sky. Effectively they form delicate silhouettes within the landscape.

Celebrate high key

This is a style of photography that emphasises the lightest tones. It is often associated with studio photography, but some extremely evocative landscape work can also be presented high key. It conjures an almost spiritual feel and can appear both mysterious and moody. For it to work, not only does the sky need to be light and featureless, but the landscape also. Pale landscapes are not so common, but water viewed under moderately high stratus clouds will inevitably reflect the muted high key tones in the sky, presenting a wonderfully holistic image. The

Figure 27 **Oyster beds**. High key landscapes promote an almost spiritual response in the mind of the viewer, which is why they prove so alluring. The white and featureless sky is reflected in the water, which helps to introduce a sense of unity throughout the image. Including the posts serves as a relief to the overwhelming sense of lightness.

quieter the mood, the more mystical the picture. While I am never too keen on post-production intervention, a little adjustment in Lightroom or Photoshop can subtly lighten the tones even further, although it is important that with any high-key image none of the highlights are completely blown. It certainly pays to check your histogram. Occasionally you will encounter a pale landscape, it could be a beach of light sand or possibly a salt-plain, which of course makes a perfect subject under these particular lighting conditions. Whether you are shooting water or a high key landscape, always include some small dark element that serves as a relief to the overwhelming lightness in your picture.

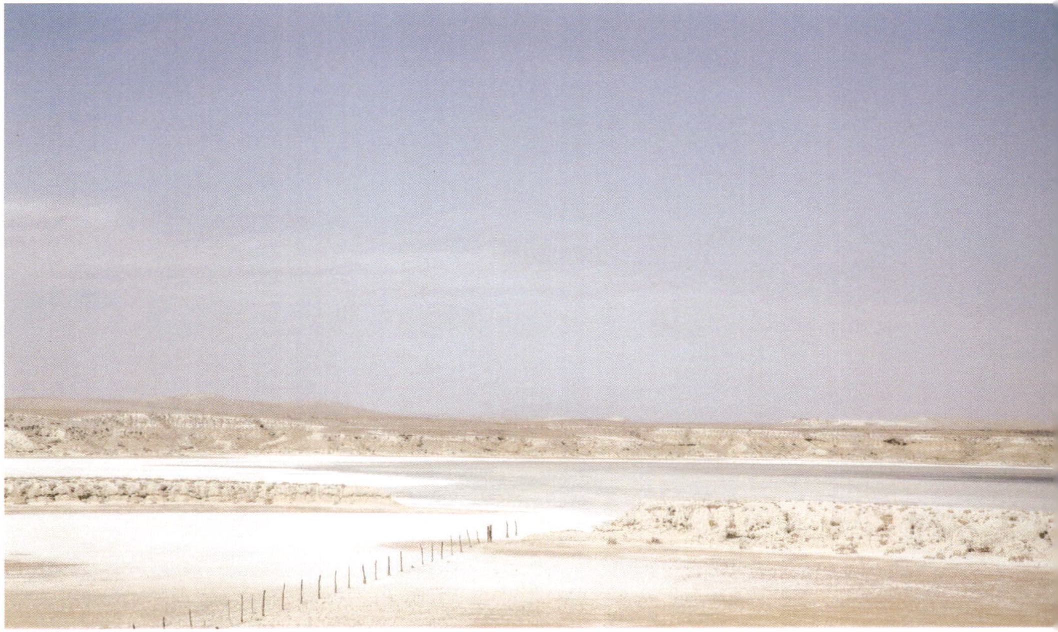

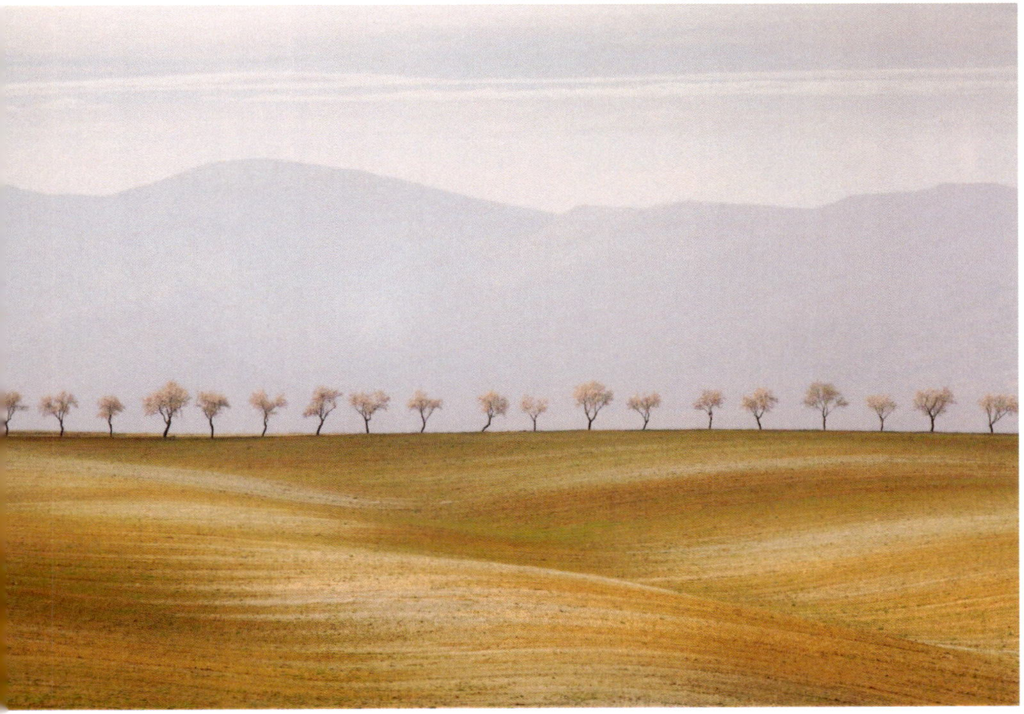

Figure 28 (Above) **Pale estuary**. While the thin stratus cloud had started to burn off, the sky remained pale. Viewed against this light and almost featureless estuary, an almost dream-like landscape has been created. The inclusion of the line of posts in the bottom of the composition adds a subtle but much needed additional element.

Figure 29 (Left) **A line of almond trees, Almeria**. A pale and delicate landscape celebrating spring, the foreground has been deliberately lightened in order to enhance the gentle tonality of the sky. This is precisely the sort of landscape that would not have benefitted from being photographed under a heavy sky.

Figure 30 **Receding posts**. Water, when photographed under moderately high stratus clouds, will inevitably reflect the muted high key tones in the sky, offering a wonderfully holistic image. The gently lapping water echoes the minimal detail visible in the sky. When indulging in high key work of this nature, it is important to take care to ensure that none of the highlights are completely blown; it certainly pays to check the histogram.

CUT OUT THE SKY

As you will already be aware, the term 'grey sky' covers a variety of options, however the most difficult of these is a featureless grey sky. These low stratus clouds are a uniform grey and are not dissimilar to fog and mist, except that it is a cloud cover that does not touch the ground. One rarely encounters rain under these conditions but it is quite common to experience a light drizzle. From a photographic standpoint, without any tonal modulation or variation, such skies can be a nightmare. This kind of weather occurs when the cloud cover is particularly low. If you have high ground relatively close by then it might be possible to rise above the cloud level, but this is not always an option. Moreover, one's visibility is restricted due to the excess of moisture in the air. In these circumstances, many landscape workers decide to abandon attempts to take photographs and wait for the conditions to improve.

So, what is the solution?

First, consider the emotional impact this sort of weather promotes and choose your subject accordingly. The range of subjects you may want to photograph will not be too dissimilar to those taken under grey skies. Often in these circumstances there is a temptation to minimise the amount of sky included, but the results will be disappointing. If you point the camera towards the ground, the camera's metering system will largely ignore the brightness of the sky resulting in an underexposed foreground but an overexposed sky. Far better to select a small feature within the landscape such as a wind-blown tree or an abandoned building and include a large area of sky. The results will be minimal but often that can convey a mood.

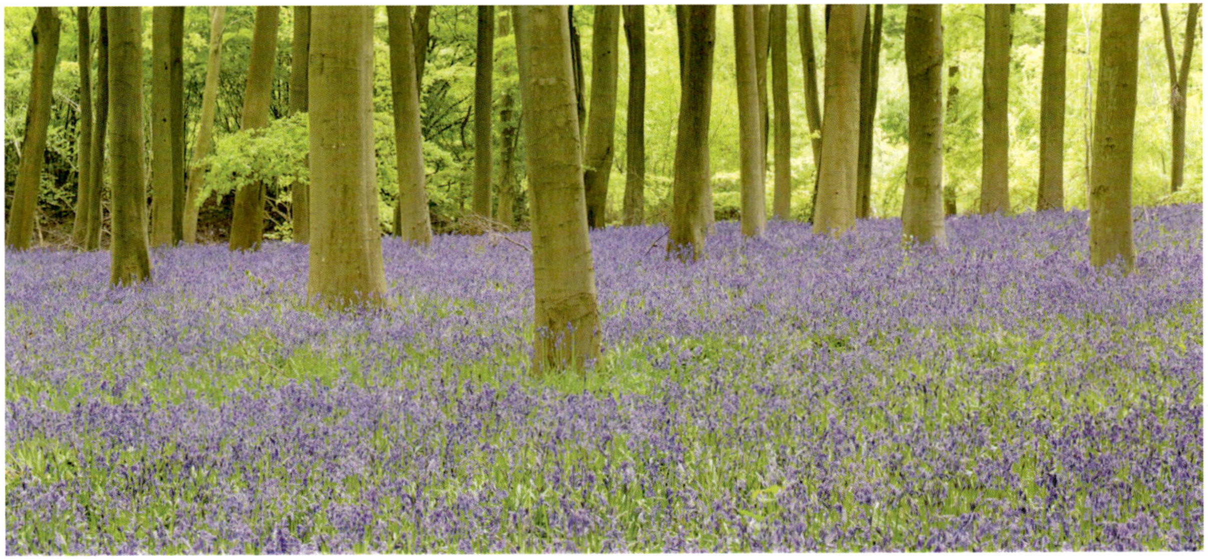

Figure 31 **Bluebell wood**. There are numerous occasions when photographing landscape where there is no need to include the sky. In this example, the 'horizon' is created by the rich display of bluebells in the foreground and the beech trees in the distance.

The alternative is to do the opposite and exclude the sky entirely. Within landscape photography, there is an over reliance on pointing the camera towards the horizon with often predictable results. Occasionally landscape benefits by excluding the sky entirely. This creates what is known as an 'intimate' landscape, because the photographer tends to focus on some smaller element. If you want to include a much larger part of the landscape, but need to exclude the sky, interesting images can be achieved by climbing onto a structure that offers a higher vantage point. Climbing just a few metres can make quite a difference.

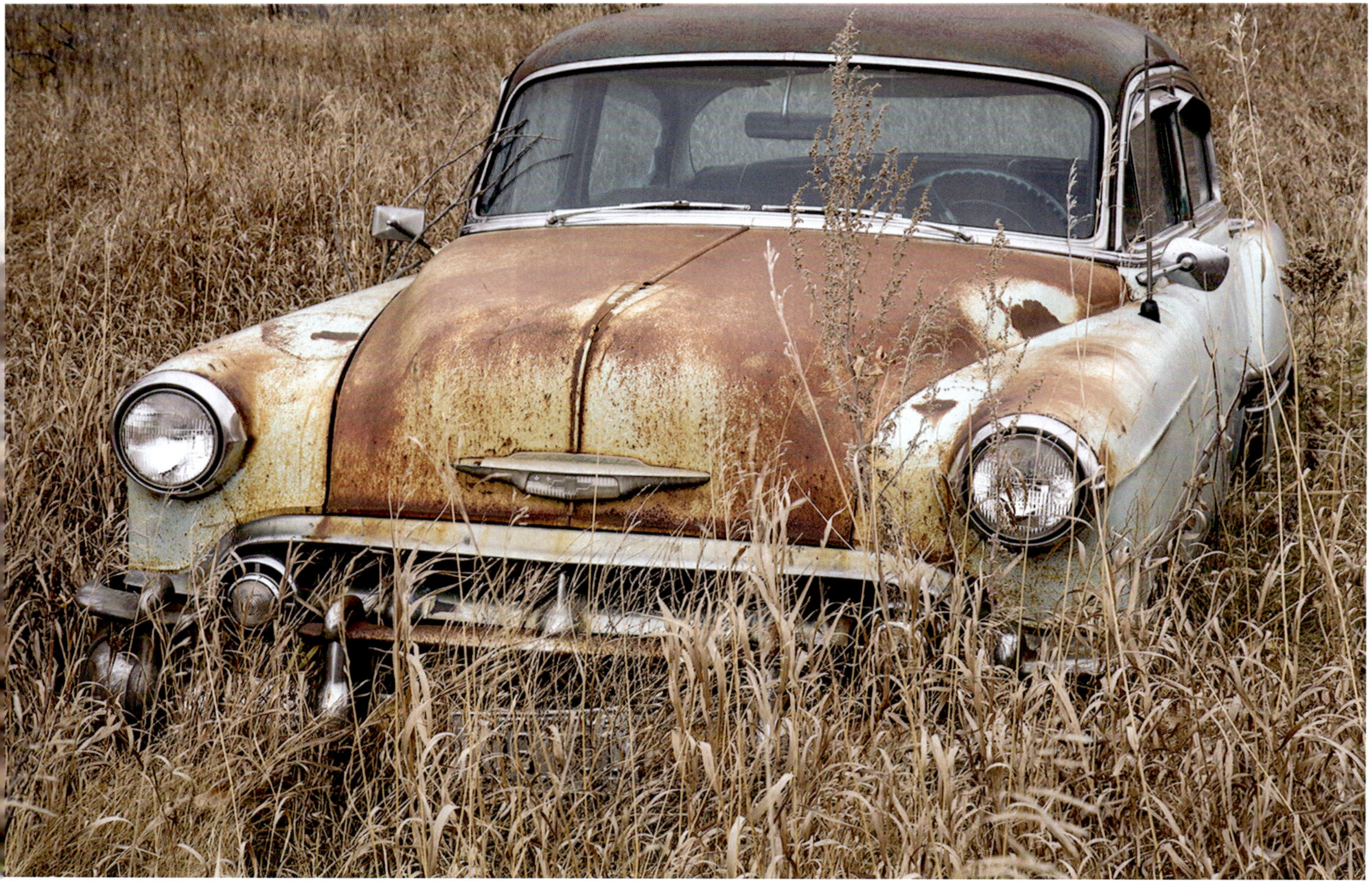

Figure 32 Wrecked Chevrolet. This is a classic situation where pointing the camera downwards produces an interesting alternative. The sky on this occasion was bland and featureless so focusing on the car made far more sense.

Figure 33 **Andalusian landscape and single tree**. Once you secure a moderately high vantage point, you are able to see the landscape from quite an interesting angle. On this occasion the sky offered very little so, looking over this valley, I was able to concentrate on the graphical qualities this cultivated location offered.

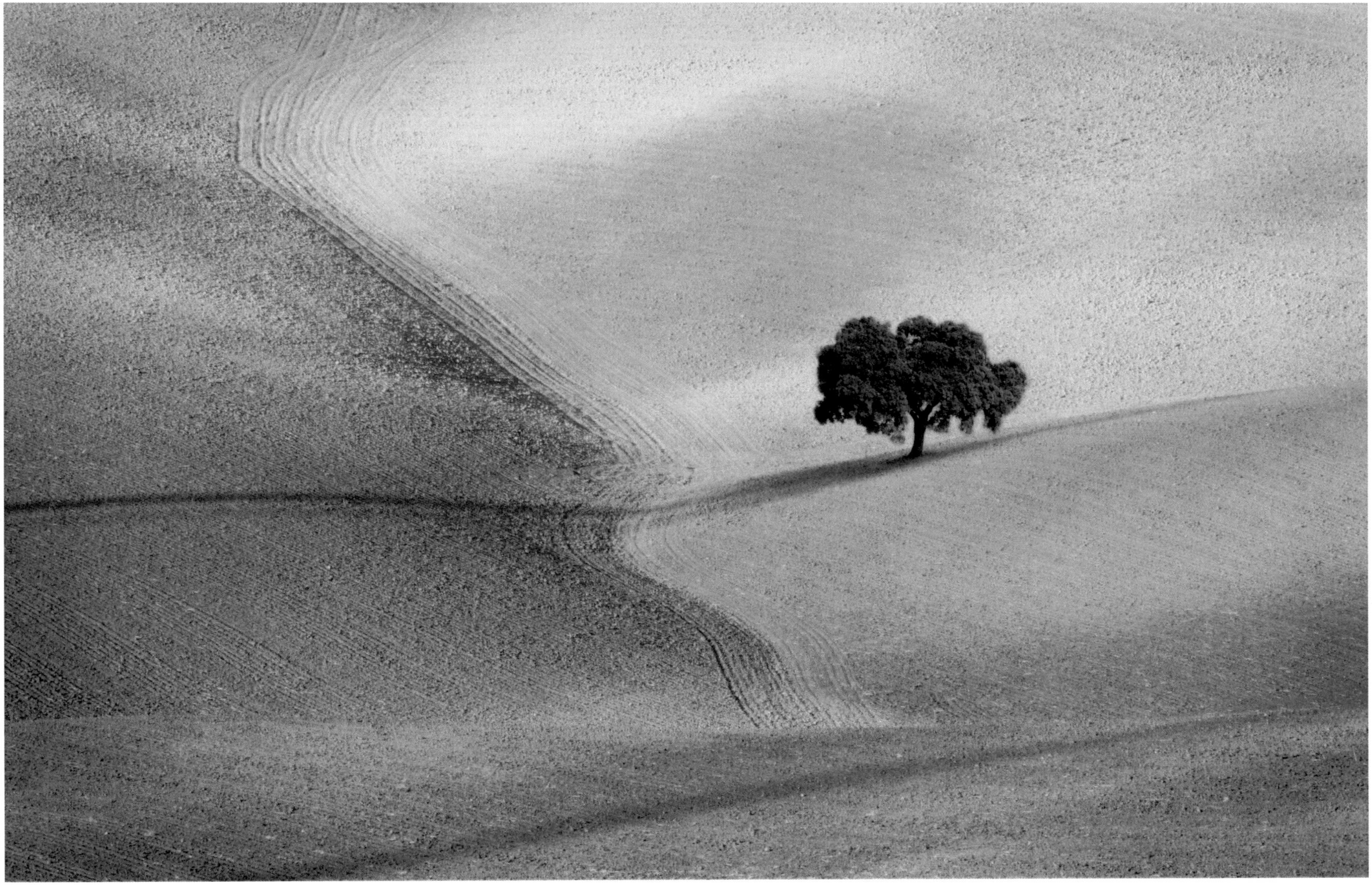

THE THINLY VEILED SUN

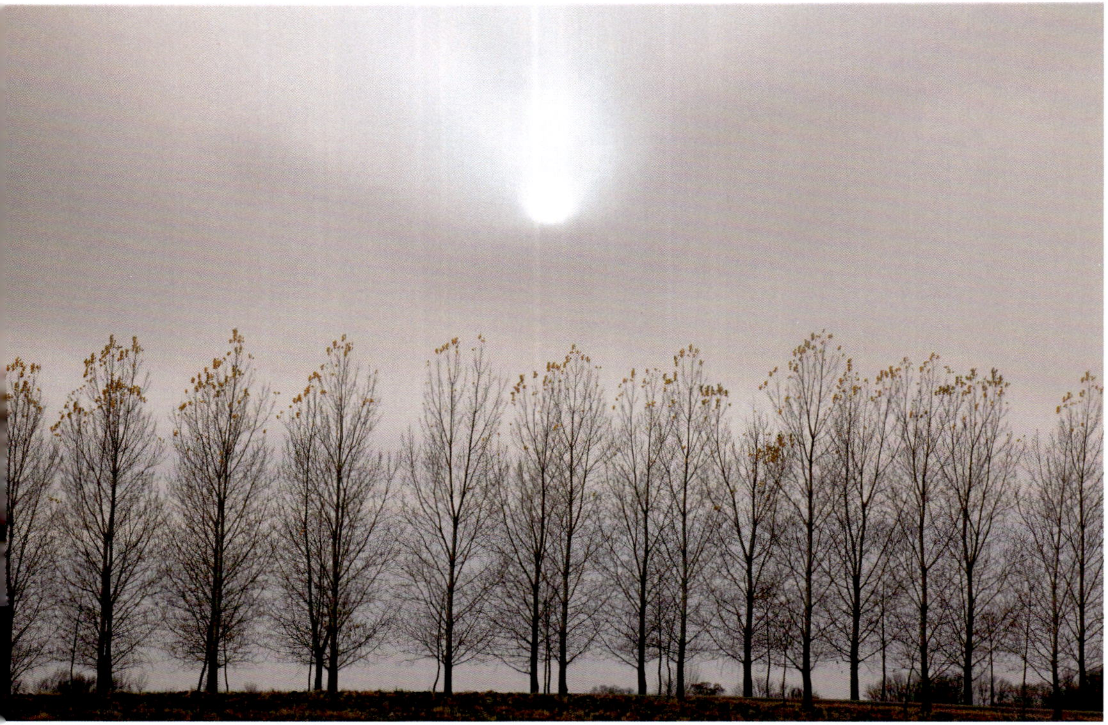

Figure 34 **Line of trees**. There is certainly something quite spooky about altostatus translucidus. It is one of those weather features that is often used to spice up a mystery or horror film.

An interesting feature that often occurs when you are experiencing altostratus clouds is that the sun in daytime, or the moon at night, begins to gently emerge as a thinly veiled element in the sky. This is a metrological phenomenon known as 'altostatus translucidus', which produces a thin grey-blue cloud that covers much of the sky. It is yet another weather condition that offers excellent photographic opportunities.

A rising or setting sun in these conditions will appear pink or orange and can usually be viewed without needing to wear shades. It occurs as a result of the cloud formation warming and slightly rising. It is certainly one of those rather interesting weather conditions that evokes a unique mood. Colourless and grey, such skies can often appear 'spooky'; think of those many films that include shots of the appearing and disappearing sun. Such images certainly appear unsettling. Conscious of the emotional impact such skies can have, think carefully about how well the foreground empathises with the general mood; a wind-bent tree, a ruin on the horizon, or possibly a rakish figure will all work well under these fascinating lighting conditions. Don't overlook the opportunity to create an interesting black and white image.

Technical issues to consider

The most challenging technical issue is getting the right exposure. The moment you point the camera towards the sun, no matter how veiled it appears, you are likely to experience underexposure. Set your camera to Manual Mode and then overexpose by between 1/3 and 2/3 of a stop. If the sun is too bright the highlights will appear blown, so only attempt to photograph the sky when you can comfortably look at it without squinting your eyes. Your exposure will not only be governed by how bright the sun is, but also by how much sky you choose to include in the composition. The more sky you include, the more you should overexpose. It should also be noted that as you are pointing the camera at the source of light, the images will all be *contre jour*, therefore foreground detail will appear silhouetted.

Aesthetic issues

1. Where to place the sun relative to the features within the foreground. Often placing the sun centrally works well, while placing the main feature(s) within the foreground either to the left or right.

2. A pale sun usually appears through low lying stratus clouds. It is an indication that the cloud cover is beginning to be burnt off.

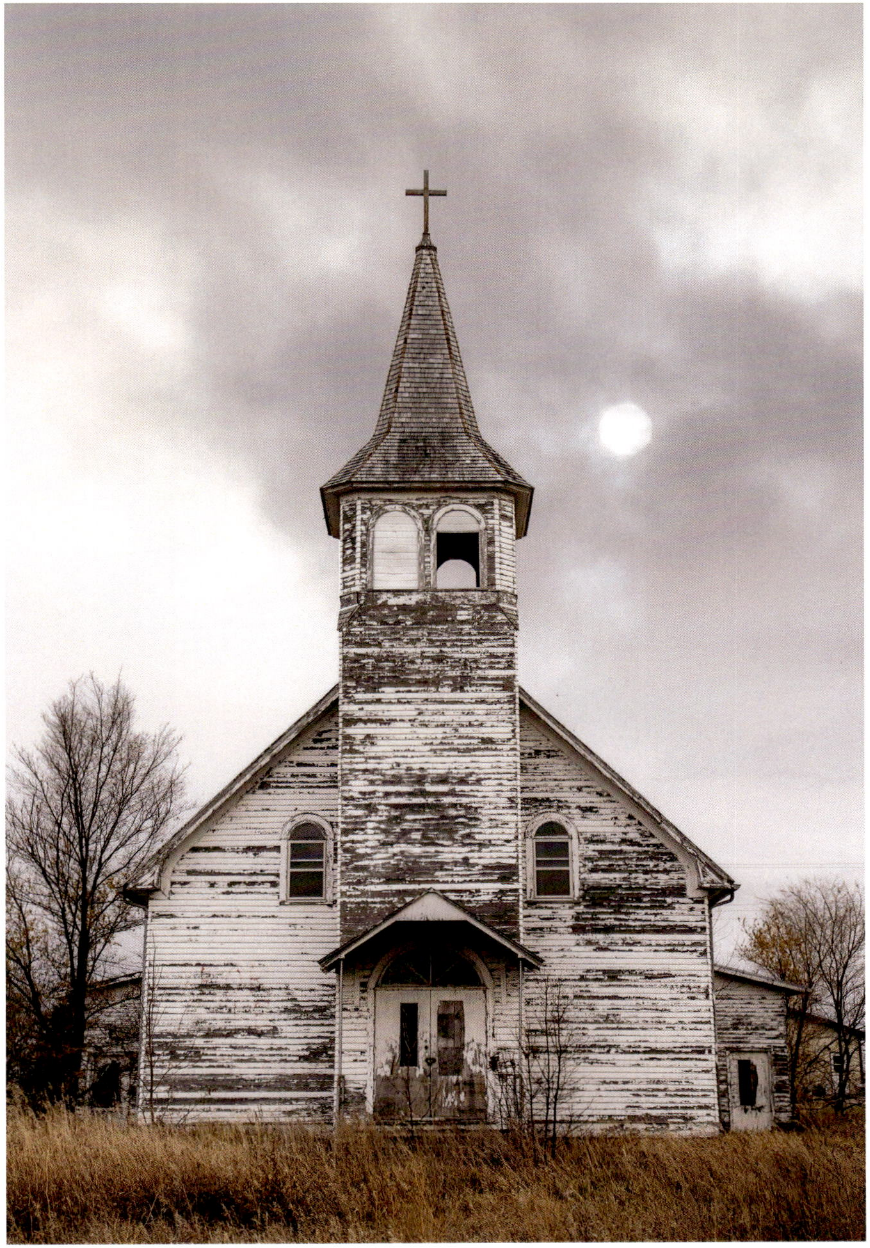

Figure 35 **Old church**. As the sky breaks up the sun will increasingly start to emerge. Only take your shot when you can still comfortably look at it without squinting your eyes, otherwise you will experience significant underexposure.

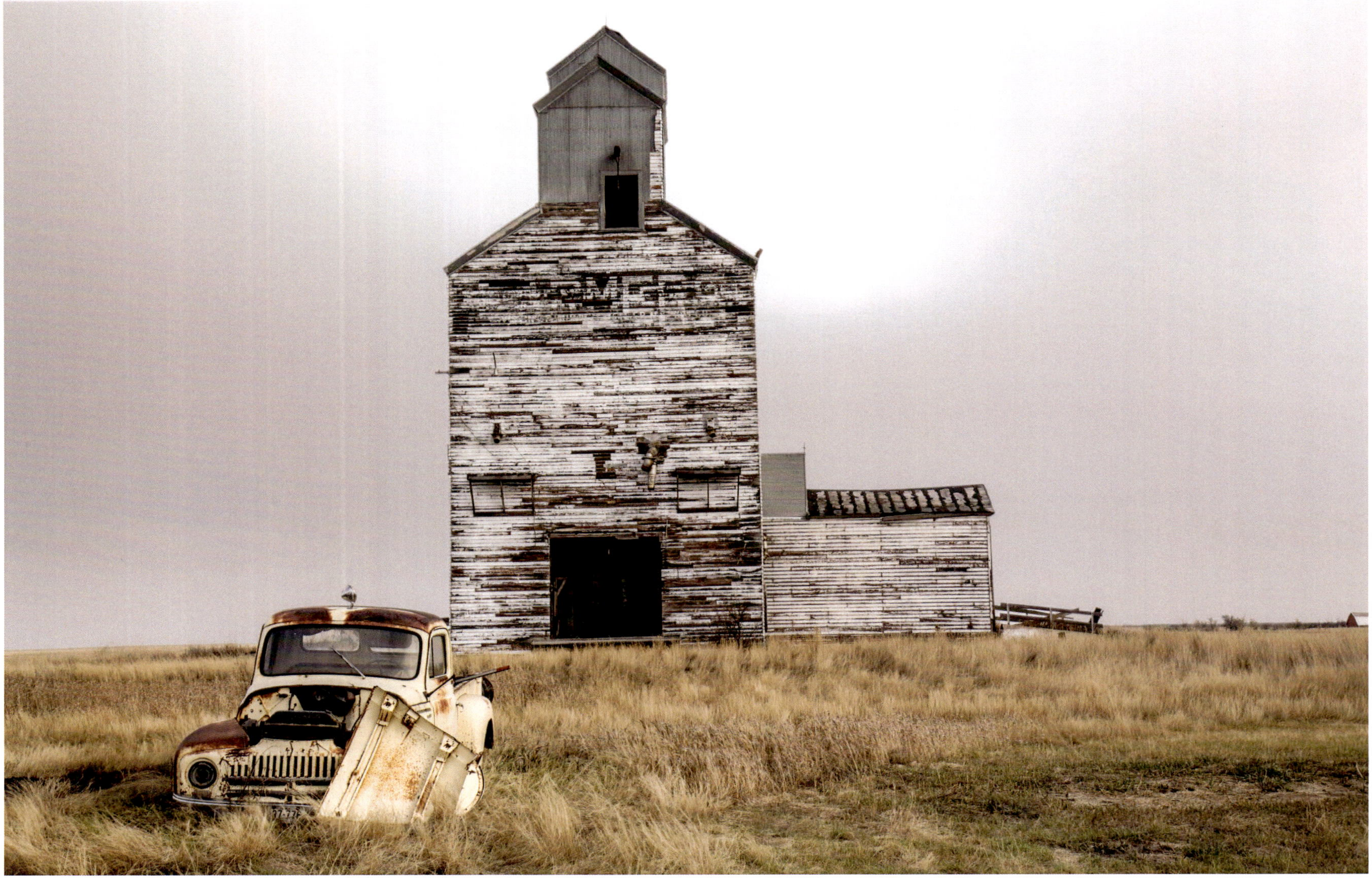

Figure 36 **Grain elevator**. My main problem was to ensure I was able to achieve an even exposure for both the foreground and the sky. To overcome this I used a soft graduated ND filter (see Chapter 1).

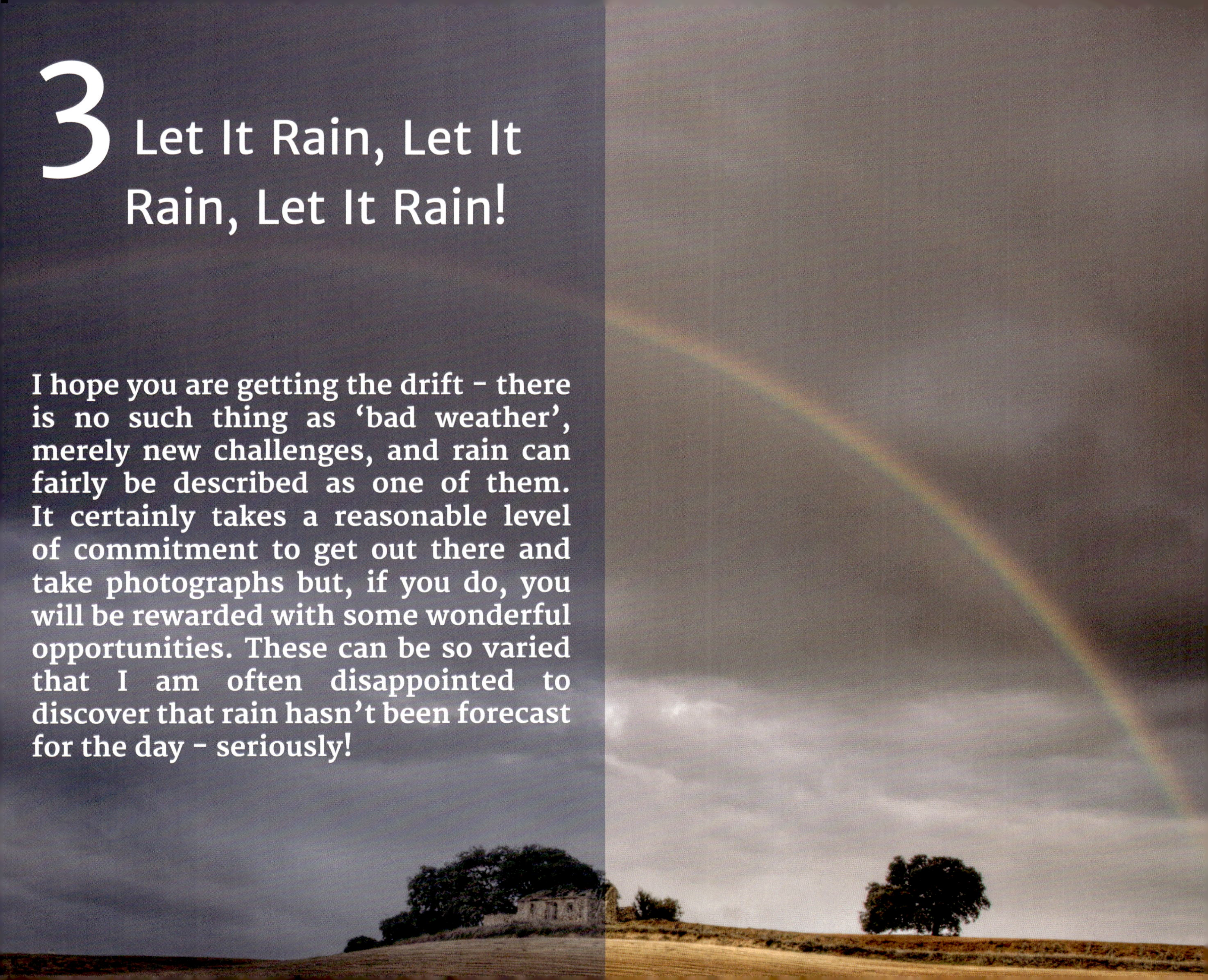

3 Let It Rain, Let It Rain, Let It Rain!

I hope you are getting the drift – there is no such thing as 'bad weather', merely new challenges, and rain can fairly be described as one of them. It certainly takes a reasonable level of commitment to get out there and take photographs but, if you do, you will be rewarded with some wonderful opportunities. These can be so varied that I am often disappointed to discover that rain hasn't been forecast for the day – seriously!

PHOTOGRAPHING RAIN

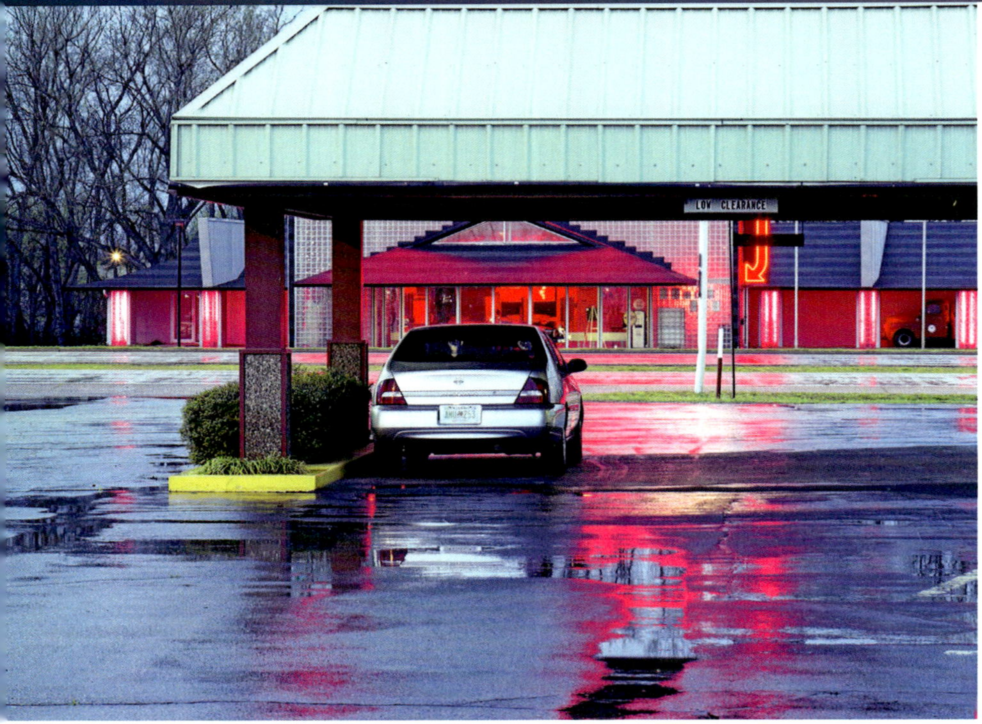

Figure 1 **Parked car and wet tarmac**. Shot at dawn, I was fascinated by the rich colours of the nearby neon reflected in the wet tarmac. While it is easy to assume I was exposed to the elements, I was sheltering underneath the canopy of my motel room. Using a telephoto zoom, I was able to take my shot in reasonable comfort.

In common with grey skies, rain offers many varieties, each of which presents unique challenges. We can experience a gentle rain right through to a full-blown deluge. When considering the latter not only is it desirable to keep yourself dry but also your camera. It is difficult to muster the enthusiasm once you are drenched and, on a similar tack, most DSLR cameras are particularly vulnerable to heavy rain and can sustain serious damage if they are not adequately protected.

Varying sorts of rain

1. Drizzle

Drizzle is the lightest form of rain and relatively easy to work in. The droplets of water are smaller than raindrops and it can often be confused with mist. The ground will appear wet although, in light drizzle, the water can evaporate quite quickly.

2. Thunderstorms

Thunderstorms are considerably more violent and, while they are difficult to work in, they can present excellent opportunities for original photography (partially because so many photographers are not willing to work in such conditions). They are created by the formation of cumulonimbus clouds and are frequently associated with thunder and lightning. They can occur at any time of the year but are more common in late spring and summer, particularly during the afternoon and evening.

3. Wind and rain

Wind and rain is possibly one of the most difficult weather conditions to work in, particularly if the direction of the wind fluctuates. It is possible to work with your back to the wind, but you will find it does have a habit of changing direction. Once again, if you are prepared to brave the elements, there are great opportunities to be had.

4. Steady rain

Steady rain is possibly the easiest of the rain conditions to work under, and one that offers the best possible results.

The secret is to look to the ground as the reflections and enhanced colour saturation open up all sorts of creative possibilities. Free of wind, you should be able to work quite comfortably providing you take precautions.

Useful precautions

Most if not all cameras can withstand the odd drop of rain, but few can withstand a prolonged downpour. If you are inclined to try photographing in the rain (and I would seriously suggest you do) then there are various precautions you should consider.

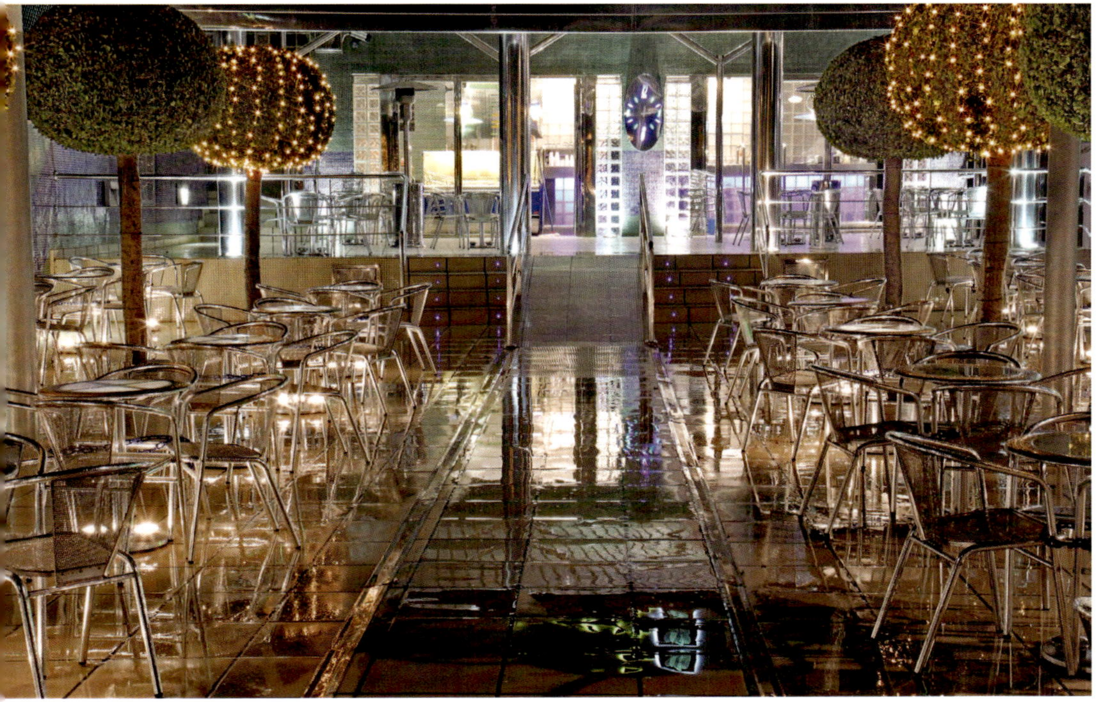

Figure 2 **Spanish cafe at night**. It is quite amazing how rain, particularly when photographed at night, can transform an otherwise prosaic location. Seen earlier in the day, I barely gave this cafe a second glance.

1. You can buy purpose-made plastic units to fit over your camera and lens. By visiting the internet you will find numerous manufacturers offering weather-proof covers for your specific camera; prices vary depending on the sophistication of the kit. It is, of course, quite easy to construct something yourself. Using something as simple as a clear polythene freezer bag, or possibly one of those cheap clear plastic shower caps (the sort that come free in hotels and motels), often suffices. Using something as simple as an elastic band to secure the bag in place is all that is needed.

2. Just using an umbrella is all that is required. If you are using a tripod, then you should be able to hold an umbrella while taking your shot. Alternatively you may consider buying a golf umbrella holder. While these are designed to be attached to a golf trolley, they can also be fixed to your tripod, which, of course, will free up both hands. Also, if you are shooting with a friend, why not take it in turns to hold the umbrella over the other?

3. Particularly within an urban situation, you are likely to find some form of shelter such as a doorway that allows you to take photographs while remaining dry. This might slightly compromise your vantage point but, if you are using a zoom lens, it is surprising what you are still able to take.

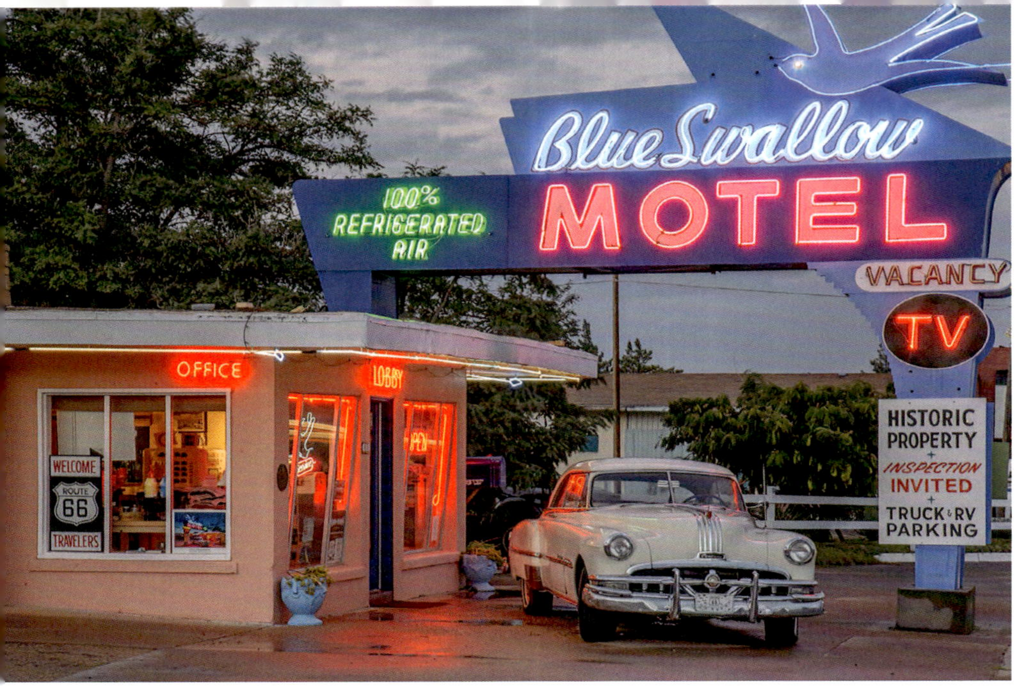

Figure 3 **The Blue Swallow Motel**. You do not necessarily need a torrential downpour to get an interesting shot in the rain. In this example there was just a light drizzle, but it was sufficient to offer a reflective surface for the gaudy neon lighting.

4. Always make sure the lens is protected by fitting a UV filter. As these filters make very little difference to the colour of the image they should be kept on at all times, as one way of protecting the much more valuable lens.
5. One of the great irritations when photographing in rain is getting droplets of water on the lens, although occasionally that can prove beneficial. Think how often you have watched news footage on a storm and seen obvious droplets of water on the lens. Such distortions heighten the sense of drama. On a slightly different tack, if you wear glasses what can prove annoying is getting water on the lenses, which of course makes viewing difficult. For this reason it is always a good idea to keep a microfibre cloth to hand, either to clean your spectacles (if you wear them) or to remove droplets of water from the UV filter.

Suitable subjects

Itemising a list of possible themes that one might seek to photograph in wet weather may suggest that the opportunities are limited, but nothing could be further from the reality. It should be possible to photograph most landscape situations in rain, although some, of course, stand out. Here are some obvious ones:

1. Wet tarmac. The urban environment can appear spectacularly more interesting when photographed in the rain; tarmac surfaces in particular become more contrasty and quite reflective. If you can find a slightly raised vantage point, moving traffic can add further interest. Pedestrianised areas also offer rich pickings as the passing figures are so concerned about remaining dry that they are likely to be unaware that you are photographing them. The reflections they create can be especially appealing.
2. Interesting shots can be achieved by capturing moving vehicles and the spray they create. Clearly you do not want to be too close to the action, which is why a long lens becomes useful. Shots such as this can be taken from an open window or possibly from an upper floor of a multi-storey car park.

3. Boardwalks and jetties are often constructed of wood and can appear particularly reflective in rain. Usually constructed near water, they offer excellent photographic opportunities. Piers make ideal subjects when photographed in the rain, if only because they tend to be deserted in such circumstances.

4. Sometimes it is just too wet to venture out. If so, then don't overlook photographing the window as a possible subject. The secret here is to focus on the droplets on the glass pane while throwing the landscape outside out of focus; select a wide aperture. By focusing precisely on the small cluster of droplets they will serve as an informal prism of the landscape outside. If you try this, keep your lens parallel to the surface of the glass when taking the shot.

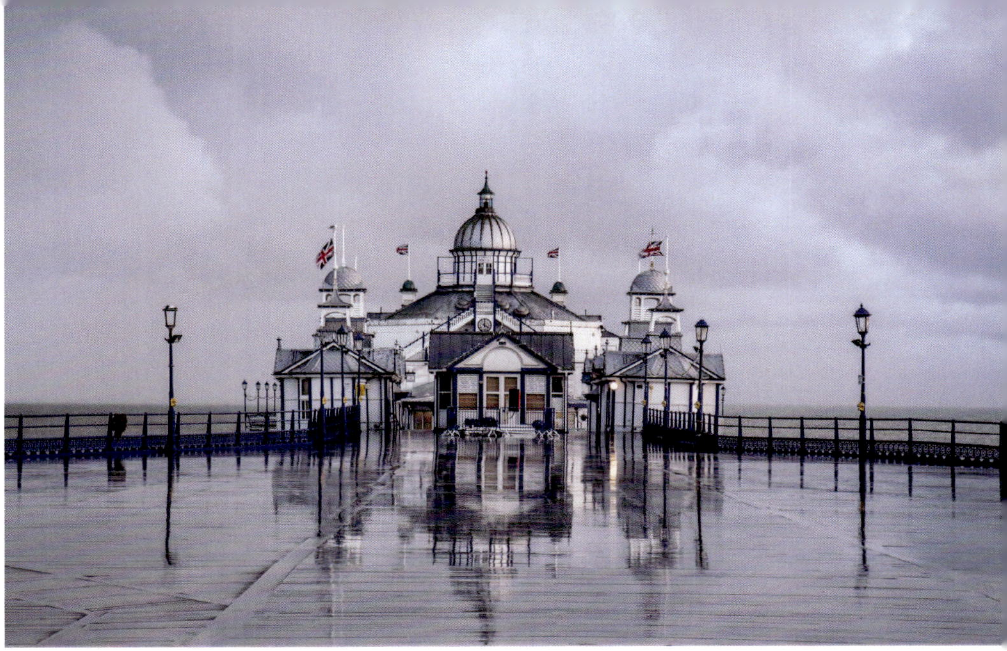

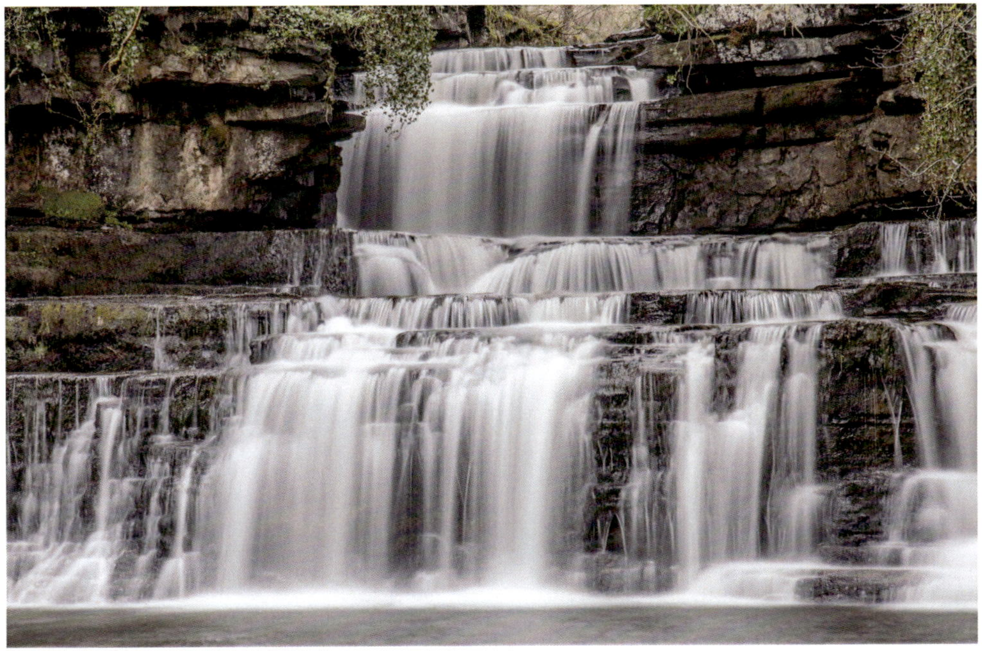

Figure 4 (Left) Waterfall. Waterfalls make excellent subjects to photograph when it is raining. They are best photographed when using a slow shutter speed in order to capture the silky effect of flowing water; this is best achieved when the sky is dark and heavily clouded. Also, the amphitheatre surrounding the waterfall is sodden causing the colours to appear more saturated.

Figure 5 (Above) Eastbourne Pier. Jetties and piers can make excellent subjects to photograph in the rain, particularly if they are constructed of wood. I had nowhere to shelter when taking this shot so, by ensuring that my ISO rating and aperture were pre-set, I was able to take my camera out of the bag just at the last moment, thus minimising its exposure to the rain.

5. If you are in a rural setting, don't overlook the opportunity to photograph flowing water. Cascades and waterfalls often look their best when it is raining. First, moving water is best photographed when using a slow shutter speed (between 1/4 and 1/2 second seems to work best). With darkened skies the amount of light is considerably limited, therefore it is quite possible to use a very slow shutter speed, even in the middle of the day. Second, as the rain dampens the surrounding landscape, the colours appear more saturated as a consequence. Dull scenarios appear vibrant and interesting as a result of the rain. Finally, if it has been raining heavily for a period of time, the amount of water flowing through the waterfall will have substantially increased, leading to a more dramatic scene.

Figure 6 **Spanish plaza**. When you are in an urban environment at night look to the ground. The wet surfaces will reveal an amazing display of colour.

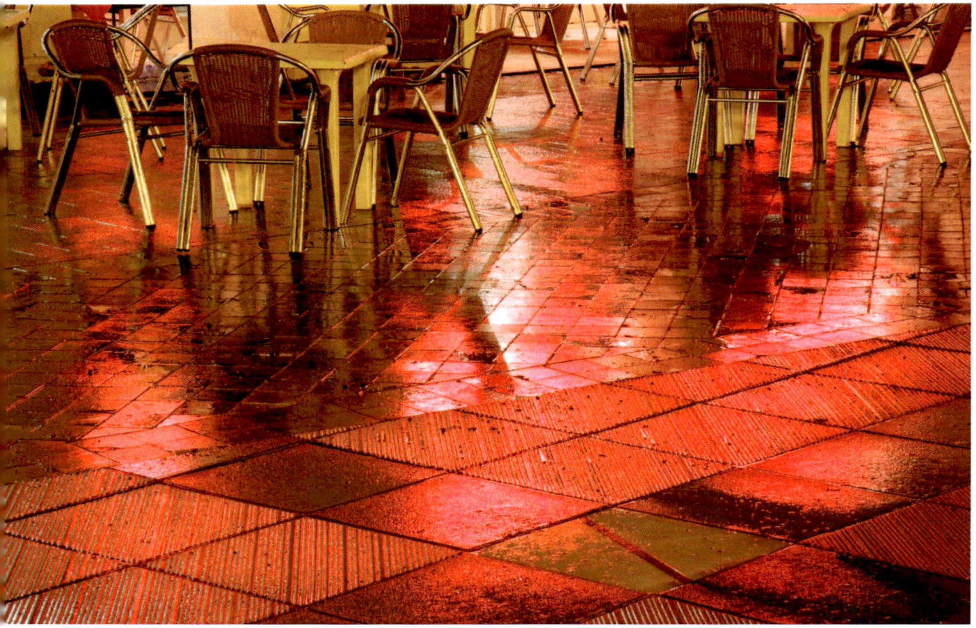

6. Unquestionably one of the best opportunities when photographing in the rain is an illuminated urban area at night. The wet surfaces serve as reflectors, offering interesting opportunities for abstract photography. If you find a location near a brightly illuminated building or structure, you will be amazed at how many interesting photographic opportunities you can find. Often within an urban location you are able to take your shot from some nearby shelter, which overcomes some of the challenges of shooting in the rain.

Figure 7 **Motel car park**. It was raining quite heavily as I took this shot but, of course, because of the long exposure the camera was unable to record the movement. The strange colour in the sky is as a result of the tungsten street lights diffused in the low rain clouds.

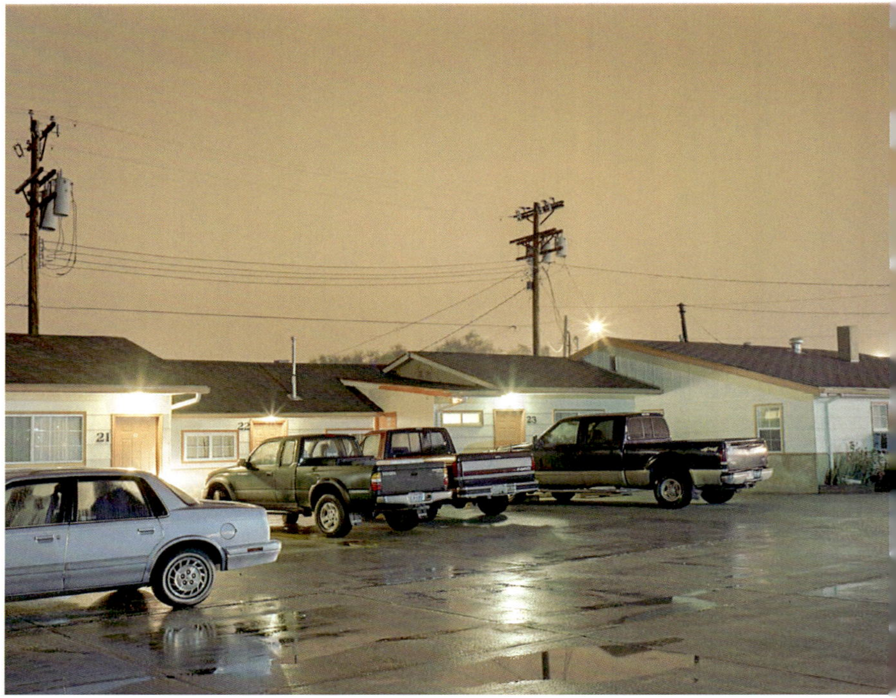

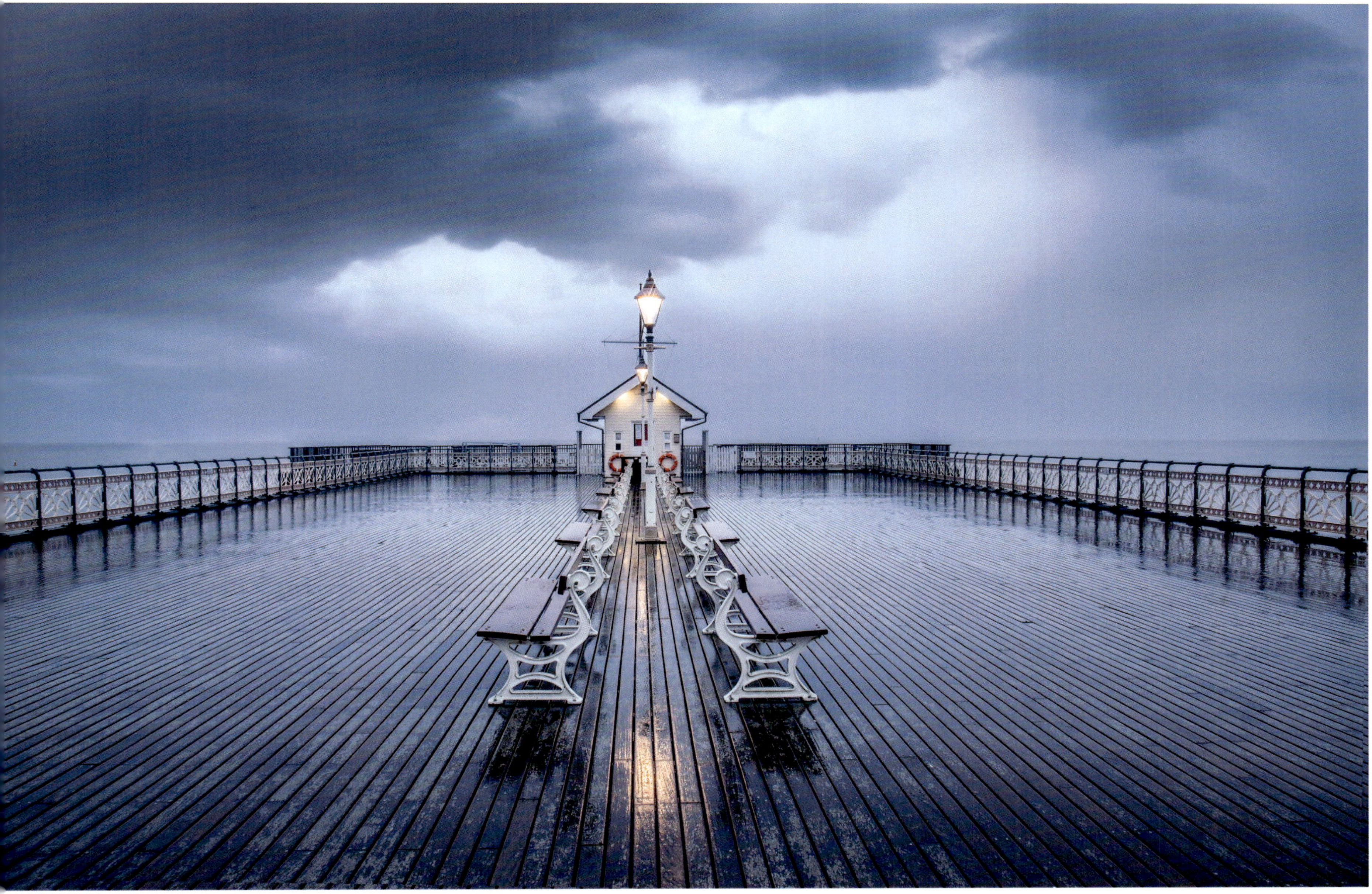

Figure 8 **Penarth Pier**. When I took this shot, not only was it raining heavily but it was quite windy as well. Fortunately, I was with a fellow photographer. We each took it in turns to hold the umbrella while the other took photographs.

CAPTURING LIGHTNING

Capturing a good shot of lightning is perhaps the ambition of most landscape photographers. It is certainly one of nature's most dramatic events, although to do it successfully is a little more demanding than you might imagine. Lightning, of course, can occur both in daytime and at night.

Photographing lightning in daytime

This is undoubtedly the most challenging time as you need to react quickly. The first task is to assess where in the sky the majority of the activity is occurring. Sometimes this can be confusing because, as you point your camera in one direction, the lightning occurs directly behind you. Normally lightning tends to gradually move across the sky, which makes this decision reasonably straight forward. Shooting a single flash of lightning is almost impossible as our reactions aren't quick enough. However, if the bolts strobe, then you are in with a fighting chance.

With regards to your camera settings, lock the focus on infinity, then set the aperture and shutter speed for the ambient lighting conditions. If you are hand-holding, I would certainly use an ISO rating of at least 400 to give yourself plenty of latitude.

A technique you may wish to consider is to set the camera to a fast continuous shooting mode. Normally a lightning flash will occur every 15 seconds so, by using this option, you will of course need to discard quite a lot of images afterwards, but if in the end you are able to grab a great shot, who's moaning?

Lightning triggers

If you anticipate taking this genre seriously why not buy a 'lightning trigger'? It certainly makes the task of shooting in the daytime considerably easier. They are designed to react to sudden changes of light far quicker than you can react. These small units are attached to the hot shoe of your DSLR allowing the automatic hands-free recording of storms. Further details are available on the internet.

Photographing lightning at night

The ideal time to shoot lightning is in relatively low light, ideally early morning or in the evening. Set your camera onto a tripod and just point it in the direction of greatest activity. Select an uncluttered viewpoint that gives you the best view of the sky. If you are able to include something interesting in the foreground, such as a small tree, it should offer an interesting focal point.

Camera settings

Set the camera's aperture and ISO rating to allow you to select a shutter speed of 30 seconds. This will give you a good chance of securing a great lightning shot almost with your first attempt. Setting the shutter speed to Bulb will also offer more flexibility. It is also important to set the lens to Manual, otherwise it could go into Hunt Mode, particularly at night.

Stacking your images

A big advantage of setting your camera on a tripod is that you can 'stack' your lightning shots, which results in a more exciting file. With an exposure of 30 seconds or more, you could experience two or possibly three separate lightning strikes, which, of course, will appear on a single file. Alternatively you can use stacking software that allows you to combine various files into a single composite image. From a visual standpoint the results are identical to capturing various strikes on a single file, except that you have much greater control over the distribution of the various layers.

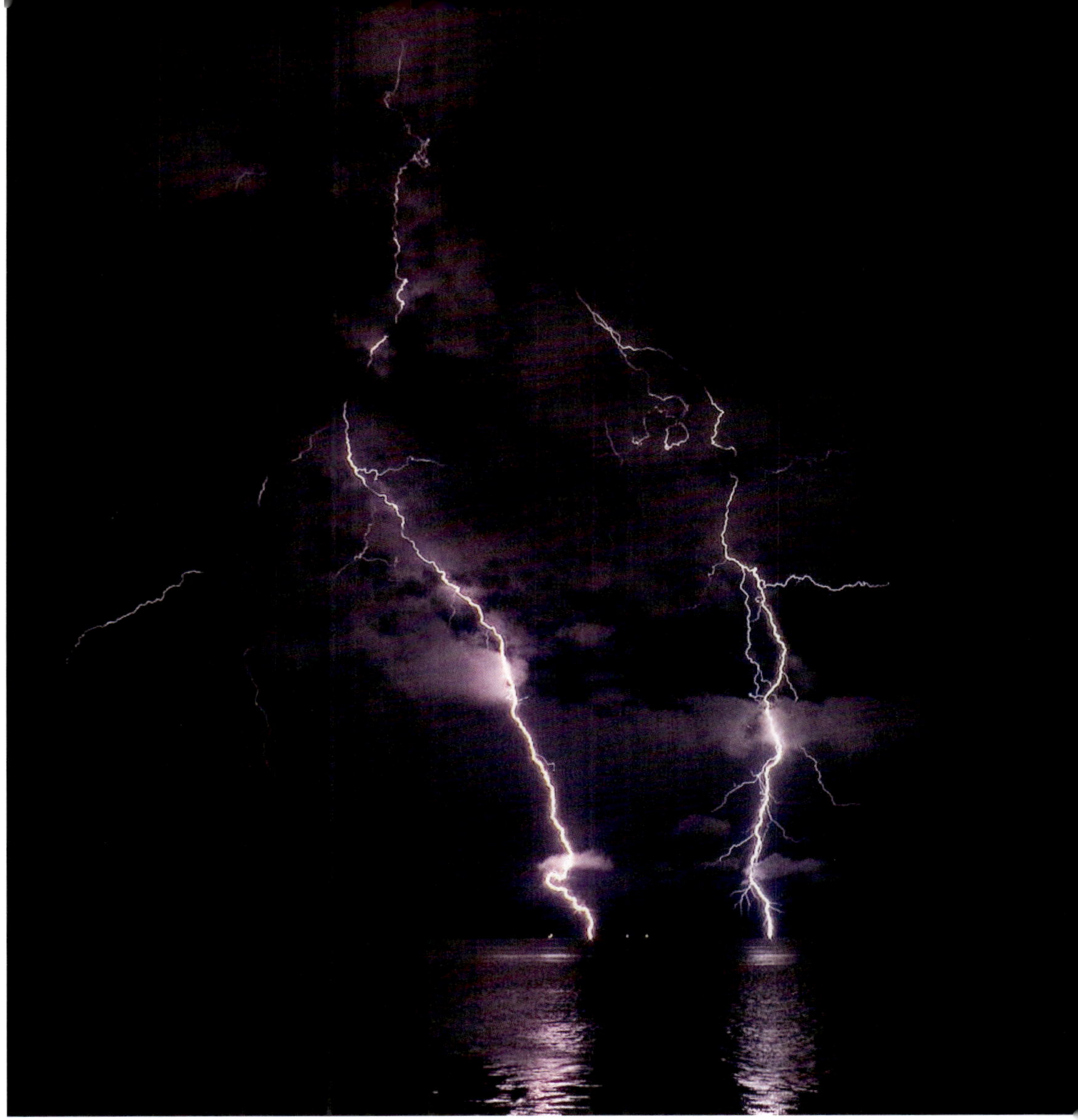

In the middle of the night we had a lightning storm, so I decided the smart thing to do was to go take pictures of it. Little did I know the lightning was less than a mile away; the strike you see here was certainly hitting the water. The sound of thunder followed almost immediately. Attribution: *By Ian Boggs from Astoria, US (Lightning on the Columbia River) [CC BY-SA 2.0 (http://creativecommons.org/licenses/by-sa/2.0)], via Wikimedia Commons*

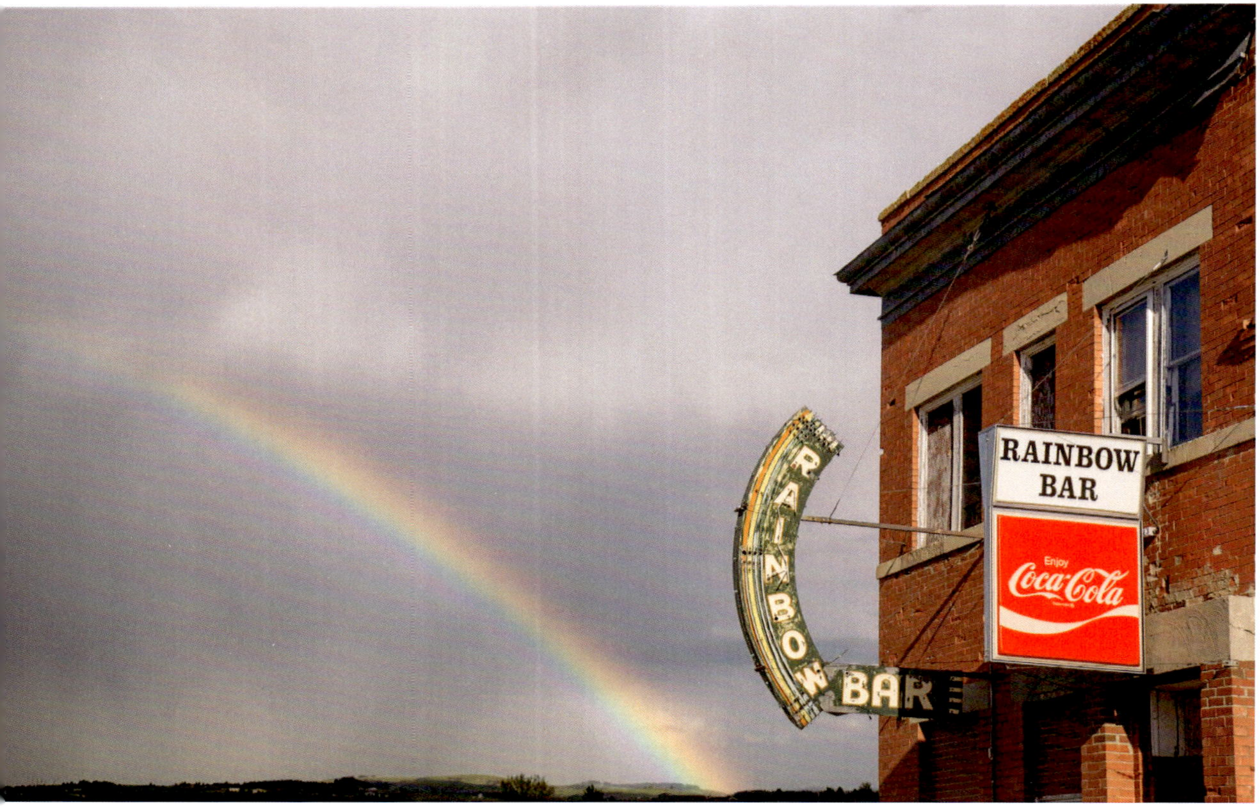

Figure 9 **The Rainbow Bar**. While the rainbow normally takes precedence, just occasionally you will encounter a foreground that is its equal. As I was driving to find the best location to shoot this rainbow from, my attention was so drawn by the beauty of the rainbow that I nearly passed by this most appropriate of locations.

Nothing illustrates the saying ‘there is a silver lining under every dark cloud’ more eloquently than a rainbow. Having endured the inconvenience of heavy rain, being rewarded with a dash of dramatic colour seems fair and just. A rainbow is a meteorological phenomenon often seen after heavy rain, appearing as a multi-coloured arc always in that part of the sky directly opposite the emerging sun. It is caused by the reflection of water droplets caught in the shafts of direct sunlight. It is possible to capture the full circle of a rainbow but, more commonly, we see just an arc or partial arc. Remember that, if there is no sunshine, then there will be no rainbows. While we see the light radiating from the sun as ‘white’, it actually emits varying colour wavelengths, namely red, orange, yellow, green, blue, indigo and violet. Sometimes we are able to witness the constituent parts of light broken down into these seven colours and rainbows are an example.

A single or 'primary' rainbow shows red on the outside of the arc with purple on the inner side, but if we are lucky enough to be rewarded with a double rainbow then the colour order is reversed. Generally the second rainbow appears slightly less saturated than the primary rainbow. We enjoy seeing rainbows, not just because they are such a spectacular meteorological phenomenon, but also because they are so intrinsically tied up in myth. It is hard to imagine an illustrated child's book that doesn't feature a rainbow somewhere within the pages. When photographing rainbows, consider the following points.

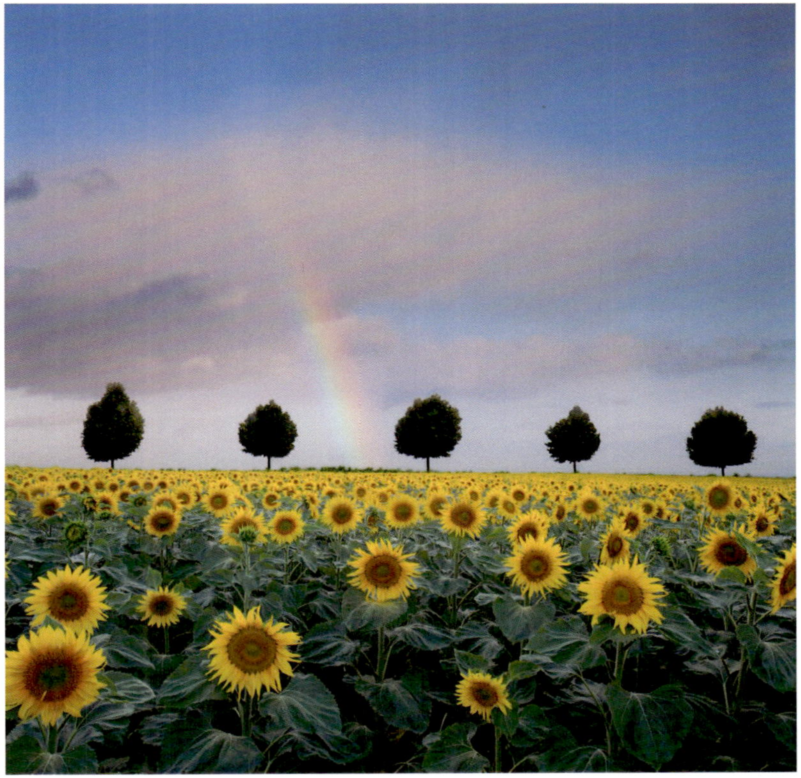

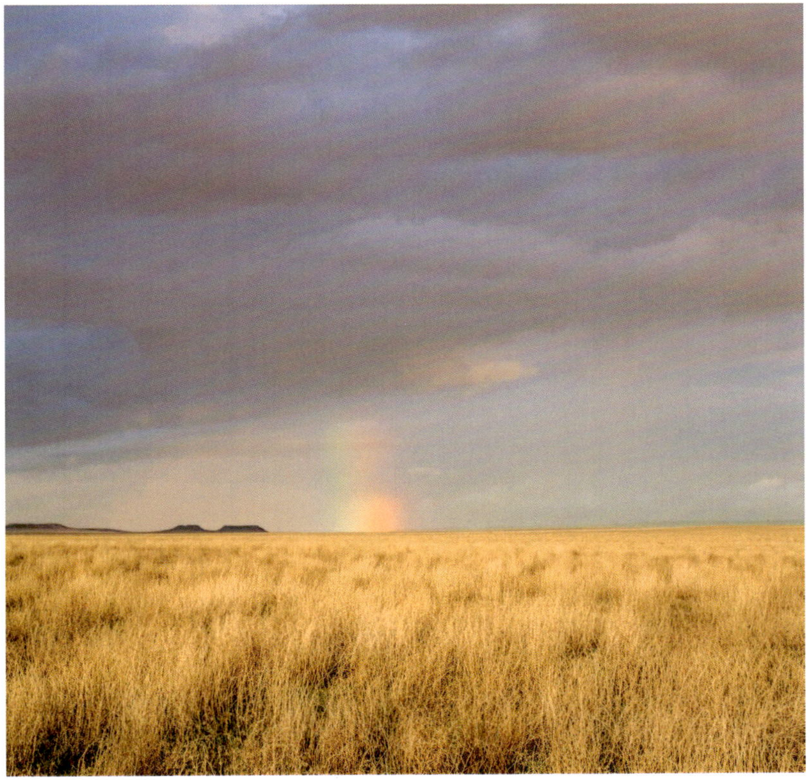

Figure 10 (Left)Emerging rainbow over the prairie. Don't always assume that you need to capture a full-blown rainbow; occasionally a more subtle emerging rainbow can prove equally evocative. When photographing a rainbow within a landscape, the foreground should be as uncluttered as possible.

Figure 11 (Above) Sunflower field. The showers that cause rainbows tend to be more common in summer than in the winter months, which is fortunate as this is often when the landscape is at its most impressive. The dramatic primary colours in the foreground are subtly echoed by the rainbow in the sky.

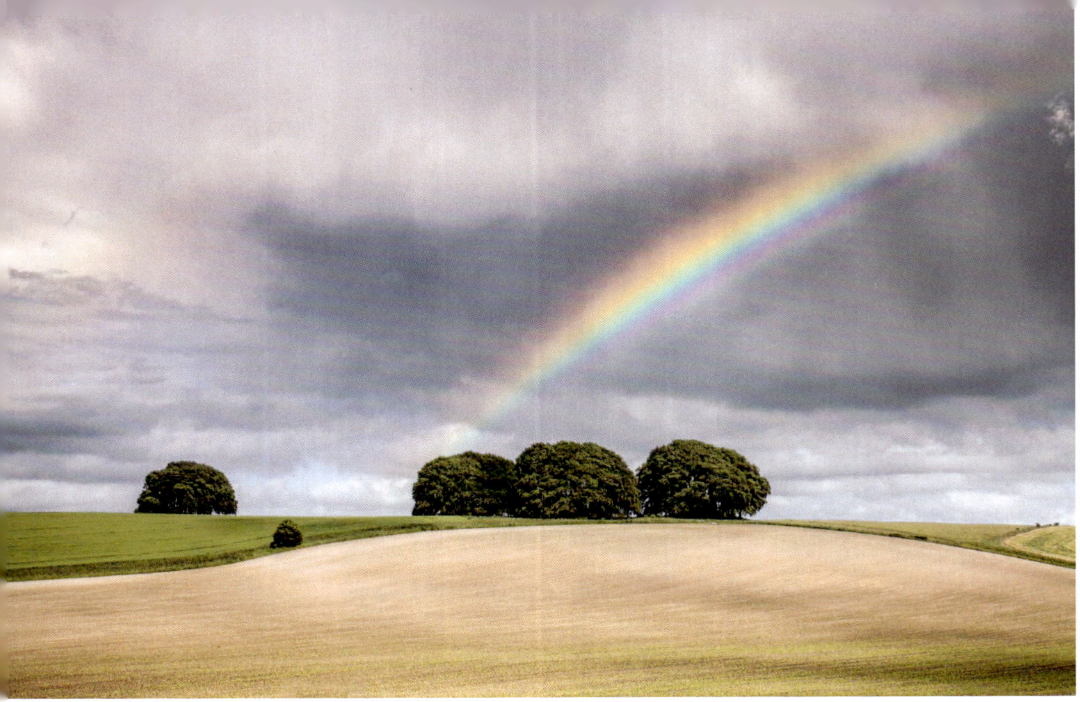

Figure 12 **Dramatic rainbow over copse of trees**. From a compositional standpoint, it certainly helps if you can organise the image so that the end of the rainbow appears over the main feature. In this example I was particularly fortunate that it appeared directly over the three trees on the horizon.

1. Rainbows are notoriously ephemeral so do not spend too much time thinking about elaborate compositions; it is not like photographing a river or waterfall that will always be there. It can help to compose the image, but not at the risk of losing the rainbow entirely. Depending on its beauty and the clarity of the rainbow, drop the horizon and make sure the rainbow is the dominant feature within the image. Essentially, keep it simple. One of the major problems when photographing rainbows, particularly within an urban setting, is to find a vantage point that does not impede the view of the rainbow. Ideally what you want is a flat and featureless horizon.

2. If you are able to, think carefully about where you want the end of the rainbow to be positioned. From a compositional standpoint, it can be used as a glorified 'lead-in line'. There may be an obvious tree on the horizon, or possibly a building, so positioning yourself so that both elements meet will strengthen the image. This is another one of those occasions when using a telephoto lens could prove useful. By zooming in on a specific part of the landscape, you are able to simplify the image while making the rainbow a more dominant part of the composition. If the rainbow is sufficiently flamboyant, dispense with the horizon completely.

3. If you have a polarising filter, experiment by rotating the filter to see how it effects the overall image. Issues such as the relative colour saturation or overall contrast will become apparent. Your aim is to make the rainbow stand out as much as possible. Polarising filters are at their most effective when they are used at right angles to the sun, while rainbows, of course, are seen at 180 degrees to the sun but, despite this, some measure of polarisation will occur. If you do opt to use a polarising filter, you need to understand that it can cut out the amount of light reaching

the sensor by a factor of 3, so it might be necessary to use a tripod. Once again I would remind you that rainbows are notoriously ephemeral, so do act quickly. Another filter you might consider is a soft graduated neutral density filter; this darkens the top of the sky and thus emphasises the luminescence of the rainbow.

4. With the appearance of the rainbow, you may be lulled into thinking that all precipitation has ended, but that is not always the case. Absorbed by its splendour, a drop of rain on your filter might easily go unnoticed, which could ruin an otherwise brilliant shot. It is quite normal to point your camera upwards when shooting rainbows, which will make it more vulnerable, so it is certainly worth checking every once in a while.

5. It should also be noted that mini-rainbows can also appear over waterfalls, as precisely the same process of refraction occurs as a result of the fine spray of water many of them produce.

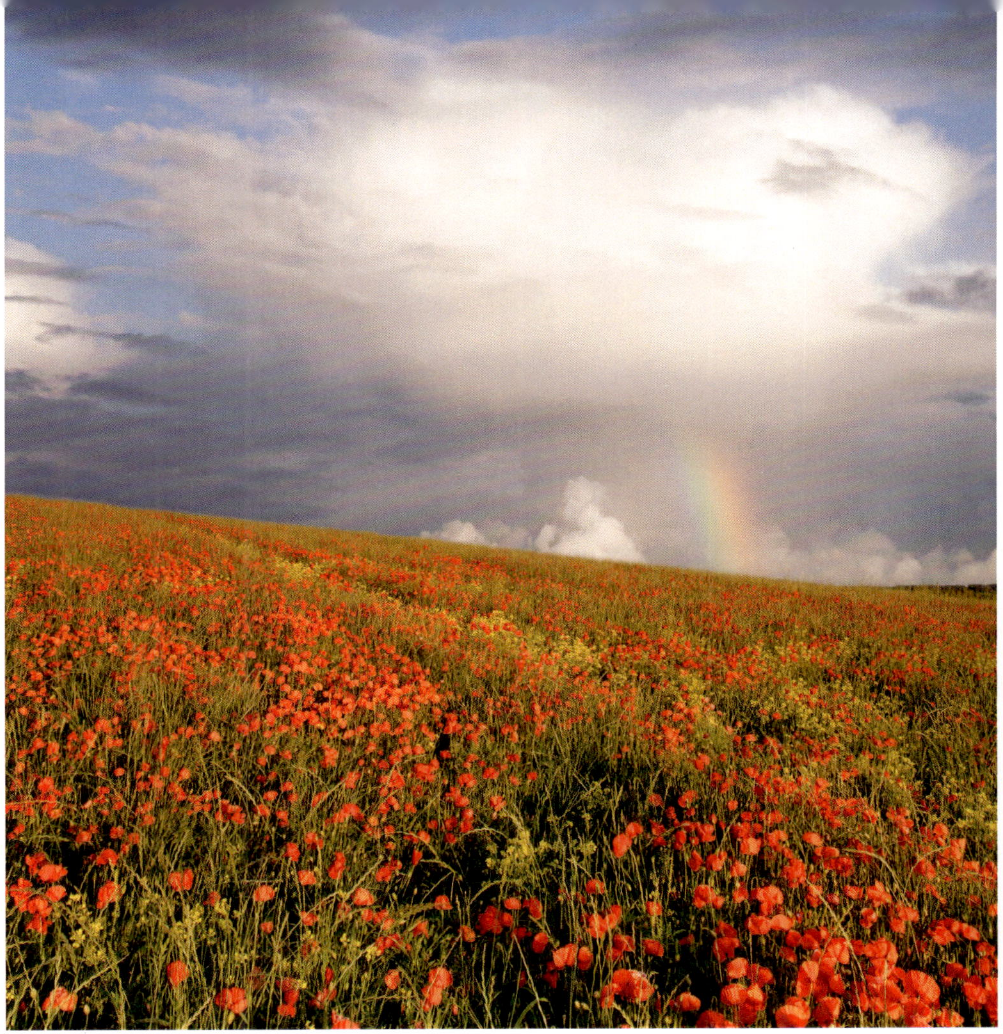

Figure 13 **Emerging rainbow over field of poppies**. Often the rainbow proves to be the dominant feature within the picture. However, in this example, as there is so much vibrant colour in the foreground, the rainbow can afford to be a little less showy.

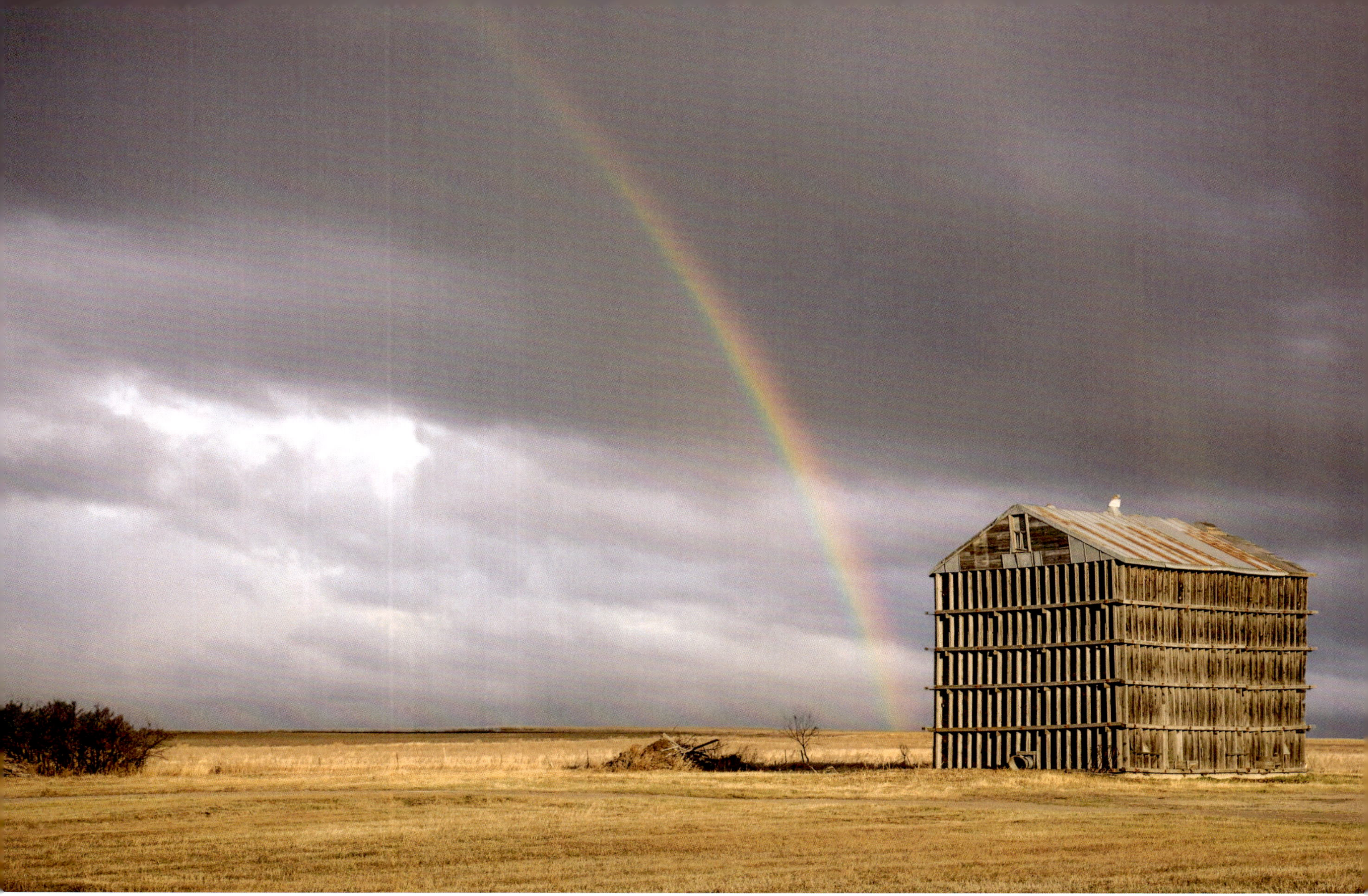

Figure 14 **Lone barn**. Rainbows only occur in that part of the sky which is at 180 degrees to the emerging sun, so the entire landscape appears bathed in a rich glowing light.

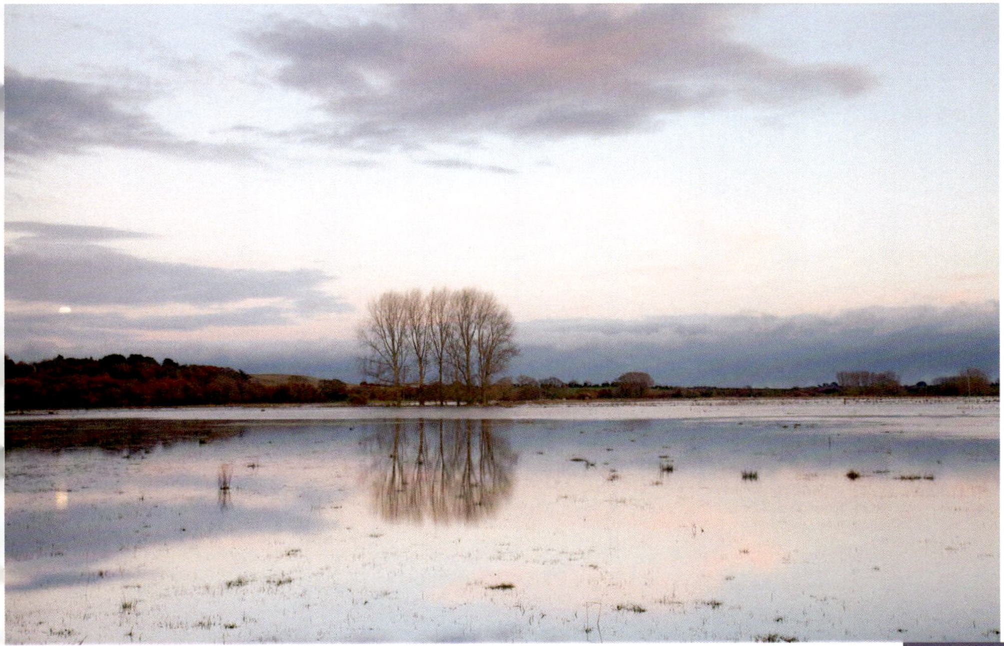

Figure 15 **Flooded field 1**. Photographed on the outskirts of the town where I live, I was able to pick the right moment to take this shot. I waited for a still evening when there was subtle detail in the sky. The rising moon was an added bonus.

Possibly as a consequence of global warming, the incidence of flooding appears to be increasing. One hopes that much of this is managed and that not too many lives are effected, yet it is another of those transformational features that, temporarily at least, has an effect on the landscape.

It should be noted that there are two kinds of flooding. The first and possibly the easiest to predict is in areas that regularly flood such as estuaries and water meadows. Flooding tends to occur in the winter months. By way of contrast, flooding can also occur quite unpredictably as a result of a relatively short but very violent thunderstorm. With the drainage systems unable to cope, large and destructive volumes of water cascade downstream, often causing quite serious damage. This can occur at any time of the year.

Figure 16 **Flooded field 2**. Taken just 24 hours after Figure 15, the water had already started to drain away. In common with so many weather conditions, the effects of flooding are notoriously short-lived so take your opportunities while you can.

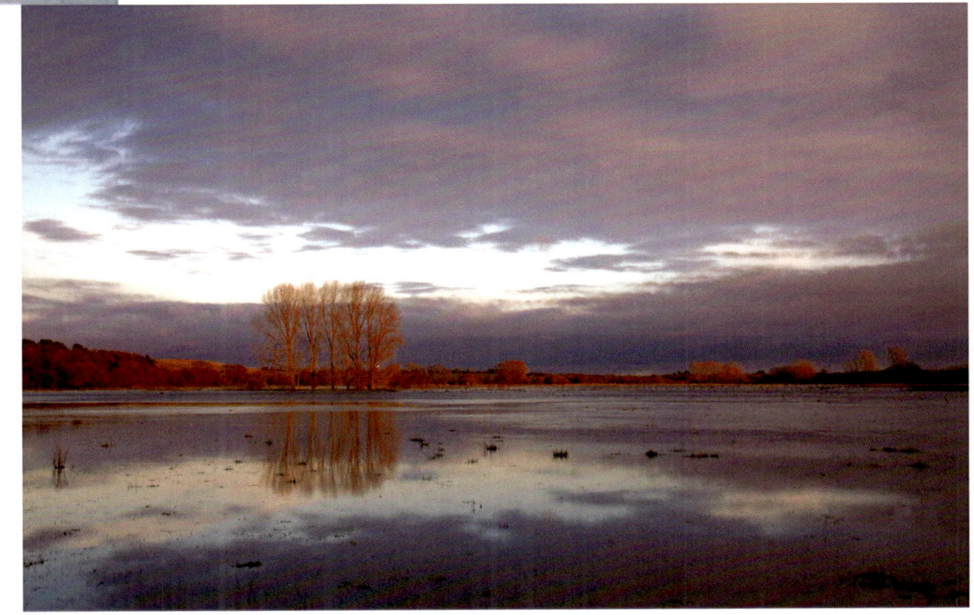

Photographing areas of managed flooding

Certain areas are more prone to flooding than others. Land near an estuary is likely to be flooded almost on an annual basis and so, of course, are water meadows. Just occasionally, land adjacent to a river or stream can be flooded but, thankfully, that is a little less common. The vegetation in areas that regularly flood is well suited to the conditions, comprising largely of reeds and tall grasses. While dowdy for much of the year, water meadows can appear spectacularly beautiful in late spring and early summer, often carpeted in flowers, because the soil is both fertile and damp.

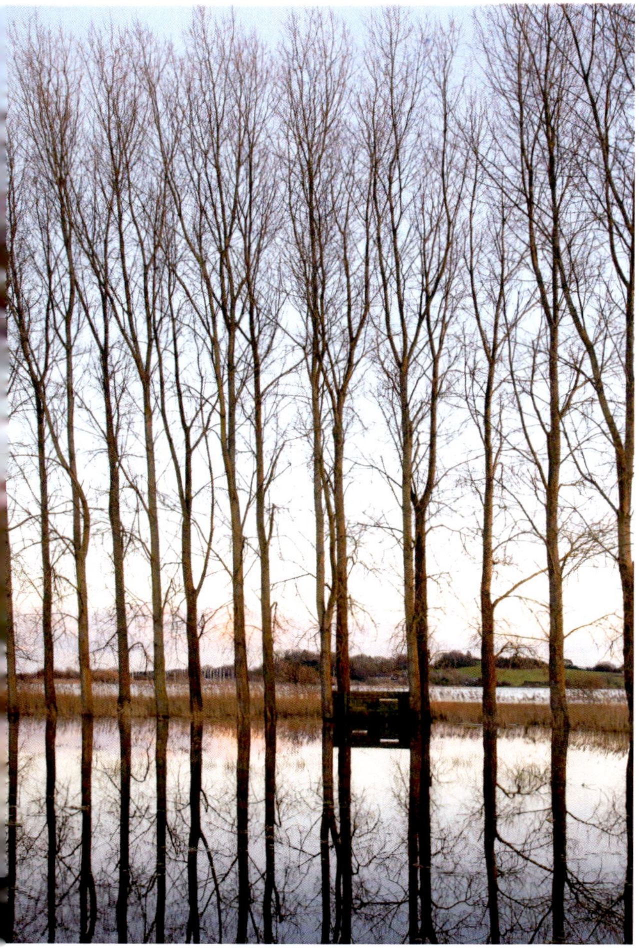

Figure 17 Line of trees. This is a common sight during the winter months. With the increase of rainfall rivers, particularly near estuaries, will burst their banks. If you are able to photograph these scenes on a calm and windless day it is possible to capture interesting mirrored effects. The calmness of this scene is enhanced by the gentle evening light.

Areas that flood rarely remain under water for long, so you need to take your chances while you can. The best time to take your shots is early in the morning or during the evening as the sun is setting. If you are able to find a location that faces either the rising or setting sun, you should be able to capture some spectacular reflections. It also helps if there is little or no wind; even a slight breeze can create ripples that diminish the clarity of the reflection.

Points to consider:

1. As the best time to photograph flooded locations is at dawn or dusk, as this is the time of day the sky will appear at its most dramatic, the strength of the lighting will be considerably reduced so use a tripod. If that is not possible, then you will need to increase your ISO rating.
2. When photographing estuaries or water meadows, the ground is likely to be extremely boggy, so wear Wellington boots. Moreover, it is not an environment that makes it easy to change lenses (it is not as if you can place your camera bag on the ground), so decide to work with one lens and stick with it.
3. From a compositional standpoint, flooding has the capacity to simplify the landscape, which of course can add interest. Features such as trees and posts are left marooned in the water and make obvious focal points. As the water is unlikely to be deep, it remains relatively still, resulting in dramatically mirrored images.

4. While there is a temptation to venture into a flooded area, don't overlook the opportunity to use a long lens. Using such lenses not only offers some measure of convenience but also allows you to photograph relatively distant objects.

5. Water meadows and flooded estuaries are a magnet for water fowl or migrating birds, which of course opens up additional photographic opportunities. Whether you capture them flying in formation or swimming on the surface of the water, interesting shots can be had.

6. This is another occasion when using a polarising filter might help. A polarising filter not only increases colour saturation, but it is also useful for cutting out unwanted reflections, particularly in the flooded areas of the landscape.

7. On a similar tack, don't overlook the advantages of using graduated filters, particularly if you want to include sky in your photograph. The exposure difference between the sky and the foreground can typically be as much as three stops so using a 0.9 soft graduated filter is one way of overcoming this.

8. If you are able to capture the detail of the sky perfectly reflected in the still water, don't worry about the rule of thirds and instead place the horizon in the middle of the composition. In this way you are making a clear statement about the relationship between the still water and the sky.

Damaging floods

As these tend to be unpredictable, they are rarely photographed unless you are unfortunate enough to be in its path. If you have witnessed such events, you will be aware that fast-flowing water can carry away anything including fallen trees and even stranded cars, so if you are taking photographs it is as well to stay clear of the water. If you are able to find a safe vantage point then clearly there will be interesting photographic opportunities.

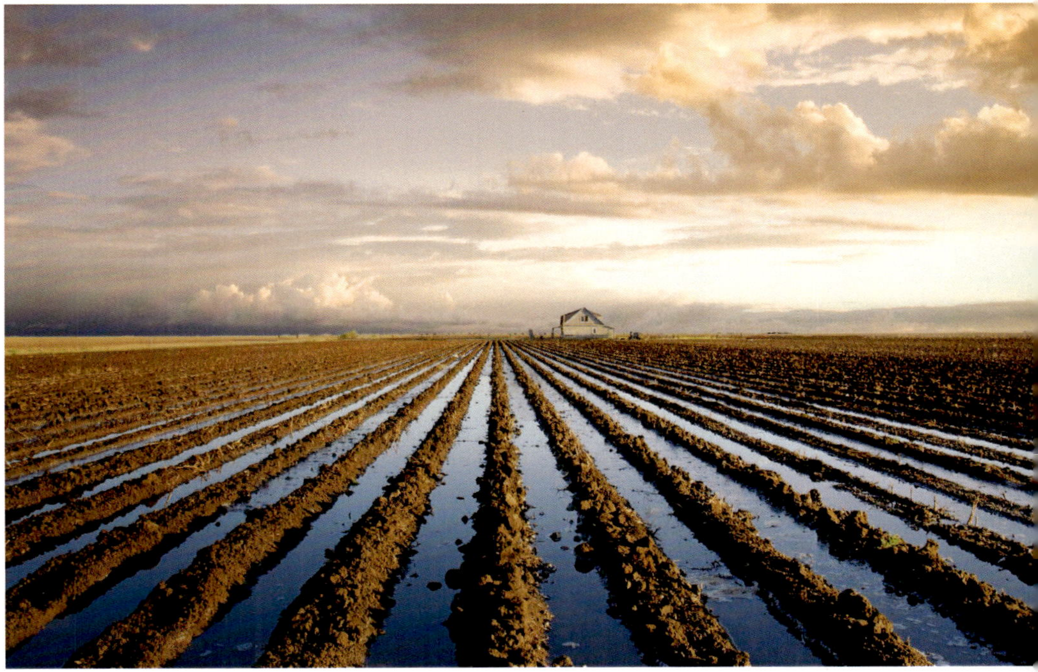

Figure 18 **Saturated field, Texas**. After the deluge had passed these furrows were left totally saturated although, with the emerging warm sunshine, the water quickly evaporated. It nevertheless offered an interesting photographic opportunity.

AFTER RAIN

I remember a prominent photographer I greatly admire being asked 'when is the best time to take a landscape photograph?' and his reply was 'immediately after rain'. Before rain the sky is murky and nebulous but, once the rainstorm has passed, we enter period of unparalleled clarity. Whether you are lucky enough to witness a rainbow or not, that period immediately after a rainstorm is truly magical. Rain appears to enhance the colours creating a truly vibrant landscape. As the sun emerges you will encounter stunning photographic opportunities from the moment you step outside.

Figure 19 **Roadside after a storm**. Moments such as this are extremely ephemeral so, when you do see an opportunity, you need to react quickly. Under normal circumstances I may well have driven past this location, but seeing it in this theatrical light convinced me that even the most unpromising locations will have their 'golden moment'.

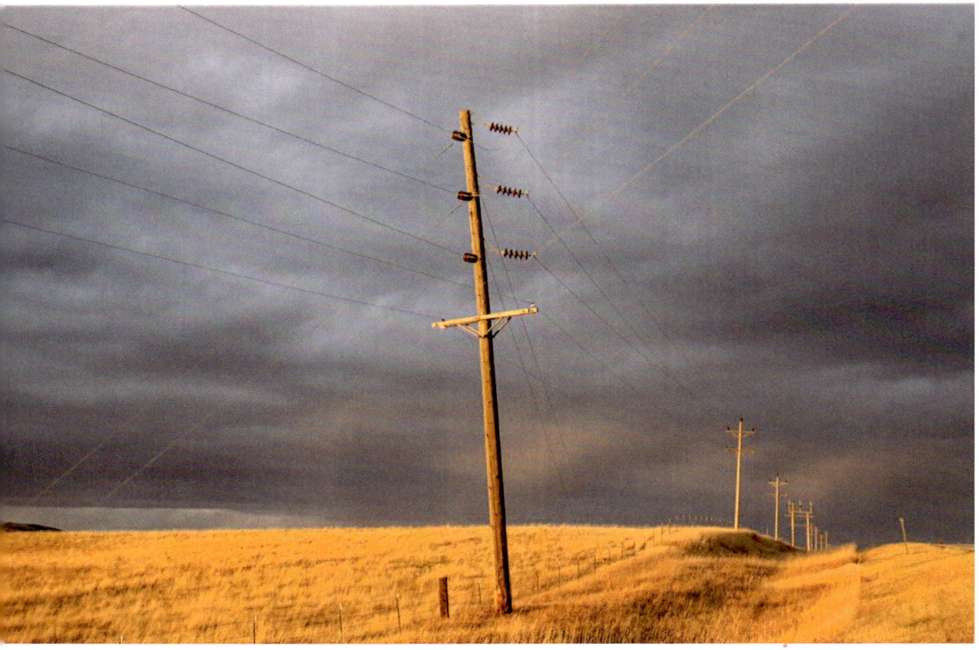

Opportunities you may wish to consider

1. The theatrical blast of light

The moment a rainstorm passes the sky will start to clear from the direction the storm has come from. The relative lighting between the area still under the storm and the area bathed in sunlight is quite extreme, offering a moment of sheer magic. The contrast between the warmth of the sunlight and the dour storm clouds lasts for just a brief period but it is one of those special photographic moments and, with just a bit of practice, it is something we can all anticipate. Occasionally, the exposure difference between the dramatically illuminated landscape and the sky is so great that it goes beyond the latitude of the sensor, resulting in either an underexposed sky or an overexposed foreground. In such circumstances, you may be required to wait until the sky lightens marginally or, alternatively, use a graduated filter.

2. Dramatic cloud formation

The cloud formations one often sees immediately after rain are so dramatic that they can provide images in their own right. Just point your camera up into the sky and don't worry about including a foreground. Typically we see towering cumulonimbus clouds that can appear especially appealing if taken in early morning or late afternoon light, as the warming colours of the sun are much more apparent.

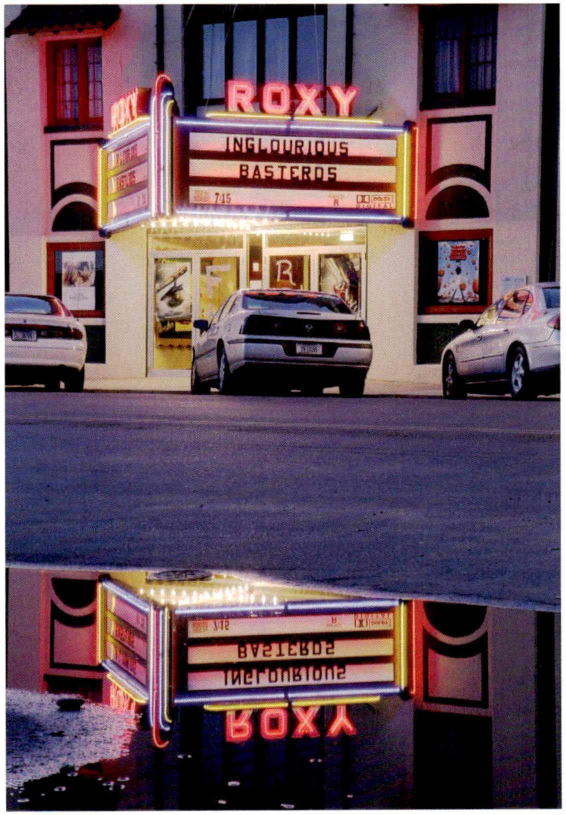

Figure 20 **Roxy**. One of the great features of a passing storm are the puddles it leaves in its wake. Whether in a landscape or an urban environment, great opportunities for photography abound. In this example the water was completely still, but interesting shots can be taken even if the water is moving.

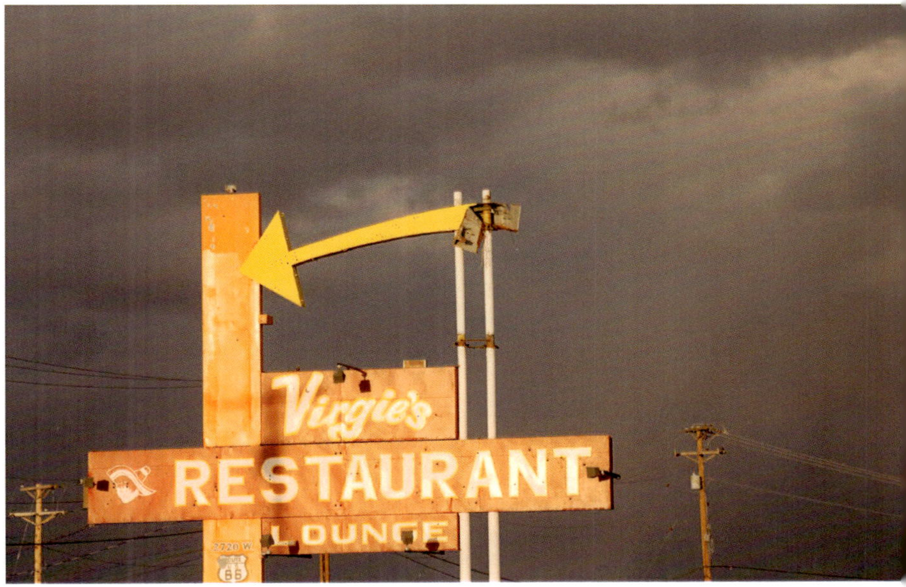

Figure 21 **Vergies Restaurant**. The light immediately after rain can appear particularly dramatic. As the storm passes the sky begins to clear, allowing the sunlight to illuminate parts of the landscape. The contrast between the areas bathed in sunlight and dark clouds offer one of those truly special magical moments.

3. Enjoy the mix of rich clouds and blue sky

Shortly after the storm has passed small areas of blue sky emerge that beautifully compliment the broken cloud. Still illuminated by the warm rays of the sun, one often sees clouds tinged with orange and this is especially evident early in the morning or late in the afternoon. As orange and blue are complimentary colours it can be a particularly attractive colour combination. It is often argued that dramatic skies best define a landscape and it rarely gets much better than this.

4. Photographing puddles

The rain has passed and the theatrical lighting often associated with the end of a shower has also subsided, so now what do we photograph? Whether you are in an urban location or in the country you will see plenty of puddles immediately after rain and the opportunity for great landscape photos abound. As they are so common they are often overlooked as possible photographic subjects, which is a shame. Often the air is quite still after a period of rain so the puddles create wonderful natural mirrors. Get down as low as you can, circling the puddle in order to find the best angle. Don't assume that the viewpoint you see as you approach it is necessarily the best. Even the smallest and most insignificant puddle can be made to look dramatic if you are prepared to get up close. Photographing puddles can be done in a variety of ways.

A common approach is to accord equal value to the reflection with the sky. If you want to ensure that both the puddle and the distant landscape are sharp then you will need to use a small aperture – close it down to f16 or f22. This might be the perfect opportunity to pull out your wide-angle lens. There is, of course, no need to include the sky at all and to allow the puddle to completely fill the frame. The image you capture will appear upside down but, of course, it can be inverted at the presentation stage. Landscapes captured in puddles can appear especially enigmatic, particularly if you do decide to invert the image. While many photographers prefer to photograph puddles when the water is still, interesting abstract or 'impressionistic' effects can be captured when there is a breeze. Finally, while the water in puddles can be inches deep, even wet surfaces such as tarmac, concrete or marble can make excellent reflective surfaces that you may wish to explore.

Figure 22 **Derelict service station**. It had rained overnight but by the time I awoke it had passed, although the rain had left some very tempting puddles in its wake. By placing the horizon approximately in the middle I was able to balance the reflection with its source. Even the most mundane location can appear interesting when photographed in this way.

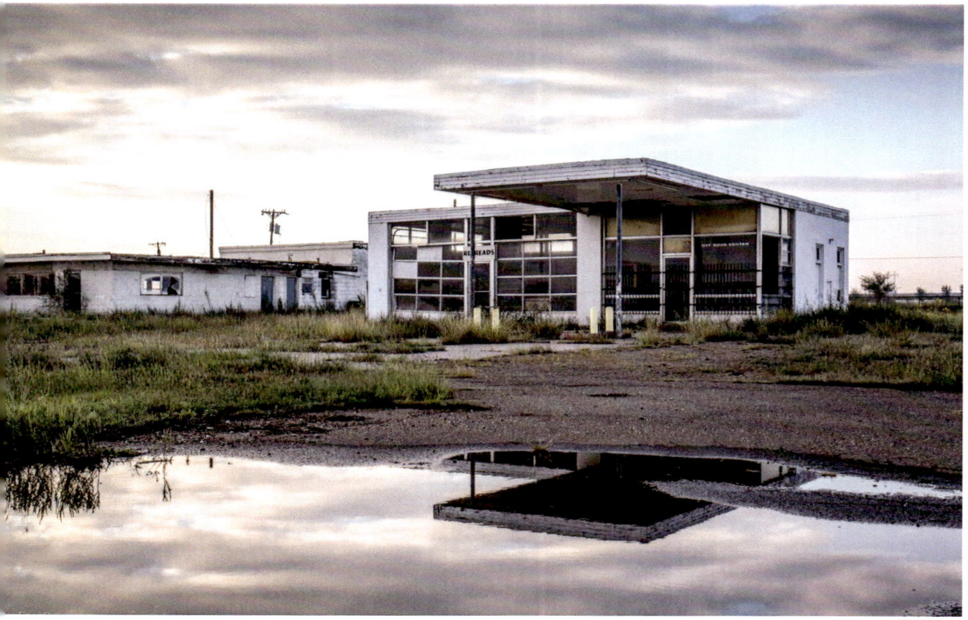

Figure 23 **Distant grain silos and evening sky**. The interlude after rain is usually followed by a period of unparalleled clarity, with the increasingly thinning clouds gently dispersed across a blue sky.

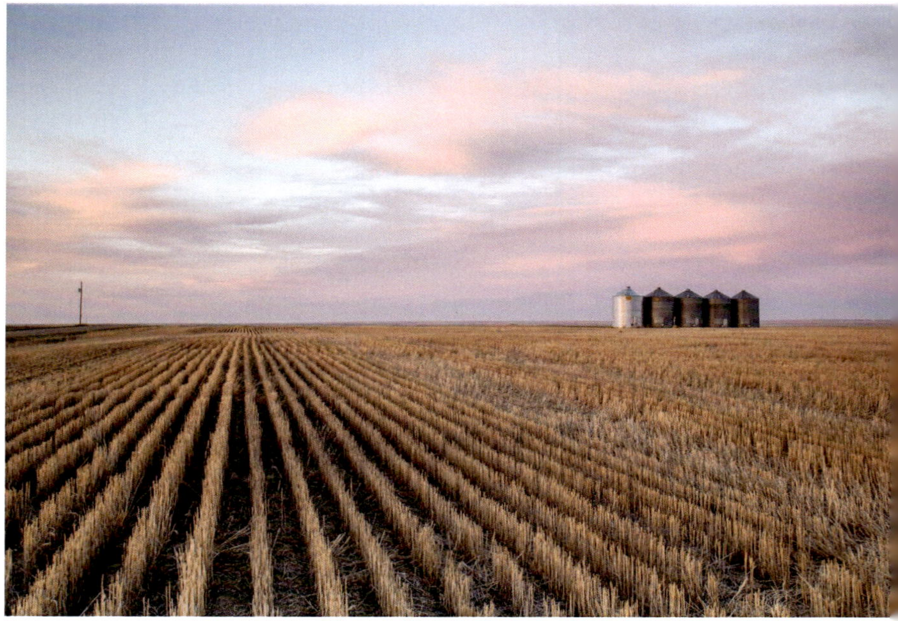

Figure 24 **Puddle and distant lighthouse**. Rather uncharacteristically a wind continued to blow after this rainstorm, ruining any possibility of a stunning reflection but, nevertheless, the puddle created a much-needed highlight in the otherwise very dark foreground.

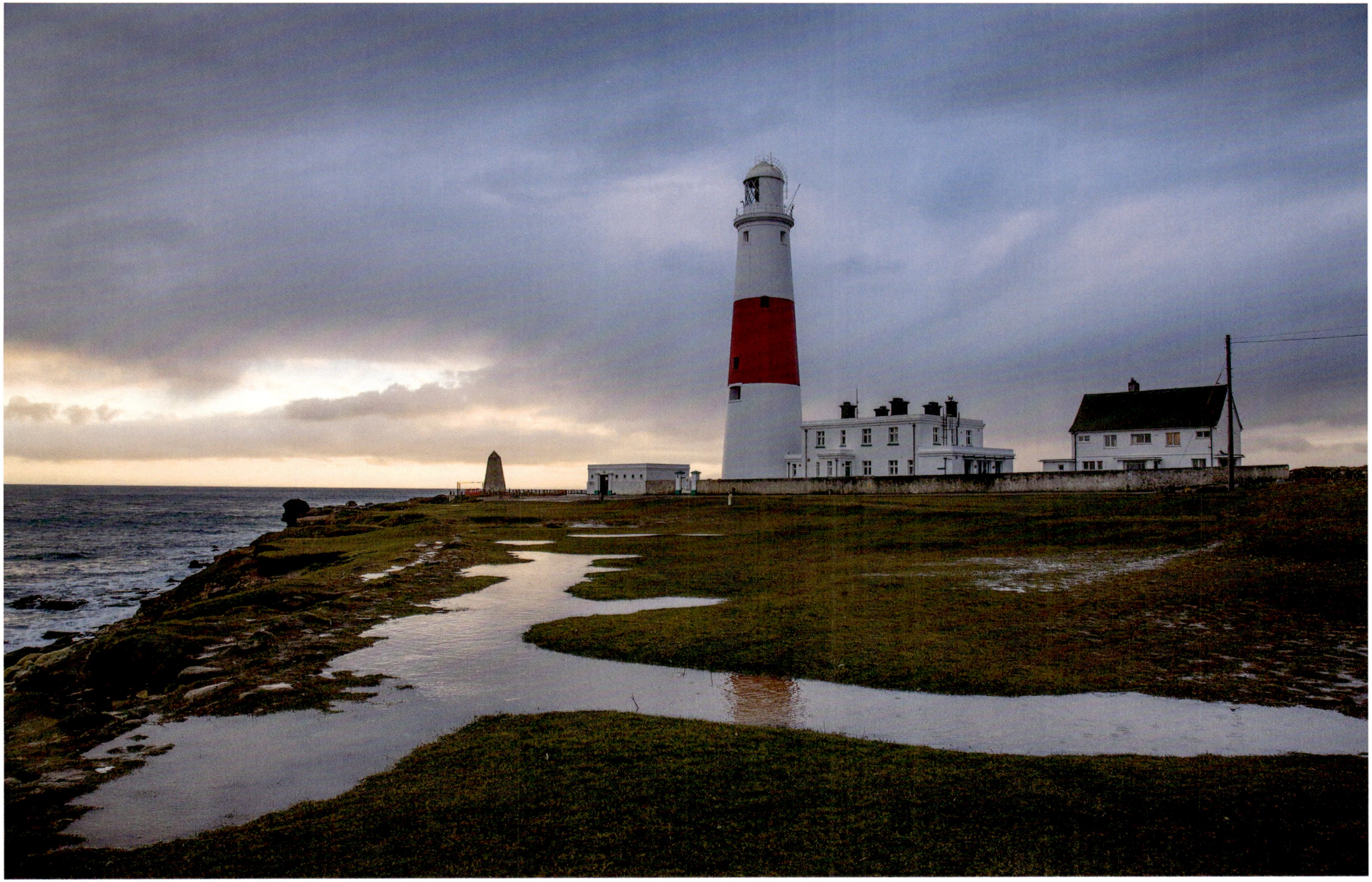

4 In Fair Weather or in Foul

Photographing in strong winds certainly has its drawbacks. For example, if you are using a tripod, a sudden gust of wind can ruin a good shot. If you are outside in cold weather the added discomfort of wind chill can persuade many to give the opportunity a miss. If you are working in a dusty location or perhaps on a beach you risk particles getting into your camera. With such drawbacks one wonders why anyone would want to photograph in strong winds but, if this publication seeks to achieve anything, it is to encourage you to continue taking photographs irrespective of the weather conditions. It is simply a matter of turning a negative situation into a positive opportunity.

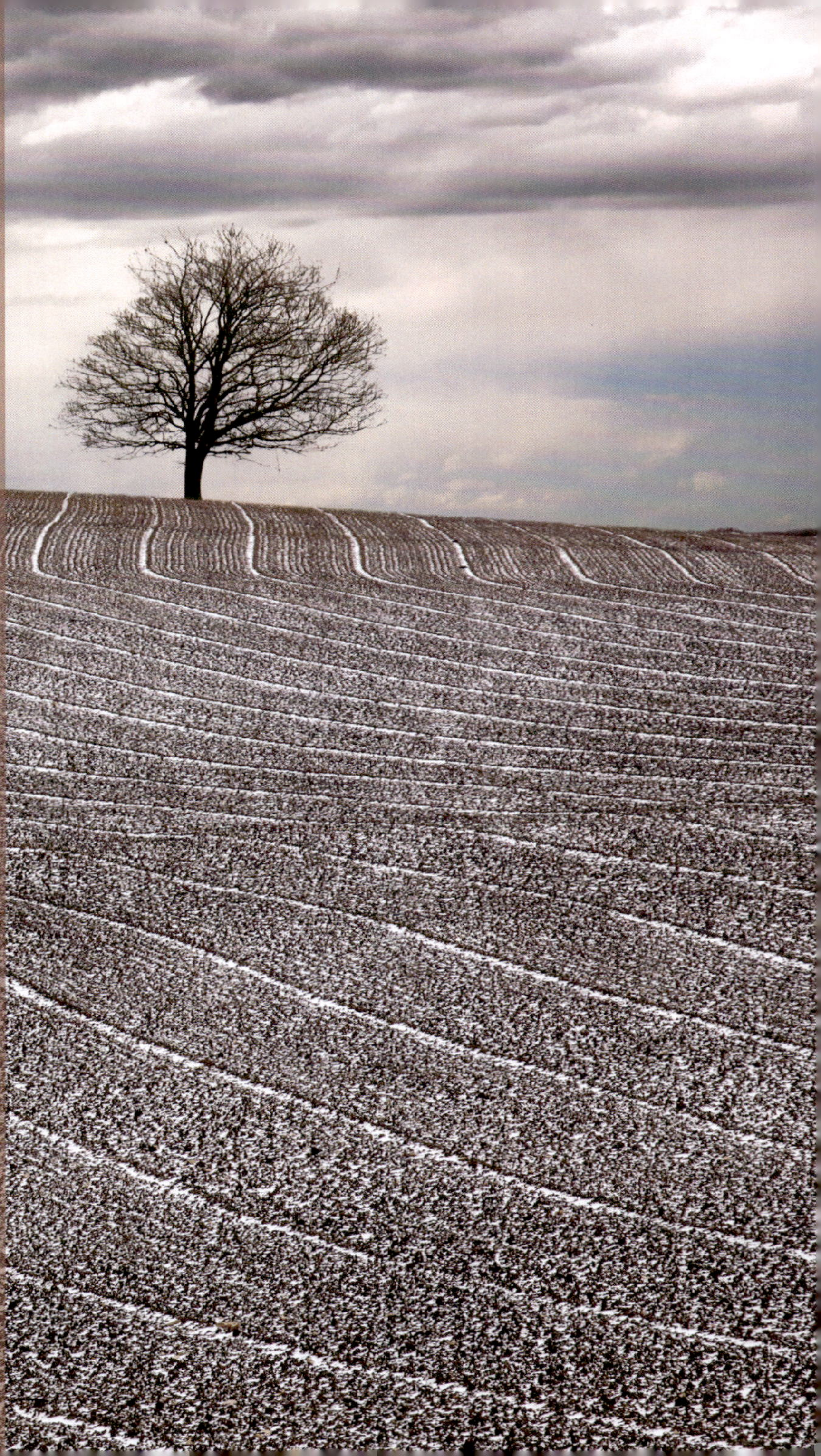

Like rain, winds will, of course, vary in intensity; whether you are experiencing a gentle breeze or a full-blown hurricane, each reveal unique characteristics. As photographers we are capturing a brief moment in time and it is a matter of how we use that instant to capture the wind.

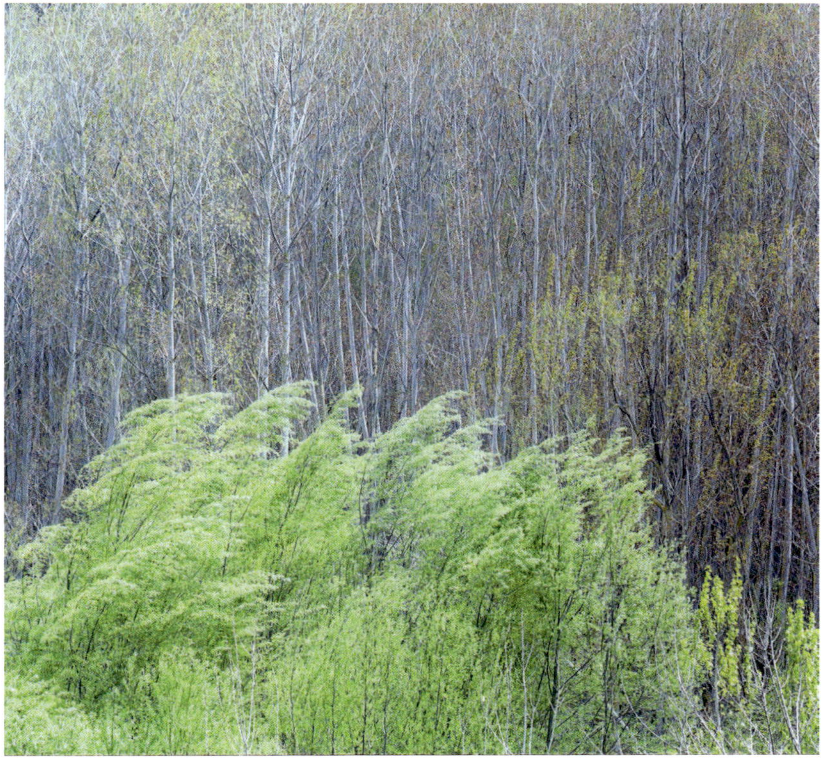

Figure 1 **Wind passing through the trees**. The task when photographing wind is to capture something that is moving within a single static frame. By watching how these green saplings in the foreground are bent by the wind, the sense of its power is graphically conveyed.

Technical issues

First, remember that you do have a variety of shutter speeds to play with. As wind is moving your choice of shutter speed is very important. Landscape workers often decide to use the AV rather than the TV option as they consider controlling the depth of field to be more important. While, in many situations, that is the right thing to do, when photographing in wind it often proves more useful to consider the shutter speed as your first priority. It could be that you want to photograph some object being blown in the wind, which requires a fast shutter speed. Alternatively, capturing the moving clouds might be another way of illustrating winds, which requires using a long shutter speed.

Sudden gusts of wind can pose a problem, particularly if you are using a tripod, so find a natural barrier. If that proves impossible then use your body as a shield by standing between the tripod and the prevailing wind. The weight of your tripod will have a bearing on its capacity to withstand wind (the heavier it is the better) but it should also be possible to anchor the tripod down by using your camera bag. Many tripods have a specially adapted hooks for this.

Don’t overlook image stabilisation. Whether it is part of the lens or integrated into the body of the camera, make sure your image stabilisation is switched on as it can go a long way to countering the problem of a sudden gust of wind.

If you are hand-holding your camera be prepared to increase the ISO rating to overcome any camera shake caused by strong wind. You are particularly vulnerable when using a long lens. The general rule of thumb is to set the shutter speed no lower than the focal length of the lens so, if you are using a 100mm lens, set the shutter speed no less than 1/100th second. If, however, you are shooting in very gusty winds, be prepared to double that. This should significantly reduce unintentional camera shake.

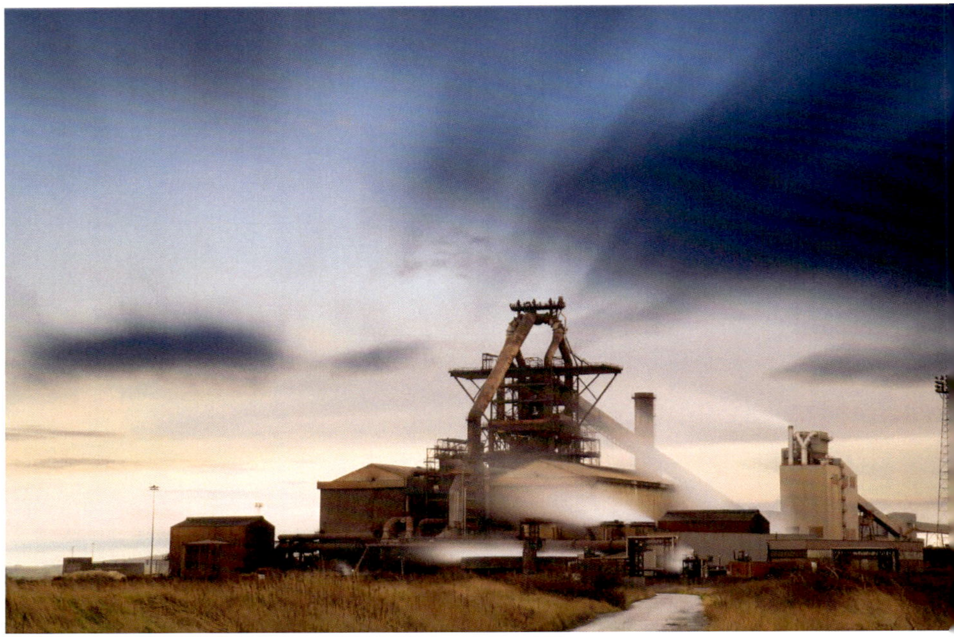

Figure 2 (Below) **Power station**. I'm sure many of you have been fascinated by the billowing steam emanating from a line of cooling towers being blown in the wind. The drama of the scene is enhanced by photographing it in low light, allowing the steam and wind to fuse together. This image required a 74 second exposure.

Figure 3 (Right) **Industrial landscape**. Something similar to Figure 2 has been achieved with this image, except that it was taken in the middle of the day. By using a strong neutral density filter I was able to extend the exposure to 138 seconds. This has not just helped to illustrate the movement of the vapours but also the clouds in the sky.

Figure 4 **Wind turbines**. If I had chosen a fast shutter speed the turbine blades would have appeared static so, by opting for a much slower one (in this case 1/5th second), a positive sense of movement has been conveyed.

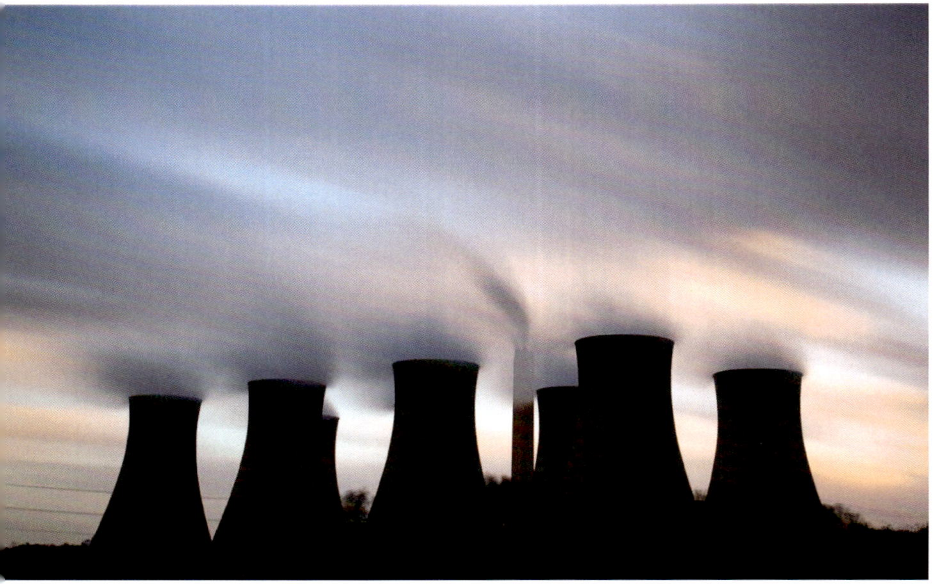

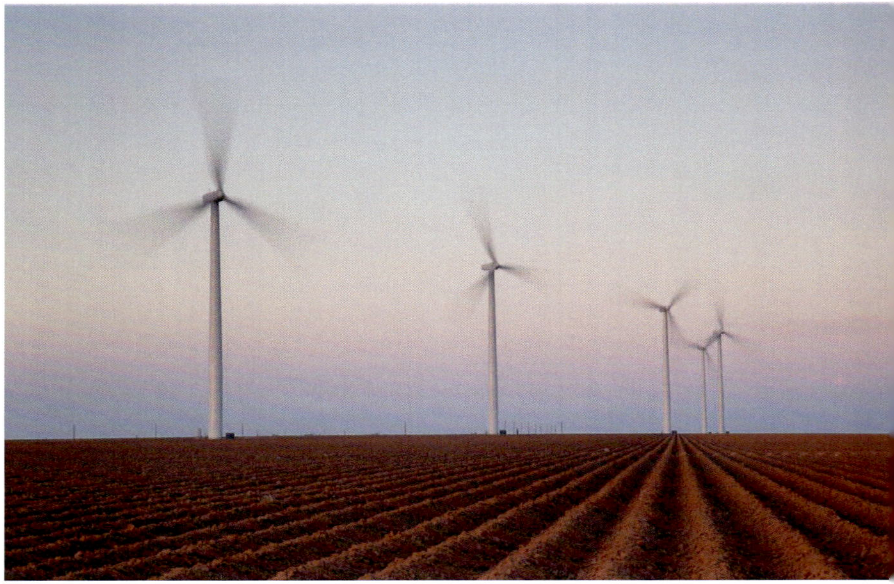

Just occasionally a bit of deliberate 'camera shake' can enhance the image. By deciding to use a lower shutter speed and moving the camera during the exposure quite interesting effects can be achieved. If you decide on this option don't be half-hearted or it could look like a mistake.

Consider the following possible locations

Bushes and trees

When we are driving we quickly become aware of the strength of the wind merely by seeing the trees and bushes yielding to its power. When photographing foliage you could, of course, opt to use a standard shutter speed of 1/60th second or more, although an interesting alternative is to use a much slower shutter speed (1 second or less) and capture the blurred movement instead. The visual impact can often prove far more revealing. Of course you will need to use a tripod.

Autumnal leaves

Few scenes convey the power of wind more effectively than leaves being blown, so this is another approach you may wish to pursue. The choice of shutter is important; you may decide to use a fast one in order to freeze the movement of the scattering leaves or, alternatively, select a slower shutter speed in order to capture a blur of movement. However, you cannot afford to use a shutter speed much less than 1/8th second as the blur will appear over-exaggerated.

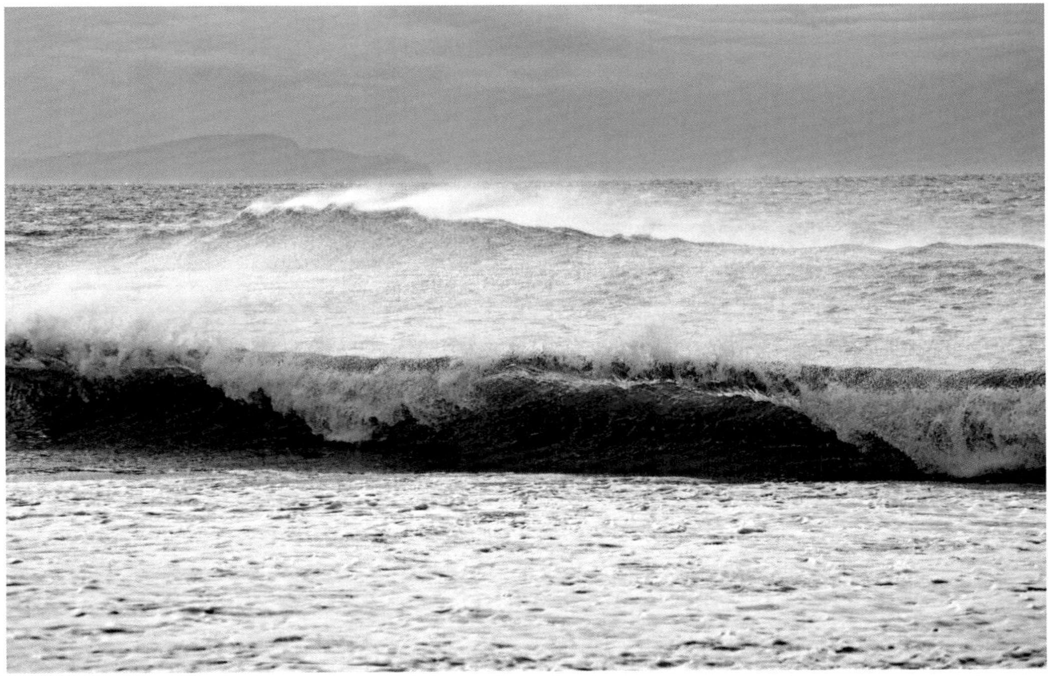

Figure 5 **Waves**. The power of the wind can be explored by photographing a tumultuous sea. Not only do the size of the waves increase when it is windy, but a rather telling spray appears, highlighting the wind's direction.

Grasses and cereal crops

On a similar tack, the motion of the wind can be graphically captured by photographing it blowing through a field of cereal crops. By doing this one comes to appreciate that the motion of the wind is not constant but irregular. For a brief moment, while parts of the field will be effected, others will remain static. This is another situation where experimenting with shutter speeds helps. Particularly interesting results can be achieved using a shutter speed of 1/8th second.

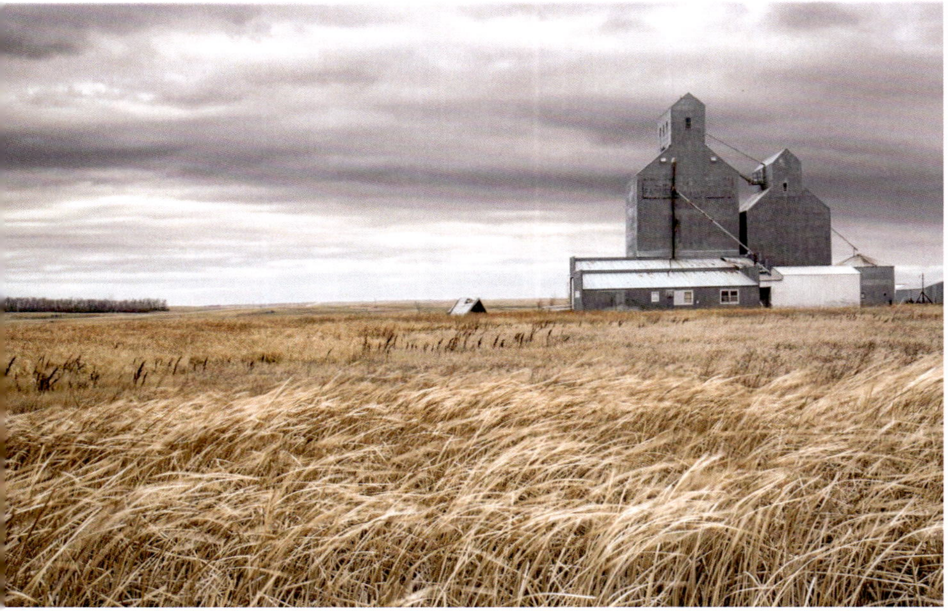

Figure 6 (Above) **Blowing grasses**. Wind is invisible and yet, from a visual standpoint, its evidence is so apparent. In this example, while the silo in the distance remains static, the grasses in the foreground are being whipped by the wind.

Figure 7 (Right) **Lone tree and sky**. By using a long exposure the movement of the clouds can be dramatically illuminated. In this example an exposure of over two minutes was required. Your choice of shutter speed is an important consideration when photographing wind.

The beach

Sand is particularly prone to wind and wonderful pattern pictures can be captured even in a light breeze. Generally the moving sand tends to remain quite low. However, never underestimate the damage sand can do to your camera. The general rule in this situation is to photograph the beach with your back to the wind and, more importantly, resist the temptation to change lenses.

The sea and waves

If you own a long lens it will be particularly useful when photographing the sea from a distance. In strong winds it is not uncommon to see breath-taking examples of breaking waves battered by the prevailing wind. Few sights exemplify the effects of weather more graphically. Once again, it is important that you exercise caution. Find a location that shelters you from the potentially damaging sea spray. There are few things more damaging to your camera than salt water.

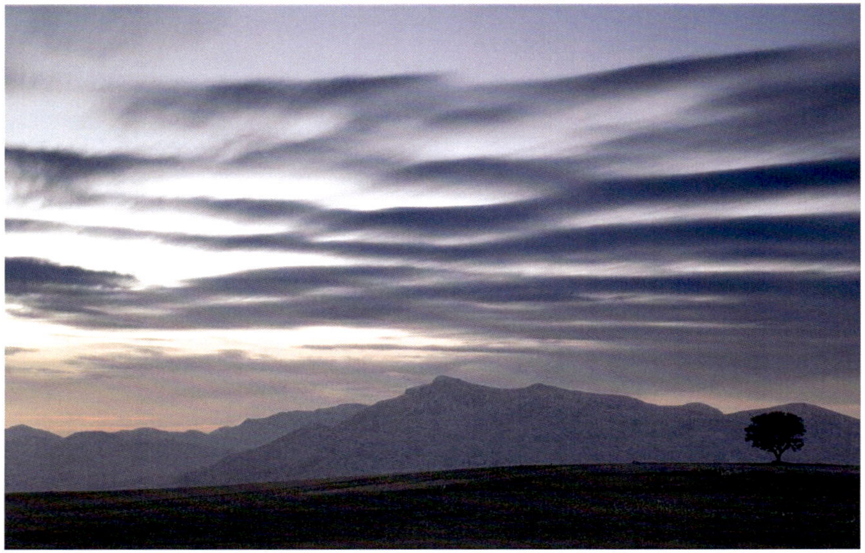

Powdery snow

Winter offers us many opportunities, particularly when there is snow on the ground. Strong winds have the capacity to sculpt awesome shapes on the sides of roads and fields. With careful selection, one is able to capture a physical incarnation of the movement of the wind. If the snow is particularly powdery even the lightest breeze will create patterns that graphically reflect the movement of the wind.

The urban environment

Even in the streets of our towns and cities there are excellent opportunities for capturing wind. Watch how figures bend into the wind, struggling to prevent their umbrellas from being blown inside out. Even without figures, litter is sent spewing out of bins and skips – certainly not beautiful but potentially very 'atmospheric'.

Industry and billowing smoke

Not all of us have access to areas of heavy industry but, if you do, you should be able to capture some stunning images, particularly in strong winds. The best time to photograph industry is in low light, late in the evening or pre-dawn. With your camera attached to a tripod, you are able to capture the billowing smoke and vapours, particularly if you are prepared to use a long exposure. If you want to capture something to rival Dante's Inferno, this is it. Don't overlook the opportunity to photograph industry in the middle of the day; in order to capture the movement of the fumes, attach a neutral density filter to the lens. This has the effect of greatly reducing the amount of light getting to the sensor, thus allowing you to use an exposure of many seconds.

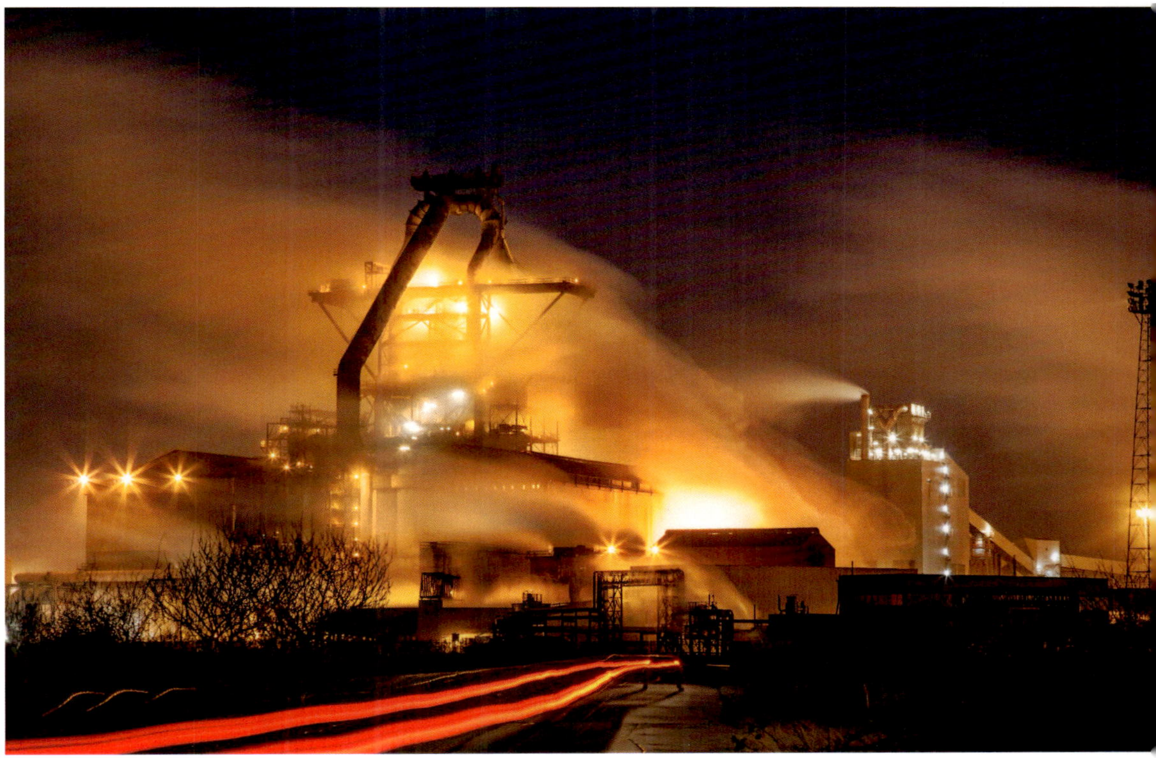

Figure 8 **Blast furnace at night**. Not all of us have access to areas of heavy industry but, if you do, you should be able to capture some stunning images, particularly in strong winds. The best time to photograph industry is in low light, late in the evening or pre-dawn.

BECALMED

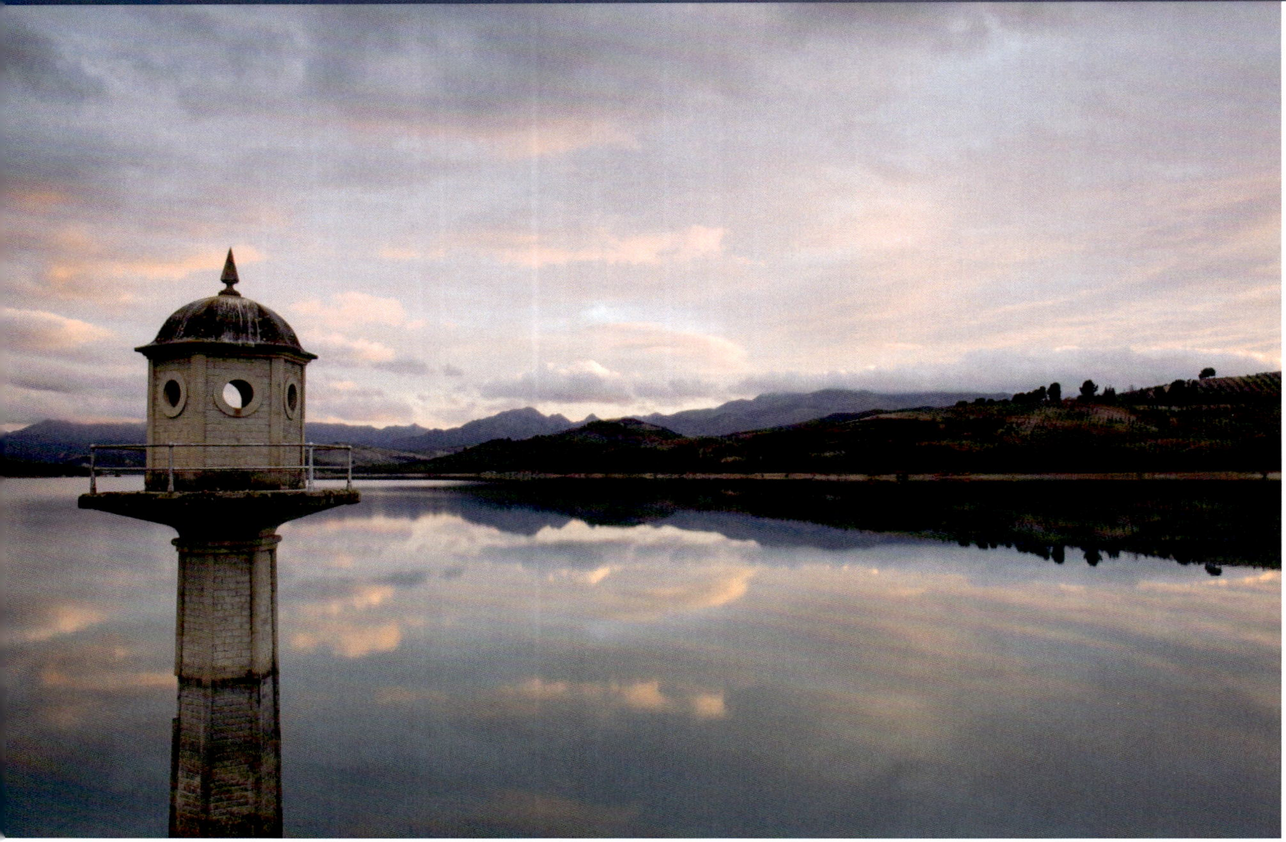

Figure 9 Reservoir, Andalusia. I had passed by this location on many occasions unaware that it might offer interesting photographic potential. As it is a large stretch of water there was always too much movement to make it interesting. It was only when I passed by just before dusk that I could see it was gradually becalming. Within just 30 minutes it calmed to an almost mirror-like surface.

Once the wind has dropped we enter a period of calm, but to capture this photographically is quite a challenge. How do you capture 'calm' in a still photograph? Taking a scenic shot of a building isn't going to work nor, indeed, is a shot of trees. Just because they appear static in the photograph doesn't mean there isn't some movement in the air. In order to capture absolute stillness we need to include elements one would normally expect to move, even in the slightest breeze. The two most obvious elements are vapours and water. Smoke rises vertically when there is no wind present. On a similar tack, it is only when the air is completely still that you are able to photograph water free of ripples.

Photographing water

It is often assumed that truly becalmed conditions are relatively rare, but it is surprising just how common they are. Wind is created by varying pressures -that is to say, air moves from an area of high pressure to an area of low pressure. When there is a measure of equilibrium between two masses of air then the winds drop. Normally we experience our strongest winds when we have low pressure, as the air from the high pressure areas flows into the low. For similar reasons winds tend to lessen in areas of high pressure. It can, however, be far more localised than that. Even when the wind is quite noticeable in the daytime, it can often calm down about 40 minutes after sunset. Moreover, those of you who are used to walking pre-dawn will have noticed how much calmer it can be prior to sunrise. This is as a result of what is known as 'atmospheric decoupling'. What this means is that winds in the daytime are created by the relative temperatures of the surface of the land and the air above. In the evening, or pre-dawn, the temperature of the surface of the land decreases so, consequently, the relative temperature of land and air are much closer, resulting in less or no wind. As photographers, the benefit of this is that we are able to photograph becalmed water almost on a daily basis, except that we do need to operate at those inconvenient times pre-dawn or shortly after dusk. The rewards however make this worthwhile.

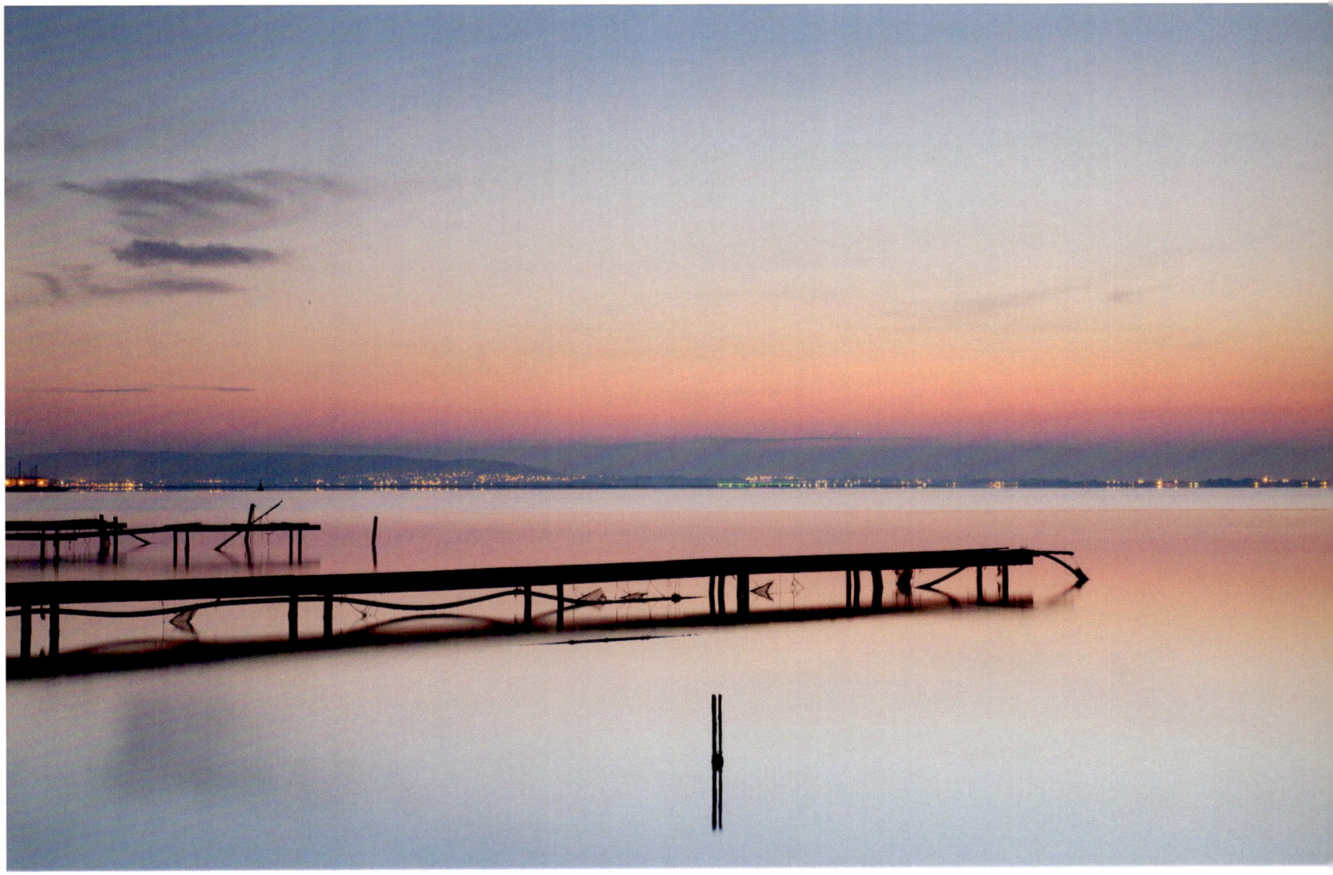

Figure 10 Pier near oyster beds, Southern France. While this was photographed in a sheltered lagoon, the water is still likely to ripple even in the slightest breeze. However, there are periods, often before dawn, when you are likely to encounter a complete calmness when everything appears still.

Figure 11 **Becalmed waters**. Even with a gentle lapping of the water a wonderful sense of calm dominants this image, helped in part by the highly restricted tonal range. The emphasis on high-key certainly contributes in this respect.

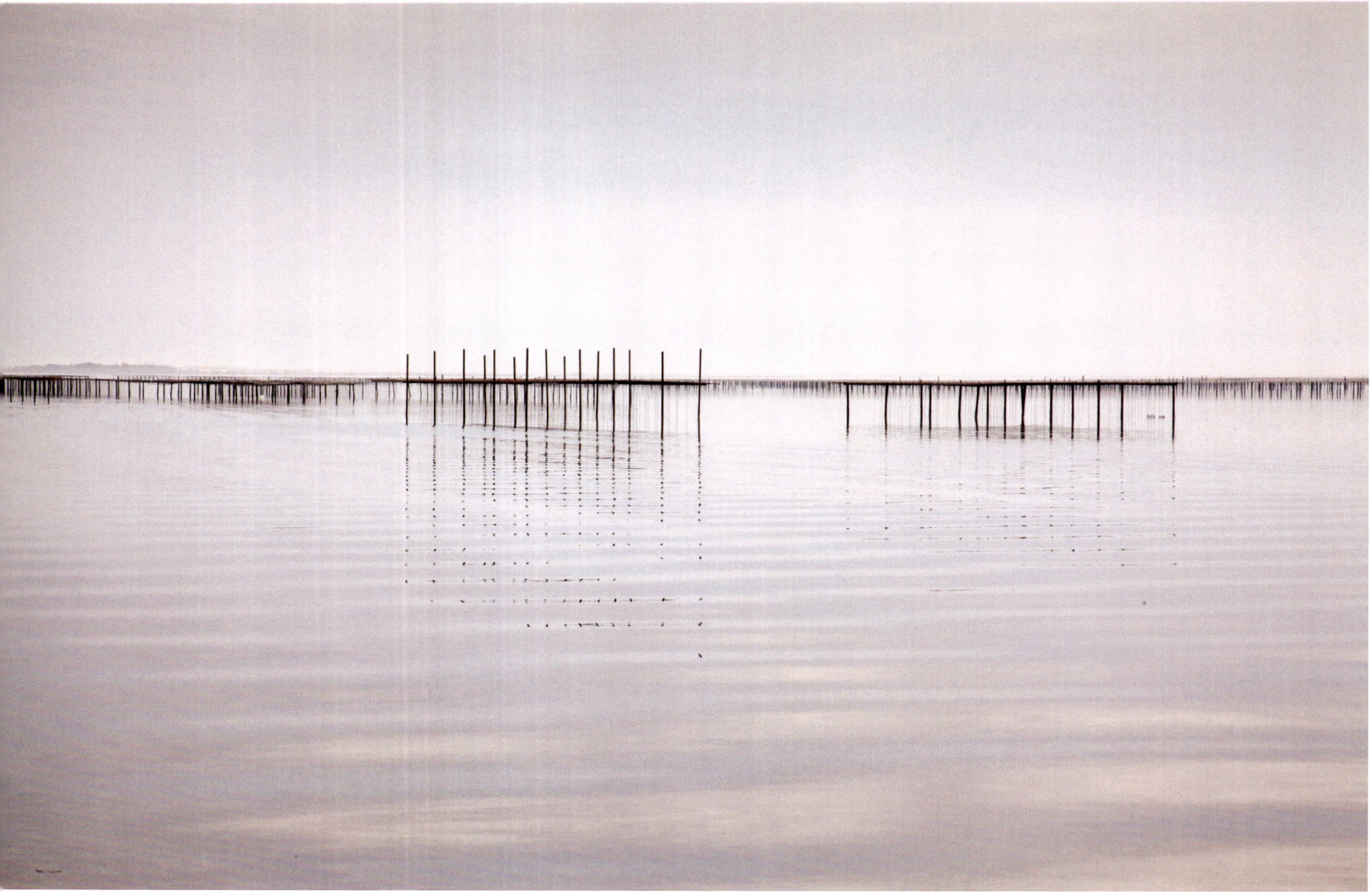

PHOTOGRAPHING IN MIST AND FOG

While the purpose of this publication is to highlight the opportunities for photographing landscape in bad weather, to describe fog or mist as such is just perverse. Even the most inexperienced landscape photographers rise to the challenge when experiencing a typical 'pea-souper'. Fog is caused by minute droplets of water in the atmosphere, although it can sometimes be confused with smog, which tends to occur only in heavily industrialised areas. Fog is defined as having a visibility of less than 1,000 metres but, for the purposes of photography, a reduced density of 100 or even 50 metres offers the most interesting opportunities. The incidence of fog occurs for a variety of reasons and being able to predict it certainly offers advantages.

Radiation fog

The most common type of fog is known as 'radiation fog' and this usually occurs during the winter and when the air is still. As the air cools overnight close to the surface it is less able to absorb moisture so, consequently, when you wake up in the morning you are greeted by a low-lying blanket of fog. It is important that you are able to anticipate its formation because it can evaporate quite quickly once the sun starts to rise.

Valley fog

The causes of 'valley fog' are not dissimilar to those of radiation fog. As its name would suggest it tends to occur in the bottom of valleys, particularly when there is a temperature inversion, i.e. the air at the bottom of the valley is colder than the air directly above. Such fogs can last for days.

Coastal fog or sea fret

The third likelihood of fog occurring is when warmer moist air passes over a very cold surface as, for example, when air off the sea passes over land covered by snow. Similarly, a coastal fog (or sea fret) occurs when warm moist air is blown over cooler water.

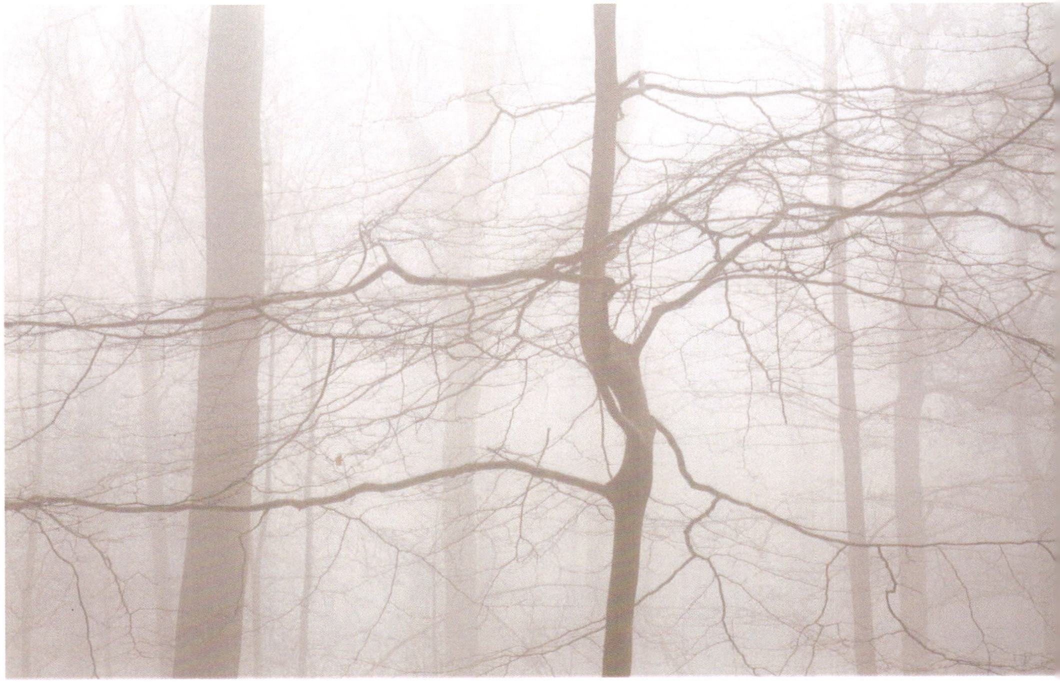

Figure 12 **Beech trees in mist**. By using a long lens I was able to greatly simplify the photograph, creating an almost graphic image. Because of the lack of colour this picture is almost 'monochromatic'.

The important point to remember is that, however the fog is formed, it offers amazing photographic opportunities.

The photographic opportunities offered by fog are considerable

1. As fog tends to considerably reduce colour saturation, a much stronger emphasis is placed on the tonal values. One often finds that images taken in fog can be very successfully converted to black and white. If you retain your photograph as a colour image, the hues will appear wonderfully subtle.
2. When photographing in fog you are able to explore a visual phenomenon known as 'tonal recession'. What this means is that distant objects appear considerably lighter than those nearer the camera; this is especially apparent when photographing a forest in mist. The tonal interplay between the trees in the distance and those nearer the camera can prove particularly evocative.
3. Because of the reduced visibility, the images captured tend to be much more simple and graphic in nature. Trees and wooded areas in general lend themselves particularly well to being photographed in fog.

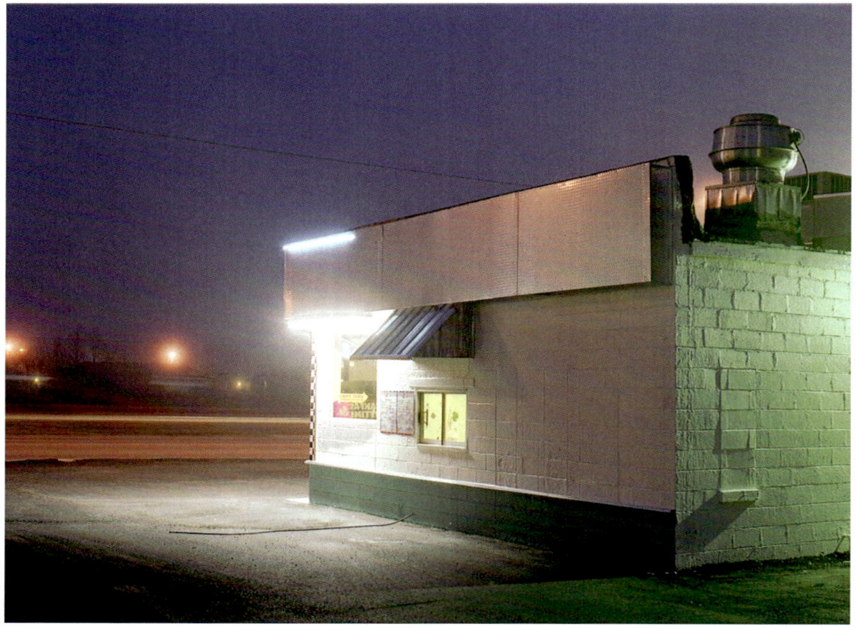

Figure 13 **Kiosk, photographed at night**. Mist and fog can prove particularly evocative when photographed at night, promoting an almost eerie atmosphere. It also has the advantage of subduing the harshness of artificial lighting, particularly within an urban environment.

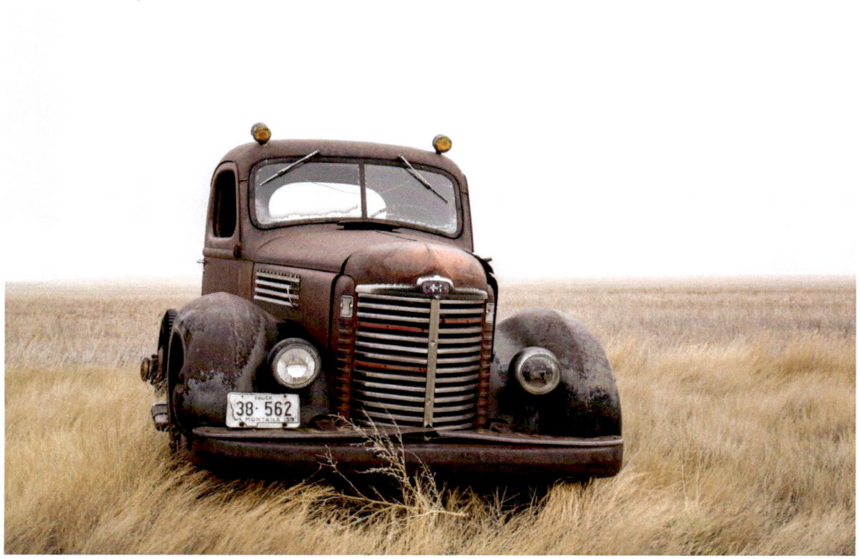

Figure 14 **Abandoned pickup, northern Montana**. Some might be concerned by the empty white sky, but this is one of the features when photographing in a heavy mist. There is something rather claustrophobic about working in these conditions as you cannot see much beyond your immediate environment.

4. This is often overlooked but, if you are able to photograph fog or mist at night, you should be able to capture images rich in atmosphere. Artificial lights that normally appear too bright are tempered by the mist or fog, creating quite ethereal effects. As the ground is likely to be wet, it is possible to capture beautifully subtle reflections. As the mist swirls around the sources of light the rays are subtly distorted, creating almost dream-like scenarios.

5. Photographed at night or in daylight, the urban landscape can appear especially interesting when photographed in mist. Traffic, only visible by dipped headlights, appears to amble through the silent, monochromatic streets offering strange and enigmatic photographic opportunities. Buildings receding into the distance can appear alarmingly unfamiliar. One has only to consider those highly evocative movies of the 1940s and 50s to appreciate the potential that this sort of lighting has to offer.

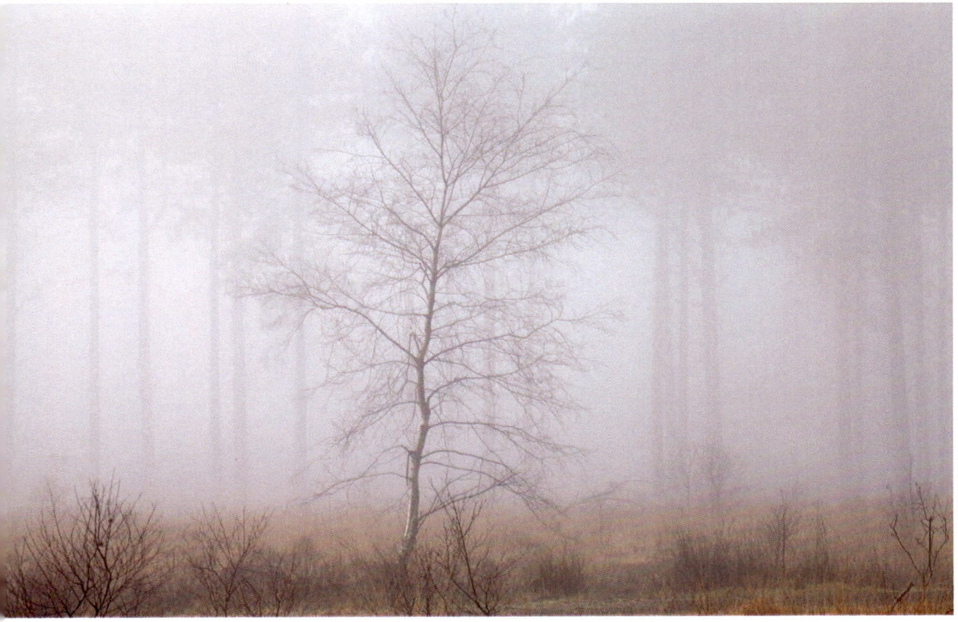

Figure 15 **Deciduous sapling in forest**. Detail that is often unobserved in normal light can become considerably more apparent when seen in fog. I often pass this spot but it wasn't until I experienced a thick fog that I truly appreciated the delicate beauty of this sapling.

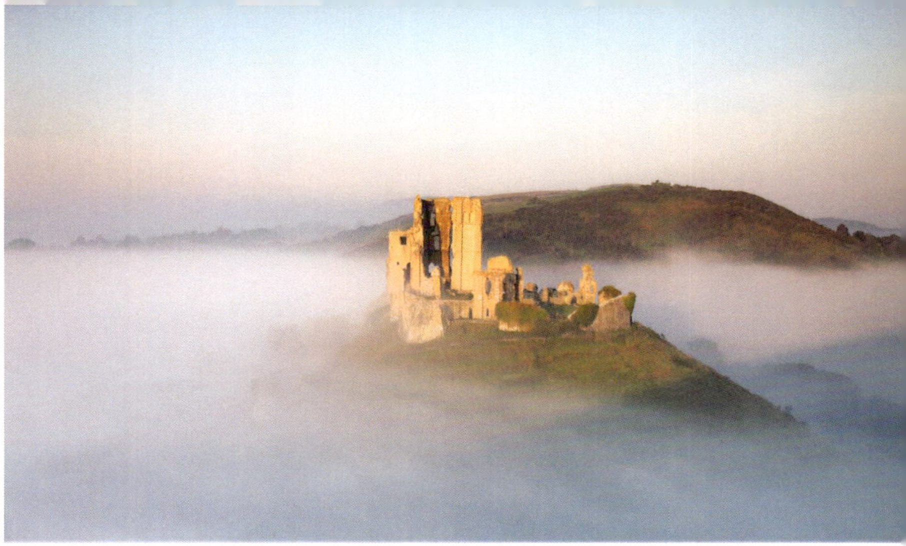

Figure 16 **Corfe Castle emerging from the fog**. Mist and fog tends to be low lying, therefore hills or tall structures can often appear above it. In this example I needed to find a high vantage point that got me above the mist in order to photograph this ruin.

6. Look for subtle silhouettes. Fog has the capacity to simplify forms and reduce texture. Consequently, objects, even those relatively close by, appear almost silhouetted. From a visual standpoint a scene blanketed in mist undergoes a process of simplification.

Technical considerations

It is of course a personal judgment but I suggest using a long lens in order to maximise the effect of tonal recession. It also draws the foreground and background closer together. The light in a thick fog can often be diminished so use a tripod, particularly if you do opt to use a long lens. But do not overlook the opportunities for taking great shots using a basic camera. Some photographers keep a cheap camera in the car permanently, just in case they encounter interesting weather conditions. Also, that which can be captured using a humble mobile phone can often prove quite illuminating. If you have good foreground interest then use it. This is where a standard or wide-angle lens becomes useful. The sky in mist often appears quite featureless, so it might serve you better to point your camera downward in order to minimise it.

Look for a sequence of regular objects that recede into the distance. A line of trees, buildings or telegraph poles assume a strange and unifying beauty when shot in mist. Using a telephoto lens will compress the effect, although equally interesting photographs can be had by using a wide-angle lens as well.

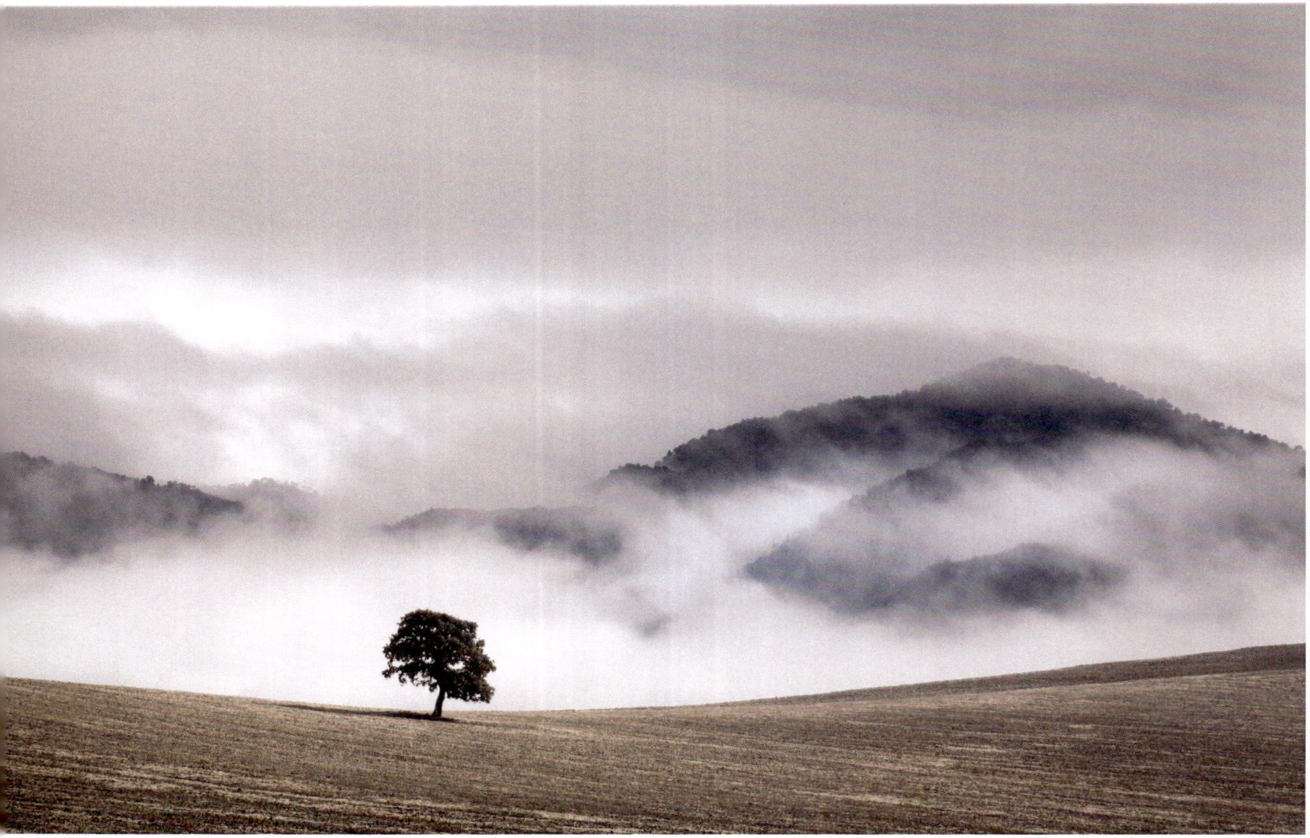

Figure 17 Rising mist and lone tree. Fog or mist can appear particularly interesting when photographed near hills or mountains. As they form on lower ground, the peaks often emerge out of the clouds offering images of great simplicity.

It is good practice to always attach a UV filter to your lens, but this will prove particularly beneficial when photographing in fog. Ideally, keep your lens cap on for as long as possible or moisture will build up on the filter, thus reducing the clarity of the final image. Carrying a microfibre cloth in your camera bag really is essential.

Mists and fog are notoriously ephemeral and can very easily disappear within an hour, particularly in the morning. There is often little point looking for photographic opportunities during a period of fog as it will probably have disappeared by the time you find a suitable landscape. It is far better to seek out possible locations prior to the anticipated fog, so that you can go there directly once one emerges.

Rising or descending mist

While we all want the fog or mist to last as long as possible, there are great photographic opportunities to be had either when the fog starts to rise (usually in the morning) or when it begins to descend (most likely in the early evening). Essentially, a fog or mist is just a very low stratus cloud so, if you are close to high ground, the visual effects can be spectacular. Mountains can be particularly prone to rising or falling mists.

The biggest problem you are likely to encounter is underexposure. The metering system in your camera is programmed to capture a notional 18 per cent grey, which often means that your shots in fog are underexposed. The easiest solution is to select the Manual Mode, then set the camera to overexpose by between 1/2 – 1 stop. Your image might appear a tad bright in the monitor, but it is far better to err on the side of lightness if you want to capture the right mood.

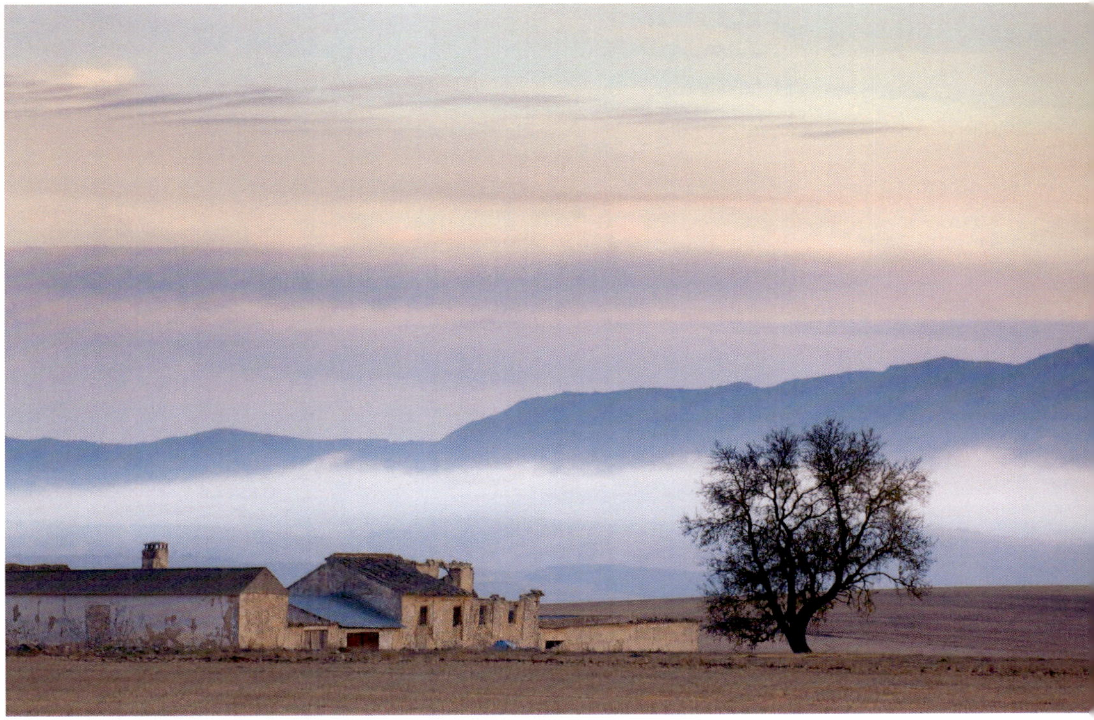

Figure 18 Descending mist and abandoned farm. It is too easy to imagine that fogs are confined to mornings, but they are just as likely to occur in the early evening as well. In this example, as the land increasingly cooled, the mist began to accumulate over the lower parts of the landscape.

HOAR FROST

Like fog, hoar frost is another of those splendid weather features we tend to see during the winter months. It is a condition that occurs when the ambient temperature falls below 0°C (32°F). The main characteristic is the icy deposit that forms, although this does not necessarily occur if the air is very dry so, in addition to sub-zero temperatures, one also requires relatively high humidity. The third characteristic is still air; frosts rarely occur when it is windy.

Look outside and the first signs of a frost are likely to appear on your car but, by exploring the countryside, you soon become aware of hoar frost forming on low-lying vegetation.

Figure 19 **Lone tree in frosty landscape**. If the ground is covered in frost the appearance is not dissimilar to a light covering of snow, so point your camera towards the horizon. Remember, frosts can prove quite ephemeral and quickly disappear with the rising sun.

In even moderately cold conditions hoar frost can form quite thickly on the ground, looking not too dissimilar to a layer of snow. Examine the frost with care and one becomes aware of fine feathers or needles that clearly offer fabulous photographic opportunities. Hoar frosts initially form on the tips of leaves and plants, but it can quickly spread.

A frost hollow

There are specific locations that appear more prone to frosts, and these tend to be in lower lying areas. Often, on a winter's evening, cold air drains from relatively higher land down into pockets, creating frost hollows or frost-pockets. As the air immediately above is slightly warmer, the cold air remains trapped. In fact if you drive around the countryside you can often see frost-pockets. If you are travelling along a ridge on a clear but cold day it is quite common to see a hollow topped with a layer of stratus cloud. If you are able to access the area you will undoubtedly encounter a heavily frosted landscape. Finally, it is worth noting that frosts are much more common inland than they are by the coast.

What should I photograph?

The panoramic landscape

Hoar frost offers numerous photographic opportunities. Whether you wish to work in detail or concentrate on a more panoramic view much, of course, depends on the thickness and severity of the frost. If it does resemble snow point your camera towards the horizon, as the ground and most of the uprights will be covered by a thin white layer that can transform a familiar and possibly unremarkable landscape into something truly special. This is the ideal opportunity to indulge in high key landscape photography, celebrating the beauty of pastel colours.

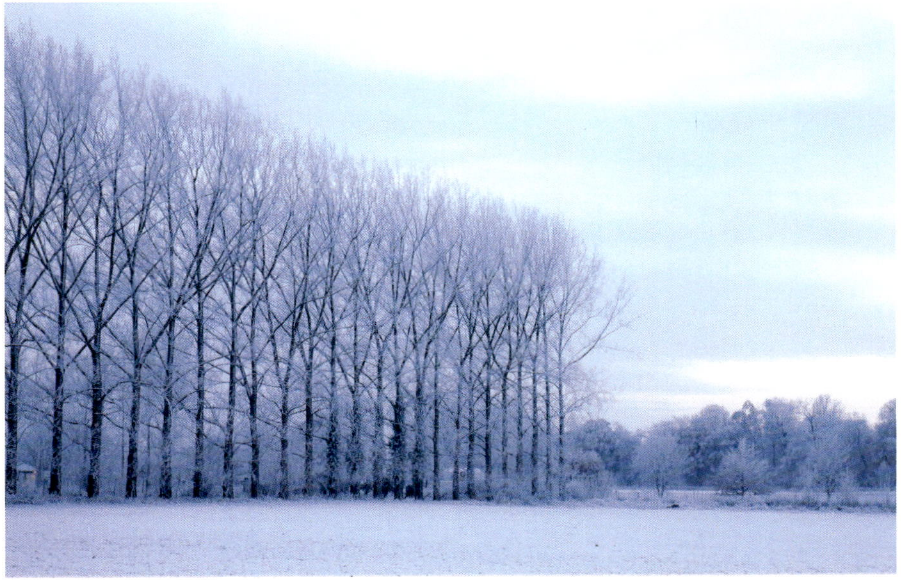

Look for detail

If you own a macro lens, or have a macro setting on your zoom, then you should have no difficulties finding good photographs. Working on this scale, you will enter a ‘winter wonderland’. Plants such as ferns or simple grasses are beautifully transformed when covered in frost. Sometimes it is quite difficult to divorce a single plant or leaf from its surroundings, in which case pack a small sheet of card in your camera bag that can be used as an improvised background. If you try this, select a wide aperture so that the background is thrown out of focus.

Explore your own garden

If you are unable to get out into the countryside don’t overlook the obvious. Your garden, your windows at home or even your car will offer good photographic potential. If you have a macro lens then you will be spoilt for choice. Dead flowers in the garden are especially interesting as, indeed, are small puddles that can often appear as strangely abstract linear patterns in sub-zero temperatures.

Figure 20 **Frost covered line of trees**. Driving along a dual carriageway, I suddenly encountered a fabulous location heavily covered in hoar frost. I pulled off the road and took my shot and then spoke to a local farmer. He explained that the hoar frost was caused by a near-by power station. As steam was released into a sub-zero atmosphere it froze and then fell to the ground. The incidence of frost can be very localised.

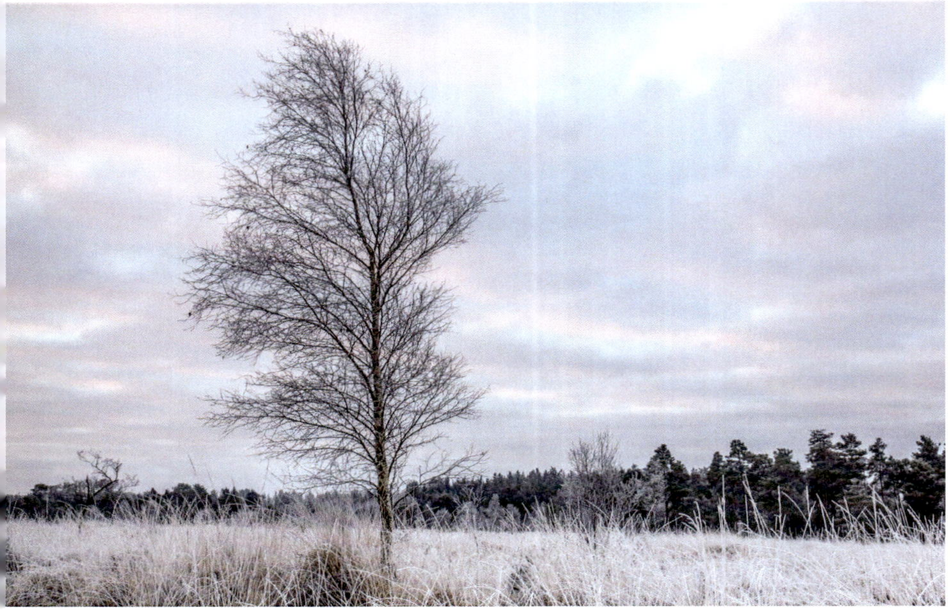

Figure 21 **Lone tree in pre-dawn light**. Often the most interesting time of the day to shoot a frosted landscape is pre-dawn. That is the time when the sky appears at its best. Shortly after taking this the sky filled in with a dull, featureless blanket of grey.

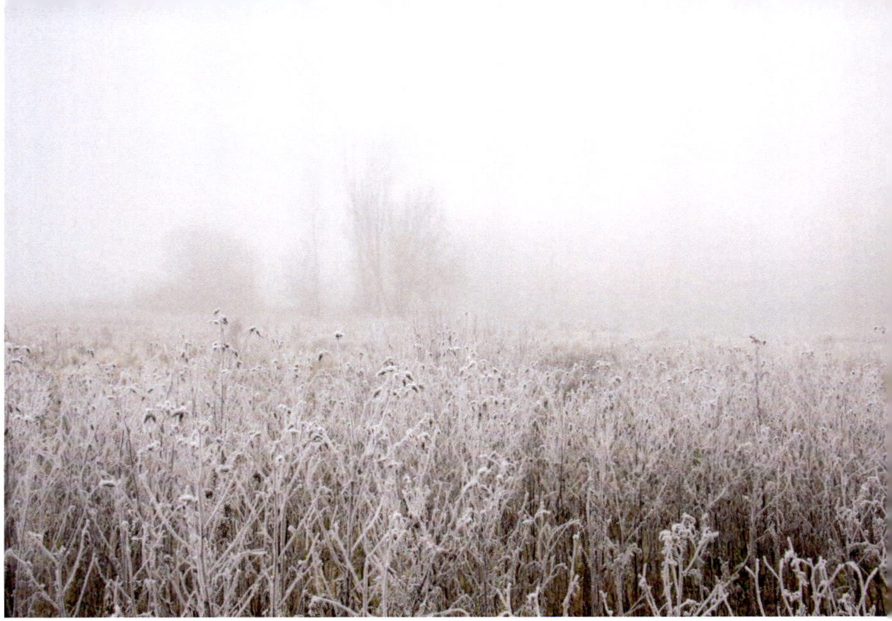

Figure 22 **Frozen grasses**. It is not uncommon to experience a substantial fog in hoar frost, which has the capacity to completely transform an otherwise familiar landscape. Minimalist in conception, the almost invisible cluster of trees in the background add a much-needed element to the composition.

Technical and practical issues to consider

1. First, most obvious, is to wrap up warm. It is difficult to concentrate on photography if you are feeling cold. On a similar tack, the camera's battery can malfunction when the temperature falls below zero, so keep your camera away from the cold for as long as possible. Keeping the battery in your pocket, close to your skin, is one way of keeping it warm.

2. In common with photographing fog, it is easy to underexpose when photographing a frosty landscape so, once again, set your camera to Manual and then overexpose by between 1/2 and 2/3 of a stop. Check your histogram from time to time. It should bunch to the right but remember that, while you are aiming to achieve a high-key image, none of the detail should appear blown.

3. The similarities with fog continue as morning frosts are equally ephemeral and can quickly disappear as the sun rises, so the best advice is to get out early. In fact some of the most beautiful images of frost are taken pre-dawn while there is still interesting colour in the sky.

4. Explore the possibilities of backlighting in frost. What this means is that you are pointing the camera towards the sun. The rim-lighting effect you able to capture can be particularly attractive.

Figure 23 (Below) **Fallen branch and pine trees**. It is quite strange how often debris in the landscape assumes a certain charm when covered in a layer of frost.

Figure 24 (Right) **Lone tree under blue sky**. Often when we wake to see the ground covered in frost the sky will appear blue and cloudless. To make best use of the situation get out early before the sun's rays melt it away.

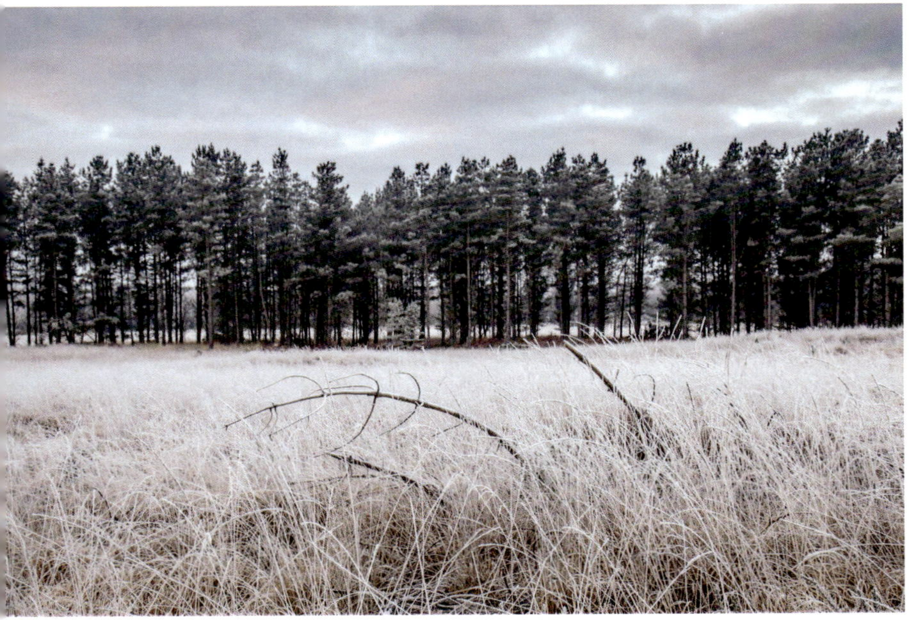

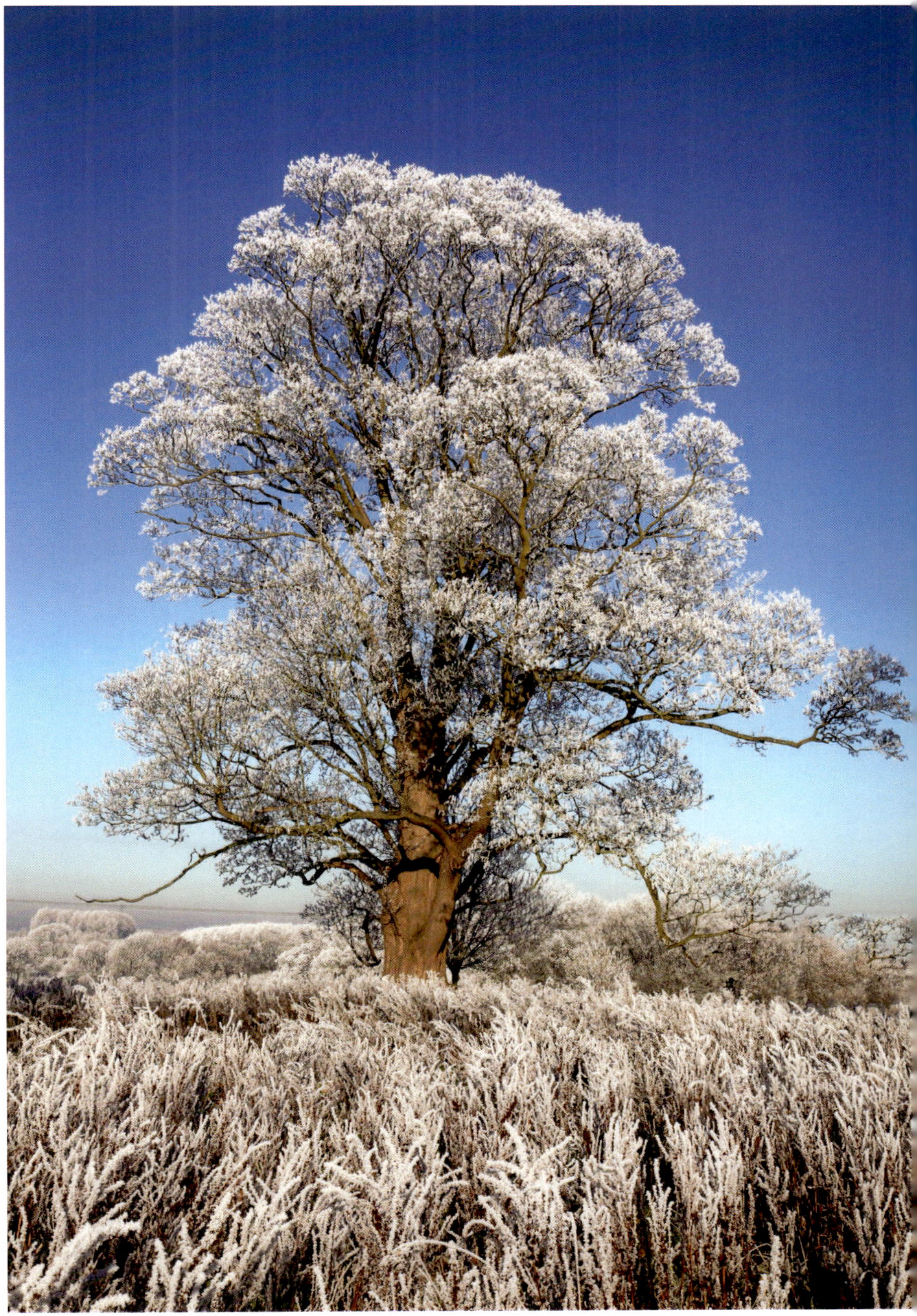

SNOW AND ICE

While certain landscape photographers are positively discouraged from taking photographs in what might be termed 'adverse weather conditions', snow must surely be the exception. Even if the camera has not been used for 11 months it comes out when it is snowing and that is hardly surprising. A snowy landscape retains a charm few can resist. You only have to look at the many Christmas cards that feature snow to appreciate its appeal. Predicting snow is not too difficult. In fact, the Met Office often proves surprisingly accurate in this regard. A product of winter, snow tends to fall during a period of low pressure.

Precautions when photographing snow

The obvious consideration, of course, is to stay warm, so you need to wrap up well. There is a temptation to wear heavy gloves, but that can hinder your control of the camera. It's far better to wear a thinner pair instead. For reasons previously explained it pays to keep your camera warm for as long as possible, and to be aware that batteries drain faster in cold weather so keep them warm inside a coat. Newer lithium batteries are less prone to cold weather, but it is still worthwhile bringing a spare one just in case.

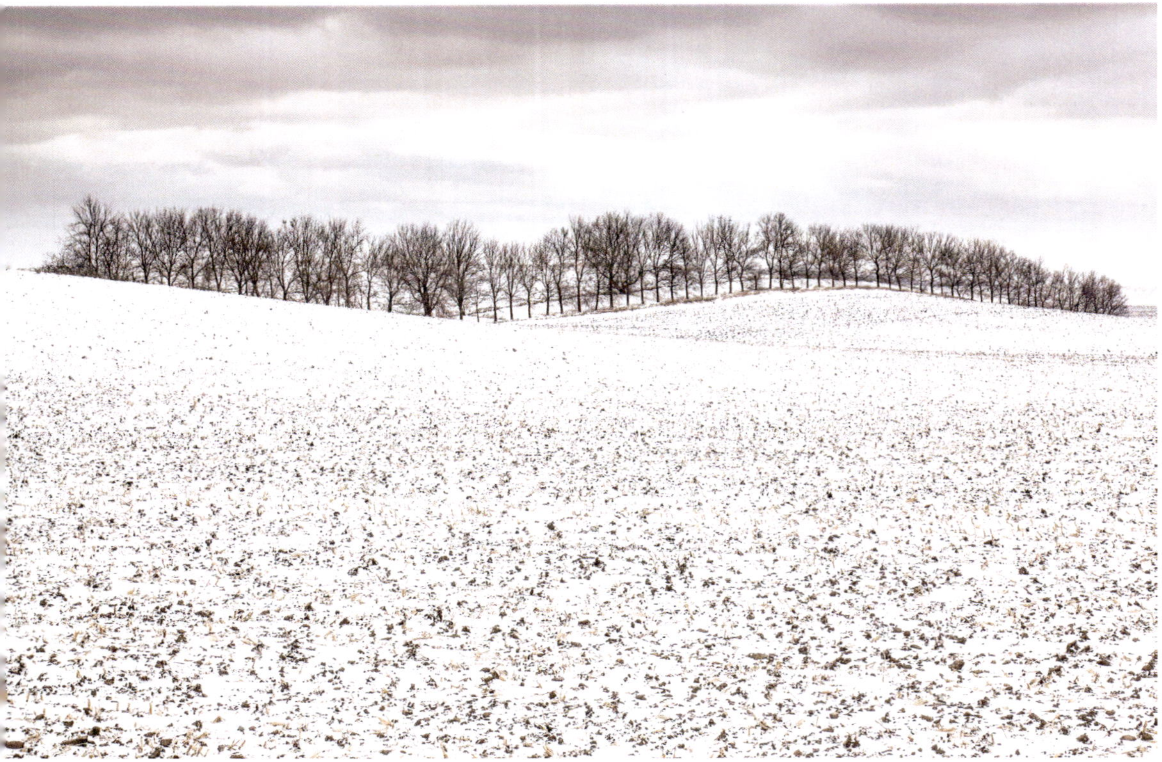

Figure 25 **Trees in snow**. From a photographic standpoint, one of the great features of snow is its capacity to transform the landscape, reducing it to a simple graphic design. The harshness of winter is far more effectively conveyed when photographed under a grey sky.

Manipulating your camera in cold temperatures can often pose problems, so try to anticipate the ISO rating you need prior to setting out. Also decide whether you want to use either AV or TV priority. Ideally you should be in a position to just lift the camera to your eye, take the shot, and then put it away.

What do I photograph?

Look for the graphical potential

Once you set out into a snow-covered landscape it is difficult to know where to start; there appear to be magnificent photographic opportunities in whichever direction you look. Landscape often assumes a marvellous graphical quality, particularly if the snow cover is moderately light. Farm tracks, ploughed fields, remnants of harvested fields leave distinctive marks that offer amazing photographic potential. Similar effects can be captured within an urban setting. The distinctive lines created by vehicles can also prove to be a useful subject to photograph, particularly if you are shooting from a higher vantage point.

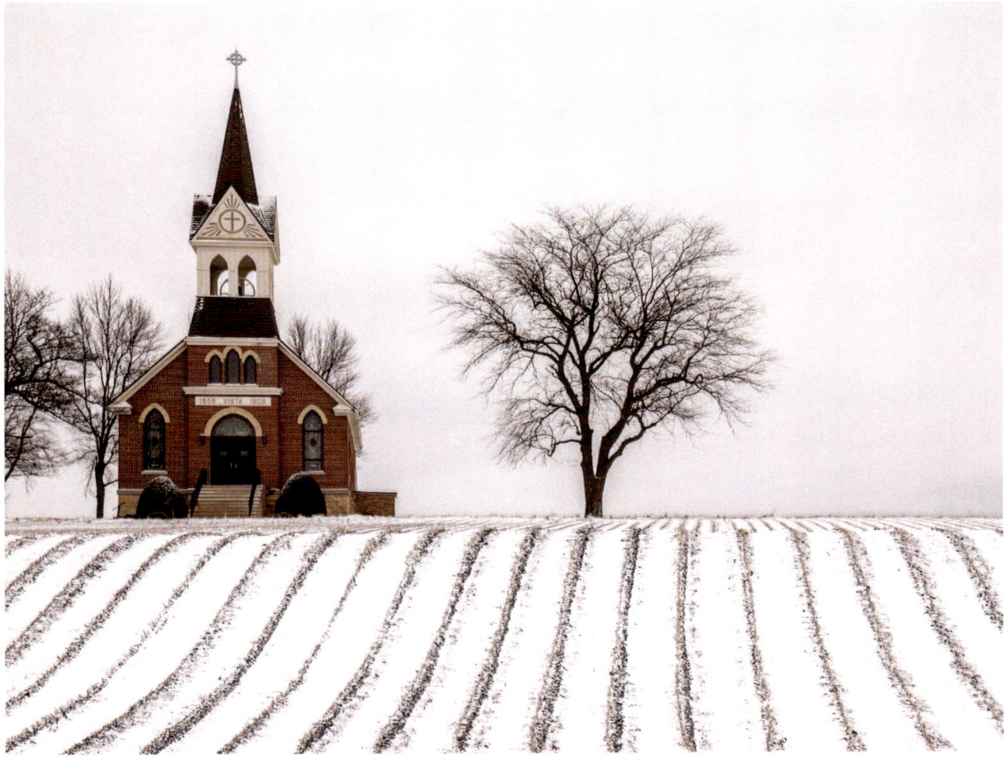

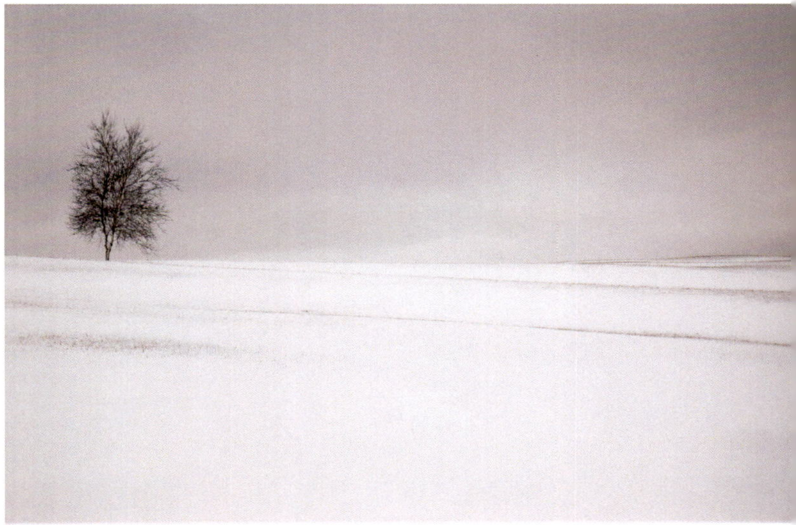

Figure 26 (Left) **Chapel in the snow**. Agricultural land can appear especially graphic, particularly if the snow fall is relatively light. The muted red of the building offers the only suggestion of colour.

Figure 27 (Above) **Single tree**. Snow has the capacity to greatly simplify the landscape offering excellent opportunities for 'minimalist' photography. Devoid of any colour, this reflects a cheerless side to winter.

Look for foreground interest

The deeper the snow the more difficult it is to find, but establishing some feature in the foreground helps to add interest to the composition. A fallen branch or possibly a frozen stream can help to lead the eye from the foreground through the picture towards the horizon.

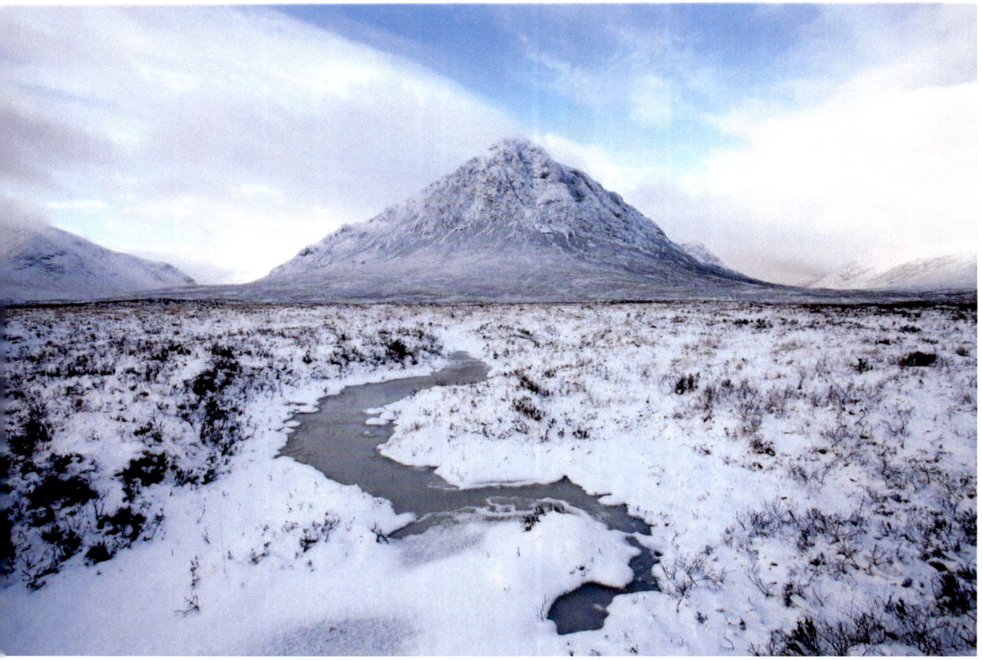

Figure 28 (Above) **Frozen stream**. The 's'-shaped stream not only offers foreground interest, but it also serves to lead the eye toward the mountain in the distance. In this example, the snow appears blue, which strictly speaking is a 'colour-cast'. This could have been remedied in the Raw Convertor, but I have chosen to leave it as the blue heightens that sense of coldness.

Figure 29 (Right) **Beech trees in winter**. If the sky isn't interesting, find a location that doesn't need one. As I walked through this area of woodland, I noticed that the trees that were north facing were totally covered in snow and ice, resulting in a Japanese-style graphic design.

Exploring minimalism

If the landscape is covered in a thick blanket of snow many features disappear, resulting in a scene of sublime simplicity. It appears overwhelmingly white, with just the odd areas of dark punctuating the light. Minimalism is a highly respected genre of photography that celebrates the maxim 'less is more' but, to be successful, you need to balance the elements with great care. The high-key nature of the images also helps to contribute to this minimalist approach. If you have metered your landscape correctly and then checked your histogram, you will see that the tonal values are bunching up on the right. With a very limited tonal range and very few visual elements you should be able to produce images of stunning simplicity.

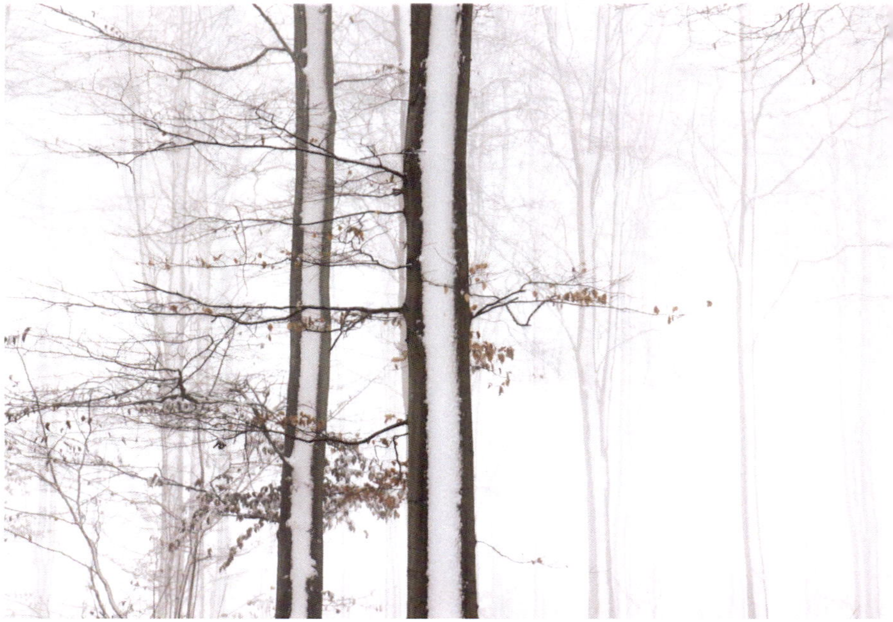

The beauty of blizzards

Snow storms vary considerably and, while it is quite common for snow to fall gently, sometimes it comes in the form of blizzards. Stirred up by strong winds the snow is whipped up into dramatic shapes, very often by the side of roads or hedgerows. Temporarily frozen, the shapes a blizzard can leave in its wake can often prove spectacularly beautiful.

Photograph snow in late evening or at night

It is commonly assumed that snow is white but, of course, that depends on the quality of light in which we view it. Taken in full daylight snow will appear white. However, if you take your photograph early in the morning or much later in the day, the landscape will show a definite bias towards blue. Moreover, because of the highly reflective nature of snow, it is possible to photograph a snowy scene at night although, of course, you will need to make a lengthy exposure requiring the use of a tripod.

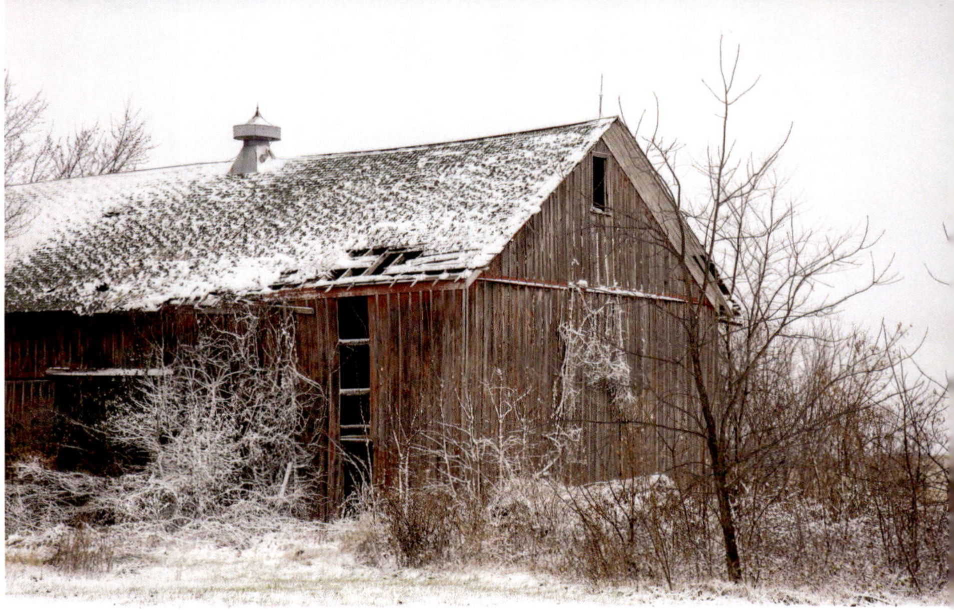

Figure 30 (Above) Derelict barn in snow. Locations and buildings we are normally familiar with can often look quite different when covered with snow. It has the capacity to simplify the landscape, helping to focus attention on textural detail.

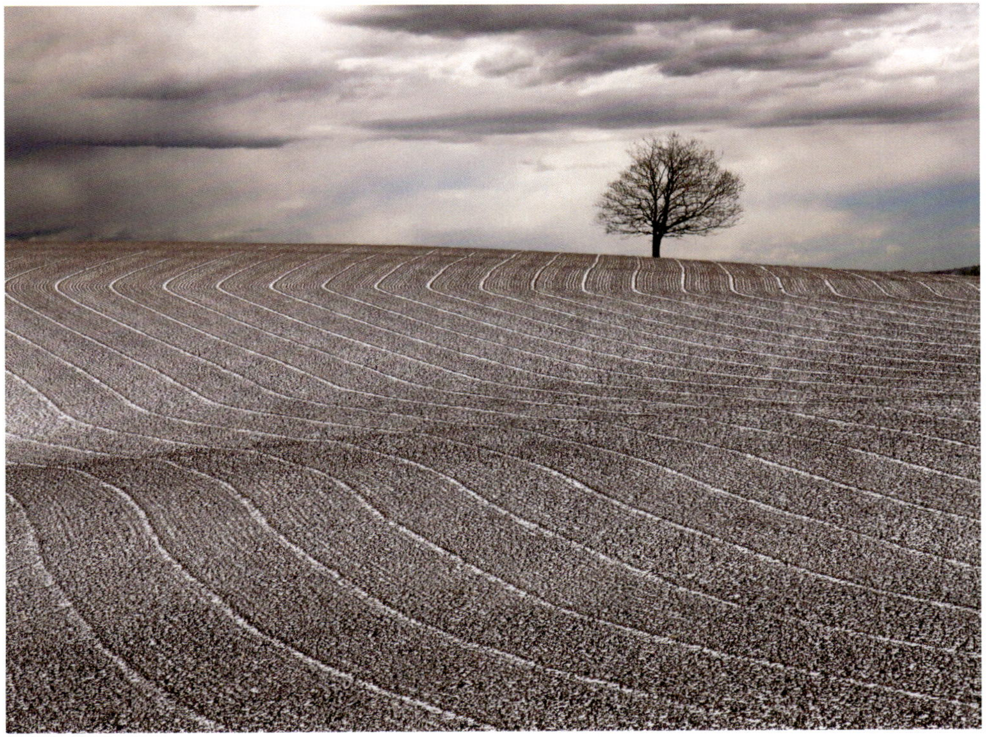

Figure 31 (Left) Undulating lines in snow. Even the lightest covering of snow can create some marvellous graphic effects. This has been exaggerated by the compressing effects of a long lens.

The unique beauty of alpenglow

To reinforce this idea that the ‘colour’ of snow is governed by the time of day, one of the most beautiful periods to capture a snow-covered mountain is pre-dawn or just after the sun has set. If the sky is clear and you are experiencing a dramatic sunrise or sunset, the snow will assume the warm hues seen in the sky, usually a warm pink or peach colour, which is referred to as 'alpenglow'. The pinkish light is what we commonly refer to as a sunset, created by the sun dipping below the horizon. The purple blue part of the sky is the shadow of the earth that increases the further the sun sets. It should be noted that the nearby clouds assume the same colour change as the snow-capped mountains, which really adds to the splendour. It is possible to see the same dramatic pinkish glow of alpenglow at lower elevations but it tends to disappear more rapidly.

Shooting 'alpenglow' is relatively straightforward. Obviously the hard part is getting to the right location on time. Meter as normal. However, it is during post-processing that much of the interest can be added. Whether you work in Lightroom or Photoshop, gently increase the Saturation in order to heighten the vibrancy of the colours.

Try photographing snow as it falls from the sky

The conventional way of capturing a snow landscape is to shoot it once the storm has passed, but exciting images can also be captured while it is still snowing. If you photograph the falling snow you will need to

Figure 32 **Andalusian mountain**. If photographed pre-dawn or shortly after sunset, a snow-capped mountain will assume the glorious colours of the sky; this phenomenon is known as 'alpenglow'.

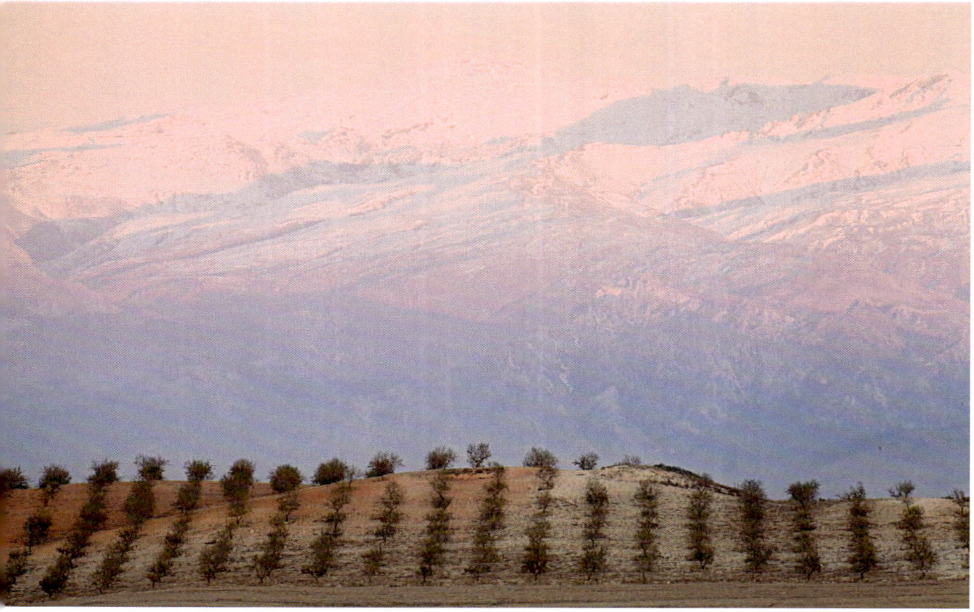

Figure 33 **La Calahorra, Andalusia**. Often wonderful images can be shot when only the distant mountains are snow-covered. In this example, I used a telephoto lens to make the mountains appear much closer to the fortress on the hill.

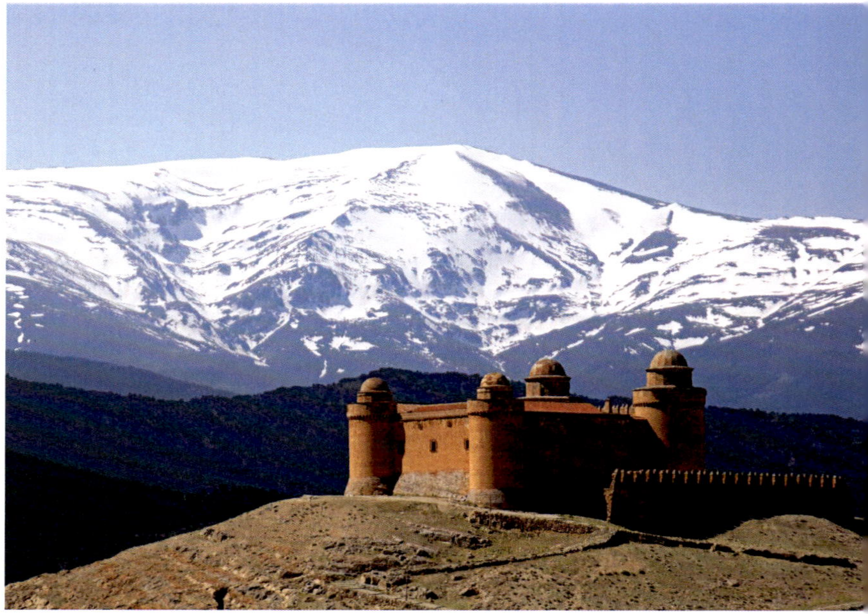

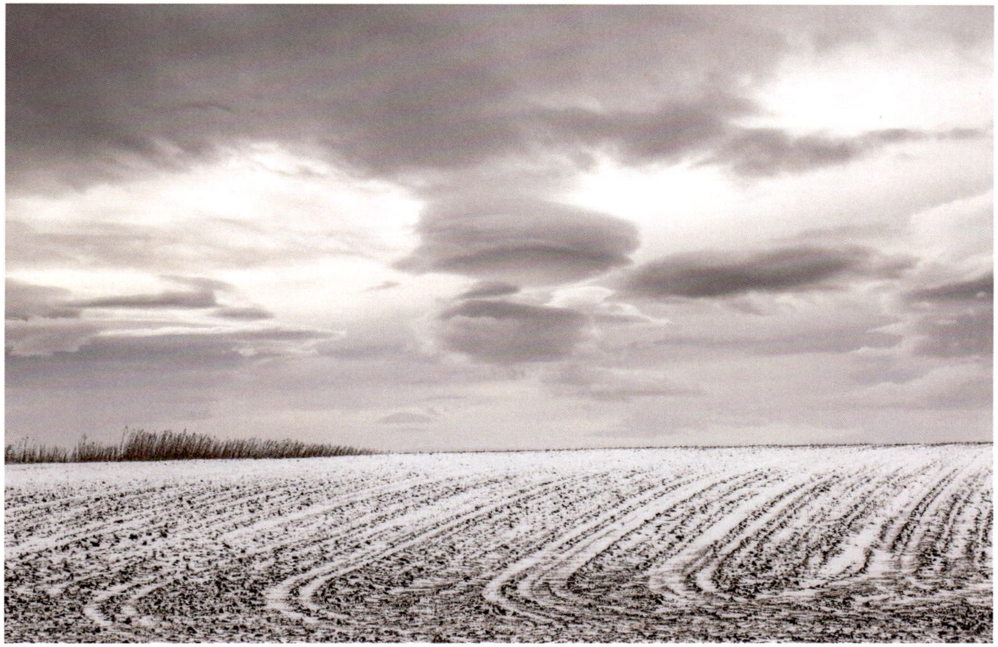

Figure 34 Ploughed field and grey sky. Even the most unpromising landscape appears interesting when covered in snow. Providing it is not too deep, the rilled texture left by the farmer's plough creates an interesting pattern in an otherwise featureless location.

select a shutter speed of at least 1/400th of a second, which can pose problems as the amount of light available will be considerably reduced. If you decide to go down this route you will certainly need to use a high ISO. One alternative is to use flash. Bizarre and strangely beautiful images can be captured with the snowflakes floating to the ground.

Metering in the snow

The camera's light meter is accurate in most circumstances, although there are certain exceptions. If you are shooting in either a very light area or a very dark one the light meter will aim to compensate for these extremes, thus giving an inaccurate reading. In snow it tends to underexpose resulting in potentially over-darkened images. While the monitor offers a great deal of information, nothing tells you more than the histogram. Ideally, you should ensure that the highlights are not blown although, if it is very sunny, a small area of pure white in snow is acceptable, and it is certainly better than allowing the snow to appear grey. It is also one of those occasions

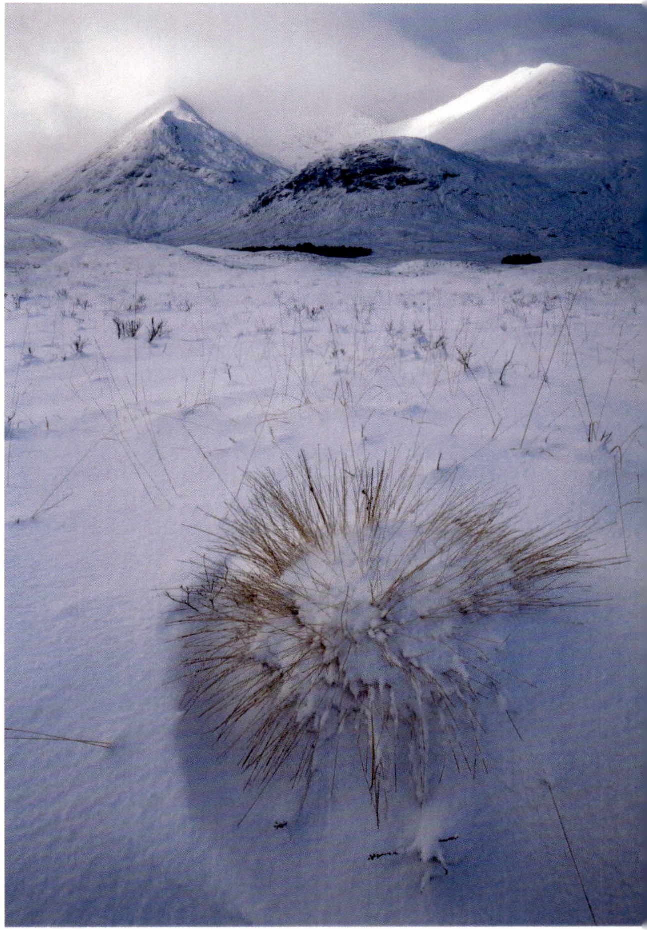

Figure 35 Tufts of grass and distant mountains. Captured just as dawn was breaking, the shadowed landscape appears overwhelmingly blue. If you are able to find a foreground feature, no matter how inconsequential, a greater sense of depth is created.

when you ought to be shooting Raw. This way, if you do make an exposure error, it can be easily remedied in either in ACR or Lightroom.

A simple guide to getting your exposures right

1. Select a part of the image that appears 'grey', spot-meter that area and then use that for the overall exposure.

2. Set the metering to Manual, then deliberately overexpose by a factor of between 2/3 to 1 1/2 stops depending on the brightness of the snow.

The White Light Balance

I normally set my White Light Balance to 'Auto', although sometimes you will need to override it and photographing snow is such an occasion. It is a matter of whether you are happy with the slight bluish cast that snow often produces. If you are shooting under grey skies then a hint of blue conjures a sense of cold that often helps to establish a mood. If, however, you are shooting snow under blue skies, and want to achieve a 'neutral' white, you might consider using the Flash setting in the White Balance. Once again, if you think you have set the wrong White Balance, this can be remedied in ACR, providing you are shooting Raw.

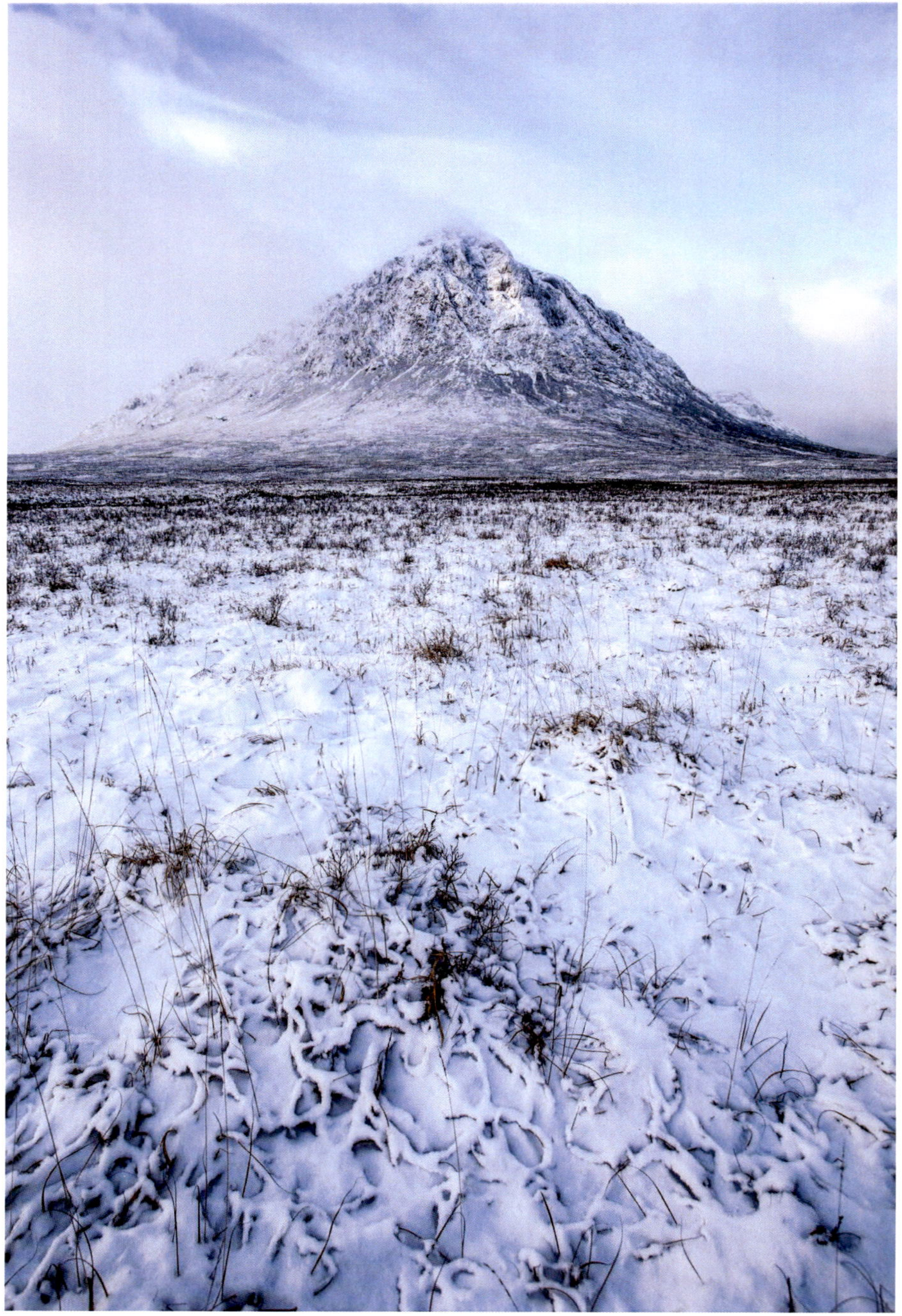

Figure 36 **Latticed grasses and mountain**. Ice and snow have a wonderful capacity to transform a landscape, often creating fascinating shapes and patterns. The vegetation in the foreground has been frozen and then covered in a layer of snow resulting in this strangely beautiful latticed pattern.

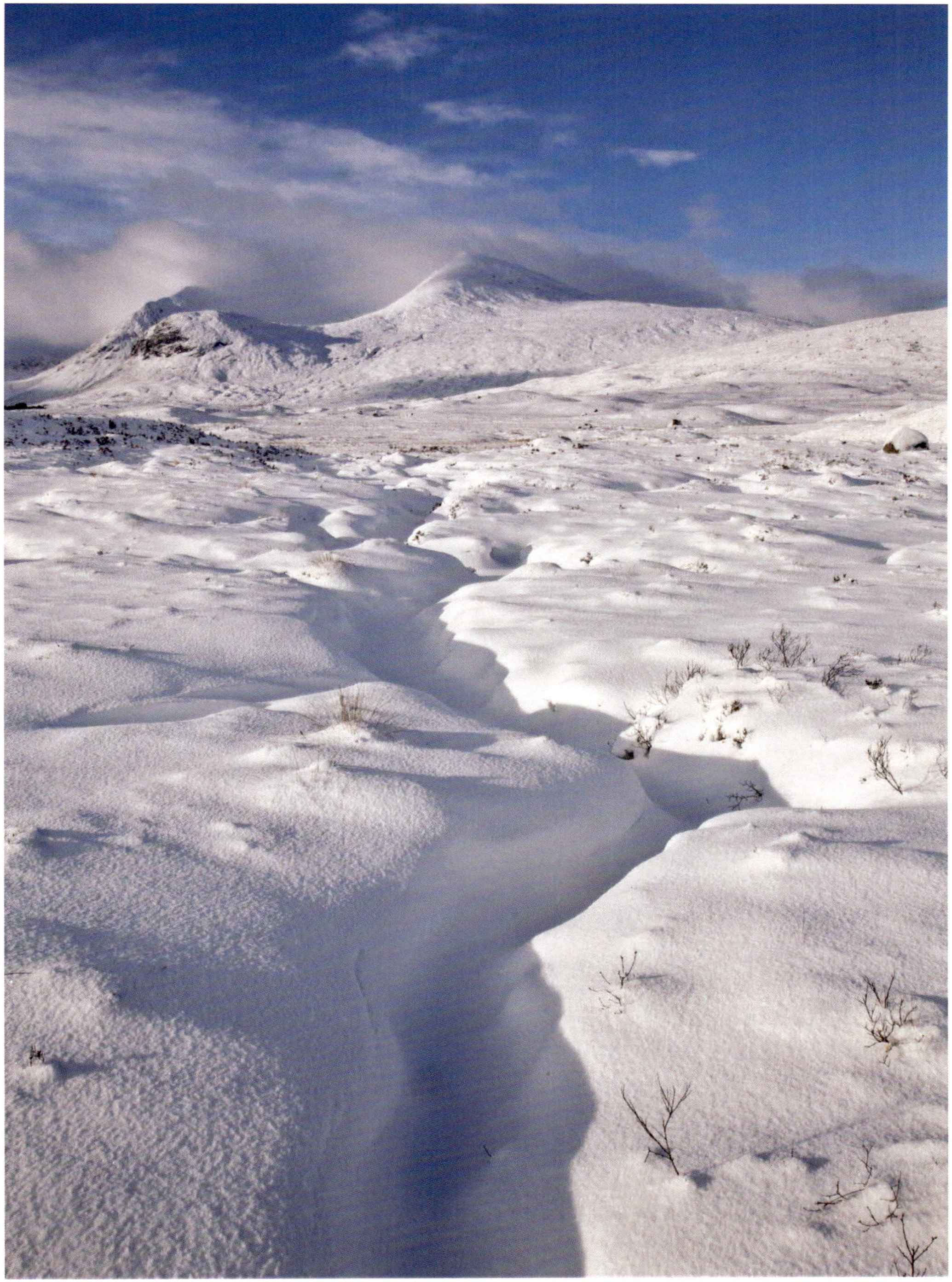

Figure 37 **Ditch covered in snow**. While your monitor can tell you a great deal, nothing tells you more than the histogram. Ideally you should ensure that the highlights are not blown-out although, if it is very sunny, a small area of pure white in snow is acceptable. In this example I was interested in the way the ditch appeared to 'snake' its way towards the distant peaks.

PHOTOGRAPHING LANDSCAPE IN FULL SUNSHINE

It is easy to assume that photographing in full sunshine offers the best photographic opportunities. After all, look at the many glossy brochures illustrating blue skies and you may believe you should be taking most of your landscapes in full sunshine but, of course, that is a gross simplification. In fact, I might suggest the reverse; it is more difficult to communicate a sense of 'mood' when shooting under a clear blue sky, although to ignore the opportunity entirely seems perverse.

So, how do you induce mood when shooting a landscape under a blue sky? I suspect 95 per cent of photographs of landscape are taken under a blue sky and for good reason. We associate it with warmth and summer, and seeing such images promotes a sense of wellbeing (i.e. a positive/happy mood). There are practical considerations too; no cold to endure, no risk of buffeting winds, no possibility than our shots will be ruined by droplets of rain. It is hardly surprising then that the majority of photographs are taken in full sunshine.

Which subjects work best under a deep blue sky?

Blue, of course, is a primary colour. Therefore, if you want to make best use of this, select a landscape that has colours that compliment blue. The opposite colour to blue is orange; what this means is that orange is the colour most unlike blue. Therefore, if you want to achieve maximum contrast, photograph a landscape that sets blue against orange. This is, of course, why pictures of golden beaches are usually photographed under a blue sky; the visual contrast

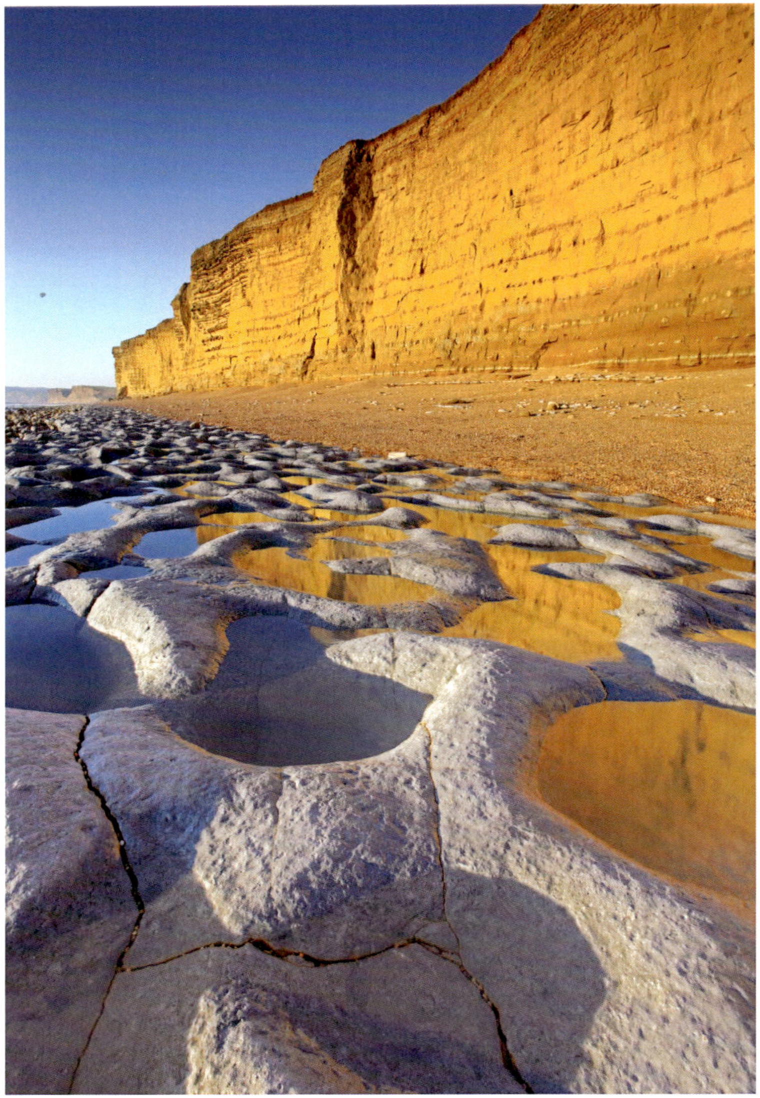

Figure 38 **Golden cliff at Burton Bradstock**. Shot in the late afternoon, the colours in both the sky and the golden rocks appear considerably more saturated than if I had taken the shot in the middle of the day.

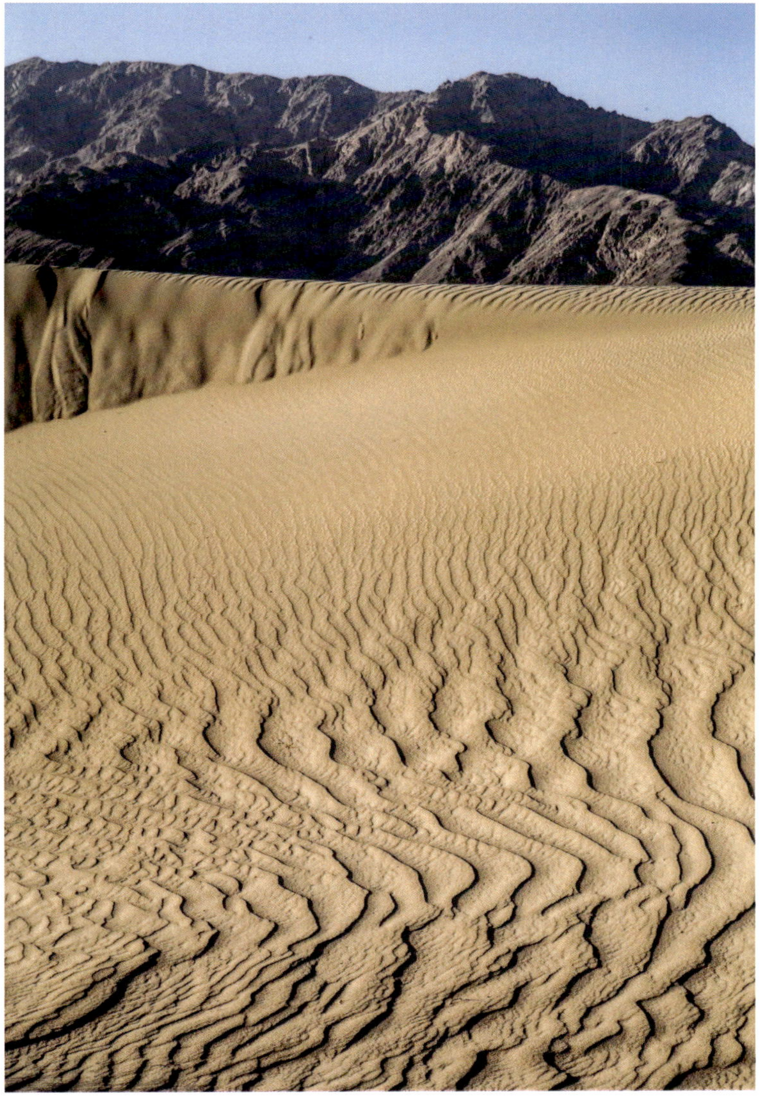

Figure 39 **Dunes, Death Valley, California**. What really sets off these beautiful dunes is the inclusion of the blue sky. Gold and blue are opposite on the 'colour wheel' forming a compelling contrast. Imagine the dunes devoid of that strip of blue at the top of the image. Without it the impact is lost.

is immediate and appealing. There are countless other landscapes that can appear equally engaging. Whether they are coastal or in deserts, sand dunes appear fabulously dramatic when photographed under a blue sky and, on a similar tack, so does a golden field of wheat or a field of sunflowers. By understanding that contrasts work best when photographed in full sunshine, other related colours to orange such as red and yellow can also be used to similar effect. So, for example, a field of red poppies also looks stunning under a blue sky.

Technical issues to consider

1. When photographing under a blue sky point your camera away from the sun. As you look at the sky you will notice it appears much paler in the direction of the sun. Moreover, when facing the sun, the contrast between the sky and the foreground is too great. If that was not bad enough, you will also encounter flare.
2. Even if you are facing away from the sun, a blue sky can appear insipid if you photograph it in the middle of the day. The sky appears much richer when photographed early in the morning or during the late afternoon.
3. A filter you may consider using is a polarising filter. This has the effect of dramatically darkening a blue sky while subtly saturating the colours in the foreground. The effects can be especially attractive if you have a smattering of white clouds in the sky. These filters work best when the camera is pointed at 90 degrees to the sun, although you can experience problems when using a wide-angle lens as it can exaggerate the contrast between the areas nearest and furthest from the sun.

4. Be aware of the shadows that are created when photographing in full sunshine. While they can sometimes help a picture, on other occasions they can prove a distraction. Be aware that shadows shorten or lengthen depending on the time of day.
5. It may seem bizarre but, occasionally, it does help to use fill-in flash in strong sunlight. The contrast one experiences in full sunshine can sometimes leave certain parts of the image appearing to be too dark – for example, uprights often appear poorly illuminated relative to the sky. Using a small amount of fill-in flash is one way of overcoming this.
6. A question I am frequently asked is where to place the horizon. A safe bet is to place it on the thirds, although you can be more imaginative than that. If the sky reveals a beautiful cloud formation, and the horizon is flat and featureless, why not bring the horizon down as low as you can. As I have frequently suggested, sometimes the sky is so impressive that it can serve as a subject in its own right.

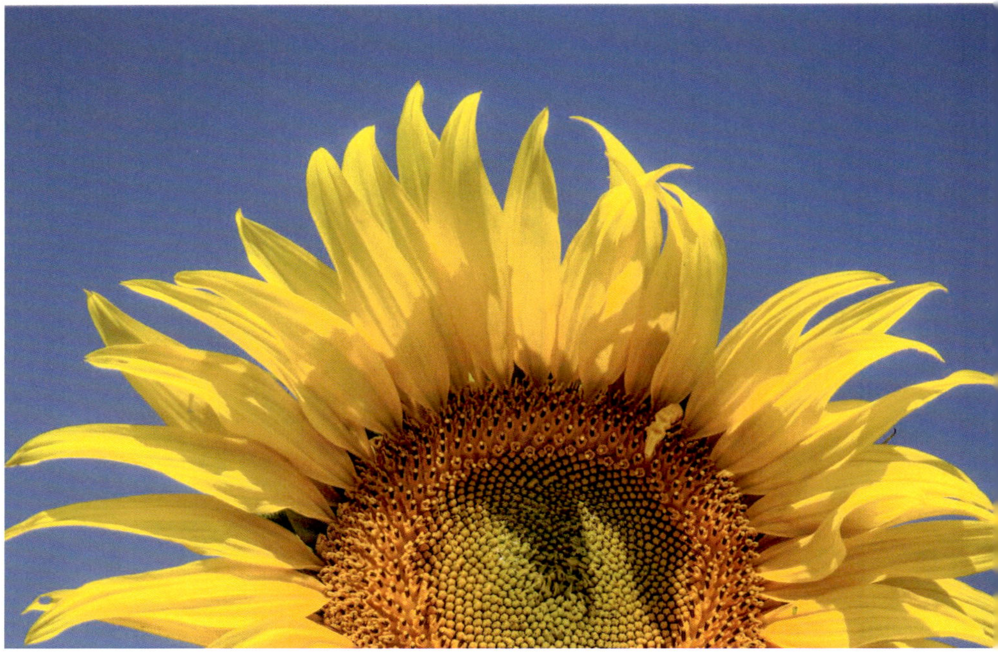

Figure 40 (Top right) Sunflower. One almost senses that nature designed the sunflower to look perfect under a blue sky. The vivid orange petals contrast magnificently when viewed against it. This is an ideal situation to use a polarising filter, as it not only increases the overall colour saturation but it also reduces any reflections off the petals.

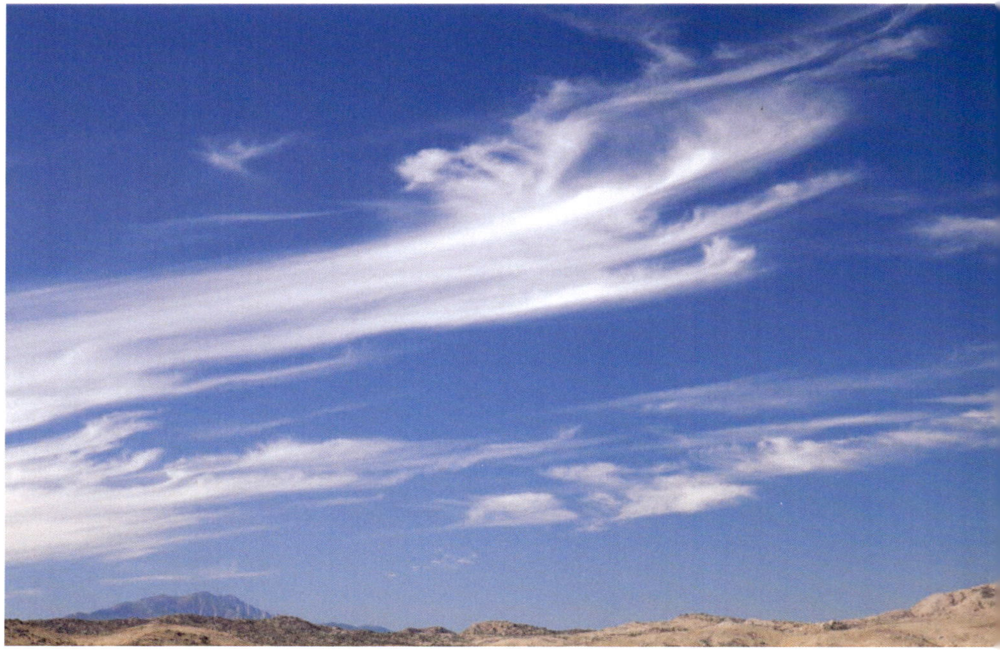

Figure 41 (Bottom right) Blue sky and white clouds. Sometimes a blue sky is filled with a lovely display of white clouds that makes it a worthy subject in its own right. If so, then lower the horizon in order to place greater emphasis on the sky.

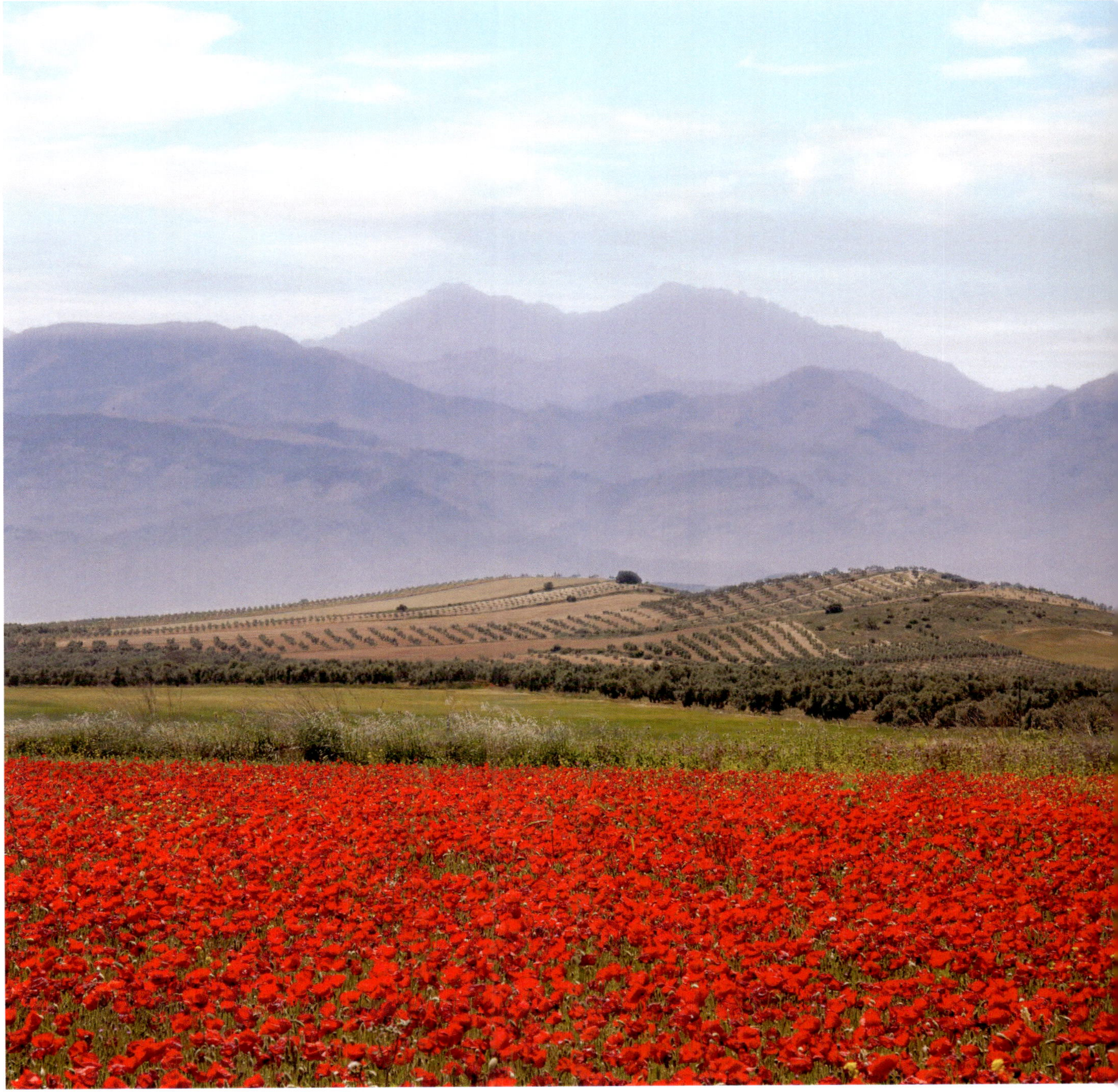

Figure 42 Blue sky and poppy field. Primary colours such as red offer a dramatic contrast to a blue sky. We associate such skies with warmth and summer. Seeing such images promotes a sense of wellbeing so it is hardly surprising that many amateur photographers restrict their photography to when it is sunny.

A DRY AND BARREN LANDSCAPE

We can feel heat, but can we see it? How do we shoot a landscape that conveys temperature? A simplistic solution might be to include a blue sky – after all it is always warm when it is 'sunny'. However, as we all know, there are many occasions when it can be bitterly cold even when the sky is blue so, clearly, that isn't the answer. Yet, as we travel insulated in our cars, we can often sense when it is warm outside. How, you might ask?

A heat haze

The answer of course is simple – any reasonably perceptive person can see heat, most noticeably as a heat haze. This is an effect of the sun that makes it difficult to see distant objects clearly. It is a strangely beautiful visual phenomenon that creates a unique quivering distortion. Areas in the distance can look strangely liquid, which is why people who have been trapped in a baking desert report seeing a lake of water in the distance; as they moved towards it, it appears to move away. This is a classic mirage.

A mirage is not a result of hallucinations – it is a genuine optical phenomenon. Cold air is denser than warm air and has a greater reflective index. As the light rays travel near the ground surface they are bent upwards towards the colder air, thus creating the distortions. One only ever sees this effect just above the surface of the ground. It tends to be more visible where the ground is flat. Light from the sky is refracted, making it appear as if the sky is reflected on the ground and our minds interpret this as water, hence the illusion.

Heat hazes are much more apparent on roads, particularly in the distance. The heat can build up quite noticeably on tarmac, which is why we tend to see heat hazes above it. The effect can be particularly interesting if you can see a distant vehicle, as it will look as if it is travelling in mid-air. A line of posts can also appear strangely distorted; because the build-up of heat is more apparent nearer the surface of the ground, the distortions are much more apparent at the base of the posts. While you can capture the effects of a heat haze with most lenses, as it is relatively distant a telephoto lens will work best.

The appearance of some landscapes can also suggest heat

Certainly images of large sand dunes under a deep blue sky could suggest warmth, although you do not need to be quite so obvious. Any terrain devoid of vegetation that appears dry and baked will also suggest heat. This will be particularly apparent if all available moisture has been evaporated. Areas revealing cracked dry earth, as if the land has been scorched by a baking sun, can certainly evoke a sense of warmth.

In the same way as a blue landscape can suggest cold, any landscape bathed in a rich red and orange light will appear warm, as red and orange are classed as 'warm colours'.

Figure 44 (Right) **Baked earth and Factory Butte**. While the ground suggests that it had experienced rain sometime in the distant past, the baked clay conveys a period of sustained hot weather. While the temperatures might be quite tolerable, visually the ingredients of this image can easily convince you this is the warmest place on earth.

Figure 43 (Below) **Rippling dunes, Death Valley**. There are some landscapes that, irrespective of the temperature, exude a positive sense of warmth. We naturally associate sandy deserts with heat, which is not surprising bearing in mind the rich orange hues.

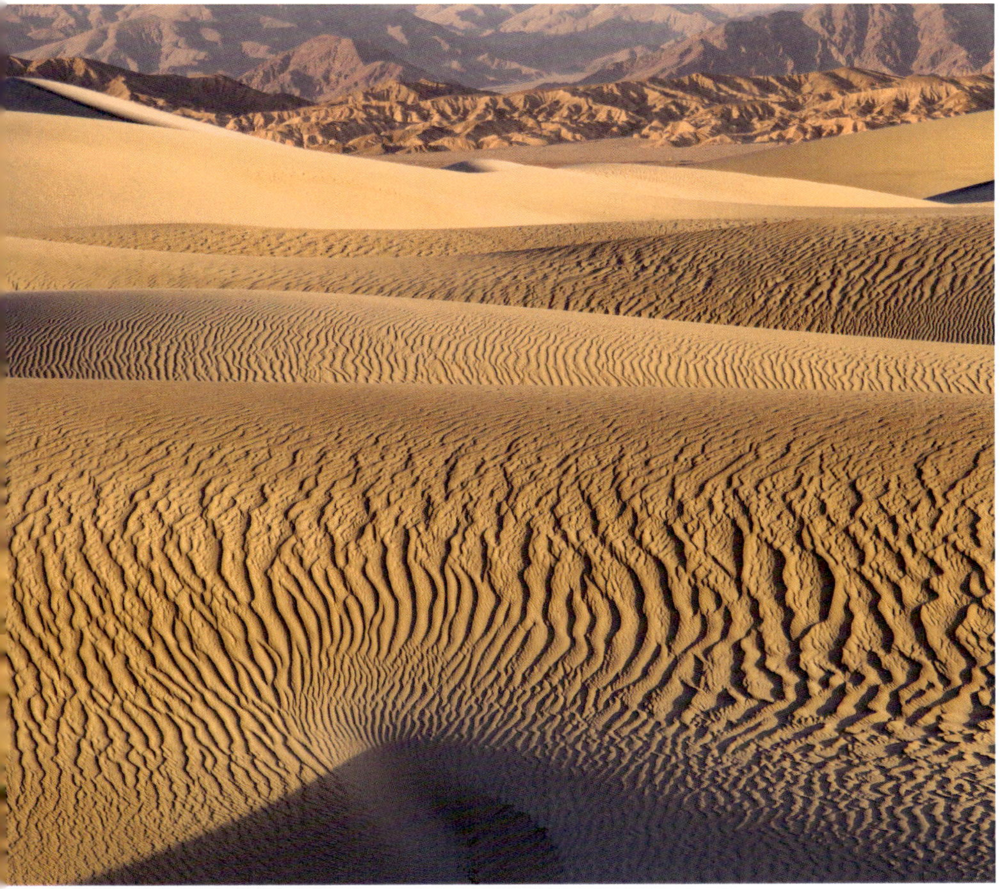

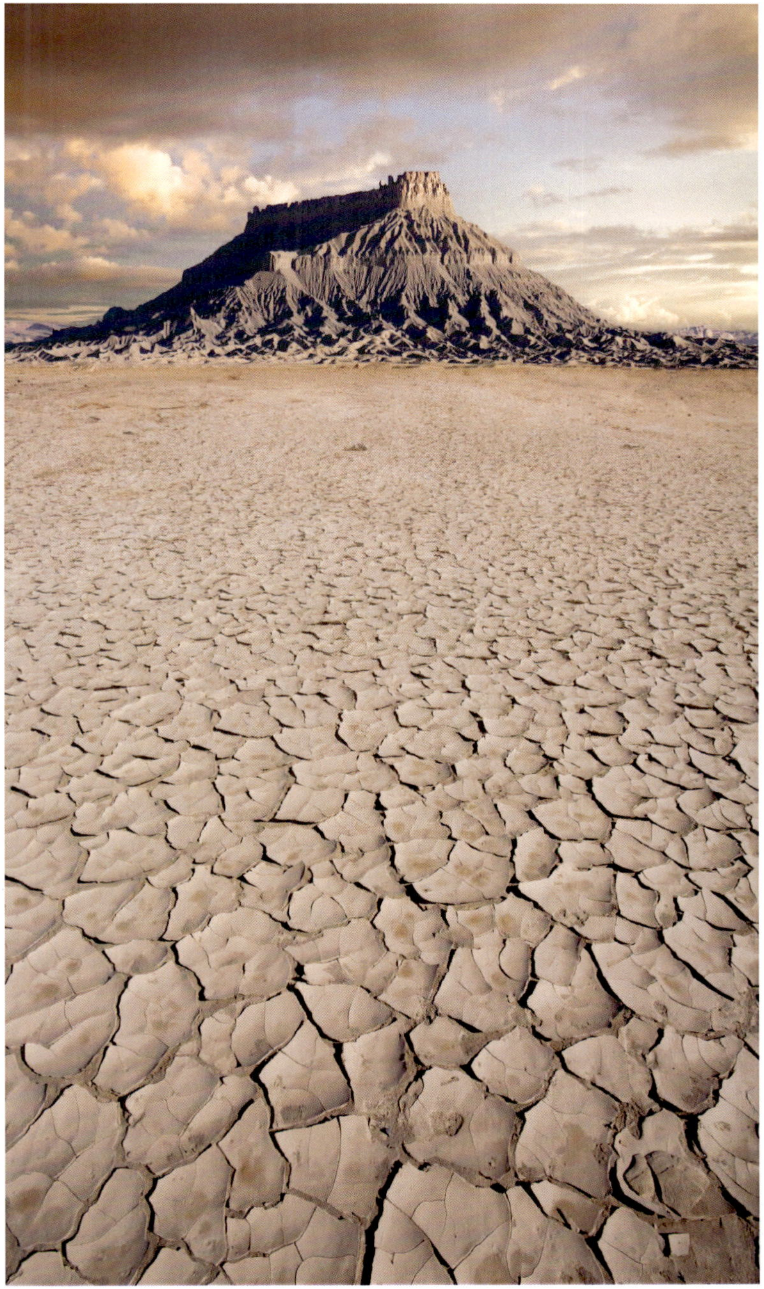

5 Adopting a Personal View of Weather

While everything we have covered so far deals with image capture, there is a lot we can do post camera to enhance the photograph. There is a plethora of software designed to help the photographer best exploit the potential of each of their shots. Although the most popular of these are Lightroom and Photoshop, the latter, in particular, is viewed as the industry standard. Both of these software programmes are immensely powerful editing tools that, if not used with sensitivity, can divorce the initial image from reality. Good weather photography should be about capturing the delicate nuances that characterise the given conditions, so it is important that no image is ever 'over-processed'.

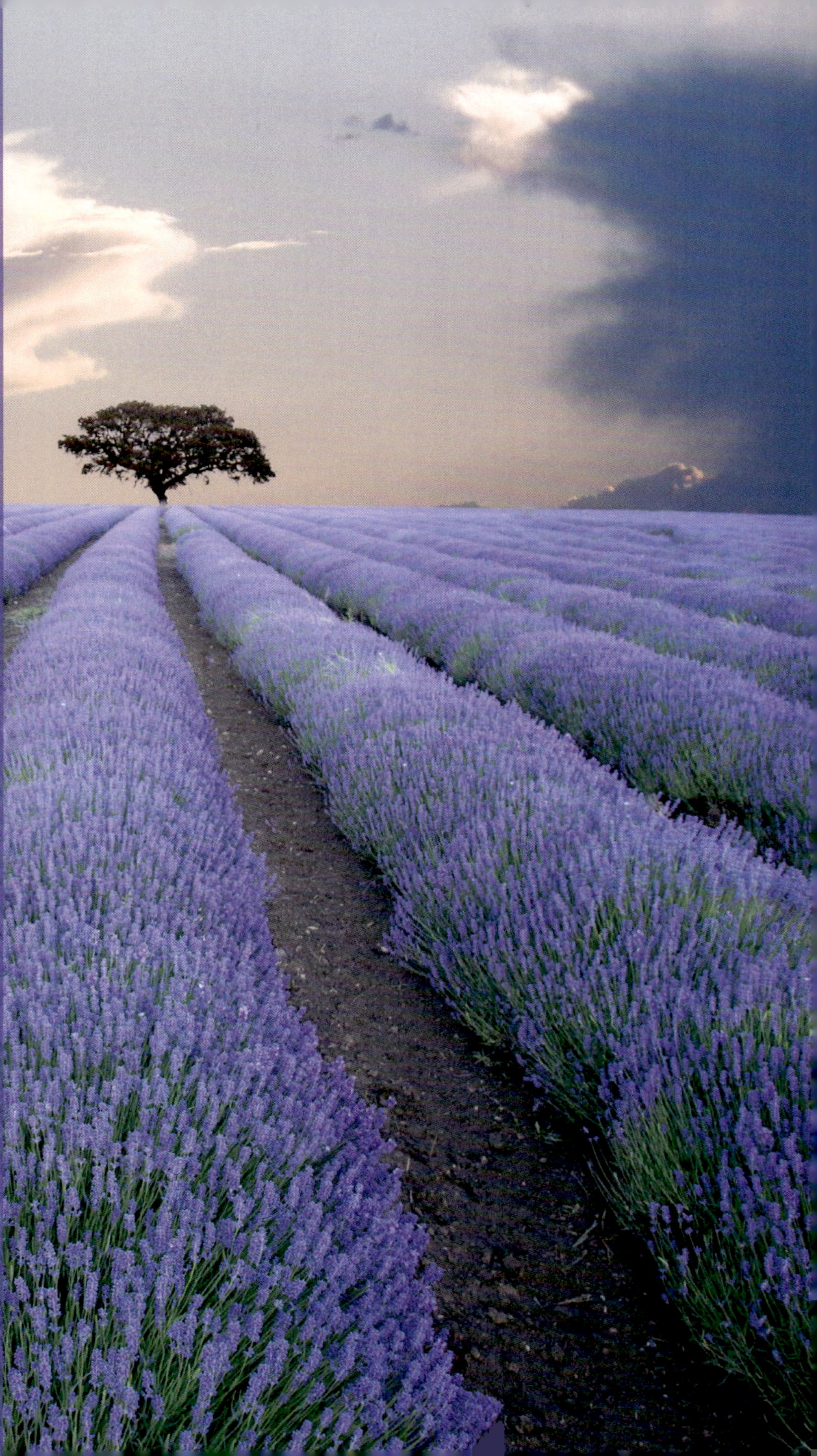

Presenting your weather file as a monochrome

If you are shooting digitally there is one post-camera processing technique I would strongly urge you to consider and that is to convert some of your images to monochrome. Expressing mood is the essence of good weather photography and one way you can achieve this is to present your image in black and white. It is, of course, a genre with a long tradition and some of photography's finest landscape shots have been presented as monochromes. Devoid of colour, a black and white photograph focuses the attention on the tonal values and, by highlighting these, the image conveys a powerful sense of emotion.

Should I use the monochrome option in my camera?

Most DSLR cameras have a monochrome setting in the menu that allows you to capture the image in black and white. However, while this might allow you to see the potential of a given location, it is not the best method of capture. Your camera will also offer specialised monochrome filter effects that you might have used if you were shooting using traditional film, such as a red, green or orange. Once again these are useful in so far as they alert you to the potential of the situation but, in order to maximise the potential of your digital file, continue to shoot in full RGB and then desaturate the image in your preferred editing software.

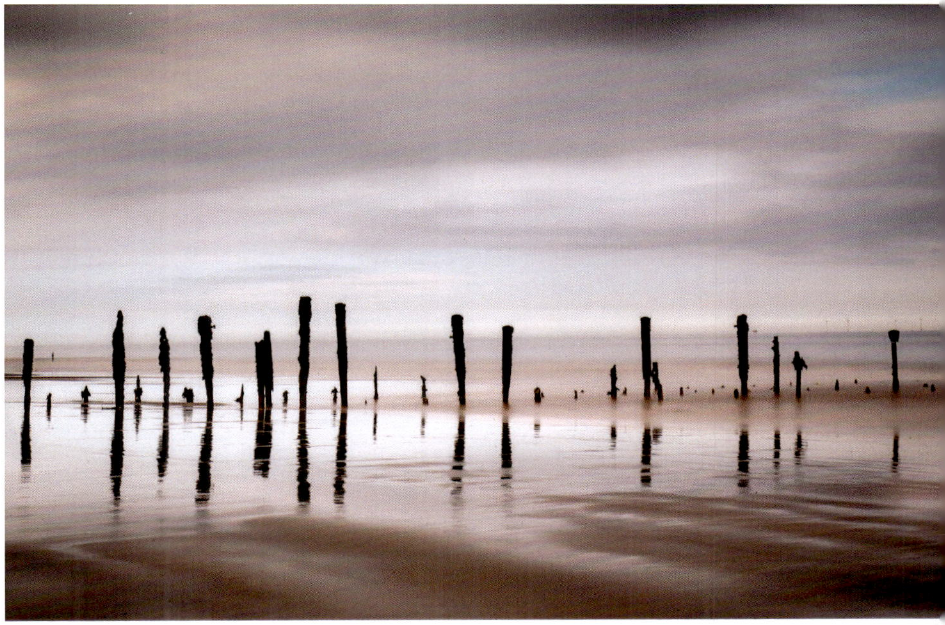

Figure 1 **Black and white conversion**. Lacking any real colour but rich in tone, an image such as this would make an ideal subject to be converted from colour to monochrome.

Which software allows me to convert my image from colour to black and white?

For reasons already explained, it is far better to shoot in full RGB (preferably Raw) and then to convert the image to monochrome. This can be done using a variety of editing software such as Lightroom or ACR, however Photoshop is probably the software package most photographers are familiar with. Whether you are using this or some other software, the process is virtually identical.

Converting an RGB file in Photoshop

With your image on screen, make an adjustment layer and select the Black and White command. The image will then immediately default to black and white. Then, by using the range of channel sliders, you are able alter the tonal values of the image relative to original colour. So, if you wanted either to lighten or darken a blue sky, this can be achieved by manipulating the 'Blues' slider.

Using Levels to create more contrast

Monochrome images are much more forgiving than colour images when increasing the contrast. In order to add 'punch' to your black and white image, make a second adjustment layer and select Levels. Most black and white images are improved when there is a small amount of pure white and a small amount of black within the image. To do this expand the tonal range from 0 to 255. This is usually achieved by dragging in both the Highlight slider and the Shadow slider so that they clip both the lightest and darkest parts of the image. Also, by carefully adjusting the Gamma slider, you have one further tool allowing you to introduce mood into the picture. By dragging it to the left, the image will lighten incrementally while, if you pull it to the right, it will darken. In this way you are able to 'interpret' your weather shot.

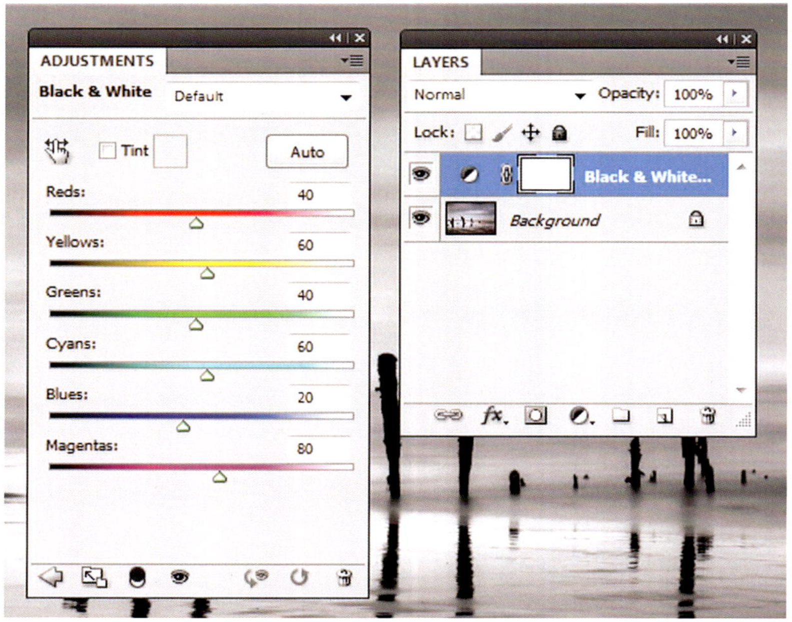

Figure 2 The black and white command dialogue in Photoshop. By adjusting the various Colour Channels quite noticeable tonal changes can be made to the final image.

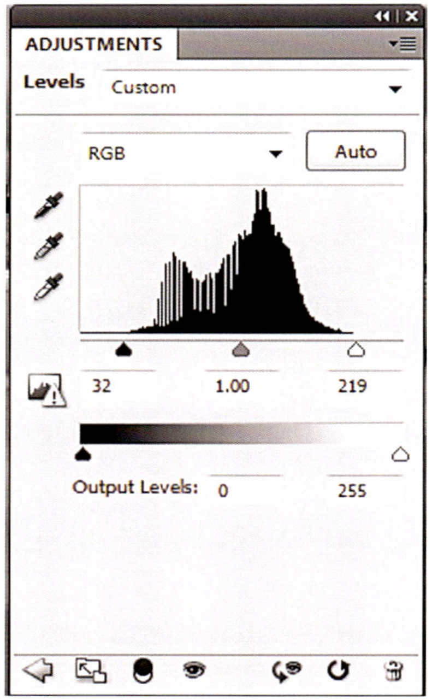

Figure 3 The Levels command. Traditional darkroom workers had the option of printing on various grades of paper ranging from Soft (low contrast) to Hard (high contrast). Using Levels, you are able to exercise the same control.

Can toning a monochrome image help?

As you will no doubt have discovered, there are various methods for 'toning' your monochrome image, either in-camera or post-camera, and the effects can be stunning. However, it is important to remember that blue toning will make the image appear cooler while sepia toning helps the image appear warmer, so think carefully about the subject in hand. For example, I am not sure that much can be gained by toning a snow scene sepia.

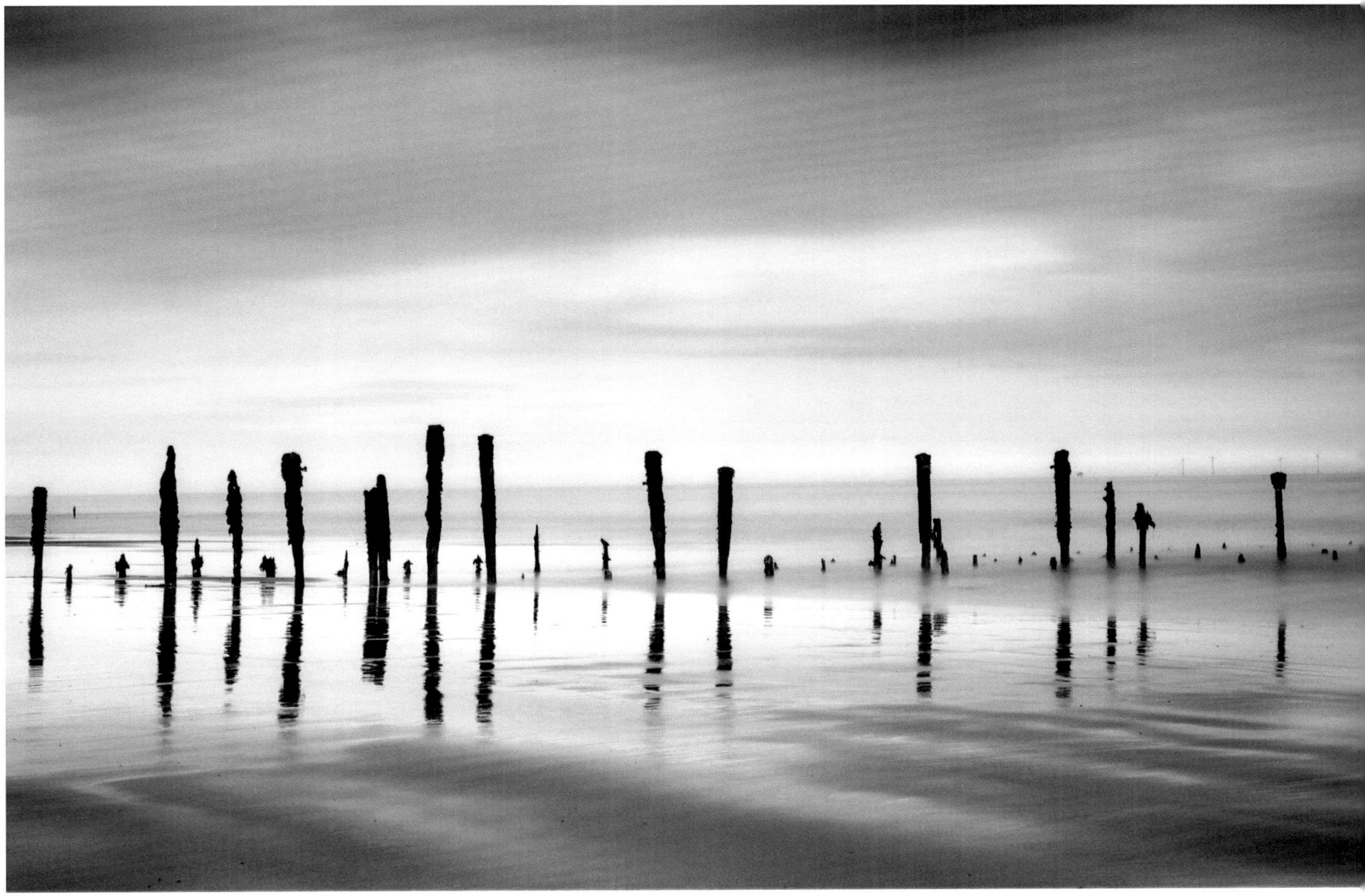

Figure 4 **The completed image**. By converting the full colour image into monochrome using the Black and White Command in Photoshop, I was able to introduce a rather attractive graphic effect. The grey clouds seem to work particularly well when translated as monochrome.

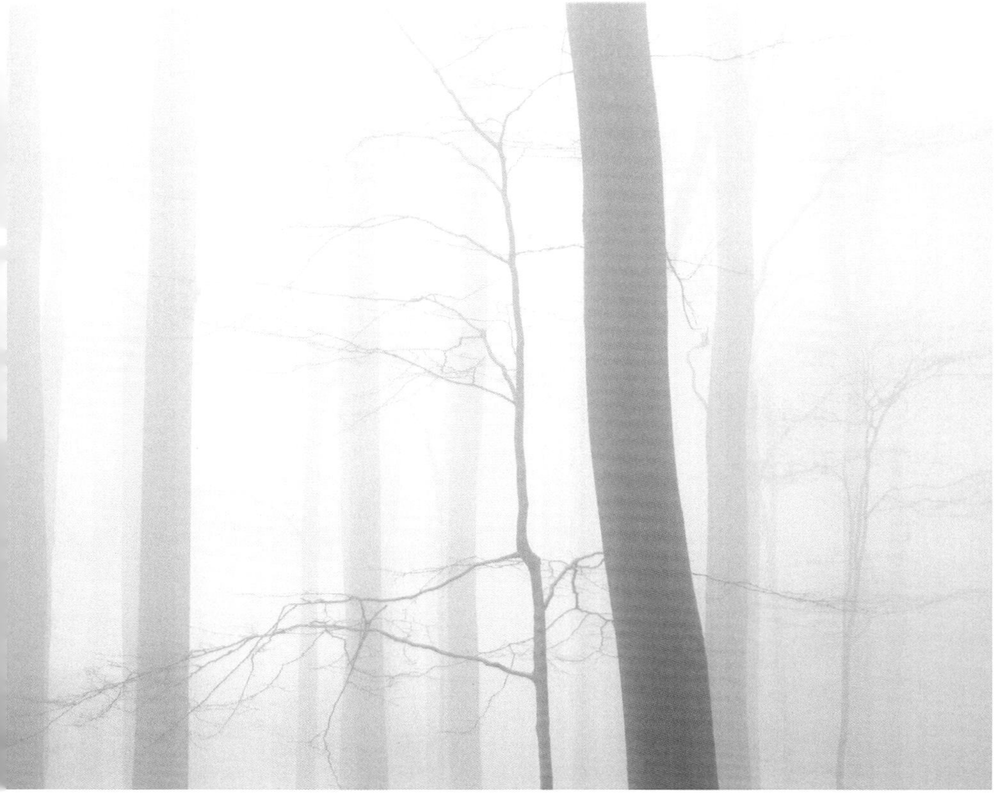

Figure 5 **Beech trees in mist**. Photographed during a thick winter fog, the original file revealed very little colour so it was an obvious choice to convert to black and white. In this example I also made a further adjustment using Levels in order to exaggerate the image's high-key qualities.

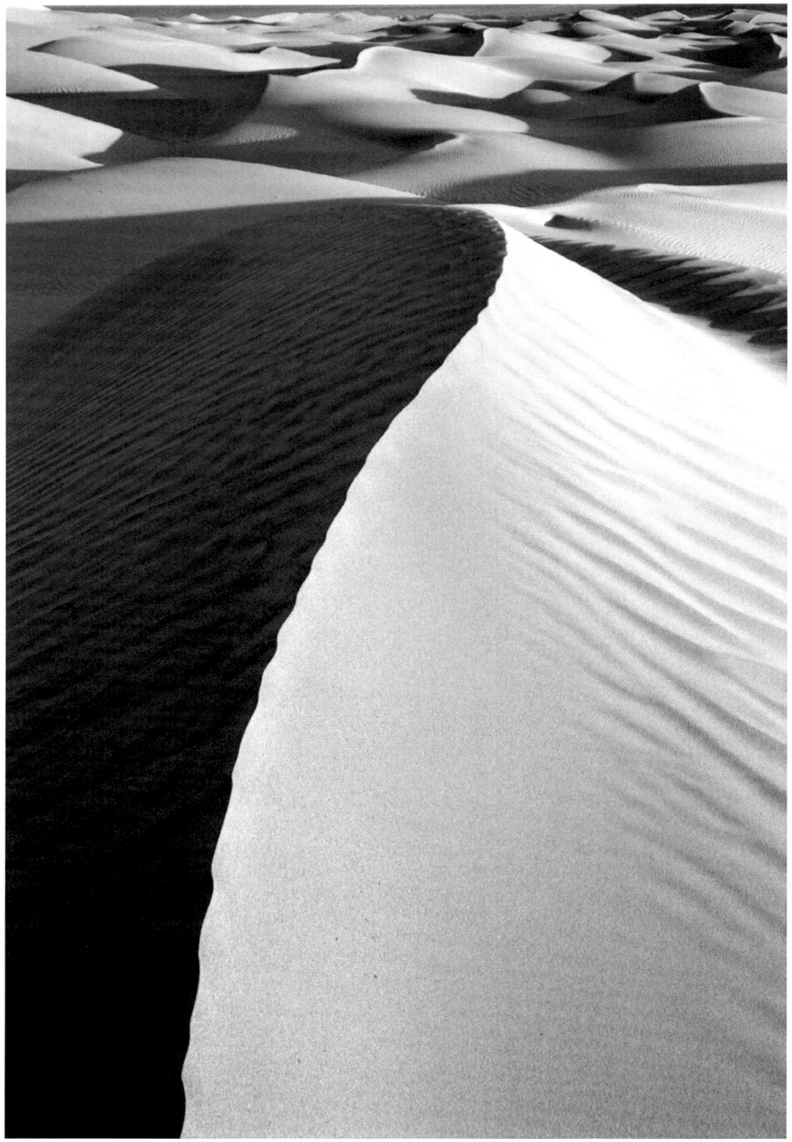

Figure 6 **Sand dunes**. Photographed in strong sunlight, this also works well as a monochrome. As there was no contrasting blue sky in the original file, the colour range was significantly restricted. By converting this to black and white greater play is made of its tonal values.

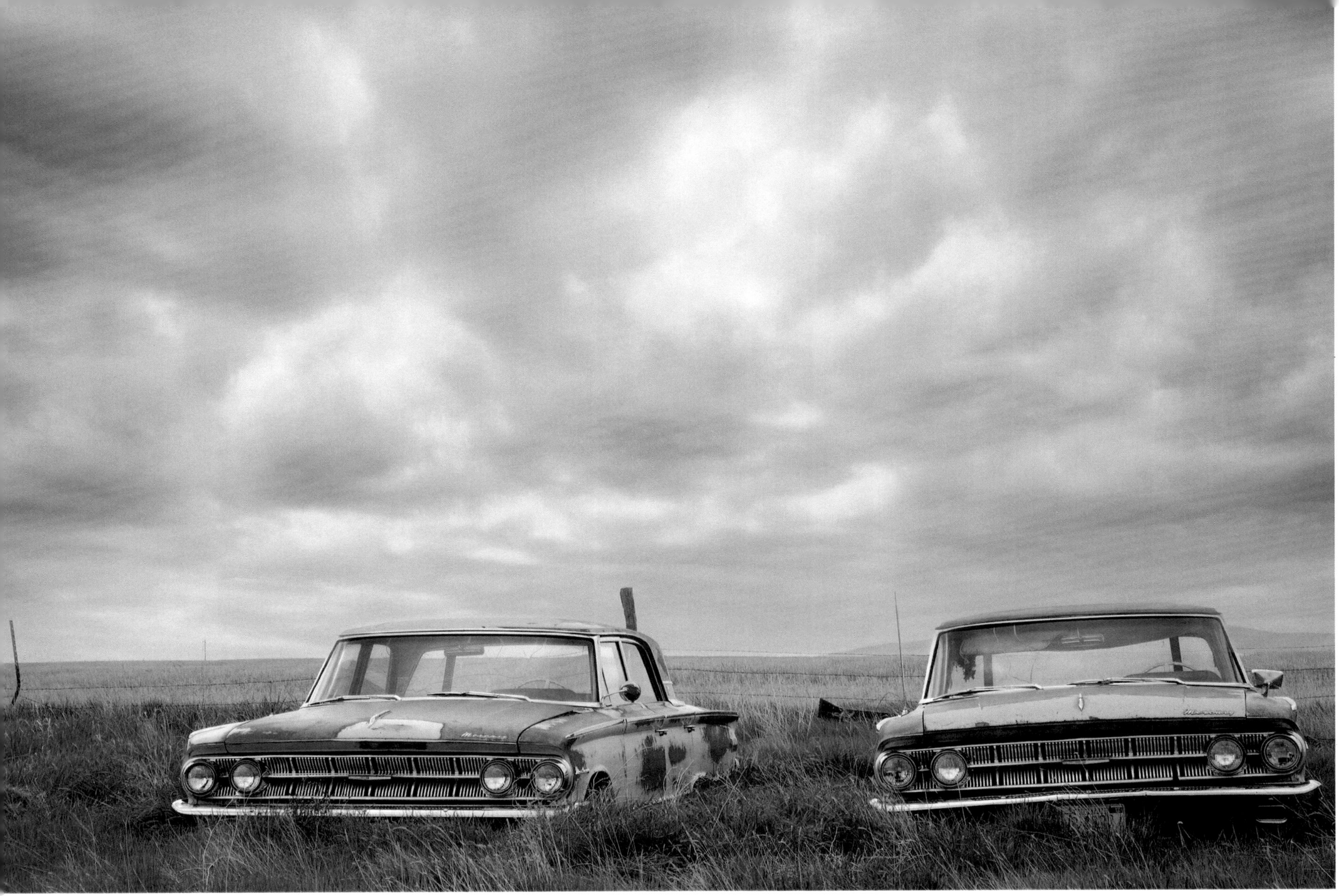

Figure 7 **Two wrecked Mercury cars under a sombre sky**. The skill of photographing interesting landscapes is to ensure that the subject chimes with the prevailing weather. In this example, the abandoned vehicles introduce a sense of pathos that is amplified by the oppressive grey sky.

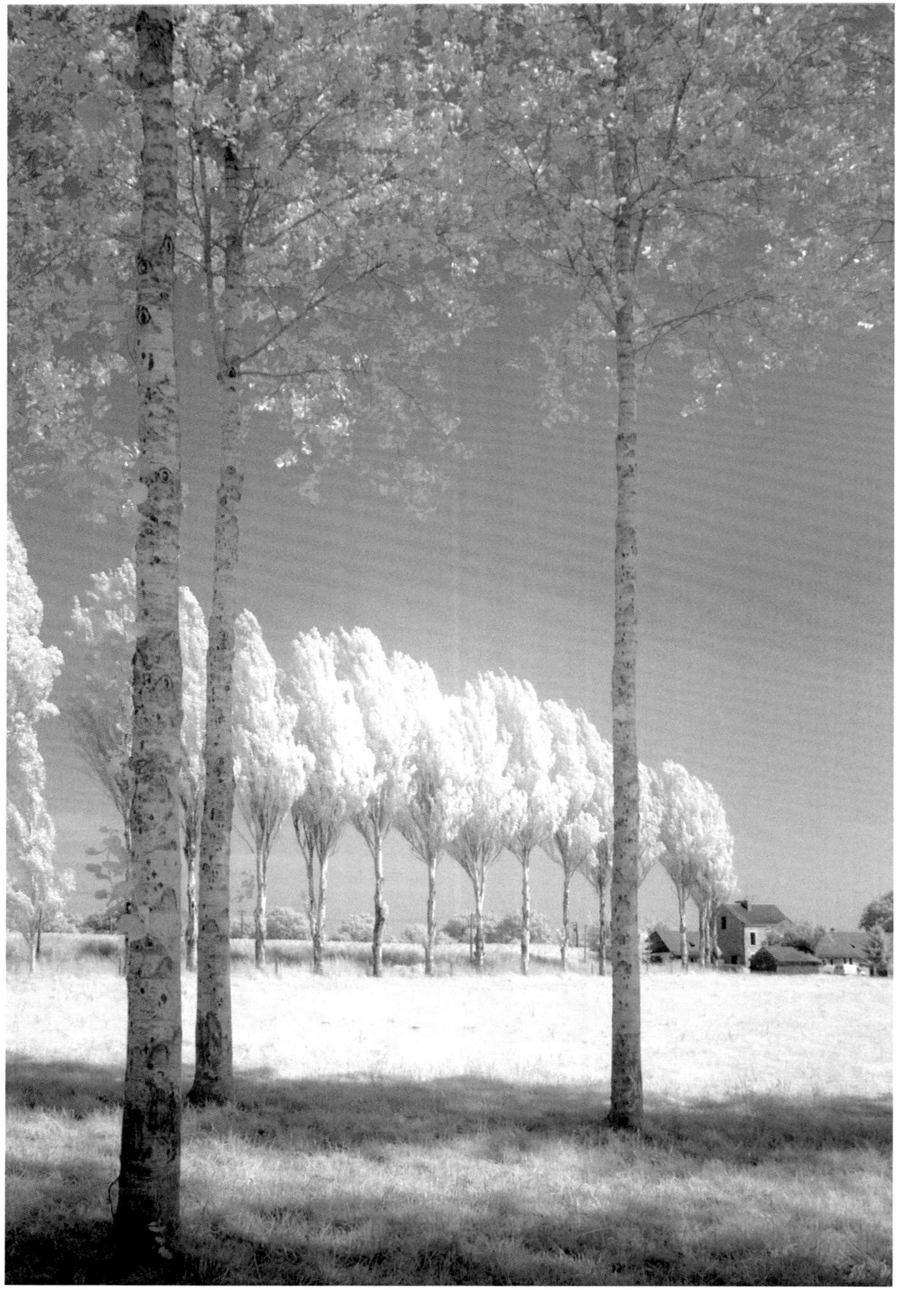

With so much emphasis placed on 'bad weather', one could easily imagine that bright sunny days have very little to offer. While colour pictures taken in these conditions might strike some as conventional and possibly boring, truly magnificent shots can be captured if you decide to shoot in infrared. There are three ways of achieving this:

1. If you are still using film, then Ilford produce a film called Ilford SFX. You will need to use a filter in order to achieve the maximum infrared effects but the results can be stunning.
2. If you are a DSLR user then you are able to shoot as normal without using any filter, but then you can use one of a variety of editing software to convert your RGB image into infrared. In Photoshop this is normally done using Channels but there are various other software options you may wish to consider such as Lightroom, Topaz or Nik Silver Efex Pro. If you want to achieve the effect in-camera, it is possible to attach a purpose-made infrared filter over the lens, although they do cut out quite a lot of light and can prove difficult to use.
3. Finally, if you are a DSLR user and wish to explore the technique of infrared photography more fully,

Figure 8 **French farmyard and a line of trees**. There is something quite ethereal about infrared that suggests an other-worldliness. Green foliage directly facing the sunlight appears white and almost iridescent then you may want to consider having your camera converted to infrared. This is, of course, quite a drastic step as it will prevent you using that camera for more conventional photography. However, as cameras have greatly improved in recent years, some enthusiasts have found themselves buying newer models and thus rendering their older cameras redundant. If so, a great way of bringing them back into use is to have them converted to infrared.

The hallmarks of an infrared image

Whether using film or a converted DSLR, the infrared camera will have an extended red sensitivity, so that the skies will appear black while green vegetation appears almost white. Infrared can also be used to capture colour but, for aesthetic purposes, most photographers prefer to present their image in black and white. The captured images are both unusual and visually stunning; they look almost like a tonal inversion with the sky appearing much darker than the land. If you decide to have your camera converted to IR you can opt for various levels of sensitivity depending on the style of photography you wish to pursue but, irrespective of the camera's sensitivity, all will work particularly well when the sun is shining and the results can appear especially graphic. If you consider photographing landscape on a sunny day boring, then shoot in IR and think again!

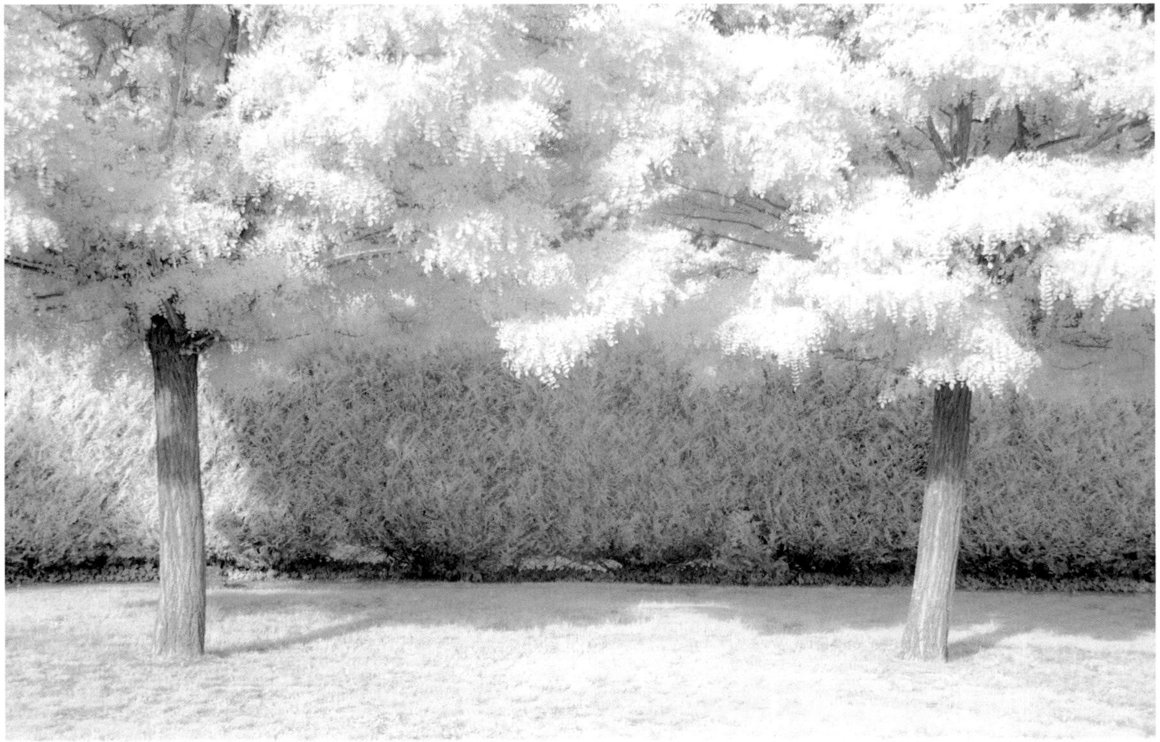

Figure 9 Two glowing trees. Photographed at the bottom of the garden, very familiar locations can appear strangely different when captured in IR. For best results, the subject should be directly or at least partially illuminated by direct sunshine.

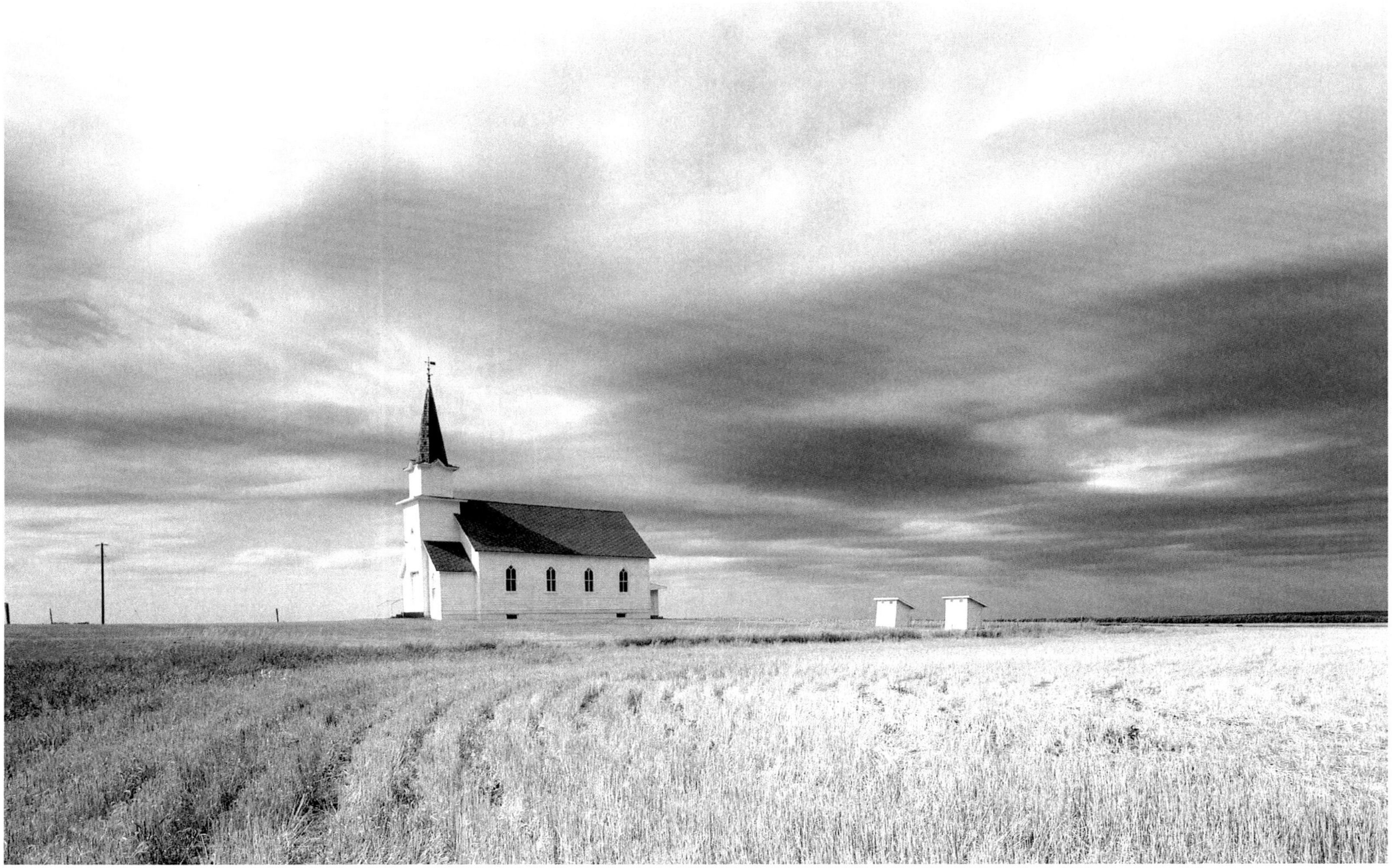

Figure 10 **Chapel on the prairie**. This was taken with a traditional camera using film. It is still possible to buy infrared film, although you may need to source it by shopping online.

USING YOUR SMART PHONE AS A CAMERA

When preparing a book of this nature it is easy to assume that everyone is using an expensive DSLR or film camera but, of course, the vast majority of images are taken using smart phones. With the ever-increasing resolution these devices offer this is hardly surprising.

While I am not arguing that we all ditch our cameras in favour of smart phones, it should be noted that, while we rarely take our camera to work or when we go shopping, most of us take our phones. I make this point because, so often, really great opportunities for taking interesting weather shots occur when we least expect them. For example, you are driving down the motorway and suddenly you notice 'the mother of all rainbows'. Without a camera it becomes another missed opportunity but, providing you have remembered your smart phone, all is not lost. If you are able to come off at the next intersection and park safely you can use your phone to capture the rainbow. Even if you are a serious photographer it is the capacity to be spontaneous that makes this worth considering. After all, it is far better to get something than nothing at all.

It is this sense of spontaneity that makes this technology so exciting. As you are walking to the office you might be enchanted by groups of children throwing snowballs. Perhaps on another day it is blowing a gale and raining at the same time. Nothing captures that scene more eloquently than a picture of people battling the gales with their umbrellas. In these situations people can become quite wary when seeing someone using a 'professional' camera but, somehow, we are much more tolerant of someone using a smart phone.

What are the advantages of using a smart phone?

More than you might possibly imagine:

1. Because of the relatively small size of the sensors, smart phones are excellent for taking close-up work. The sense of weather can often be communicated by examining small details such as icicles or, possibly, a small cluster of leaves shrouded in hoar frost.
2. Smart phones are small and very easy to manoeuvre; most now have large screens allowing you to compose your picture from an awkward position. For example, it may be raining and you cannot find shelter but, by stretching your arm backwards, you are able to locate a small spot that is sheltered. Doing this with a conventional camera would be much more challenging.
3. No doubt mindful of how many people now use smart phones as their only camera, there is an interesting range of camera apps you can get, offering things like improved stability control, a range of filter options and the ability to manually focus.
4. A measure of just how seriously this photographic evolution is being taken is that it is now possible to use third-party lenses in order to extend the smart phone's flexibility. Moreover, the smart phone I use features an 8-megapixel sensor, which reasonably compares with the first DSLR I bought just a few years ago. Downloading your images is also relatively straightforward, allowing you to further edit your images as if they had been taken on a conventional camera.

5. The real value of using a smart phone is that it positively encourages spontaneity. We rarely go out to photograph weather specifically; it springs upon us out of the blue. Being able to use a camera that most of us habitually carry ensures that we never miss any potentially interesting weather shots.

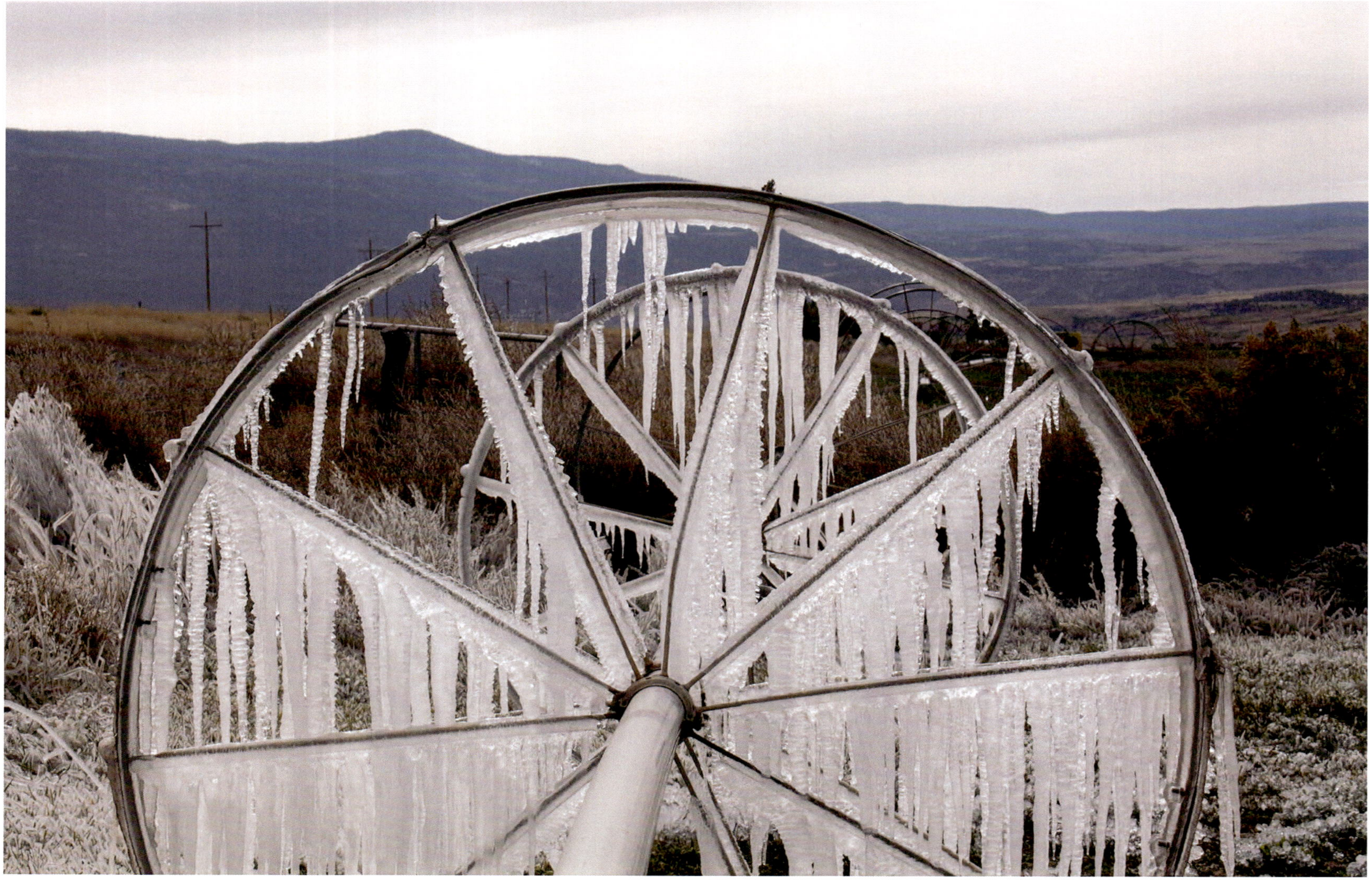

Figure 11 **Frozen irrigation wheel**. I spotted this irrigation wheel that had frozen solid overnight, even though the temperature was well above freezing the following morning. As I did, a cop-car arrived. Assuming I had parked irresponsibly and was about to receive a ticket, I was relieved to see the policeman lifting out his iPhone, and taking the same shot. Having our phones to hand served us both well.

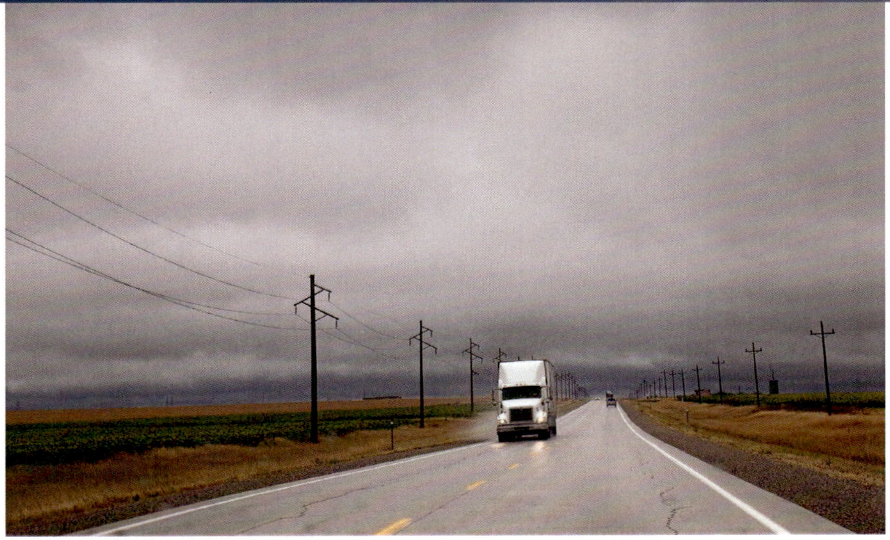

Figure 12 White truck on the highway. When travelling as a passenger in a moving vehicle you are able to enjoy a unique viewpoint, particularly when it is raining. Sharing the road with other vehicles with their headlights turned on and generating spray, the sense of weather could not be more apparent.

At first glance this may seem like an invitation to commit suicide, so let me immediately clarify my thoughts. No one should ever contemplate taking photographs from a moving car while driving. There are, however, two other possibilities. First, taking a photograph of weather from your car while it is stationary (and of course that carries with it a list of caveats). Second, taking a photograph when you are a passenger in a moving car. Let's consider the first of those options.

Photographing weather from a stationary vehicle

This might appear a bit of a 'cop-out', but there will be occasions when perhaps you are not suitably dressed and this might be a disincentive to get out of your vehicle. As you have a good view from your parked vehicle, why not take a photo from inside? If you are using a telephoto lens, it is surprising what can be achieved; wind the window down and give it your best shot. The underlining principle should always be that it is far better to get the shot than to get nothing at all. Safety must of course remain the ultimate consideration, so it is essential that you take care to park responsibly. No picture is worth a potential accident.

Figure 13 An approaching mobile home. Photographed through a windscreen covered with raindrops, this image reveals countless out-of-focus highlights creating a bokeh effect. While some 'purist' landscape photographers might view this as a nuisance, such aberrations positively enhance the feeling of weather.

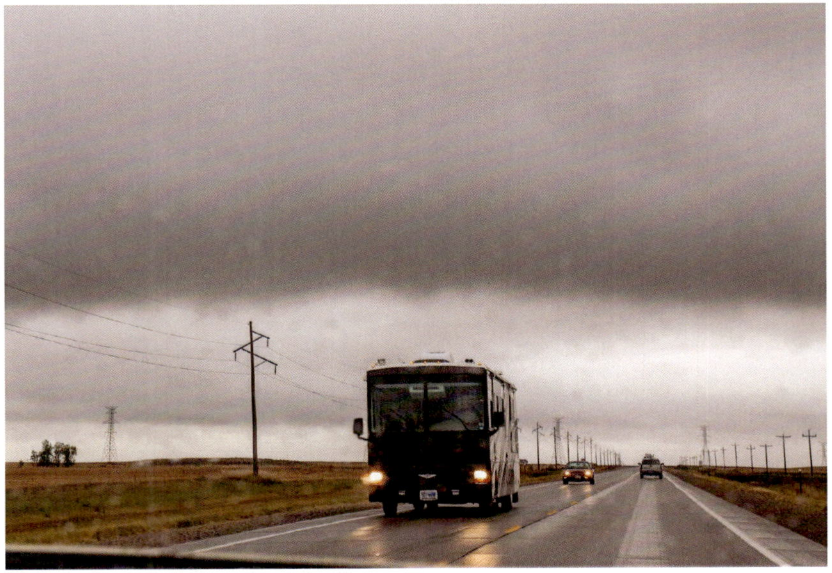

Shooting from a moving vehicle

It is pointless being overly romantic – 'landscape' is what we see as soon as we step outside, and this includes on the open road. Just think how often you have seen remarkable weather while travelling in a vehicle and, if you are a passenger, you are free to exploit this. As a passenger you have a privileged view of the landscape and you are able to see it from the middle of a road, which does offer a fresh perspective. It is pouring with rain or, possibly, you are experiencing a blizzard and the windscreen wipers are working furiously, then your viewpoint becomes even more special, so be prepared to take the opportunity presented.

Some landscape workers are only prepared to photograph using a tripod under benign lighting conditions, but they are missing out. Whether you decide to include the moving windscreen wipers is a matter of personal taste. You will be shooting through a rain-splattered windscreen but the bokeh distortions this creates are a key part of the genre. To restrict yourself to one approach in good weather is to ignore the mood and the drama that one can capture when photographing a storm from a moving vehicle. Should you want any further encouragement, this is a technique that is often used by movie-makers to communicate the experience of travelling through bad weather.

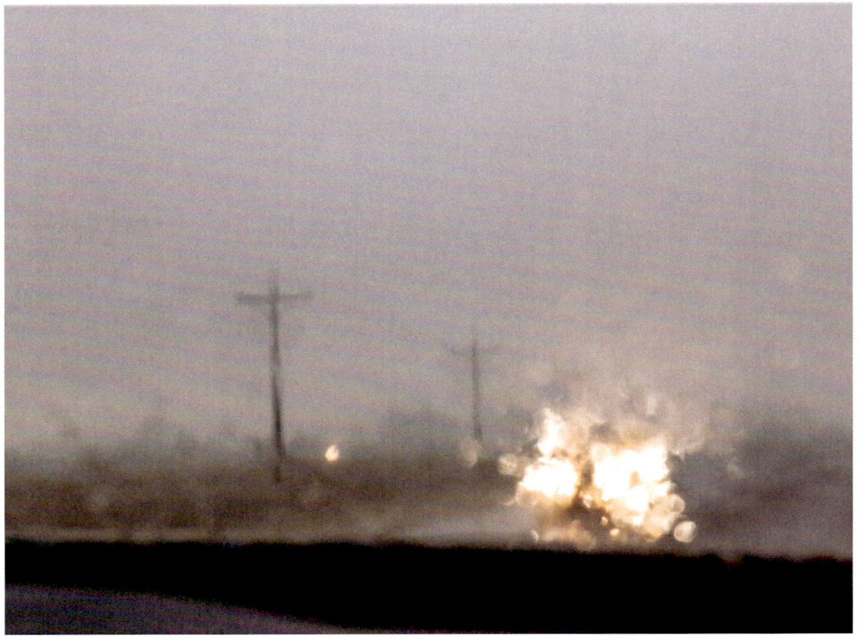

Figure 14 **Headlights**. Grainy, blurred and lacking detail, this is the kind of image one could so easily consign to the bin, and yet it conveys the very essence of travelling through a heavy storm in low light.

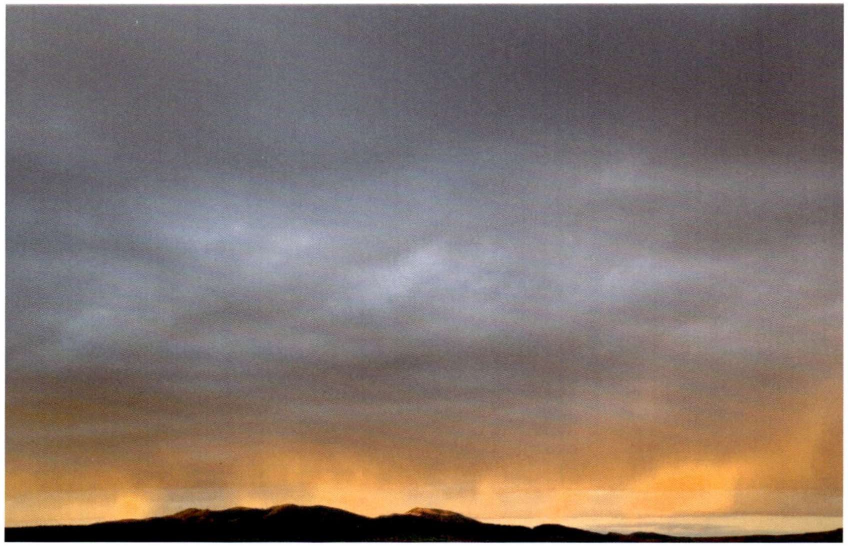

Figure 15 **Dramatic sky.** The driver was unable to stop to allow me to take a shot of this remarkable sky shortly after a storm, so I wound down the passenger window and took my photograph as the car was moving. As I was using a comparatively fast shutter speed the movement of the vehicle is not apparent.

When shooting digitally you have the choice of shooting in Jpeg or in Raw. Mindful that you are able get more images onto your memory card many users are tempted to shoot in Jpeg but, if you wish to get the best out of your weather photographs, you will be far better served shooting Raw. While I am not suggesting that you over-process your images, being able to make certain adjustments post-camera clearly makes sense. If you are shooting Raw then you are able to process all your images in ACR (Adobe Camera Raw), which offers a highly impressive range of editing tools. What some photographers do not understand is that what appears on the monitor or on the computer screen is only part of the visual information that has been captured when shooting Raw. If an area appears too light or too dark this can be very easily remedied in ACR without degrading the image. It is, of course, capable of doing a great deal more. You can access ACR in two ways:

1. By visiting Adobe's website **www.adobe.com** you are able to download the Raw Convertor for free. The Raw Convertor is not generic but camera specific, although just about all DSLRs are catered for.

2. Updated versions of ACR are available in Lightroom. This is an amazingly sophisticated and comprehensive software package and it would be impossible to cover all its features in just a few pages. However, there are two or three basic editing tools that can really make a difference to your weather shots.

Figure 16 **Start image.**

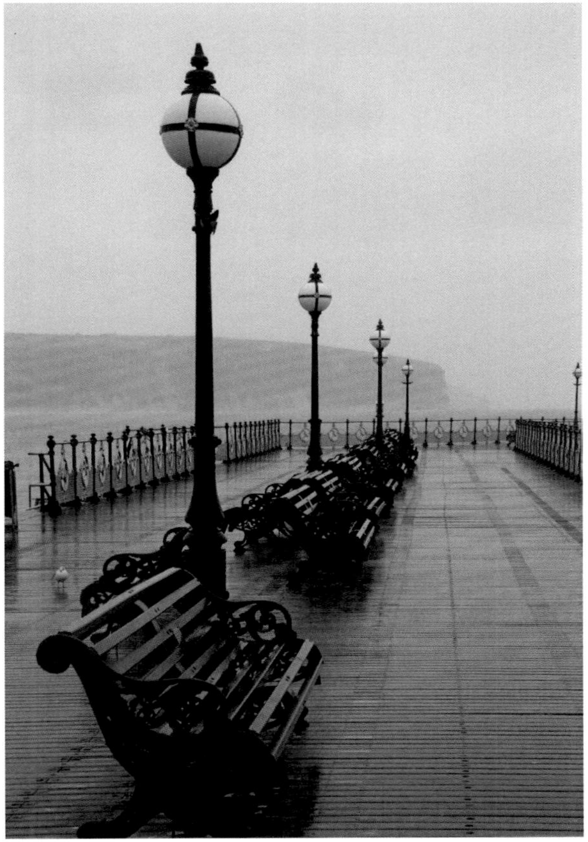

This is a typical image captured in the rain. It reveals a reasonable level of contrast except that it seems to be in the wrong places. The sky appears too light, while the foreground lacks 'sparkle'. This can be easily remedied using just a handful of tools in Lightroom. Start by transferring the image from Library to Develop.

Step 1. The sky in the Start image appears pale, while the shadows in the foreground are too dark. In this example I have reduced the highlights by dragging the Highlight slider positively to the left. I then cautiously pushed the Shadow slider to the right, which increased shadow detail. It is very easy to get carried away, so it is important to keep an eye on the histogram (at the top of the dialog) to ensure that all the tones comfortably remain within the 0–255 spectrum.

Step 2. The sky was still too light, particularly in the upper portion. By selecting the Graduated Filter tool I was able to make a smooth incremental selection. I was then able to subtly darken the selected area by pulling the Exposure slider slightly to the left. The great advantage of using the ACR facility in Lightroom is that if you do not like what you see you can return to the earlier step by selecting Previous, or even start the entire process again by selecting Reset, without degrading the image.

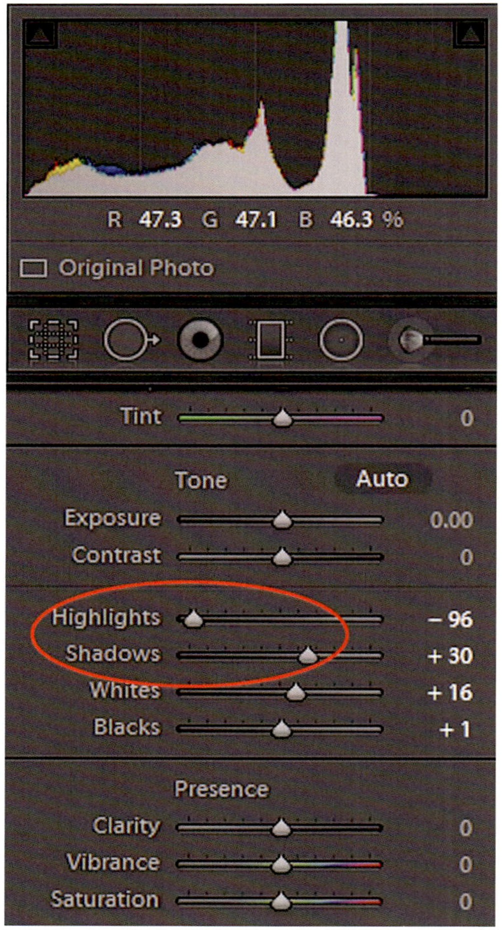

Figure 17 Step 1.

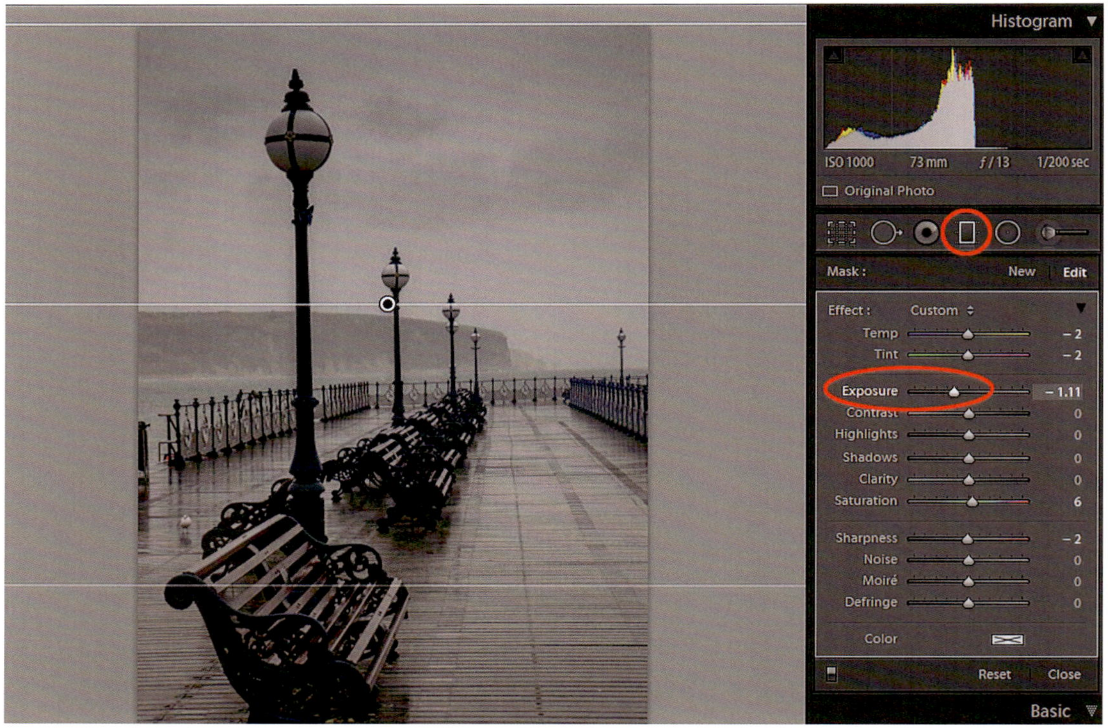

Figure 18 Step 2.

Step 3. Possibly one of the best tools available in ACR is the Clarity slider. What this does is to expand or compress the contrast within the mid-tones. In the original Raw file (see page 137) the boardwalk of the pier lacks contrast. By pushing the Clarity slider to the right, the mid-tones within this most important part of the picture have been expanded revealing its inherent textural qualities.

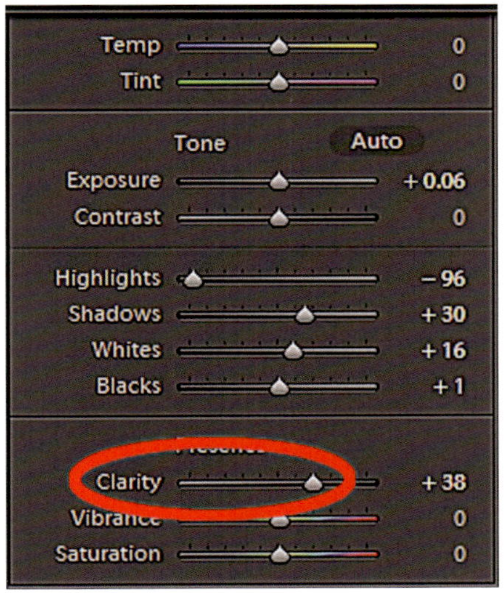

Figure 19 Step 3.

Finished image

Often qualities we saw when we took the photograph are not apparent when we view the monitor or the computer screen. By carefully adjusting selected tonal values in ACR much of the original drama that motivated you to take the photograph in the first place is revealed.

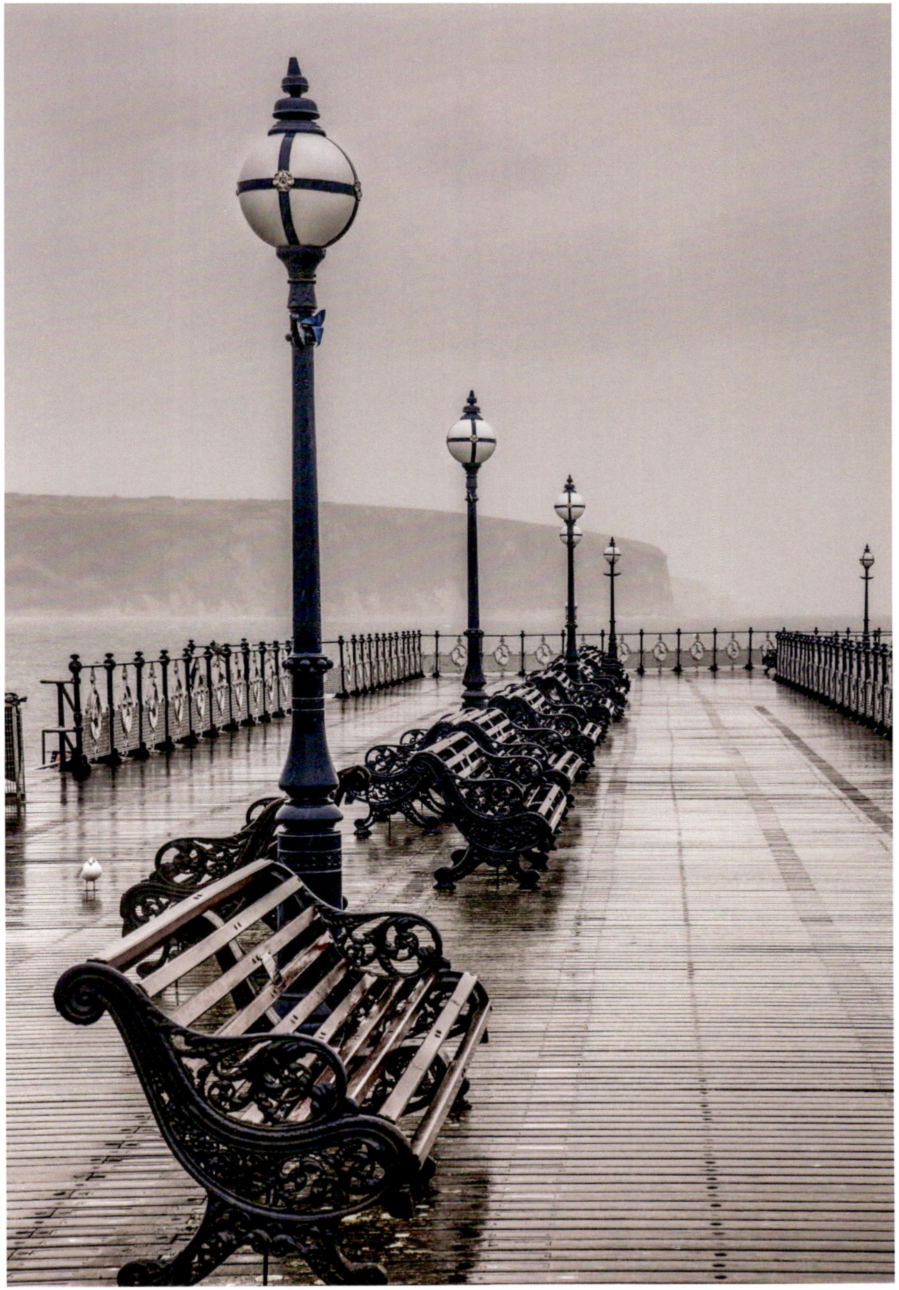

Figure 20 Finished image.

IMPROVING YOUR WEATHER SHOTS USING HDR

Excessive contrast is the bane of most landscape photography. As we have seen in the previous section, one way of overcoming the problem is to shoot Raw and then make highlight and shadow adjustments using The Shadow and Highlight sliders in The Raw Convertor. Another option is to use HDR. Why do we need this, I am sure you are asking.

The advantages of the modern DSLR camera are too numerous to itemise but, if they possess one flaw, it is the inability of so many to deal effectively with high contrast. Essentially, most sensors are ill-equipped to handle images revealing bright highlights and dark shadows at the same time. Typically, in a landscape situation for example, one can meter for the sky but, as a consequence, the foreground appears too dark. Alternatively, one can meter for the foreground instead but then risk blown-out highlights. So how do we resolve this problem? Simple, by making various exposures of the same location - typically by taking one showing an 'average' reading, another that ensures that all the highlights are fully captured and a final shot that aims to underexpose in order to reveal all available shadow detail.

If taking multiple shots proves impossible, you should be able to create three separate files by using the Exposure slider on the Raw Converter or ACR. As well as using the Default exposure, create two further files, one showing a +2.00 exposure and a second showing a -2.00 exposure. The increased latitude available within these three files should deal with most eventualities. Remember also that many DSLRs have an Exposure Compensation, bracketing mode or AEB setting that can be programmed to give you three separate exposures. This can prove particularly useful when shooting dramatically-lit weather landscapes.

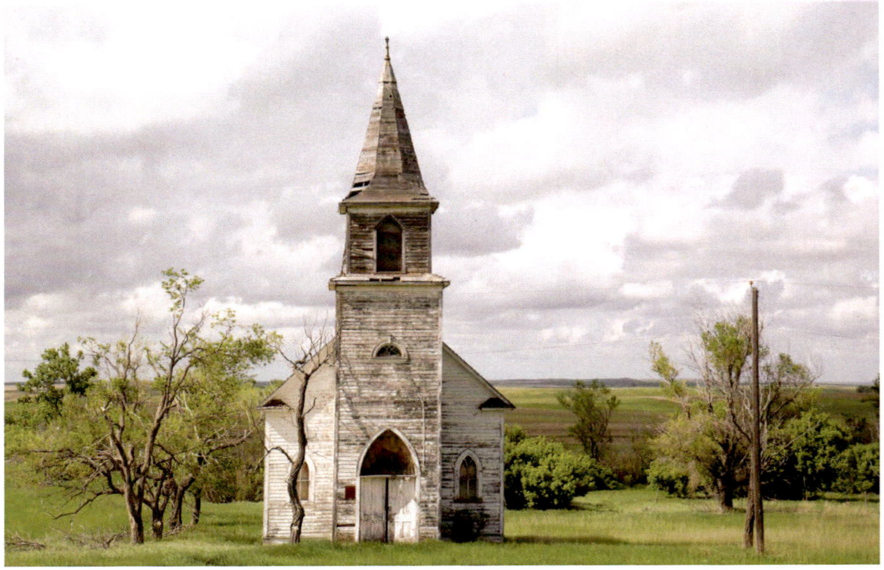

Figure 21 **Start image 1a**. Often some of our most disappointing images are taken on an overcast day. The contrast between the sky and the foreground is too great for the sensor to cope with.

Creating a HDR file using Photomatix Pro

There are various free HDR plug-ins one can access that offer excellent alternatives to Photoshop, including Picturenaut (**www.hdrlabs.com**) and FDR Tools Basic (**www.fdrtools.com**) but, within the scope of HDR manipulation, Photomatix is considered the industry standard. Its basic version can also be downloaded for free by going to **www.hdrsoft.com**. However, if you wish to be a little more ambitious with your HDR work, I would strongly suggest that you consider accessing the Photomatix Pro package. This really is a sophisticated piece of software and positively encourages creativity.

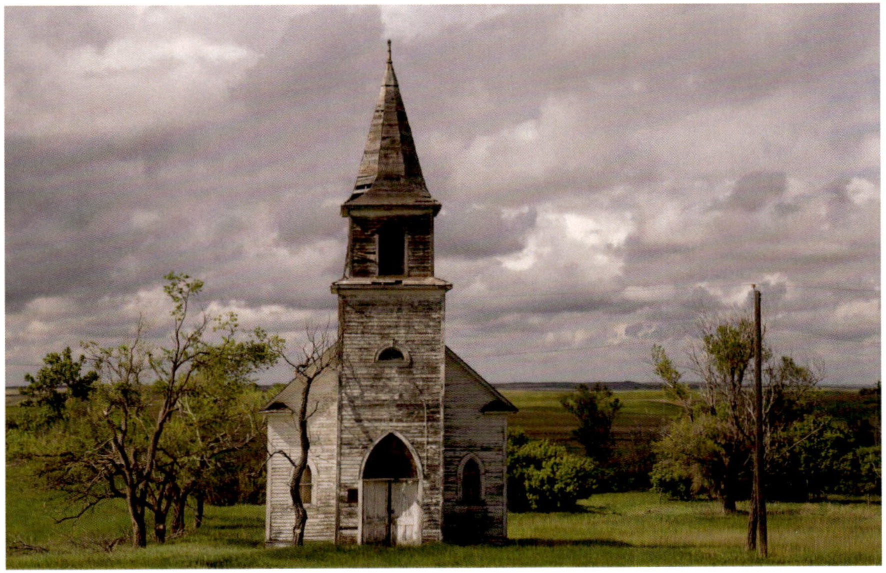

Figure 22 **Start image 1b**. By exposing for the sky all the required highlight information has been captured but this, of course, has been achieved at the expense of the foreground.

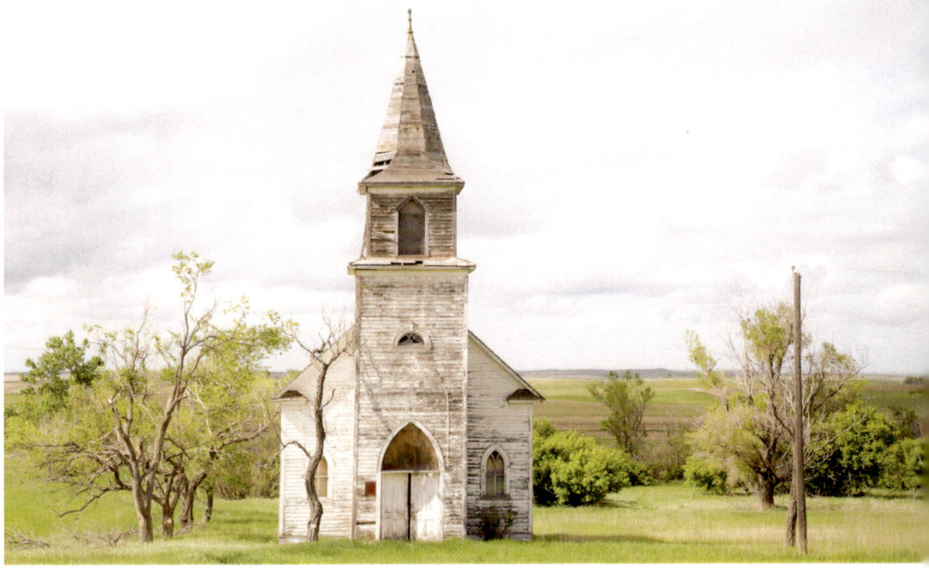

Figure 23 **Start image 1c**. This file is something of a compromise and, while there is visible detail in both the shadow and highlight areas, in parts it is very weak.

The role of Photomatix Pro is to extract the best tonal profile from each of these files and composite them into one final 'super' file.

Tone mapping

1. In Photomatix Pro, select 'Load Bracketed Photo' or 'Generate HDR image' (this depends on the version of Photomatix you are using), go to 'Browse' and then open the files you wish to use. Ideally these should be Raw files. In this example I have selected just three, but I could have used more should I have needed to.
2. By selecting OK the 'Preprocessing Options' or 'Generate HDR – Options' dialog will appear;

they are largely the same and, once again, it is a matter of which version of Photomatix Pro you are using. Make sure that the 'Align source images' box is ticked. You should also select 'by correcting horizontal and vertical shifts' or 'by matching features'. Generally I find the latter the best option. Tick 'Reduce Chromatic Aberrations' then hit OK.

3. You will then open an extremely complicated dialog offering you a bewildering array of options. Ironically possibly the most useful of these is hidden behind 'Show More Options'. Open this and you should see the White Point slider, which allows you to set the lightest part of the picture, the Dark Point slider, which lets you determine the darkest part, and the very important Gamma slider, which allows you to determine the overall tonal mood of the image. These decisions can be made for you automatically but I really would recommend that you do not derogate these choices - they are key to the overall character of the image. The pre-sets at the bottom of the dialog are particularly interesting and easier to operate than in Photoshop. In this example I have chosen to use 'Painterly' but, if you really want to go for that 'in your face' look, why not opt for 'Grunge'? It is important that you select the right process for the image in hand. A very useful facility is the pre-set thumbnails at the bottom of the dialog that offer you an overview of the available options. Moreover, if you find the effect of any one of them a tad overwhelming, reduce it by using the Strength slider that is found at the top of the dialog. Photomatix Pro really does allow you to micro-manage every aspect of the image's tonal range, actively encouraging you to develop your own personal style. Final options you may wish to consider can be found under 'Show Advanced Options'. Making adjustments using the Saturation Highlights and Saturation Shadows sliders can certainly introduce an interesting edginess to the image. When you are finally happy with what you see, select Process.

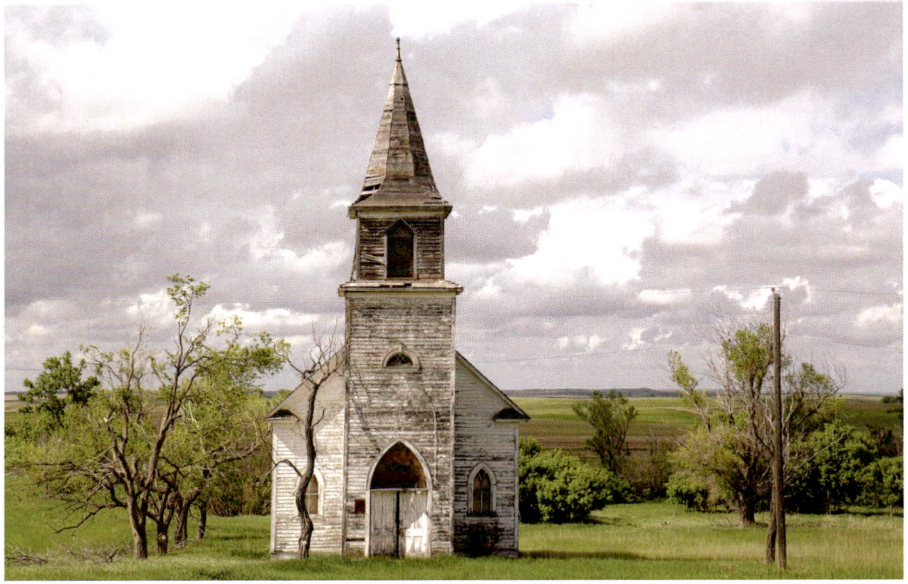

Figure 24 **The completed image**. Photomatix Pro not only helps you to overcome the exposure shortcomings of using a DSLR camera, but it is also a positive means of achieving a personal style. In this example, I have chosen to dramatise the sky in order to heighten the sense of pathos this abandoned scene suggests.

The ethos of this book is to encourage you to celebrate and capture the subtle nuances of weather but, just occasionally, we could do with a little help from Photoshop.

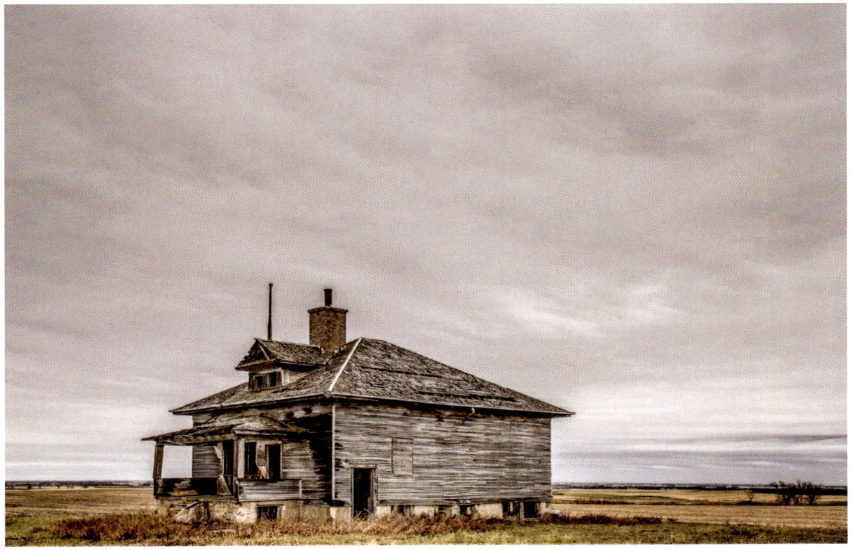

Figure 25 **Start image**. This is a photograph I took as I was driving out of Minnesota, heading west towards the North Dakota border. It was raining at the time, but capturing its effects wasn't easy. Start with a background that is dark or that can reasonably be darkened in the processing stage.

Step 1. Open the file then open the Layers Dialog and create a New Layer. Name this New Layer 'Rain'.

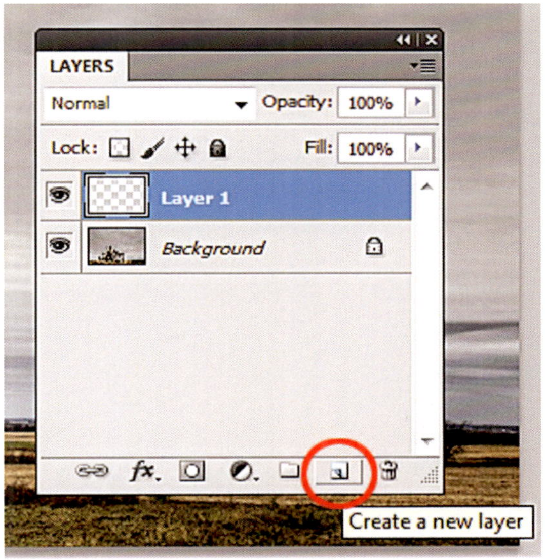

Figure 26
Step 1.

Step 2. Fill this new layer with black. Go to Edit > Fill > Black and then select OK. Your image will be temporarily hidden by the 'Rain' layer.

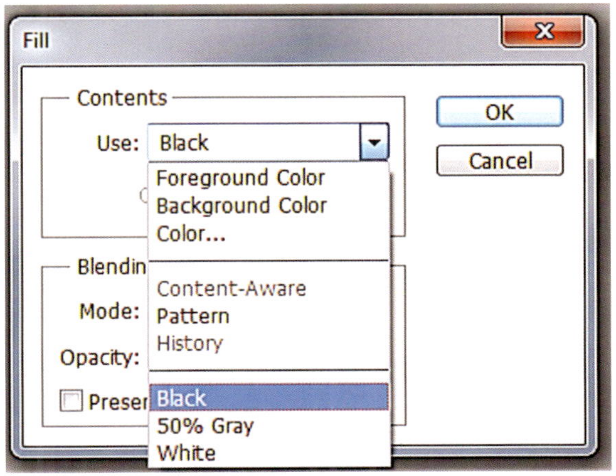

Figure 27
Step 2.

Step 3. In order to introduce the effect of rain, and with the 'Rain' Layer still active, go to Filter > Noise > Add Noise.

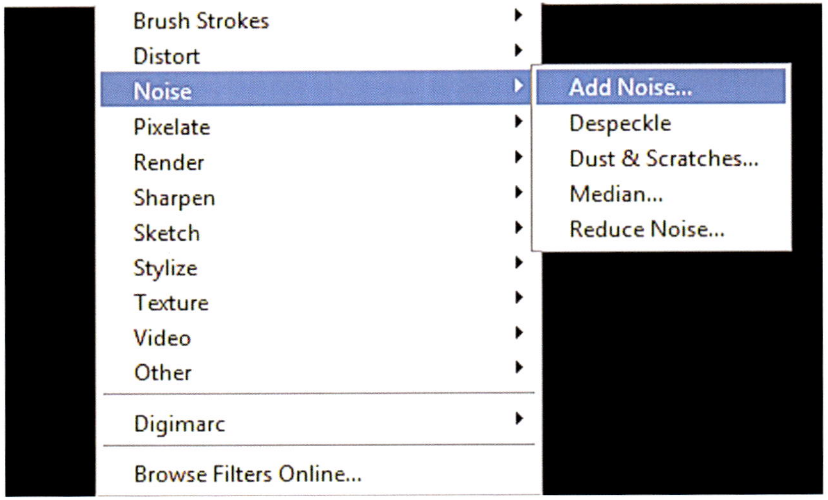

Figure 28 Step 3.

Step 4. In the Add Noise Dialog set the Amount to 25%, in the Distribution box select Gaussian and then click Monochromatic at the bottom of the dialog. Hit OK, and this will introduce the beginnings of our simulated rain.

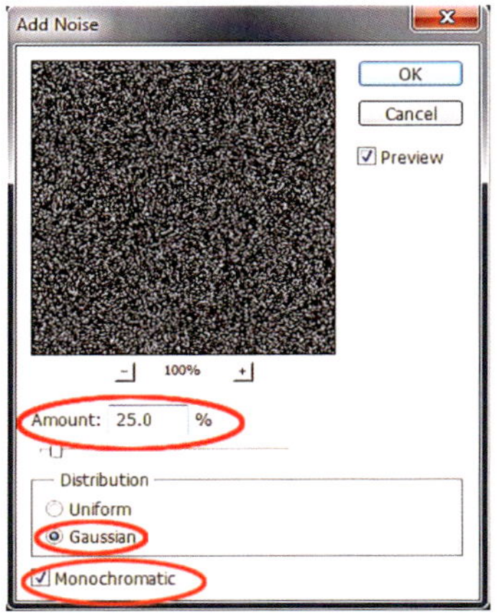

Figure 29 Step 4.

Step 5. At this stage the white dots that are to become the droplets of rain appear too small. To increase their size go to Edit > Transform > Scale. With this selected, click on the Link Icon that is between the Width (W) and the Height (H) option in the Options Bar at the top of the screen. Change the value of the Width to 400%. This will, of course, increase the Height as well, resulting in much larger grains to play with. Click the Checkmark in the Options Bar in order to accept the scaling.

Figure 30 Step 5.

Step 6. It's time we were able to see the image beneath the Rain Layer. To achieve this, select Screen from the Blend Mode. Your image will appear with a layer of white dots over it.

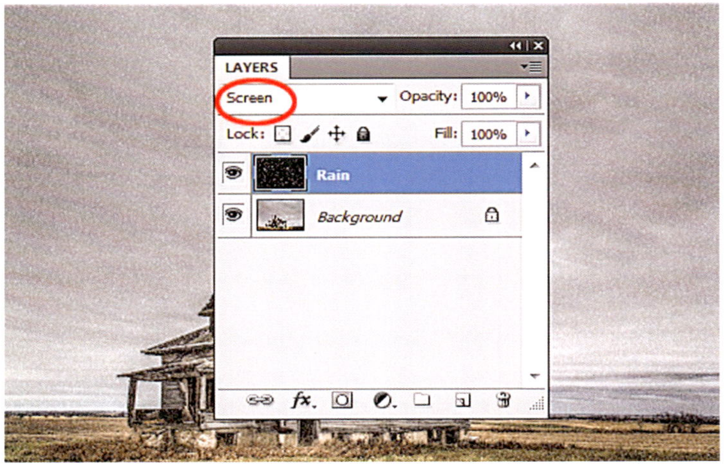

Figure 31 Step 6.

Step 7. As you might wish to adjust the rain effect, it would help to change the 'Rain' Layer to a Smart Object. To do this, with the Rain Layer still active, click the small Menu Icon in the top left of the Layers Dialog and then select Convert to Smart Object from the drop-down menu.

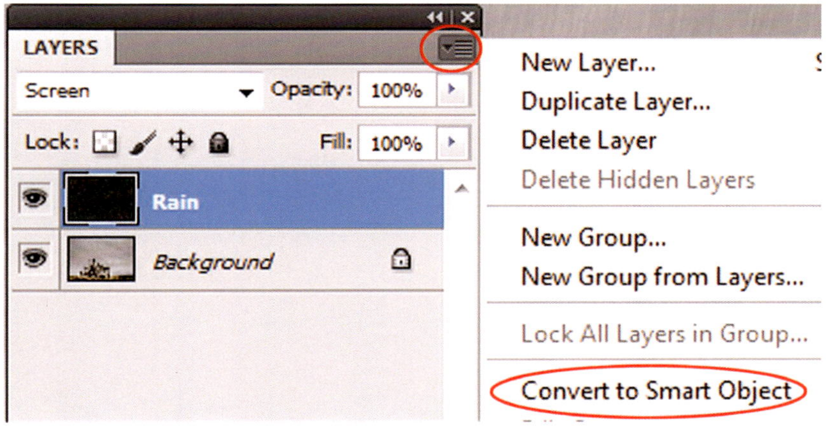

Figure 32 Step 7.

Step 8. With the 'Rain' Layer converted to a Smart Object, you can now transform the white dots into something resembling rain. To do this go to Filter > Blur > Motion Blur, then the Motion Blur dialog will appear. You have two controls -the first of these is Angle. Rain rarely falls directly downwards; more often it is angled. By adjusting this dial you can select the angle of the falling rain. The second control is Distance. This effectively elongates the white dots so that they appear as streaks. Because you have converted the 'Rain' Layer to a Smart Object, you are able to experiment to see what best suits.

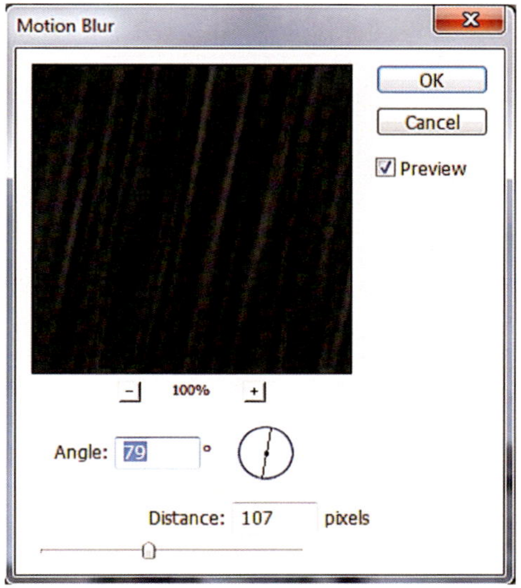

Figure 33 Step 8.

Step 9. You may well find that once you have introduced the rain effects, it appears too light. As the Rain layer and the Background layer are two independent layers you can continue to make independent tonal or contrast adjustments to each until you achieve the result you are after.

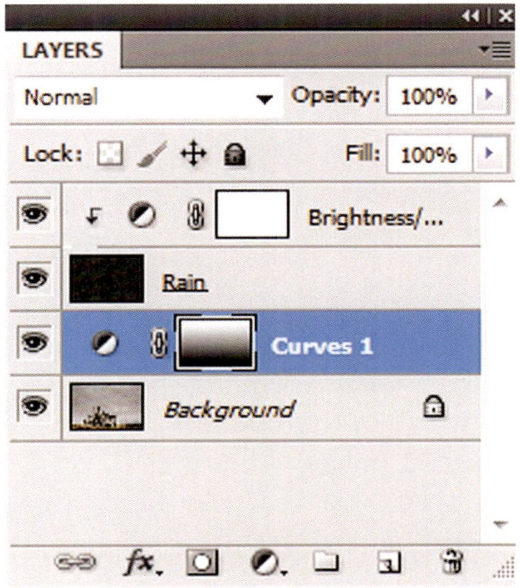

Figure 34 Step 9.

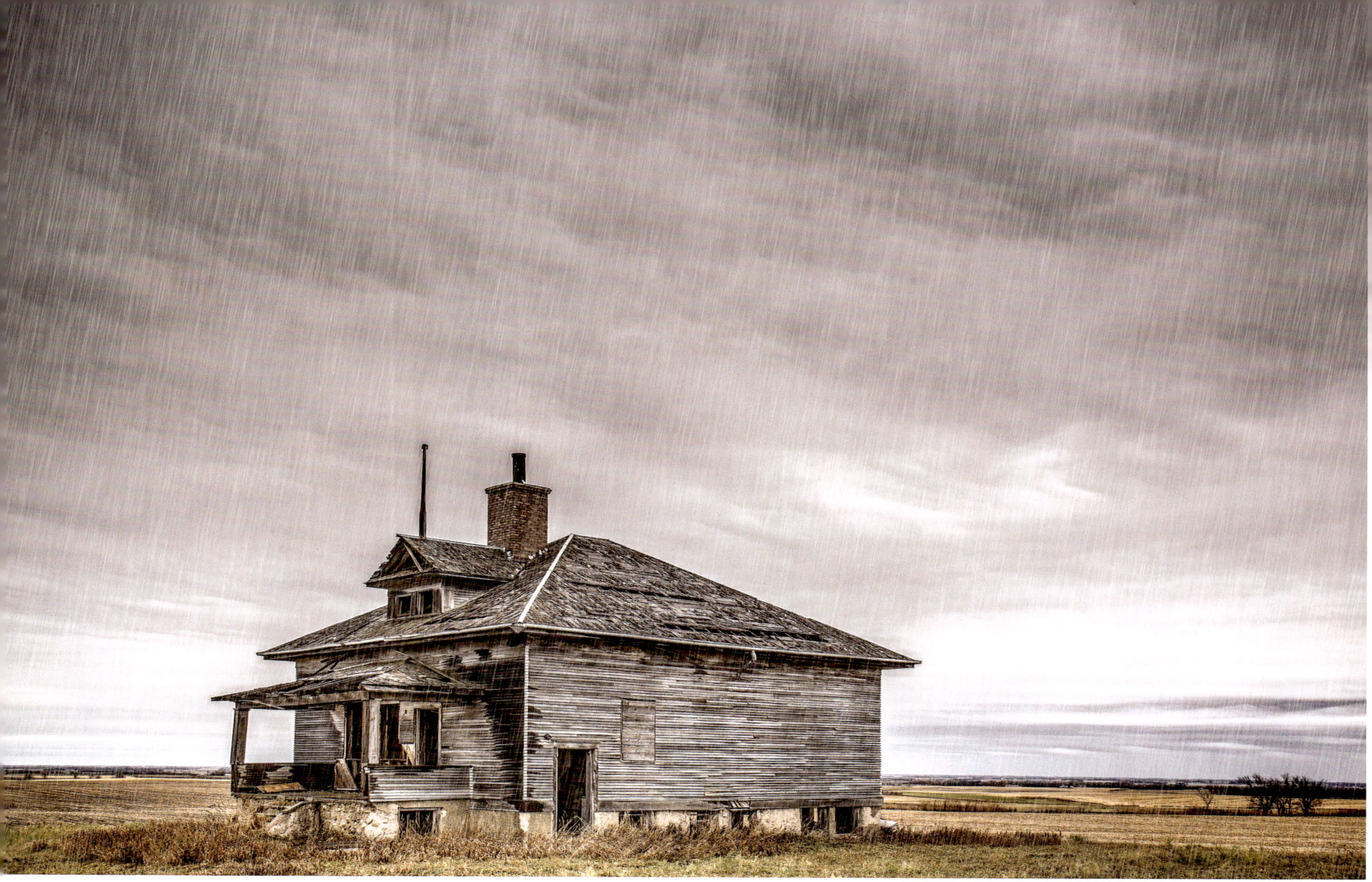

Figure 35 **Finished image**. While this is a practice I would not condone in all circumstances, occasionally a little bit of help from Photoshop can prove useful.

SHOW HOW THE SAME LOCATION DIFFERS DEPENDING ON THE PREVAILING WEATHER CONDITIONS

If the subject of our photography is weather, the location is largely irrelevant. In my introduction I referred to the great American Photographer Joel Meyerowitz who, in his much celebrated publication *Bay/Sky*, was content to photograph the same offshore horizon, dispassionately recording the subtle nuances of the ever-changing weather, not just day by day but also hour by hour. Just give it a moment's thought; a photograph taken at a specific location will never be quite the same due to the ever-changing vagaries of the weather. When you are photographing landscape, no matter how you try, it is an image that cannot be repeated.

This is, of course, a good argument for discouraging plagiarism. When viewing somebody else's work in magazines or on websites it is easy to become seduced and aim to do something similar. Often, when travelling to 'honey-pot' locations, photographers are disappointed because it is not what they had expected. I am not trying to discourage you from visiting well-known locations but, if you do, be prepared to photograph it with an open mind. The weather and lighting will be different but, of course, that works in your favour because you are then able to photograph the subject with fresh eyes.

A wonderful way to get to understand this is to follow Joel Meyerowitz's example. Identify a location you are comfortable with and take a sequence of photographs that reveal the ever-changing weather.

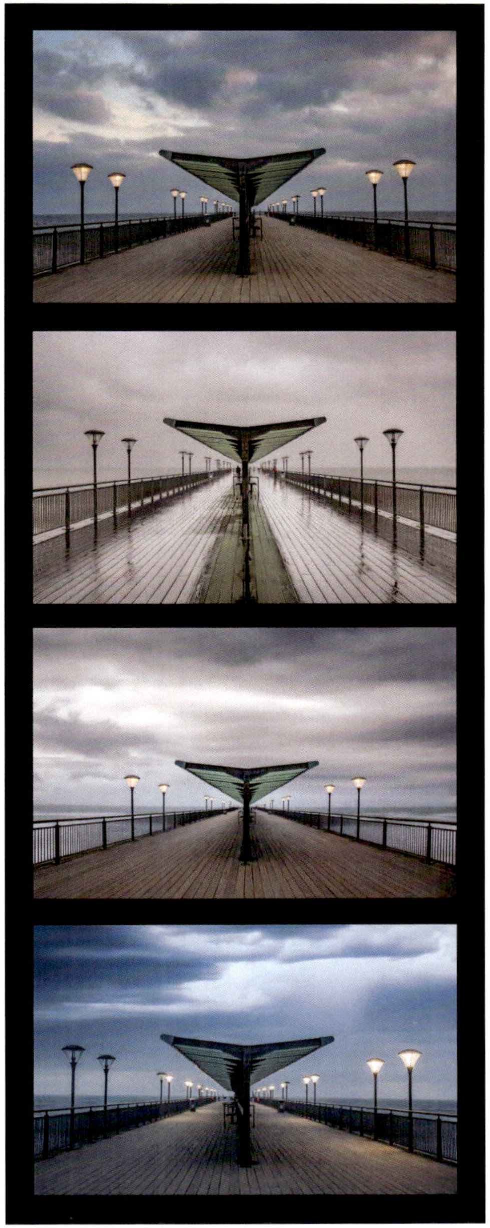

Figure 36 **Boscombe Pier**. This sequence of four shots was taken over a week, each photographed before dusk, just as the pier was scheduled to close. I chose that time because there would be fewer people around. When embarking on this task it was important to keep the composition as consistent as possible so that the viewer is less concerned with the structure of each image and more aware of the varying weather conditions. I chose this location mainly because it was relatively close to my home and because it gave me plenty of scope to capture the ever-changing weather.

Deciding on a location

1. It should be one that is conveniently close to where you live or where you are staying. There is little point in choosing a location that requires a two-hour journey. The essence of this exercise is spontaneity.
2. Once again, following Meyerowitz's example, your choice of location should be simple. The sky tends to be the mirror of the prevailing weather so choose a location that offers plenty of it. I would even suggest that if the foreground is too interesting it can deflect attention from that element you particularly wish to highlight, namely the weather.
3. How regularly should you take your shots? Clearly this will be governed by the time you have available. You might, for example, have identified an interesting location on your journey to work, so you may decide to take a shot on a weekly basis over a period of time. If you are on holiday you could decide to photograph a location on a daily basis. If a specific day is sufficiently interesting you could even accumulate an illuminating variety of photographs all taken within the space of an hour. You could decide to adopt a different method and visit your elected location only when specific weather conditions materialise, i.e. only travel if you anticipate wind, rain, snow or whatever.

Reviewing and editing your work

This is where you will truly begin to understand how weather influences landscape. Even if you decide to do nothing with the images, what you learn from the exercise will prove invaluable. It certainly helps to set the images side by side and identify the subtle difference the changing weather brings. When editing you should also consider the time of day that the photograph was taken. What might prove most illuminating is that you do not necessarily need to capture a defined weather pattern for a photograph to be interesting; it doesn't need to be iconic or dramatic. The weather could be benign but overcast yet still convey mood.

Think about presentation

Whether you decide to present your photographs as individual images or to group them together to form a composite is a matter of personal choice. If you are working in Photoshop or Lightroom you have the opportunity to group files together into a single image, which can be particularly revealing. I would even argue that this is the only way to present such images as it encourages you to make subtle comparisons and allows you to appreciate the uniqueness of each hour and each day.

Finally, if you are wondering what the point is of photographing a subject in quite such a systematic fashion, there are precedents. I have already referred to Joel Meyerowitz but a similar, although not identical, project was undertaken by a Chilean-born photographer, Camilo Jose Vergara, who decided to document the changing inner city streets of 16 American cities. The project has taken decades but, amazingly, he has been able to record quite noticeable changes. I make this point not only as a statement of encouragement, but also to show that this is a working practice that has been used by other photographers.

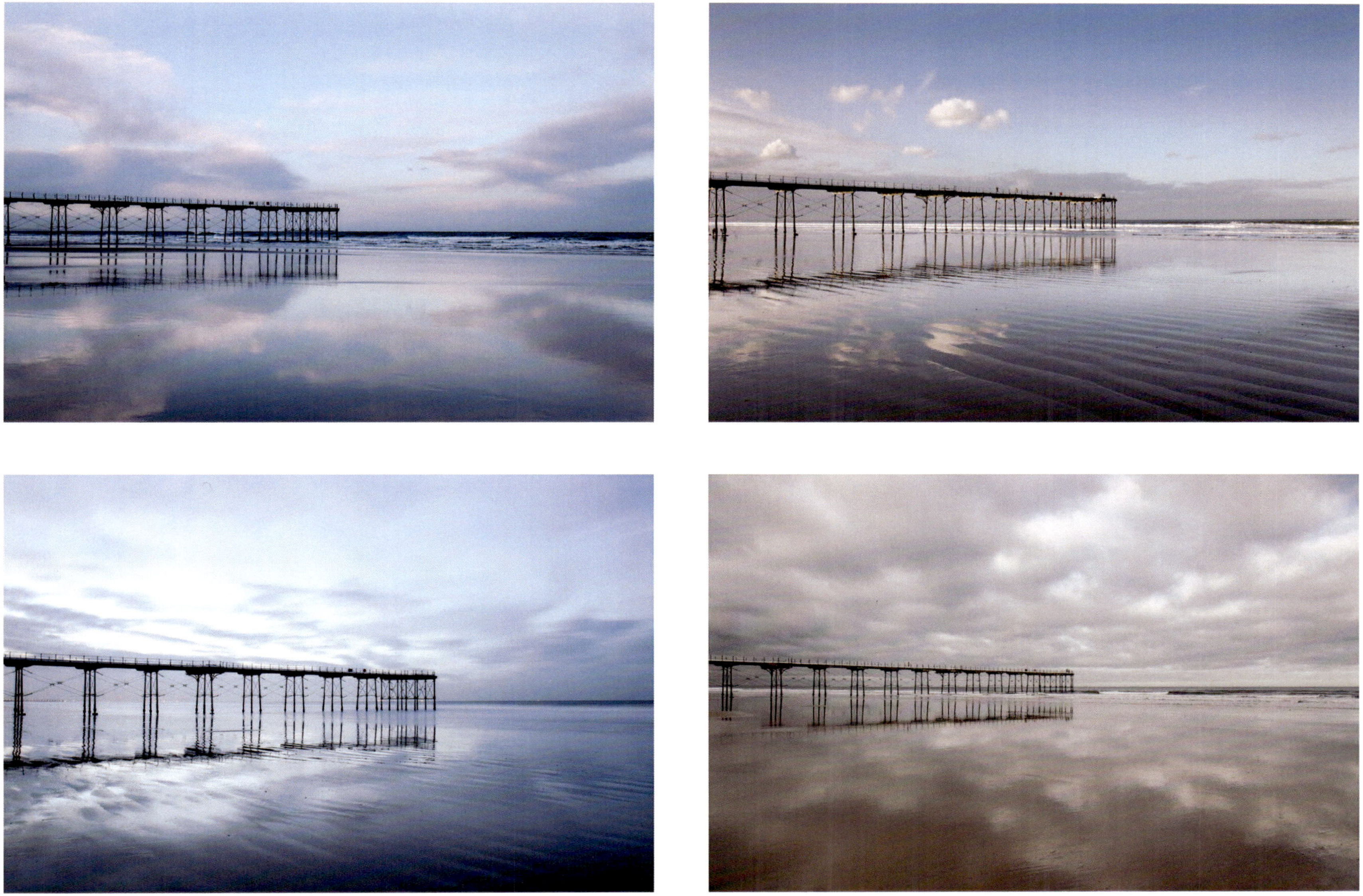

Figure 37 **Saltburn Beach**. These images were taken over several days. It was important that I captured the receding tide at precisely the same point within the cycle. While all the shots reveal broken cloud and the same compositional structure, the character of each image is different reflecting the subtle difference each day brings. Grouping your images in this way gives you a better appreciation of what these differences are.

IS THERE A MARKET FOR YOUR WEATHER PICTURES?

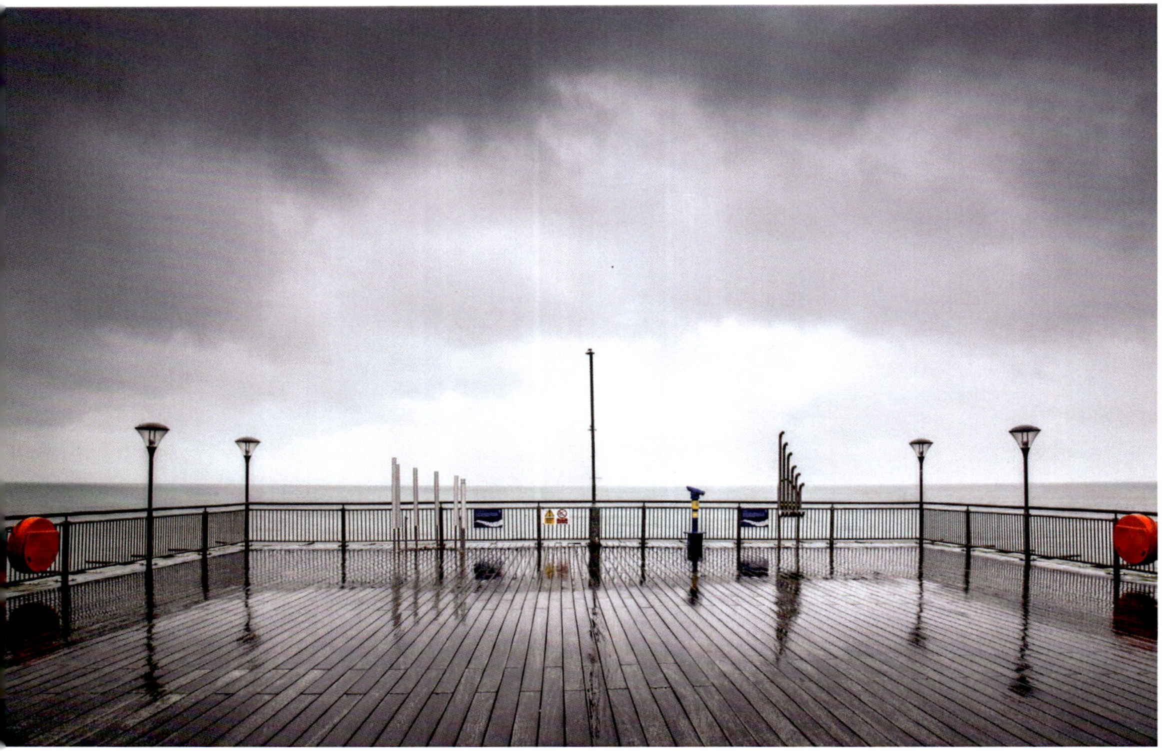

Figure 38 **End of pier in rain**. Shot in the middle of summer, the talking point in both the local and national media was how poor the weather was. Normally one would have expected to see crowds of holiday makers but the rain has discouraged them. Images such as this are both newsworthy and contemporary. To make best of it, it should be sent within hours of being taken.

The answer of course is 'yes'! It is commonly assumed that only 'professional' photographers are able to sell work, but nothing could be further from the truth. Many enthusiastic amateur photographers regularly sell their work, even though photography is not their only source of income. Weather pictures in particular sell very well because we are obsessed with it. Moreover, people are fascinated by the visual changes that weather can bring, so the market for weather images is strong irrespective of the source from which they come.

When photographing weather be imaginative. After taking a series of photographs of large waves crashing into a coastal breakwater it is easy to convince yourself that nobody else is interested, but anyone not living near the coast would find such shots fascinating. On a similar tack, if you personally are not experiencing snow then, of course, images of areas that are will be of interest to you. If you are unfortunate enough to encounter flooding take all the shots you can because they will be newsworthy. There may be other photographers taking similar shots to you but they may not have the presence of mind to market them.

Where are my outlets?

The local media

The most obvious outlet is your local newspaper and the regional TV station. The local newspaper, whether it is a daily or a weekly publication, will have a very limited number of photographers working for them and, of course, they will be limited as to the photographs they can take. As a consequence, newspapers positively invite readers to submit work, so why don't you? Unfortunately local newspapers rarely pay photographers but it might be your first experience of getting your work published. Local television stations are also unlikely to pay you for your weather shot (unless it is truly spectacular) but, once again, it does no harm to have your images shared with a million other viewers. The early morning or evening weather forecast regularly showcases the work of a local photographer. The key of course is that it needs to be contemporary; there is little point in sending them an image that was taken several days ago.

The national media

As you get more experienced, why not submit your work to a national newspaper? They are just as interested in weather as your local newspaper and, if your image is sufficiently interesting, they will pay, sometimes very generously.

Stock agencies

There are numerous stock agencies (or image banks) that accept submissions from both professionals and amateurs. As you might expect, they all require a certain standard of photography, but it will offer you the opportunity to earn money from your much-prized images. While each agency will have their own specific requirements, they generally operate in the same way. When visiting their websites you will be invited to submit work. Very often they will stipulate a specific number of samples that will be checked for quality. If they like what they see you will be invited to submit more. As your images will be sold to highly demanding clients there can be no room for sloppy craftsmanship. Each agency might be responsible for marketing up to a million images so, in order to ensure your image gets noticed, it is important that you

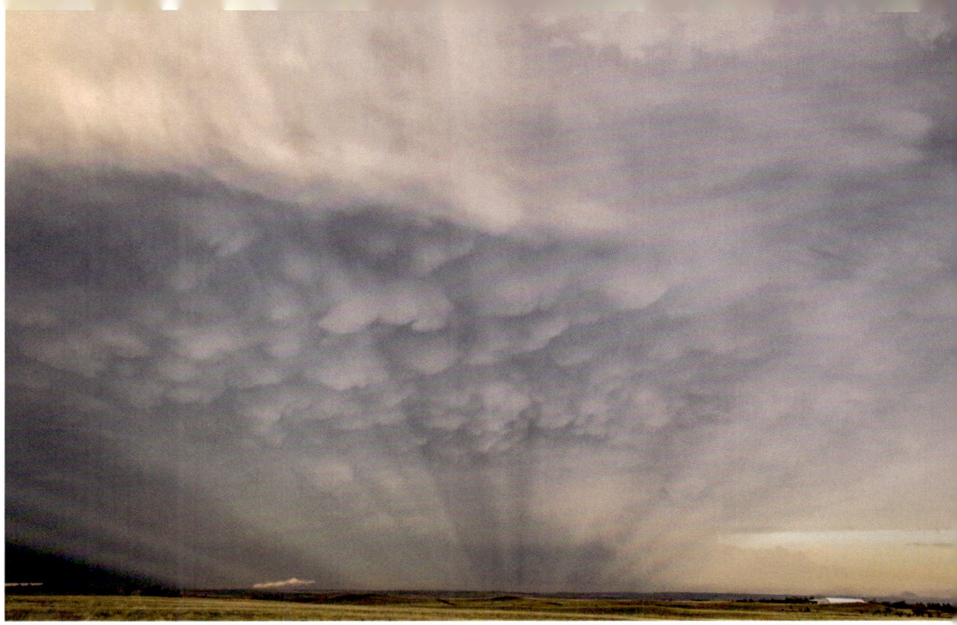

Figure 39 **Dramatic sky**. Local TV stations and newspapers are always looking for dramatic sky pictures as a lead-in to the daily weather forecast. If you have a spectacular shot that epitomises the weather for that day, send it in. You may not get paid for it but it is nice to share your work with other readers or viewers.

'word-tag' each one you submit. What this means is that you attach a sequence of words that describes all the aspects your photograph appears to illustrate. It is often suggested that the process of word-tagging is as important as taking the photograph. After a period an agency will send you a statement (usually every 6 months) itemising your sales for that period.

Suggested agencies

Alamy. Of all the large agencies, Alamy is possibly the most accessible but, of course, you will be competing with thousands of other photographers. You need to visit their website **www.alamy.com** and see what the current conditions are. Follow the link 'How to sell your images'. Some of your photographs will be of general interest and could be used at any time. Others will have immediate interest such as, for example, a small tornado that has damaged buildings near where you live and is currently in the news. If so, then you need to be spontaneous, as the shelf-life of your photograph might only be a matter of 12 hours or fewer. Send it off immediately.

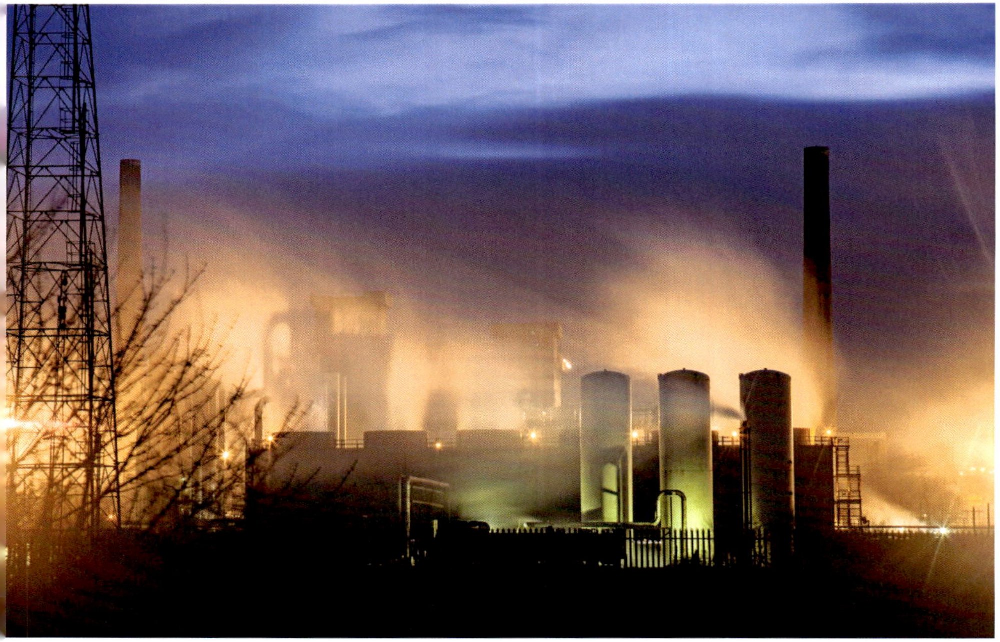

Figure 40 **Industrial vapours blowing in the wind**. Agencies such as Alamy welcome an enormous variety of images, particularly those that many other photographers may choose to ignore. With toxic gases drifting in the wind, this image certainly has a story to tell.

Goto Foto. This is a relatively new agency so you might find the competition a little less severe. To access their website go to **www.goto-foto.co.uk** Submitting images is relatively easy and you begin by registering. This is an agency that particularly stresses the value of accurate and comprehensive word-tagging.

Getty. Getty is possibly the most prestigious of all the image bank agencies and does not welcome submissions from the general public. You are invited to submit a sample of your images and, if it is of a sufficiently high standard, they will be prepared to market your work. So, if your work is up to scratch, why not give them a go? Getty can be contacted by going to **www.gettyimages.com**

Arcangel or **Trevillion**. Another possibility is to consider sending your images to a specialist image bank such as Arcangel or Trevillion. Both these agencies deal almost exclusively with book covers,

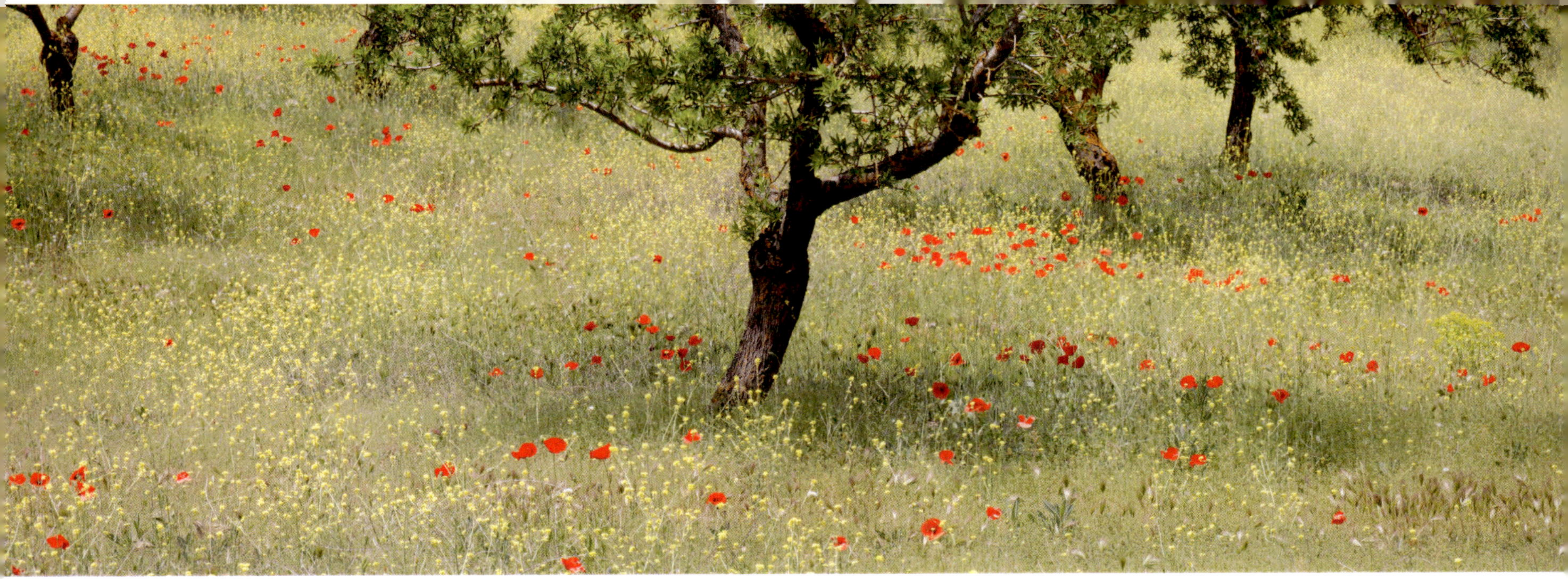

Figure 41 **Andalusian pasture with almond trees**. Don't be discouraged from taking shots when the sky is overcast; often it can prove to be a great advantage. With a much softer light, there are no ugly shadows to obscure the delicate floral detail. It also helps to consider the format you are using as panoramas are often favoured by greeting card manufacturers.

largely novels, but it is surprising just how many feature landscapes shot in interesting weather conditions. To contact either of these go to: **www.arcangel.com** or **www.trevillion.com**

At first it can be quite daunting submitting your work in this way, but if you don't try then you will never know. The overwhelming majority of contributors to all these agencies started as amateurs. Moreover, I have just offered you a sample; there are countless others you might wish to contact.

Greeting cards

You will no doubt have bought a greetings card and occasionally thought to yourself, 'I've got a better shot than that'! In reality you probably have, so why not submit your work for consideration? In addition to images of cute puppies and kittens, a surprising number of cards feature a landscape photographed in interesting weather conditions. Because cards tend to be small (A6 or A5), the design needs to be simple and eye-catching.

Just flick through the range of cards currently being marketed and you will quickly get an idea of what is required. Similarly, while greeting card publishers are listed on the internet, their details will also appear on the cards they publish. Each company will have a preferred style so, if you think your photographs fit that mould, give it a go.

Self-publishing

Until recently this would have been an expensive option, but there are now numerous printing companies specialising in short runs. If you think your images are good enough, why not give this a go? Check out some of your local galleries, gift shops, etc. and see if you can use these as an outlet.

The important point to remember is that all agencies, whether card manufacturers, image banks or your local newspaper, depend on people like you to submit work - effectively you are their lifeblood.

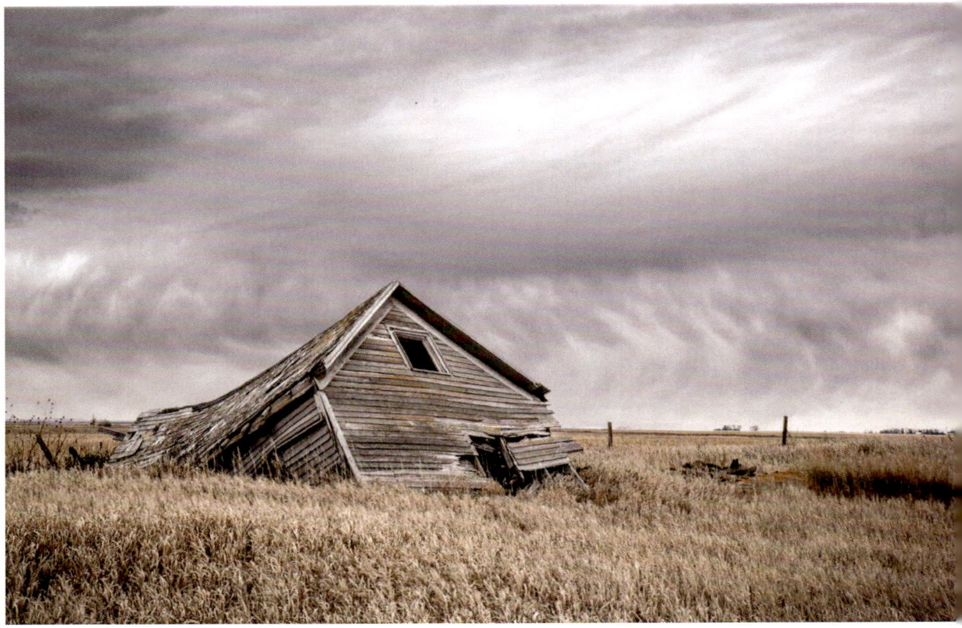

Figure 42 (Top Right) Tumble-down homestead. Dramatic weather will always be of interest and have some commercial value. If you are able to capture a theme that in some way echoes the mood of the sky, it will prove advantageous.

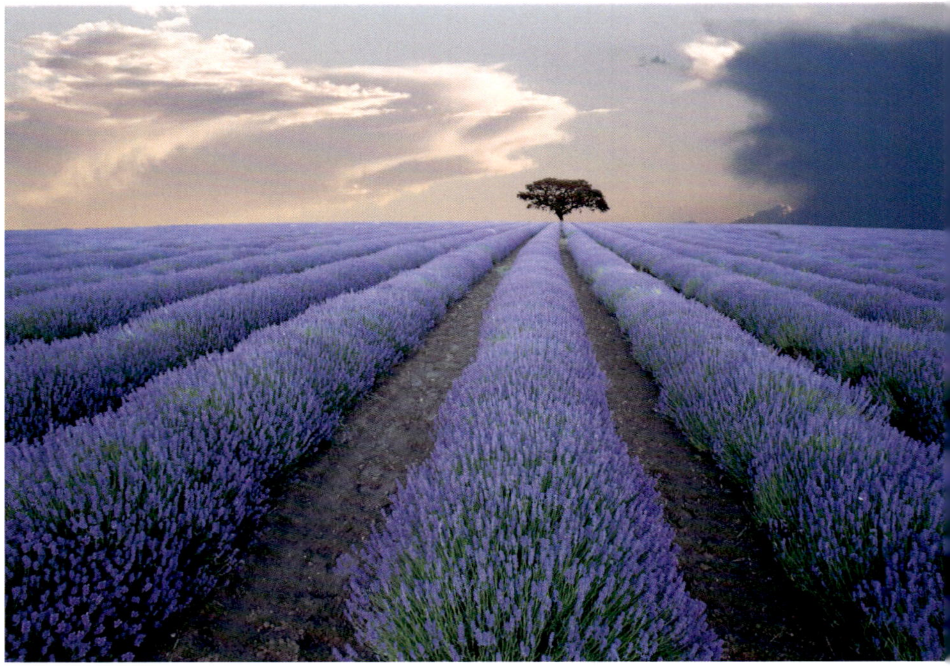

Figure 43 (Bottom Right) Field of lavender. The most marketable weather shots tend to be the most simple. There are very few elements in this image, just the receding rows of lavender and a dramatic cloud formation in the sky. Images such as this can very easily be reduced in size for greeting cards and postcards.

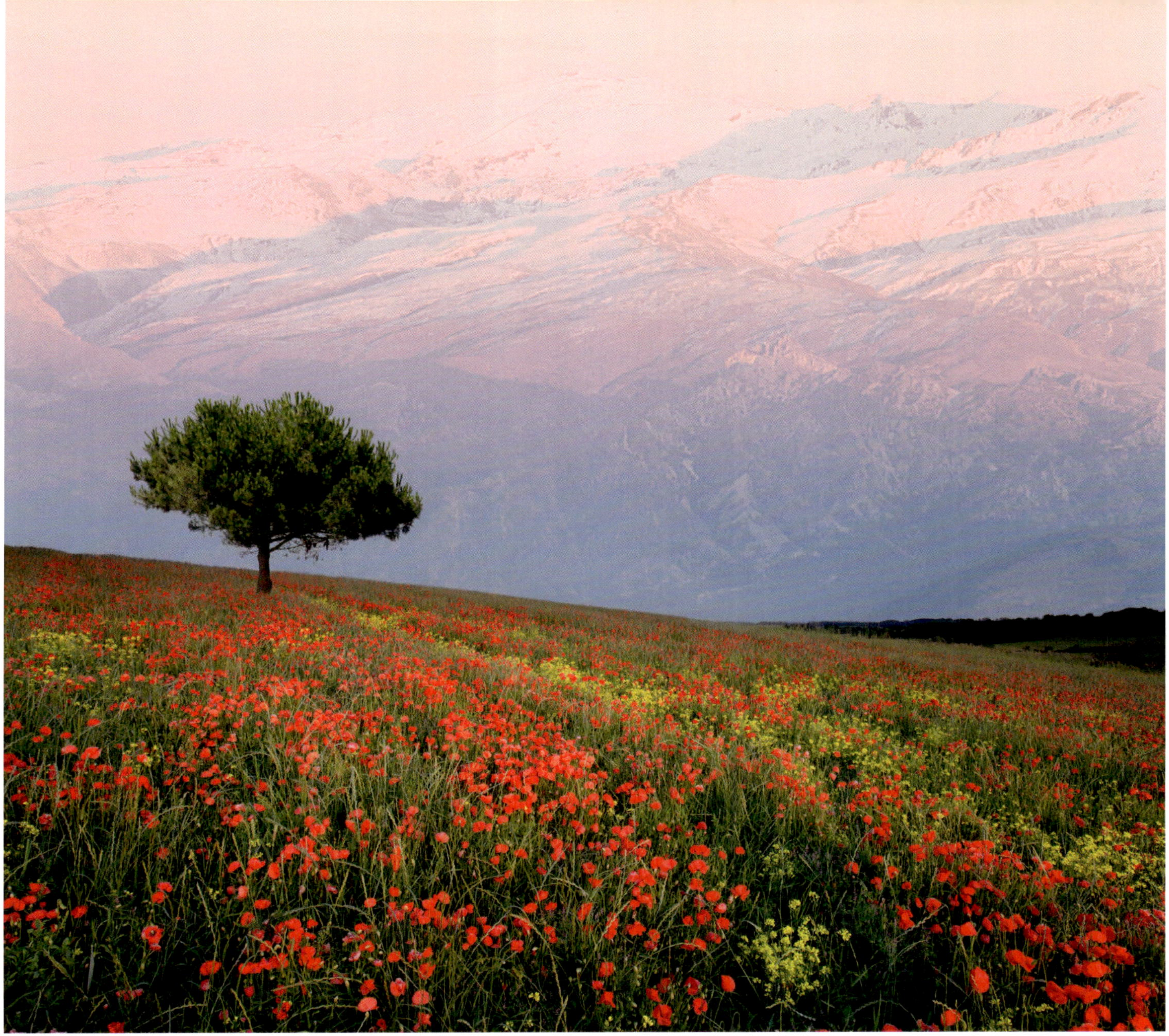

Figure 44 **Field of poppies and the Sierra Nevada**. Calendar printers are constantly looking out for interesting and 'up-lifting' images that can easily represent a month or season. Most calendars will feature the work of a variety of different photographers so, if you have something special, why not submit it?

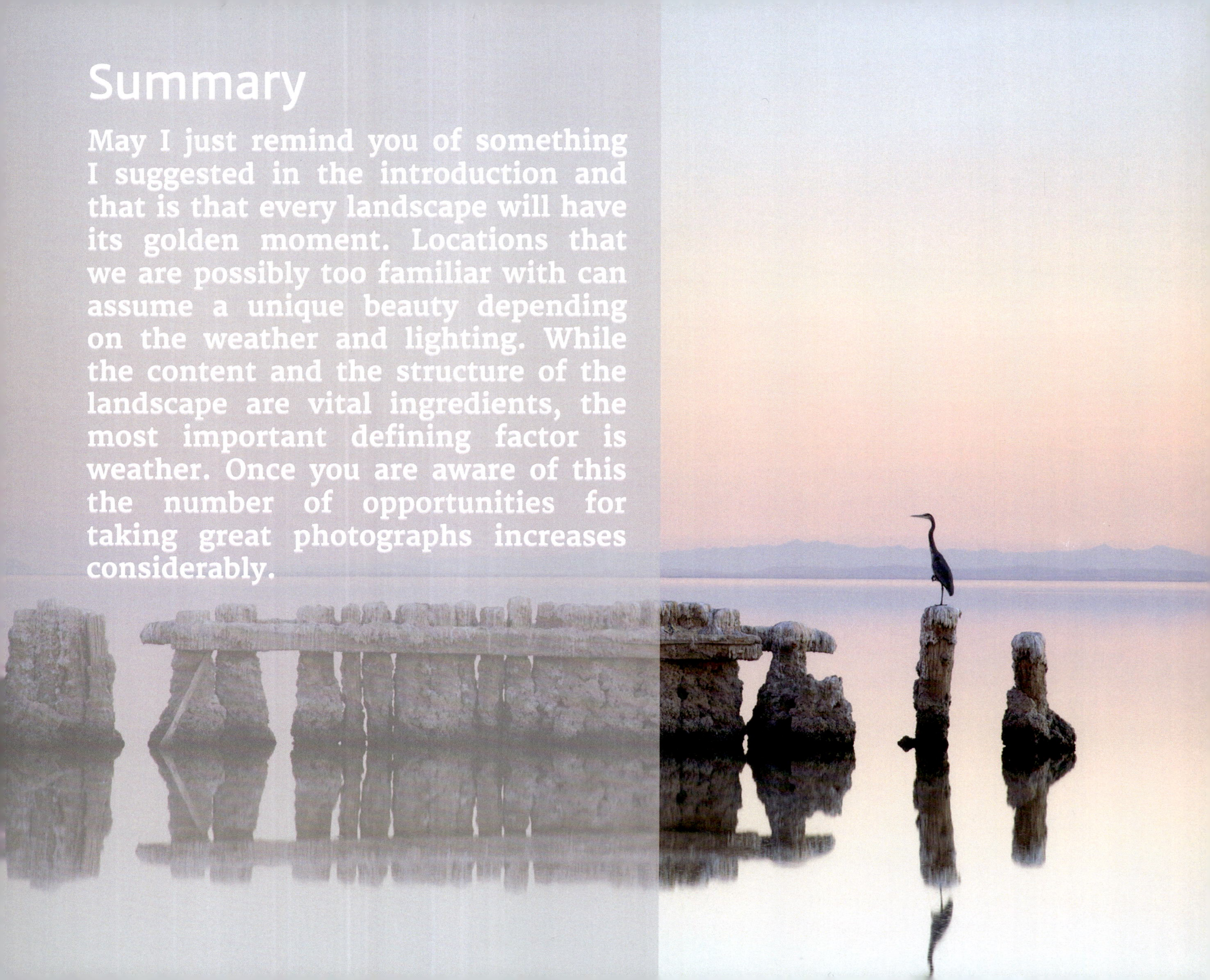

Summary

May I just remind you of something I suggested in the introduction and that is that every landscape will have its golden moment. Locations that we are possibly too familiar with can assume a unique beauty depending on the weather and lighting. While the content and the structure of the landscape are vital ingredients, the most important defining factor is weather. Once you are aware of this the number of opportunities for taking great photographs increases considerably.

Celebrate the weather, whatever it offers

Adopting the right mental attitude is so important. When you look out in the morning and see that it is raining, that's a real cause for celebration. When you arrive at a location and discover that it is shrouded in thick mist, ponder on your good fortune. While travelling to a landscape you had long planned to photograph, you notice the sky is beginning to fill-in; just think of the wonderful opportunities this changing weather presents. It is so easy to dismiss the current weather as being 'ordinary', but no such thing exists. While I am perhaps labouring this point a little, if you are able to adopt a positive view of weather your landscape photography will become more interesting and fulfilling.

Make taking photographs a daily pursuit

The great joy about weather is that it is always present. In the same way as a diarist records their personal activities of the day, get into the habit of recording some aspect of the weather. By doing this regularly, not only will you be developing important photographic skills, but you will also develop a unique awareness of the nuances of the changing weather patterns. Whether you are working or a student, retired or on holiday, make yourself go out every day and photograph some aspect of weather.

Get to know your area

Possibly the most successful landscape photographs are those where the tenor of the weather matches that of the landscape. Certain landscapes benefit from being photographed under a simple blue sky while others might not. It is so important to familiarise yourself with your own locality and constantly ask yourself 'what would this location look like in frost, snow or fog?' Many features of weather are frustratingly ephemeral so it helps to have worked out in advance possible locations that you may want to visit should the weather conditions permit. Even when on holiday your first task should be to reconnoitre the immediate area with a view to taking photographs.

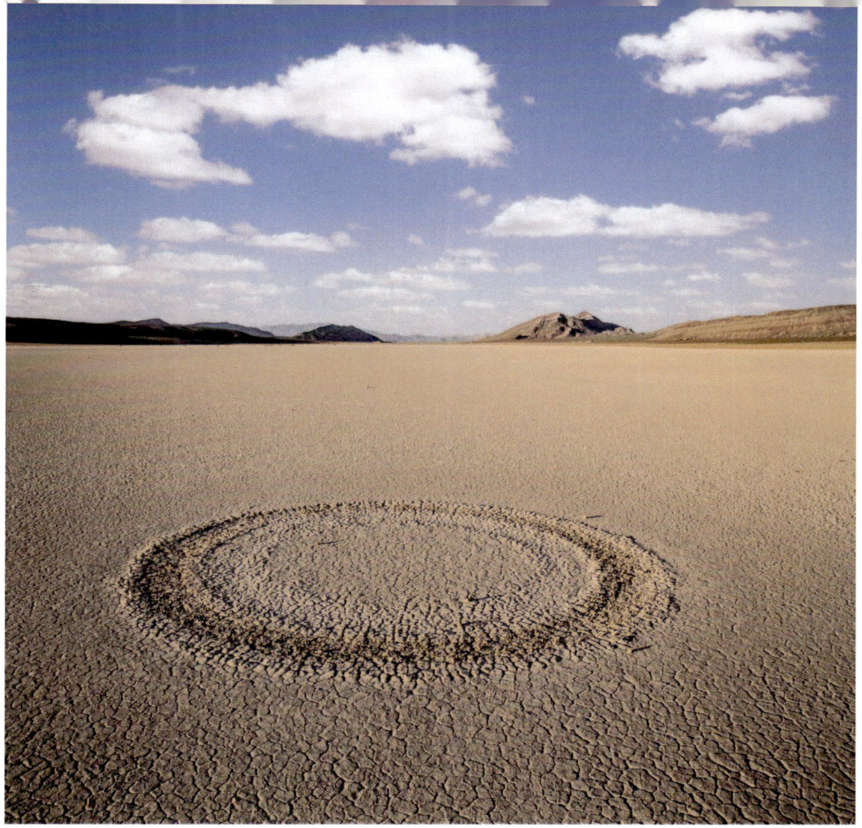

Figure 1 **Circle in the desert**. Landscape need not always be predicable. I spotted this 'man-made' circle in the middle of the desert not knowing how or why it was created but, in an odd sort of way, it chimes with the cluster of white clouds in the sky.

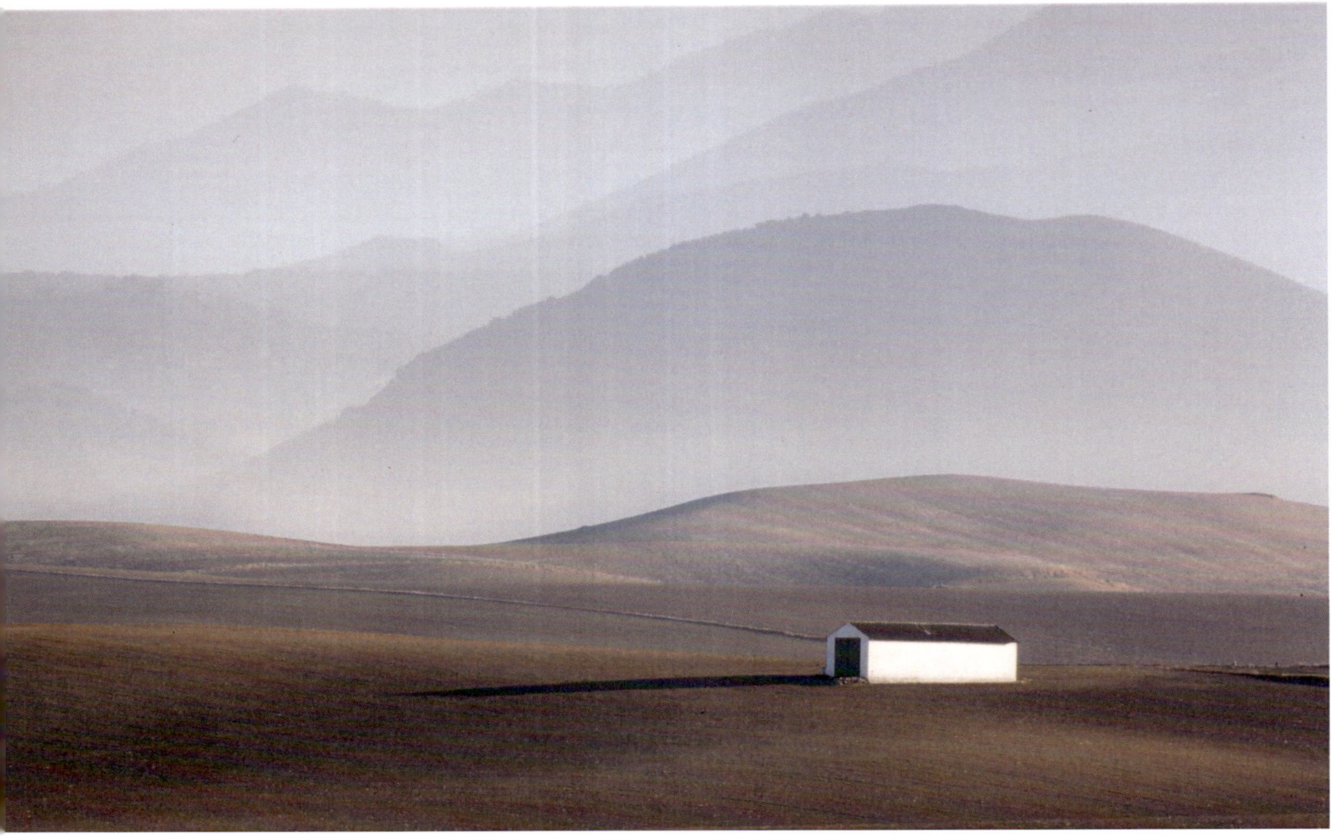

Figure 2 White barn in Spanish landscape. Each type of weather imbues the landscape with its own special character. Being sensitive to this will greatly improve your ability to photograph landscapes.

Learn to understand weather

Weather is not random. It follows a pattern and the more we understand, the more able we are to use it to our advantage. It really is the active ingredient when photographing landscape. This publication aims to alert you to the numerous opportunities weather has to offer, and the more acquainted you are with this subject the better you will be able to exploit its many moods. Weather forecasts are helpful, if rather generalised, but being able to assess what might happen from your immediate location improves your chances of getting a great shot. It also helps to understand that certain cloud formations have quite distinct visual characteristics that echo the landscape; when this occurs you are offered a fabulous opportunity for exciting photography. Finally, while there is much we can do post-camera to improve our photographs, avoid the temptation to over-process. If you are shooting Raw, your captured images will reveal an astonishing array of qualities that accurately communicate not just what you saw, but what you experienced. The skill is to bring this honestly to the fore.

Now, where are my Wellington boots?

Figure 3 **Autumnal landscape**. There are occasions when the character of the sky has little to offer, so just exclude it entirely. The soft light it produced allowed me to take this shot without the problem of unwanted shadows. It is important to understand that every weather condition offers its own unique set of opportunities and it is simply a matter of utilising them.

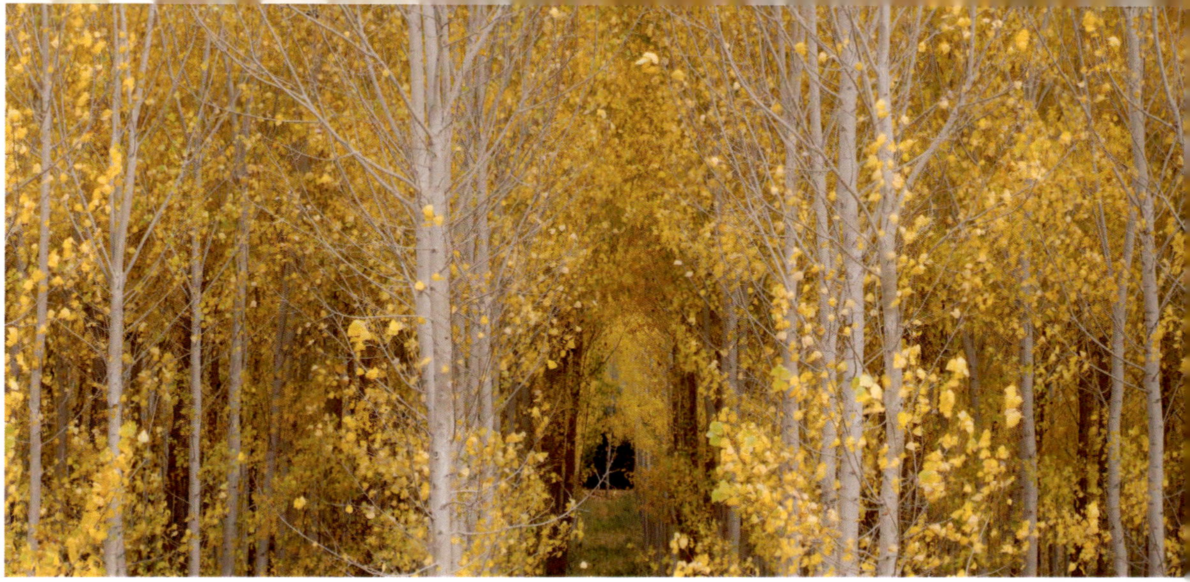

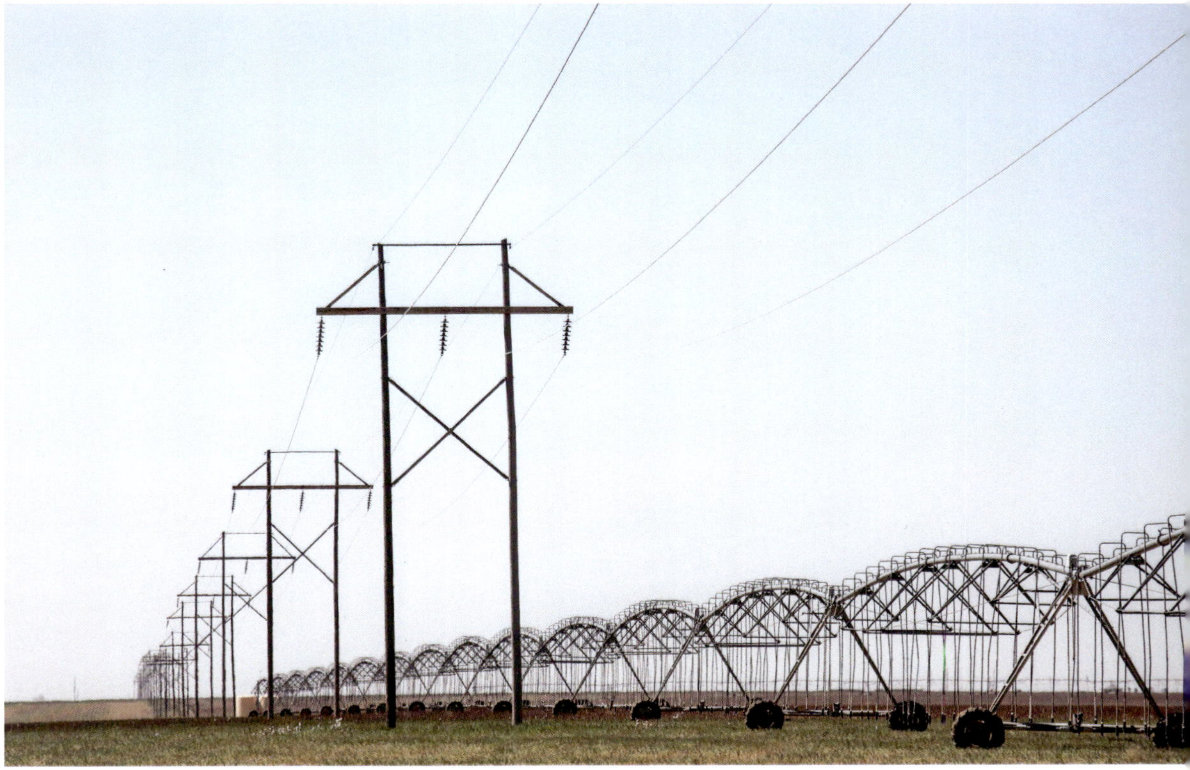

Figure 4 **Landscape with power lines**. Possibly the weather that many landscape photographers most fear is the dreaded 'white sky', but every condition offers unique opportunities. I was struck by the industrialised nature of this landscape and photographing these structures against anything other than a bland sky would have been impossible.